The Berkeley Girl
In Paris, 1968

The Berkeley Girl

In Paris, 1968

By Elise Frances Miller

To my husband, Jay

⌘

SHRP
Sand Hill Review Press

v

PROLOGUE

In 1991, my son put me on notice. He was fed up with hearing about the 60s generation. "Sex, drugs and rock 'n roll, and now there's as much racism, poverty and war as any time in history, and you pathetic suckers dealt it out!" Operation Desert Storm had commenced, and I shuddered to think that if this Middle East "operation" lasted as long as the Vietnam War, my fourteen-year-old might have to replay my guy's crushing 60s decision—draft or dodge. The right corner of his lip turned up in disgust and his pimply face swung side to side like a gate in the breeze, about to slam shut on me. Did he imagine that we'd all signed a malicious pact aimed at screwing up the world?

In the decade that Americans of several generations are obsessed with, whether it's to love it or hate it, we had a war and social strife, but most young Americans believed that our country was a good-hearted place that had, from its inception, haplessly spawned evil inequities. Just like prior and later generations, most of us were focused on finding a lover or a spouse and learning enough to make a living. So why did the myth persist that our entire generation was deliberately and confidently revolutionary?

When a TV movie called *1969* was released in the mid-90s, I gathered the family in front of the set to watch, hoping for some minimal support for my recollection about how naïve, frightened and passive I had been during my freshman year at UC Berkeley. Within minutes, I was on my feet, shouting "Everybody out! This is nonsense!" And then, of course, the family wouldn't leave.

With entertainment objectives superseding the political ones, everyone in the film was a stereotype, speaking words designed to titillate. Girls were gorgeous and mindless, aggressive she-beasts craving "free love." Guys – unless they were among the deluded soldiers and veterans – were either violent, grubby political radicals or violent, grubby drug addicts. Guys of all backgrounds were obsessed with not getting drafted—well, at least that part was true—but miraculously, they had acquired the ability to analyze every American blemish as if they'd earned PhDs in sociology. And courage! What bugged me most was the courage they all supposedly had: to change the way they looked, to expose themselves to loss of family and friendships, to attack and be assaulted physically, to risk everything for their ideals.

But I remembered. For most of us, it was not that way. Not for teenagers and college students in their early 20s. Out of over 7 million U.S. college students, estimates hover at only 40,000 demonstrating against the war. Then in January 1968, the Vietnamese Tet Offensive brought international awareness to the immoral and tragic mess stirred up by our leaders in Washington. Suddenly, at each demonstration, 10,000 to 100,000 people hit the streets, not just in America, but all over the world. The numbers grew from there and reached into mainstream society, but that was in the 1970s, when social revolutions for women, gays and other minorities were launched as well. Determined to find physical proof of the truth, I began pulling out old pictures and yearbooks from our Los Angeles high schools and UC Berkeley. Suddenly, there we were, thousands of trim-haired, neatly-dressed, conservative-looking youngsters, with perky, forced smiles, encased in identical inch by inch-and-a-quarter boxes for our children to snicker at. Only they did not snicker.

"Mom, this isn't the 60s, is it?" our daughter spoke first. "I mean, these kids are all so *conservative*. Look at the short hair on the guys, and the girls' hair. What are those little wings growing out from their cheeks?"

I laughed. "That was the 'flip,'" I said. "That was the style."

"They're all so...so middle America!"

"Look at you!" our son recognized my picture. My hair hung past my shoulders, wings nevertheless quite pronounced. I remembered pinning in the rollers at bedtime each night. Eyeliner and lipstick were carefully applied, designed to construct a face like Natalie Wood's—on the make, yet still an innocent young girl.

"What happened to hippies and commies and anger?" our son asked. "You all look like a bunch of nerds. You don't look like you could fight your way out of a paper bag, let alone defy cops to save the world."

I came to put my arms around them both and drew them in with a tug. "This is real," I told them. "Remember it the next time you see those more exciting versions in the movies." But our son moved away from the yearbook, shrugged his shoulders and grew silent. Our daughter was still flipping through the book, disappointment furrowing her brow.

That was the night I decided to create a work of fiction to convey my recollections about how we looked, felt, struggled and persevered. How every day those conformists photographed in the Berkeley yearbook confronted awkward questions, beckoning quests, and critical decisions. And how all over the world in the spring of 1968, there was unavoidable turmoil as abrasive as stone and change as unstoppable as time itself.

CONTENTS

≈PART ONE≈
California

ONE

Berkeley

The first time I saw UC Berkeley, I held fast to Aaron Becker's arm with both hands as we strolled beneath Sather Gate and over to the side of Strawberry Creek bridge. Above us, the Berkeley hills shimmered in green and gold, the buildings rose white and majestic, and the promise soared as large as the picture on a giant movie screen—football games and fraternity parties and sunlit arms heavy with textbooks. Wasn't I the lucky one to be on campus, a senior in high school visiting my college boyfriend for the weekend? Then, as I leaned against Strawberry Creek's retaining wall, a crisp paper flyer crackled against my hip. I glanced down at a boldface word—"protest"—and gave out with a startled "ohh." But before I could back away for a better view, Aaron wrapped his arms around me. He stroked my hair and placed a strand neatly behind my ear. His warm breath on my cheek steadied my own. "Never mind about all that," he whispered. "You'll hear about it soon enough. I'm so happy you're up here with me, Janet. Just let me hold you..." My heart pounded wildly at the mere thought that by next fall, I would join Aaron for his final year at the university. We kissed passionately, then once again more tenderly, as if to seal a bargain we had made about our future.

That sunny spring weekend in 1967, Aaron was my academic advisor, tour guide, and basketball buddy. I stayed in the dorm with the daughter of Mother's friend. In the evening hours before dorm lockout, Aaron and I snuggled up on the broken-down sofa in his studio apartment, sipping Lancer's rosé from juice glasses and listening to his hi-fi set. Simon and Garfunkel's Homeward Bound awoke a feeling in both of us that here, together, would be our true home.

Aaron had been in the scout troop with my brother Matt from Cubs to Eagles. The gangly boy had grown tall, with a Paul Newman-tapered body, light brown hair and deep, dark brown eyes. For over six months, since we rediscovered each other on one of his vacation visits back to Beverly Hills High, Aaron had enchanted me with his stories about the magic of "Cal." His campaign of long-distance phone calls and color postcards of bay views at sunset succeeded in their purpose, and I set my sights on Berkeley.

So, in the fall of 1967, I came north for my freshman year, cherishing a vague, Victorian version of romantic fulfillment. Like nineteenth century Daguerreotype portraits. Wedding cake couples, slightly blurry around the edges with touched-up blushing cheeks. From my dorm room on the sixth floor of Freeborn Hall, the San Francisco Bay spread out in front of me just as in those dozen or so "propaganda" postcards from Aaron that I'd saved in the bottom of my desk drawer. But my boyfriend couldn't be with me all the time to romance me away from the grating reality all around us. His vivid descriptions of life at the "greatest public university in the nation" began to look like a Norman Rockwell with a shredded canvas, or worse, like one of those poor mangled people painted by Soutine or Munch.

On my first night as a college freshman, hours after the rosy sunset had turned to sludge over the Bay, my new roommate asked, "Do you support Johnson's war?" Her voice was tight, as if something was bunched inside her throat. Her name was Barbara Borovsky, and she was from San Francisco. We had been telling each other about our high schools and families. Across the darkened room, talking between beds, it should have been easy to express the ambivalence that was in my heart.

"Well...no...but I don't think I know enough to tell them how to win it," I replied.

"Then you believe it has to be won," Barbara spat out. She was way too disgusted to be relaxing into a good night's sleep. "How do you feel about the American military just making a quick exit, getting the hell out right now?"

"Well"—I always used words like 'well,' 'perhaps,' 'I think,' and 'maybe.' I had read in Cosmopolitan Magazine that those words signaled that you lacked self-confidence. So natch, I tried not to say them, but they continued to pop out. I stopped talking for a moment, and then I told her, "I just got to college. What do I know?"

Barbara was silent for what seemed like a long time, except for quick, deep nose breathing, like a girl running laps for gym class. Then, with a hard edge to her voice, she said, "If you don't mind, Janet, let's not talk politics in this room. No war. No politics. And no religion either."

"But, you seem to be interested, and I'm not...not..."

"We have to co-exist here," she said matter-of-factly. "And I, for one, have a very busy year planned."

So that was my potluck roommate. Barbara Borovsky was short and stocky, with frizzy orange hair, and I soon noticed, she dressed in pants every single day. In a way, she was what I had always wanted to be: sure of herself. From the moment she stepped off the bus from her home in the big city across the San Francisco Bay, she knew what she wanted to accomplish at Cal. She was there to learn about societies and politics and to master effective writing and speaking skills. Her parents were against the war, and she fell naturally into a pattern of extracurricular activity that gave her a cadre of friends with a common purpose.

After that first night, Barbara was never mean, she just ignored me. I tried to accept the fact that I would never be my roommate's friend. She would hear the words "snooty and superficial" in my high-pitched, little-girl voice, and see it written in my appearance—cashmere sweaters, long, wavy black hair, and green eyes that I emphasized with black eyeliner, just as I had done in high school. After all, I did think I made a more attractive impression that way.

But it bugged me. The distance between us was more than superficial. Underneath layers of hair spray and scalp, my gray

15

matter felt like it was all wrapped up in one of those Ace bandages that protect sore muscles from movement. Barbara's brain would contract, breathe, bleed and crackle, and it might just as well configure itself into a big electric neon sign that screamed, "Here I am!" Basically, I was scared to death of her. I went around ashamed of despising Barbara. I comforted myself with the assumption that she despised me back.

The second week of the quarter, I finally got up the nerve to talk to Aaron about Barbara Borovsky.

We were having coffee in the Bear's Lair. Its woodsy ambiance seemed like a good backdrop for sharing. After sipping in silence for a few seconds, I set my cup down as if the heavy mug were made of rare porcelain. "I've got a problem." I hesitated.

"I've got a solution," he quipped. "Well, maybe. Try me." He blew into his steaming cup.

"I've been assigned a radical for a roommate."

Aaron's head jerked up from his coffee. We sat next to each other in the booth, so he turned awkwardly toward me. Concern creased the space between his eyes. "Go on.

"A few quick words in the morning and a quick 'g'night Janet' isn't normal for roommates, is it?" I continued. "And when I walk into the dorm lobby I see Barbara through the double doors surrounded by her hordes of friends in the study lounge. I can see that messy orange halo of frizzy hair hunched over some newspaper story or SDS leaflet like a lamp illuminating a sacred treatise. I want to stop and say hello. I want to be friends, but there they all are," I whined. "And I'm as shy and spineless as a...a...a nematode."

Aaron laughed. "Zoology 10 is really increasing your vocabulary, isn't it?"

"Don't laugh at me. Please? I had hopes that my roommate would be my best friend. Like a sister. I've never had a sister..." My voice faded as I fought against tears. Dammit, why did I always sound so junior high?

Up until now, Aaron hadn't even liked to discuss the protests against the war. Up until now, occasionally or rarely would have suited me fine. Aaron had worthy ambitions in scientific research and he didn't want an arrest record or any shoddy FBI file messing up his diligently planned future. I couldn't blame him for that, not if it wasn't going to help end the war anyway. And that's what he believed. And I? I believed in Aaron. I waited for his "solution" to come.

Aaron cleared his throat and exaggerated a straight face. "Here's the real problem," he said. "Every single girl in Freeborn Hall was in the popular crowd in high school. And as amazing as it sounds, they were all radicals. Popular radicals. That was one of the toughest prerequisites for admission, like passing Algebra 2. You lucked out, Janet. They waived the requirement for you. And you got the only official waiver, so just remember that."

Sarcasm was Aaron's way. His joke snapped me back to reality. Cracked me up. I punched him on the arm in a fit of faux resentment. Heavens! Had I actually been feeling like they were all high school "popular crowd radicals"?

Opening up to Aaron, I was never shy. I gazed at my boyfriend's square jaw and his straight sandy brown hair, cut at a moderate, in-between length. He wore Levis and a clean, button-down cotton shirt, blending right in with most of the guys at Cal. At least, I reflected, those not trying to prove a point.

I sipped my coffee. Aaron was still grinning at me. True, it was a cockeyed, sarcastic smile, but it took me in like I was part of his joke on the world. I went on, "Je comprends, je comprends! I should forget about Barbara and look around for girls not interested in politics."

"Sure," he encouraged. "There are plenty of them. More of them, in fact."

"But the thing is, I am interested in politics." Aaron's brows lifted about a mile, but I pushed bravely on. "And I admire Barbara's activities, kind of. And I think I agree with her views, maybe. But it's frustrating not being able to discuss things with her. She cuts me off. She's so all-or-nothing."

Aaron nodded attentively. "Absolutist. That's how they are."

"Yes. Well, that's how she is. And she's out there on the Plaza so much that I don't know how she's ever going to pass her exams. Barbara Borovsky. Remember that name because she's going to be famous some day."

Aaron chuckled. "That's quite a mouthful."

"Yes, well..."

"Famous and in jail, eh? Well, it has to be a public performance. That's the radical's strategy."

I shuddered at the word 'performance.' "In a way," I said, "I envy Barbara. I'd like to be like that, to work on something significant, to have more faith in myself and to have lots of friends. But do you think she could be a card-carrying Communist?"

He choked a bit on his swallow of coffee. "President Johnson,"—his lip curled cynically at his own mention of our president—"wants the public to believe that the majority of students are radicals. And that all students who are war protesters are Communists. Or drug addicts, nymphomaniacs, or bomb-toting criminal anarchists. And lazy and work-averse..."

"...like Maynard G. Krebs. With dirty hair, of course." I said with a giggle.

"You've got it," he said. "His strategy is to lump us all together."

"But we're not all like that. And no one is all those things, are they?"

"Of course not," he soothed. "So about your roommate, you might want to avoid knee-jerk reactions. She might hate the war, but not be a member of the Communist Party."

"Of course you're right!"

"You can just ask her, can't you?"

"Are you kidding? She might have squeaky clean hair and hate the Communists as much as Daddy, but still, she can be sharp as a Bowie knife."

Aaron nodded, then polished off his coffee. The brown liquid in my cup was cold and unappealing. I slid the cup around in its saucer, not knowing what else to say. It sloshed on my finger, and I swiped at it with my napkin.

"I'm sorry your roommate has been so tough on you," Aaron said earnestly. "Maybe if you tell her that you're better at listening than talking when it comes to politics? I mean, if you really want to understand her...

"I do, but..." I sighed, then slumped in my seat.

Aaron put his arm around my shoulder and squeezed. "Probably best not to get involved," he advised. "Some of those people break laws. But honestly, you don't have to be afraid in your dorm. Remember, your roommate has her nightmares, too. Nightmares are the common denominator these days."

So that's where we were, Aaron and I, caught in the vise between radical youth performance and Johnson administration propaganda, and wanting more than anything else to be left alone to live a normal life. I hadn't understood him one bit about the nightmares then, but I hadn't wanted to admit it.

About five weeks into the quarter when a simple, one-page letter from Mother arrived, I finally understood the comment about the nightmares. The letter informed me—in Mother's neat, tiny script—that Matthew, my only brother, my childhood companion, would be shipping out to Vietnam.

The first reading was downstairs in the dorm when it was already time to set out on my daily walk to class. Forcing myself to place one foot in front of the other, I tried to find the strength to stop being numb. The traffic light on the corner of Bancroft and Telegraph Avenues turned green and I was swept forward by the crowd. I reached into my pocket and scrunched the paper. How dare Mother and Daddy write this in a letter! Would the expense of a telephone call bankrupt them? I knew the answer: my need to hear a voice, to cry into a receiver, was exactly the scene they wanted to avoid. At least, I thought, I'll be able to cry on the one shoulder I can count on in this world. My date that night with Aaron would be my solace.

On the other side of the intersection where the crowd spread out, I peered across Sproul Plaza to Sather Gate. Fighting my way back to high school senior year, I remembered the two of us walking through the Gate and Aaron talking in that habitual, show-off way of his with his arm wrapped protectively around my back. The memory of a sweet kiss on Strawberry Creek bridge brought tears to my eyes.

Crumpling onto one of the slatted benches by the side of Sproul, I began to sob, both grateful and dismayed that no one in this bunch of strangers paid any attention. I took deep breaths and blew my nose, realizing that life as I knew it was gone. If I tried to revive it now, it would feel like a Frankenstein, a creature pieced together from dead flesh. One had only to read the Daily Cal or to be in the Plaza at noon to perceive the nightmare that I had until today—with no little help from Aaron's exalted perspective—scrupulously avoided.

As I caught my breath and wiped my eyes, I was furious with myself that I knew so little about what would soon be Matt Magill's war. Instinctively, I frowned at the books in my lap. What good were these thick textbooks if they didn't teach me anything real about my life? I would go today—right after class!—to read up on Vietnam. There must be whole books and magazines on the subject in the Main Library.

With a burst of determination, I prepared to rise. Further up the Plaza, I spotted Barbara Borovsky sitting behind the Students for a Democratic Society table, as usual. She had explained why SDS was an appropriate name for the organization. It was one of the few real conversations we'd had that month.

But on the morning that I learned my big brother had been drafted, I suddenly began to notice more than the busy-frizzy head of my roommate. Down toward Ludwig's Fountain, around card tables and rows of barren sycamores, stood clumps of students with mouths agape, hands flying with emotion or wrapped securely around heavy stacks of books. And I asked myself, quite simply, why wasn't I out there with them? It was the first time I had asked myself that question, even considered the possibility of joining the protesters. Why had I always rushed through the Plaza? Why had I never been over there searching for answers?

Dazed and depressed, I rose and moved forward until I stood about ten feet from the nearest table, twisting away and back again, not daring to focus for too long on the material in front of me, nor to make eye contact with those standing or sitting there. I squinted through the crowd in a deliberate effort to appear as if I were waiting to meet someone. All the radicals, I decided, male or female, were going to be argumentative, aggressive people, who would talk me into things I didn't want to be talked into and make charges that I was ill-prepared to refute.

But what, I now asked myself, would I refute? That civil rights for Negroes was not a noble cause? That Vietnamese people weren't humans with brains and families who had the right to decide among themselves how they wanted to live and die? That this war, in which Americans had used chemical weapons—disgusting and scary things like napalm—should not be stopped? Even I had heard about napalm. God knows where though.

A new thought hit me with high voltage. What was the point in being afraid of people who called my family the enemy, if the enemy was perpetuating the war that would send Matt to kill and be killed, and might even, some day, do the same to Aaron? I approached the row of wobbly card tables with signs taped across the front legs.

I scanned—stacks of literature, mimeographed sheets, Xeroxed pamphlets with black, boldface letters arranged as inflammatory phrases, or more sedate brochures, paid for by national organizations. I listened—certain words and phrases jetting through the crowd, absorbed like fists to my stomach: "Military-Industrial Complex," "Negotiations Now!" "Immoral War!" "Black Power," "Arms Race." All of these provocative words attacked the established culture that fed and clothed me.

Mother and Daddy stood in the shop window of my mind like well-dressed mannequins, their frozen smiles behind the glass. Jean and Marshall Magill. They hung back behind my own reflection, unreachable and insentient. My throat was dry and thick with questions. The muscles in my knees felt weak. Hugging my notebook and texts, I made my way over to Ludwig's Fountain. The brown, floppy-eared pooch for whom the fountain was named lay a couple of yards away, resting on the cobbled stones as if he, too, was weary of conflict.

I sat on the ledge surrounding the circular pool and tried to play through in my mind what I would say if I decided to approach one of the tables. I didn't like the prospect of being harassed by hotheads. Would I be able to keep up with their rhetoric? Would I embarrass myself, as I had with Barbara Borovsky? Worse, would I get involved in something I didn't want to get involved with, be forced to march, protest, make speeches in front of people, waste my time with these activities? Yes! Waste my time! Was I smug and self-satisfied like Barbara thought? No! I just found it impossible to imagine that I, Janet Magill, Cal Freshman, would be able to end the war in Vietnam.

But what if no one spoke out against the war, ever? What if none of these people were here? I swallowed hard, stood and squared my shoulders behind my load of books, and taking a step forward, tripped over a solid brown obstruction that had just risen and waddled over toward my feet.

Ludwig howled and I felt the burn as I caught myself on my hands and knees. I must have yelped as I sprawled out across the cobbled stones, with my books and purse now about two feet beyond my skinned hands. A half-dozen people came running to help me, while an equal number fussed over Ludwig. "Sorry doggie, sorry," I cried out as strangers helped me to my feet and I brushed my torn tights, the new forest green ones that matched my plaid mini-skirt. Damn. Shit. All that. Here I was swearing and starting to cry with all these people around. I brushed at my hands and arms as they handed me back my books, stacked as neatly as their layers of sympathetic words. "I'm late for class," I was saying.

But then there was a young man with a serious case of puckered brow, asking me if he could help and holding out a black-and-white leaflet. His sideburns, composed of scraggly wisps of dull brown hair, extended to his sharp jawbones. His eyes were insistent. "You might want one of these. There are more important facts in here than your professor will teach you today. Read it in class!"

"Well...okay. Thanks." I tucked the leaflet into the pages of my notebook.

"It won't bite." He smiled. "Just read it. We're all in this together, you know."

I thanked him again, surprised by his gentleness. I hurried off into the crowd, heading straight through Sather Gate toward Wheeler Auditorium.

All through class, telling Aaron about Matt was on my mind. I devised conversations, then revised them as if editing a term paper. As I emerged onto the blacktop, the Campanile bells chiming, a moment of panic slid down my throat like a bad piece of meat. When Aaron spoke to me about common nightmares, was he shielding me from his own? Could he really be shipped out, just like Matt? I quickened my pace, heading for Freeborn Hall. I needed to rest and absorb all this before I talked to Aaron. I hoped I'd have some time before my roommate descended upon our tiny room.

TWO

THAT PARTICULAR OCTOBER EVENING, I swept my cottage hearth and stacked fresh logs, cleaning obsessively as I always did just before Janet was due for a visit. Taking my guitar out of its case, I leaned it against the bookshelves, then decided the Hoyt Axton album would set the mood. Strains of "Angel Cake and Wine" filled me with a pleasant heat even before the flame caught the brushwood.

Humming along with the Axton cut, I snatched a biochem book where it lay open on the floor, along with the notebook, pencils, and empty soda bottle—A & W Root Beer, always an essential component of my midterm exam preparation. Redistributing this stuff appropriately, I began the ritual of cleaning Dork's cage, mumbling sweet nothings to quiet squawks from my humble parakeet and tugging at the removable tray. After dumping the corncob shavings, well spiced after several days without a visit from Janet, I set to work scraping and scrubbing, then positioning the whole cage under the cool shower tap. I grabbed the cheap seat on the can to watch the avian circus and to fantasize about the evening ahead.

I formed a mental picture of Janet Magill, tall and sexy, standing in my doorway with the lamplight in her Irish green eyes. Then sitting cross-legged like a kindergartener at my hearth. Then relaxing, her long legs taking over the sheepskin rug, reclining... Perhaps this would be a special night for us.

Janet loved my new cottage, a pad worth every beaker and cloche I'd wash, working extra hours in the lab to make rent. Here was the perfect setting for a romantic evening, this one and all the many to come. The place was two quick strides by four in the front room, but it had a great cold-day-in-the-woods charm. A creek stone hearth, beamed ceiling, skylight, and my additions—the aquarium, second-hand hi-fi, and brick-and-board bookshelves. In the little chrysalis of a bedroom, I'd stuffed a queen-sized bed, an objective symbol of eternal hope, like the condom I carried around in my pocket: just in case. However, given my propensity for "good girls," the type that

23

were still saving it for the big commitment, my parakeet was my only roommate. I called him Dork as a benign reflection of our familiar relationship.

Like my queen-sized bed, Janet Magill objectified hope—actually, a whole range of hopes. She had these sophisticated mannerisms, always tossing exotic proper nouns into the conversation like hothouse vegetables into garden salad. Isadora Duncan and Andy Warhol. Waikiki Beach and the Champs Elysées. And French phrases...how I turned on to something as simple as merveilleux or au revoir. But she wasn't snobbish about that or anything else. It had been a kick introducing Janet to my cottage, the university, and to the mysteries of independence—life without parents.

Barring the contingency goblins lurking over the shoulders of the even most rational scientists, now that I had Janet by my side, I was confident that nothing would deter me from achieving my goals: a successful career as a research scientist and a home and family more stable than I'd had as a kid. That vision, central to my life since Dad ran out on us, was finally within reach.

Dork snapped me back to the business at hand, bitching at top volume while he jumped around, pecking at his plumage under the spray. I wiped the wire bars down, replaced the cuttle bone and mineral block, and slid a fresh tray of shavings into the bottom of the cage. I was calming the bird with a few low whispers when I heard a timid knock at my cottage door.

"Bonsoir," I greeted Janet, swinging my arm toward the blazing hearth to usher her inside. My buoyant greeting snagged on my girlfriend's wimpery breath and she stayed put. I stepped out into the shadows.

"You can't imagine how I needed to see you tonight...that is..." she began. I stood still, bent toward her like a crowbar to better hear what came next. She hesitated, mouth pinched shut and eyes glazed with tears, bright as ice. I remembered that face from the day she walked up the hill to tell me that Woody Guthrie had died.

"Matt's shipping out to Vietnam after the holidays," she finally whispered. A vague snapshot of Janet's big brother Matthew Magill, my ol' scouting buddy, flashed through my mind. I tried to absorb what she had said.

"Jeez ... Matthew...damn..." I mumbled, putting one arm around her back. The next thing I knew she had me in a childlike grip around my middle, her head against my chest. I let her hang on, praying she wouldn't start to cry. Then gently, I kissed the top of her head and took her by the arm, guiding her inside and down onto the sheepskin rug in front of the fire.

"Couldn't his hot-shot job get him deferred?" I asked. Matthew checked meters for L.A. Gas & Electric. Janet had told me that her father, a World War II vet and a big wheel at a large company, bragged interminably about his son starting out in an American public utility.

Janet shook her head and met my eyes. "Not a chance. He's not in college, so he was fair game." Dork let out a loud, sympathizing squawk. I reached for the hi-fi, lowered the volume.

"Shouldn't we do something?" I asked. "Shouldn't I call him, extend my sympathies?"

"No, you don't understand," she whined. "You'd be better off calling to congratulate him! He's John Wayne and James Stewart rolled into one. He's right there with my parents, and you know how they feel. 'My Democrats, right or wrong.'" She paused, then after meeting my gaze, her baby-doll voice stiffened into a neatly targeted syllable: "Shit."

"Yes. It's that." I chuckled before I could stop myself. I had never heard Janet use that particular word before. "Another new vocabulary word for freshman year?" I quipped.

"It's to the point," she snapped, then shrugged her shoulders and softened her tone. "You know the thing I'm most afraid of?" I shook my head.

"That war will change Matt. Even if he was a tease and an idiot sometimes, we used to, you know, play together. Hide and seek, belly laughs at Laurel & Hardy. We shared jokes my parents didn't get. Innocent stuff. He is innocent now, the way I see it, and that's why he wants to be the big war hero. He's heard the World War II stories all his life from Daddy, and he'll kill and maim, maybe even plunder and rape..." her voice cracked like a teenaged boy's and she buried her face in her hands.

I rubbed her back. "He's not a child, Janet, and neither are we."

Her resentment wafted up from her lap. "He'll be a tough vicious man."

I whispered, "I'm sorry, Janet. But I hope so. That way Matthew will survive."

She reached for her purse and some Kleenex, mopping up, obviously attempting bravery. "Shit and more shit," she said. "I used to hate that word."

Then she slid in to close the gap between us. Her eyes were drawn to the fire, which crackled to life, oblivious to her somber situation. She turned to me and sat up straight. "Aaron? Please don't make fun of this?"

I flinched as if struck. "What kind of a sleaze to do you think I am?"

"Well. Okay, I'm sorry. But I know how sarcastic you can be sometimes." She took a big breath and let it all out in one long string of words. "They're giving Matt a going away bash during Christmas break with a bunch of Daddy's hawkish friends and they're so proud of him I can't stand it. Don't they know he could die?"

A long, mournful groan came straight from my gut. Her grateful smile faded quickly. "Please, please Aaron, will you come with me? Be my ally? I know you're not comfortable doing the big Beverly Hills social scene, so that just makes me appreciate this even more."

Janet knew what she was talking about. She and I had both grown up in Beverly Hills, but on different sides of Santa Monica Boulevard. I lived in an apartment with my mother and her complaints, while Janet lived in a big house with a father, mother, brother, terrier, and two maids.

"Okay, yes, of course..." I nodded, sliding my hands down to grab hold of hers.

Outside a motorcycle roared by, catching our attention. Then we heard laughter and the shouting and jostling of a group getting ready to depart. I had lived in the big house adjacent to my cottage for the previous two years. Tonight I was especially happy to be sprung from group life. "Students in the big house are on their way down the hill to a meeting," I explained. "Stop the Draft Week."

"I know. I've seen them." There followed a few seconds of dead silence. Janet picked industriously at strands of wool between her crossed legs. When she ceased vilifying my rug, she began staring at me with a scowl.

"What?" I reached out to her, but she brushed my hand away.

"Don't you see, Aaron? My roommate has firm convictions. I admire that. I wish I could do something, not just add to the chatter against the war, but work...work hard to end it."

I groaned, but stayed calm, reminding myself that my girlfriend had only been at Cal for a few weeks. "We've been all through this, kiddo. You know I hate this illegal war, but those dogmatic speakers and their herds of stampeding buffalo are counterproductive."

"But you hate the war more than the protesters, don't you? Aren't you ever tempted to go out there? To help them?"

"Oh sure," I snickered, trying to lift the mood. "Johnson's war machine will squeal to a halt like a hyena on a leash just because a few children are having tantrums. Trust me. It's worse than a waste of time...it's fodder for the reporters and for the hawks."

Then suddenly, as if her lit fuse had just touched powder, Janet's voice flared and echoed in the small space: "But I just don't know if you're right or not!"

I shot up on my knees and leaned toward her, shouting over Dork's noisy empathy. "Don't you know people with power have less respect for the radicals than they do for the Viet Cong? I think about what I might do to change things, and I'm sure my letters to D.C. have been transferred directly to landfill and yes! that leaves me feeling powerless. But hell, until I figure out something better, that's my way of working on it."

Janet slumped down. "I just wonder how many will die before you figure it out."

"I'm sorry, Janet. I know you want to help Matthew, but your roommate's tactics are not the way. Most students hate the war, but relatively few college students are actually involved with protest groups. There's good reason for that."

She glanced at me, shrugged her shoulders, and her gaze was drawn by the fire. I got up to get her a tissue, which she accepted and blew her nose with great fanfare. Even in this miserable condition, she outshone my dazzling hearth. Slightly parted, pouty lips, big eyes, and thin flushed cheeks, all nicely framed with a mass of long, dark hair. She knew I was smiling at her, but she wasn't returning it. I rocked back on my heels and gave her my best crock-o-shit smirk. "Hey listen. I'd stand in the middle of Sproul Plaza with a placard until my feet bonded with the pavement if I thought it would help."

But all she said was, "At least you have your convictions about the protests, and you're paying attention." I dropped to my rug again and reached for Janet's hand. She continued, "Today I read a leaflet from Sproul Plaza and took a book on Vietnamese history out of the library. Then I bought a New York Times. Have you ever heard of the Gulf of Tonkin Resolution?"

A knot hit my stomach and a snicker reached only to the level of my throat. Was it really the first time this girl had heard of the legislation that Johnson used to justify waging undeclared but de facto war? My quick reaction was to force a straight-face. "Hmm, I seem to remember. Tell me."

She regurgitated the text, fresh from her day's foray into previously ignored information, concluding her explanation with a brief but sincere measure of self-flagellation. "But that's the very first time I've read more than headlines in all these years! That's terrible, isn't it?"

"So you've been oblivious," I comforted, "but you're at Cal now, with information all around you. Be patient with yourself."

She sighed and bit her lip, her eyes focused in the region of my chin, as if she were talking to herself. "There's all this serious, life-and-death stuff going on in the world, and I'm sad because I'm missing the myth of college. What I crave is art and music and science and you and me, falling in love. And I do want to do something significant with my life. Just like you do."

"Of course! And you're a smart girl. You will. I'm sure of it."

"But with all of these new interests and ambitions, I've never wanted to think about the war, and there it stands, like Godzilla, casting a monstrous dark shadow. I've...well, I guess I've been as shallow as a puddle."

"Okay, so you've been a puddle, but now you're starting to dig deeper. It's a start..."

She giggled. "I'll be a deep puddle." Her lips puckered into a sour-candy smile. "I will read now, everything I possibly can. I want to know, not just since Matt...but being here where people talk about the world. People like Barbara and her friends. It makes me want to do something, anything. Maybe if enough people scream, the government will listen."

"Not if it's only the kids."

"The kids," she echoed, bitterly. "Like Matt, kids playing with real live ammunition." Janet held my hand with the grip of a hand wrestler. "Aaron...oh for heaven's sake! Don't you realize that you could be next? Aren't you worried?" I stared at the fire, wondering how it kept jumping in a room that felt so airless. I had always kept my head down, staying out of trouble, studying hard, cleaning up after myself. I'd made an effort to be civil around my mother, patient with my girlfriend, kind to my pet. All this behavior had succeeded in bringing me to the brink of a good and purposeful life. I refused to believe that my carefully constructed edifice could be wiped out now.

"I'll be fine," I mumbled.

"What?"

"I said don't worry. It's not fair, but they just don't waste people like me."

"But once you graduate?"

"Hey, let's run away to Paris together...just hop a plane and go!" I declared.

"This isn't funny, Aaron, maybe you should come up with a plan, a blueprint..."

"Someday we'll walk along the Seine holding hands and picking spring blossoms out of each other's hair along with the grit from not washing for a month."

Then, blessedly, she laughed. That was one of the great things about Janet. She appreciated my humor even when we both knew it wasn't bankable material. She blew her nose again. "Leslie Caron never had grit in her hair, you moron. And oui, mon amour, I do want to run away to Paris together someday. That's why I hope you..."

"Hell, you're so gorgeous," I said. "Let's not talk about the war anymore."

"But we have to talk about it, don't we?" she asked, even as she shifted her incredibly long legs to the other side of her body and removed her cardigan. Maybe this would be the night. Maybe we were both just that fed-up with the status quo. I moved in to stroke her back, my thumb snagging on the bra beneath her soft blouse.

It was smooth, the way we dropped together onto the sheepskin pelt as automatically as rain to earth, both fondling while she positioned her head snugly on my shoulder. The distant sound of bells from the Campanile reminded me that she had to be back in Freeborn Hall by eleven or be locked out for the night. I inched forward until Janet's rapt green eyes were directly in front of mine, held her face in my two hands and drew her forward for the kind of long, gentle kiss that women are supposed to love. I held her close and whispered our joke about her Wonder Glow makeup. How I loved that name...and the pleasure of warm cheeks, the fire, Axton's deep throaty rhythms, and the blazing glow inside.

The next kiss was more passionate and I thought about the phenomenal year ahead. Janet scratched my back gently with her long fingernails and I rolled on top of her. I heard a soft "whoosh" as next to our prone bodies a white-hot log fell into the soft pile of ash. I ran my hand along the lovely length of her torso, untucked her blouse from scratchy wool pants and pushed my hand up inside. Then, stroke and kiss and suffer as usual, but this time, hoping for a payoff, I whispered, "When I feel close to you like this, I want to go for it."

Deftly, Janet rolled away from beneath, leaving me with a mouth full of foul sheep's fuzz. "Oh shoot..." she breathed heavily. "I've got to calm down." She fanned herself with the bottom of her blouse, then touched the back of her hand to her forehead as if she were taking her temperature. "We've got to take it easy, Aaron."

"Why...why should we take it easy...?" I drew the condom from my pocket and held it up to her. "Do you know what this is?" I asked.

She touched it briefly, drawing her hand away as if it were contaminated. "Those things break. They're not safe. Mother told me that was how Matt got born after Daddy left for Europe." I snorted, but she whispered, "Please put it away, Aaron. I'm sorry." Above us, my parakeet tapped patiently at seed, while the aquarium motor hummed. Even the zebra danios and rainbow fish are getting some, I thought. Only Dork and I remain celibate.

"You know how I feel about it, don't you?" she asked. "I'm not ready for any big steps just yet, and..."

"Haven't I told you you're the only one I'll ever want?" I cut her off. "That more than anything, I want to be with you? And that I never want to do a repeat of my parents' divorce? This could be the start of our future together!" Abruptly, I halted my speechmaking, took a deep breath and blew it out, fighting for control. I hated how desperate I sounded.

"I remember," her voice went flat. "You were ten years old when your dad left." She stared blankly into the flames.

Suddenly I felt as cynical about love as I did about politics. "Their whole generation was repressed," I said. "And now ours, I guess. Poor Freud lived and died for nothing."

Janet reached out to take my hand. "I'm sorry," she said. "But it won't always be this way. I do hope someday. I do want you to be the one."

"I've been waiting for you to get up here, Janet, to grow up a bit. I assumed we meant something special to each other."

"We do! That's why I'm worried about you. And the draft and Matt."

How in hell did we get back to this? I wondered. "Okay, I should have understood." I got up and after two paces, searched the kitchen drawers for my stash of weed, more for the relief of activity than for the object. "Want a little smoke? I've got some weed here somewhere."

"Not tonight, thank you," she replied as politely as if I'd offered her a cup of tea.

"Or we can play guitar, sing some Dylan or the Byrds. You love the Byrds and I love to hear you play and sing. Maybe it would make us feel better."

"I don't want to feel better!" she burst out. "Why do I have that privilege when Matt...? I just can't, Aaron. I can't just sit by with my brother going over to that awful place where he should not have to go! I want to work with them, no matter what!"

"Work with who?" I asked, confused.

"With Barbara Borovsky and her friends. With others trying to accomplish what I'm desperate to accomplish. The end of the war."

"Dammit, Janet. What are you saying?"

"You have your answer, and that's fine for you. But your answer is not mine."

"By tomorrow, you'll calm down."

"By tomorrow, I'll be one of them!"

"You're a lunatic," I shouted. "You'll do this without me!"

"Of course! I wouldn't expect...I have to, can't you see?" She glared at me, breathless, as if she'd just been caught with her hand in the cashbox. She waited to see if I would arrest her, admonish her, or gently remove her hand, already gripping a fistful of bills, and let her go.

"I just worry about you, that's all. About your disillusionment, not to mention your physical safety."

"What do you mean, 'physical safety'?" she asked, as innocent as a turkey before Thanksgiving.

I sighed. "Janet, you've been reading about Vietnam. Have you read anything about the radicals, the arrests, the pummelings by the police, the Black Panther party, stuff like that?"

"Well, a little. And I haven't actually talked to Barbara about this yet."

"Good girl. All I'm asking is that you do your research first. Think for yourself. Don't be led by people just because they seem so cocksure of themselves." I put my arms around her and pressed her head a little too forcefully into my shoulder. My insides knotted and my skin itched, making me aware that nothing seemed more important to me right now than keeping this girl next to me. So I kissed the hand that I hoped to keep free from the protester's picket sign.

With a deep pang of frustration, I removed Hoyt Axton to stack a new array on the turntable, the soulful folk music and softer rock that fit the scene. Simon & Garfunkel, Dylan, and Edith Piaf—I wanted to believe that something French could still please Janet Magill.

Just before our walk down the hill, we listened as Dylan told us that the times were a'changin', and the bitter thought crossed my mind that peace and love were still trapped in the aspic of poetry. Silently, I prayed for some real change before Matthew had to leave. And before his sister slipped into the quagmire, and away from me.

A few days after Janet's visit and after the close of Stop the Draft Week, my conversation with Janet had begun to dominate every solitary meditation. Reluctantly, I decided to write to my father as a kind of plumb line. I had to begin, at least, to maneuver a way out of my approaching military obligations.

At that time Dad was living down in South America. Divorce notwithstanding, he'd been pretty generous to my mother Cora and me over the years. Cora—at her request, I've called her by her given name since the divorce, when I was ten. Dad, who is still Dad, took a job as a foreman at a big American photographic equipment factory in Ecuador, where he'd married a woman that Cora called "SS." She made up this nickname while talking to her friends in the West L.A. salon where she manicured fingernails for suburban housewives. She insisted that it stood for "Saucy Spic," but I knew that secretly she worried that the imagined Latin sex bomb would be the Gestapo that would lock away the source of our vital supplementary funds, hers and mine.

I sat down with pen and paper, opening with all the pleasantries: I'm fine, my mid-semester grades are Bs hovering temptingly near to As, how's Juanita, the kids, how is work, blah, blah, blah...and then I launched into it, trying to sound as wise and witty as possible, angling to keep his attention.

Dad, I know that even in your Shangri-La you must have heard all about the progress of the U.S. government in developing the most arcane and invidious methods that could possibly emerge from their pea brains in order to torture en masse the young male population of this country. Last year, Congress rejected Johnson's proposal for a lottery. It may happen yet, but one way or another, the military has to get its numbers up to feed the Southeast Asian beast. So the rumor is that draft deferments for graduate students may end this year, and since I am graduating in June that means the ransom on my head is rising steadily. Instead of getting a full-time laboratory job and beginning doctoral studies in biochemistry fall quarter, according to plan, I'll be shipped off to some boot camp in Alabama or Louisiana. Even if the lottery should come up for a vote again and pass, if I get a questionable number, I'll live in abject fear, trembling every time I open my mailbox for the next umpteen years until this blood sport has ended.

So let's get right down to it. How do you feel about funding a little trip out of here? I thought I would time this little excursion for after my last final but before the ceremony, and I should mention that a one-way ticket will be sufficient.

I could come to you for a visit, but I figure you and Juanita want your privacy, and anyway, French is my second-best language and Paris is a favorite destination of my girlfriend, Janet Magill.

Speaking of Janet, I don't think I've written you about her. She's a sweet, gorgeous girl from, guess where? Beverly Hills. You might remember that I was in the Boy Scouts with her big brother, Matthew. I was making one of my pilgrimages back to high school, and there she was in my old French teacher's class. I didn't recognize her at all, but she remembered me and waited for me outside the classroom until I emerged from my nostalgia-fest with Mademoiselle Katzen. Janet is still the same skinny girl, but now with just the right amount of filler and contact lenses instead of glasses. We've been dating during vacations, and now she's up here at Berkeley. Matthew, it seems, was just drafted.

And that brings me back to my original topic. Please send word ASAP. I'll be packed an hour after my last final exam. I promise you, this will not be one of those things we will laugh about when we reminisce. This is serious. This will be one of those things you will remember and be glad you did. Did I say thanks? Well, I will.

Your son, Aaron

I sealed the letter and sent it off, not showing it to Janet nor informing my mother about my plans. I couldn't decide who would be worse, but I knew I had to avoid tearful scenes, for now. June seemed far away, and I still held out hope that the escape could be avoided. I planned to begin applying for biochem graduate programs soon.

Meanwhile, protests seemed to settle down on campus as final papers and examinations loomed ahead. Three weeks, then a month after my airmail plea went out to my Dad in his Paradise, I still hadn't received a reply. December arrived, Janet and I came through exams with banners raised, and soon we were preparing to fly south for the incomprehensible festivities for Pvt. Matthew Magill.

THREE

AARON AND I TOUCHED DOWN at Los Angeles International on the afternoon of Matt's farewell party. I had asked Aaron to spend the party night at my family's house before going home to his mother's apartment for the holiday.

December weather had followed us south. There was no sparkle, no color, barely any sunlight over the city. Our taxi sloshed along Venice Boulevard, where deficient sewer drainage left a foot of dingy water and debris running lazily west toward the beach. From Venice, we drove north through the downpour and into Beverly Hills.

The cabby pulled up next to two gray figures huddled on the sidewalk. Jean and Marshall, my excited and gesturing parents, stood before the physical evidence of my emotional separation from this place, their home, no longer mine. Through my new, Berkeley lens, I perceived a cavernous, two-story crate with a weathered tile roof and a cast-iron, painted Negro jockey on the lawn. Aaron must have sensed tension. He squeezed my hand, but before he could utter the amusing final rites I knew he'd planned, I bundled myself up, brushed away my tears, and fled the cab to stand under my mother's waiting umbrella.

Aaron fed precious cash to the driver, retrieved the suitcases and followed along to where we stood under the veranda. Daddy opened the front door about two feet—not wanting, I guessed, to run up the central heating bill—and squeezed his beefy torso through, pulling Mother and me in after him. His deliberate tan gave his head the appearance of a leathery pumpkin under the foyer ceiling lights. Then he thought to reach back outside to pull Aaron through, bumping Samsonite on the door jamb and deepening Mother's frown lines until she finally whined, "Marshall, please!"

Daddy was shouting "Never mind that, Jean. Come on in you two!" His good-natured laugh exploded over the clatter of the rain and suitcases. "We're just a little absent-minded in the storm. We're not used to weather here," he told Aaron, as if my boyfriend hadn't grown up in this city.

Aaron smiled graciously. "It's been crazy, hasn't it?"

I held up my hand as if I were a crossing guard, stopping Daddy's yakking mid-sentence. "Daddy, please pay Aaron back for the cab," I commanded.

Aaron protested, "No! No, Janet. That's okay..."

"But...don't be ridiculous! Janet's right." Daddy's wallet was already out of his pocket. Aaron accepted a five-dollar bill with a simple "thanks."

Mother guided us through the foyer into the little den at the back of the house, introducing us to the new Laotian maid, who followed us carrying a tray of Cokes in tall glasses. "Cokes, Jean?" Daddy gave Mother his you-messed-up expression. "Wouldn't hot chocolate have been better on a day like this?" Mother began to ask us about that, but we instantly began gulping our Cokes. She touched her carefully waved hair to make sure that the storm hadn't mussed it. Would I ever dye my hair blonde, I wondered? I assessed her slim figure and the subtle makeup, and decided that Mother was a woman who was more interested in appearing stylish than youthful. That was appropriate, I reasoned, but her composure, no matter what insults Daddy threw at her, irritated me. Mother said little, deferring to Daddy's booming inanities.

We chatted on about the rain and Pacific Southwest Airlines and school and finals. Then I let them know how Aaron's tutoring had been my salvation in Zoology 10, and not to expect sterling silver grades my first semester. My parents exchanged those meaningful, mysterious glances that scratched up my spine.

Finally, we were led back out to the foyer and followed the maid upstairs to our respective rooms.

Once sequestered, I took in the view from the backyard next door to the neighborhood beyond. I knew the details of this view and our house like the crevices of my own body, and they had persisted in the three months of my absence. Mother had done a little remodeling and interior decorating when we moved in during my infancy, and little had been altered since. Bernard Maybeck, the early-century architect who so brilliantly fashioned the brown shingle houses like Aaron's little pad in Berkeley, knew that the word "home" meant close, natural smells of wood, fabric, charcoal, and roasting food. Returning to

Beverly Hills from Berkeley, it was easy to feel that any semblance of "home" here was eradicated by faded postwar beige and grand excesses of space. Suddenly, I laughed bitterly, if a bit hysterically. I realized that this going away soiree for Matt was to be held in a living room as large as an entire Maybeck, entered through a foyer twice the size of Aaron's Berkeley cottage.

It occurred to me now that even as a little girl, I had sensed something missing in this house. When I was fourteen, Mother had let me—no begged me—to make a room for myself that I would love. It was the only part of the house that had been completely redesigned. To make my room pop out, to counteract my plain Jane name and the low expectations that my family had of me compared to brother Matt, I chose a thick, bright red carpet as a daring complement to pale pink walls. Gritting her teeth into a smile as bleached as her coiffure, Mother had stepped reluctantly into the fair rosy field of my custom-designed floral pink, red, and white draperies, yards and yards of it needed to accent the two windows and the balcony doorway and to cover the two twin-sized beds. Even the stuffed animals were color-coordinated. White cats with ruby eyes, soft pink bears with black and white points. Five pieces of matching, expensive, laminated furniture with walnut sides and pristine white tops completed the picture.

Now with the detachment of the Berkeley-schooled, I stood there, hands dangling at my sides, thinking of all the families this furniture might have fed. But then I contrasted all that beige outside my bedroom door. Like the woodsy cottage in the hills that absolutely reflected Aaron's character, this room had once mirrored mine. Bright, bubbly, and cheerful, yet set apart from the rest of the household. Aspiring to be different, and to create my own space where I could lose my shyness. I was puzzled about how it would suit me now or in the future. For today, the semblance to a veneer of high spirits, even when my heart was breaking, was a bit too close. I stripped for a shower and let my tears run down into the sewers.

An hour later, showered and dolled up in my party dress, I lay stretched on my bed with a bottle of Weibel—a sweet, green Hungarian wine I'd found in my parents' bar—and waited for my date to knock. Soon Aaron, dressed in his one Sunday suit, peered into the glow from my bedroom.

"Hi! I was expecting you," I came forward, pecking him on the lips. A big playful grin automatically lit me up. "Gee, you do clean up beautifully," I told him. It was then that his eyes travelled to the bottle of green Hungarian wine standing uncorked on my nightstand. I pecked again just to see him wince when he connected it to the smell of my breath.

He shed his coat and climbed onto the bed, next to me. He leaned in for another kiss. I obliged, then quickly reached for my guitar. "Monsieur Becker, voulez vous jouer?"

He chuckled appreciatively at the double entendre, then came back at me with "Oh-sure-bien-sûr." "You look amazing," he said. My hair was curlier, but otherwise there was no stylistic evidence of my new life. I was wearing a bright yellow wool dress with long sleeves and a scoop neck. The A-line skirt ended just above my knees. Sitting on the bed, the silence that came between us filled with unanswered questions about the whys and whens of our sexual future. I crossed my legs to avoid giving Aaron a view up the great divide of my webbed pantyhose.

Anxious to avoid the topic, I began aping Bob Dylan's low whine in 'Mr. Tambourine Man,' while Aaron obligingly kept the beat, using the nightstand as a bongo. We went from song to song, mostly the folk and rock stuff we both loved. Dylan, Joni Mitchell, the Byrds, Stones, and Beatles, until finally I complained, "My fingers feel fumbly," and picked out a familiar melody. "O-oh-say-can-you-see?" I dragged my voice like a ten-ton weight until the last note collapsed into an ominous-sounding minor key.

"I think you've got an original contribution to make to baseball in the 60s," Aaron said.

I blew a noisy raspberry from my lips. "Let's just watch the news, even though from my recent reading I can tell you that even Cronkite is dishing a pack of lies."

"Not a pack, but lots of omissions."

I switched on the portable set at the foot of the bed. "It's hard to believe. Lots of Catholics, especially the Irish Catholics, are working against the war, but not my parents. Oh nooo," I said sarcastically. "Mother and Daddy care more about the Democrats than they do about the Church. I wish I could get them to read the articles some people are brave enough to print.

I said something about it on the phone, but they cut me right off." I found CBS and adjusted the rabbit ears.

Aaron got up and paced the floor. "I don't know if I can listen to this. Christ, Janet, isn't it a bit masochistic?"

"Let's just pretend the jungle is on Fiji," I pouted. "Come sit." I patted the bed and he complied. We lingered there for as long as possible. There was stirring in the house, but somehow the party seemed more of a threat than the television. Confronted by the inevitable nightly carnage coming across the airwaves from Vietnam, I drank defiantly, straight from the bottle. Although I occasionally offered my boyfriend a sip of the sticky, fruity stuff, my hand ungenerously maintained its grasp on the long neck of the bottle.

Just as Cronkite was giving his signature signoff, as if on cue, there was a loud banging on my bedroom door followed by Matt's voice, muffled but insistent.

"Hey you two," he boomed, "Dad sent me up here to make sure I interrupted your private party. Heh heh...!"

"Matt, oh!" I rushed to the door and squealed just as he finished his little joke. I threw my arms around his neck.

He pushed me back. "Whew! You'd better take it easy with the drinking, sis."

Then he gave me a delicate peck on the cheek. "Never mind that," I said. "It's so good to see you. And look at that uniform!"

"Yeah, I'm ready for 'em. How're you doing, Aaron?" He stretched his arm across my back and grabbed Aaron's hand.

"I'm fine. Glad to be here," he lied. "And how have you been? I mean, how's the U.S. government been treating you?"

"Hey, you want a preview?" Luckily, Matt was searching me for a reaction, missing Aaron's. "Well, I'm fit. I mean really fit. They just about kill you to make sure you're fit."

"Well...let's not talk about that kill part," I mumbled, feeling the room begin to whirl. There was an uncomfortably quiet blip.

Matt reached forward and gave my upper arm a squeeze. "Say, I need to get back to the folks. Don't be long now, sis. The party can start anytime. The one downstairs, that is." I searched for the boyish grin, but none was apparent. My sympathy went out to the straight-arrow guy who had bounced eagerly up the stairs just a minute before. "I'll see you guys later," he said quietly. He spun around, dismissing us with the wave of his hand.

FOUR

OUTSIDE JANET'S WINDOW, the wind rose and whipped a floppy maple against a charcoal and navy blue sky. My girlfriend wobbled to the TV set and switched it off with a flourish. She grinned a little too broadly. "Ready for this?" she asked. I was beginning to worry about her making it to the bottom of the stairs without falling on her derrière. We checked each other's clothes, then I linked my arm securely in hers for the slow, ceremonious walk down, down into a truly marvelous scene of synthetic closeness.

Southern California wasn't used to "weather," as Daddy Marshall Magill had said, but it didn't keep the family's social circle from showing up for the big send-off for Matthew. The Magill house had been transformed. Its corridors and open spaces were filled with glittering humanity, piles of food, glasses of sparkling champagne and scotch on the rocks, and sounds of men trying to top each other's exploits, women trying to find excuses to laugh.

The foyer, the small den, and a larger den with a wet bar, were filled to capacity. But the center of activity, where the family held court, was the living room. My eyes widened at the grandeur of it, just as they had the first time I'd seen it as a small, gangly Cub Scout. More awestruck than jealous, I used to scrutinize those maids—back then, they were two stout black women from rural Tennessee. Did they live in a small apartment like I did? Had their fathers stuck around? Matthew's mom had been Den Mother and later, his dad was Scoutmaster. I wondered what Matthew and his dad would talk about when the pack left, and what they ate for dinner at the Magill family table.

The one person I never wondered about at all was the skinny little girl who sat in the corner during the scout meetings, reading the Boy Scout Handbook through thick, pink-framed glasses. Eleven years later, when she was in high school and I was down from Cal for break, Janet and I agreed that as children we had both resented Matthew's popularity. She admitted that she was odd-man-out in her family, a black-haired Irish among the blondes, and worse, the first family member to be college-bound. This last was a source of both parental pride and endless obnoxious cracks about how studious and brainy she was "for a girl."

I stood between the floor-to-ceiling windows on one side, a flattering oil portrait of Janet's mother dressed in a low-cut blue evening gown on the other, wondering if the cost of all this wasn't justly sending a son to Vietnam. I shook my head, trying to rid myself of this nasty thought and focused on the dazzling white plastic Christmas tree in the corner—must've been twelve feet high—studded with an unimaginative array of colored balls, lights, and tinsel.

Janet grabbed my arm. Her mock whisper sprayed my ear. "You see? Matt seems excited about going!" She surveyed the crowd with watery eyes. I was about to comfort her with a reply about Matthew's enviable, mindless self-confidence, when she tugged at me again, pushing through the crowd to reach the golden-haired guest of honor. Matthew was subjected to another perfunctory kiss. Then, with enough drunken gusto for friends three-deep to hear, Janet proffered a fraught and quavering, "Poor Matty."

"Nonsense!" Matthew yelped and in a continuous, sweeping motion, he shook my hand and slapped me on the arm. Always the good guy, always the gentleman. He guided us a few steps to one of the strategically-placed waiters with a tray full of alcoholic beverages. I would have preferred a ginger ale, but I smiled stiffly at my host and reached for a nondescript tan liquid in a short, squat glass. Janet chose the same.

"Catch ya later," said Matthew, proceeding to respond to his admirers. Royalty graciously bestowing his person upon as many subjects as possible, I thought, swallowing the vile beverage. Scotch, I decided. No doubt the best that money could buy. Janet was mingling, so I decided to plant myself on one of the three sofas arranged around a huge mahogany coffee table.

It was then that Janet's eyes wandered to the grand buffet, and I froze as I saw her flesh take on the pallor of the green Hungarian wine. Three words emerged low like a growl from somewhere in her abdomen, the last bursting forth above the party chatter: "Dear God...no!"

My immediate reaction was that the scotch had sent her over the top and she was going to unload her evening's excess onto the pristine beige carpeting. Then I saw the spot where her eyes had fastened. At the center of the buffet table, laden with a five-star general's feast, were two rows of plastic soldiers: red, white, and blue. The figurines stood about five inches tall, some with fixed bayonets, others rushing with rifles or clenched fists toward the paté de foie gras. It crossed my mind that their fierce grimaces were either an indication of their zealous aversion to goose liver or their burning desire to murder North Vietnamese people. What happened next did not reflect the quality of the Magills' paté.

Janet rushed forward kamikaze-like through the amazed crowd, the shitload of spirits nearly tripping her up on the way. Swinging her arm wide with a soprano yelp, she swept the plastic up into a cataclysmic flight over the long trestle. Several figures made dull thuds on the carpet. Those less fortunate landed among various assorted cheeses and dips. One soldier had flipped upside down and rested on the point of his bayonet, which had targeted a soft stuffed mushroom.

I broke through to stand by Janet, pulling her close, protecting her even though she didn't know I was there. Jean and Marshall Magill entered the fray from opposite ends of the room. Janet went at her mother, even before Jean had seen the damage done to her picture-perfect buffet. "How dare you glorify this horrible sacrifice you are asking your son to make!"

"But we're not..."

"This is a war you're sending him to," Janet continued voce granita, her spine straight and her chin high. "It's not a cruise to Europe! Don't you see that he's going to be one of those plastic soldiers on the table? Haa!" she cried, her voice filling the room. "One of the white ones, no doubt!"

"Janet, please." Her father rushed in from the opposite direction. He attempted to skewer her emotions on the points of his sharp eyes, even as he maintained a tolerant-of-youth sneer for the crowd who stood, soaking in every word, habituated as they were to regular doses of televised drama. "We are trying to make the best of an unfortunate situation."

"You are not!" Janet shouted, her voice growing with the strength of her wine-soaked emotions. "You've accumulated so much that you're up in the middle of the night checking under the bed for teeves. But there are no teeves...no, wait..." she paused, her hands on her temples, trying to regain composure. "Thieves!" she shouted triumphantly. "No thieves. Matt could get killed, and for what? This is not our war and this party doesn't prove that it is!"

The crowd snickered audibly. I breathed my first since Janet's magnificent rout of the soldiers. Suddenly she was Jeanne d'Arc, Deborah the Prophetess, and Rosa Parks.

If Janet's dress had sported lapels, Marshall Magill's hands would have grabbed them. As it was, his fists flailed dangerously close to his daughter in a fit of lost patience. "Is this what they're teaching you at that school we pay for?" he cried.

"I'll take this, Dad. This one's mine." Matthew was by his sister's side, pulling my arm roughly from around her and cutting me off. I felt the blood rush to my face and the scotch to my head as I absorbed the meaning of Matthew's calm and completely arrogant tone. "If you are going to break up my party—and it is my party—then you listen here. What makes you think I'm not glad to fight for my country? I may be white, but at least I'm not like these cowardly yellow Berkeley bastards who want to take everything and give nothing." He glanced warily my way. "You don't have to feel sorry for me!"

Suddenly any distance I'd achieved went the way of the plastic soldiers, another of Janet's complete routs. I found my voice buried beneath several years of cynicism, like dead wood miraculously sprouting moist clusters of new leaves.

"Maybe she doesn't feel sorry for you," I said, steadying my eyes to meet Matthew's. "Maybe she feels sorry for those poor bastards in Vietnam, the rice farmers who get burned and mutilated in their own country, on their own land, by snooty Americans like you who think they own the world."

"Well, well, this is nice. Aaron Becker has an opinion," Matthew said.

I glanced over at Janet, not wanting to miss her moment of surprise. Chicken-shit Aaron Becker had stepped forward to support her in her campaign.

"But Aaron, I do feel sorry for him," Janet whimpered.

"That's it. Cry for him, cry for the innocence he will lose," I said, remembering the tears she shed in my cottage, those very words. I bent back toward Matthew, smelling his mint-fresh breath. "In fact," I went on, "you'd be better off dead than killing people who have never done anything to you, people you don't even know."

"Aaron, that's not what..." Janet tried to move forward between us but her father had a grip on her shoulders. "Aaron, CHRIST! What are you saying?!" Her cry finally caught my attention, but I knew if I could just finish, she'd feel the bond between us she'd been seeking since October.

"Janet, I'm speaking the truth. They're going to make your big brother into a murderer!" I turned away from her. The eyes of party guests and the smartass mouth of the guest of honor had fallen under my spell. "Matthew, for God's sake, what have you got to do with this war? You're Mr. Nice Guy and they're going to make you kill kids and burn villages. Don't go! Just quit, run away."

"Is that what you're going to do, college boy?" Matthew shot back.

"Damn right! I've already written to my Dad for the fare. That's a one-way ticket. If I lose my grad school deferment I'll be outta here, and I won't be back until this country gets its head screwed on straight!"

Matthew rocked back on his heels with a sneer on his ruddy lips. He began to shake his head, snickering at me like I'd just delivered the punch line to a terrific joke. His final, more hearty burst of laughter led a weak chorus of contemptuous onlookers. Pure hatred bubbled in my stomach. I hadn't known until that moment that flight had been my last, best, and only option all along. I heard Janet sobbing, but I couldn't take my eyes off the face of the doomed. I'd just dragged my bloody secret out from my heart and exposed it to the air, and it was already drying up and turning brown.

Without a decent comeback, I pushed my way through the jumble of sashed and perfumed humanity, into the elephantine foyer and up the stairs.

I went straight for my suitcase. I couldn't stay in that house another minute. Janet's furious footsteps were behind me, but they halted at her bedroom door. I stuffed my meager possessions under one arm, grabbed the case, and hauled the whole mess down the hall.

Janet was pacing. "How could you?" she veered toward me as I dropped the suitcase on her bed.

"Well, I can't be sorry for speaking the truth, can I? I mean..." I didn't know how to go on. We would just have to straighten things out later. Intent on getting out of there, I started to arrange things so I could close up the case. Suddenly, she grabbed my toothbrush out of my hand and hurled it across the room where it landed on the stomach of a white stuffed cat with rhinestone eyes. Janet's eyes glittered like the cat's.

"Those people down there are my family. That is my brother you wished death on, and he believes he's going to fight for your way of life. All the goddamned rice paddies under creation can go up in smoke before I would want to see him dead."

"Hey, you started that big scene. You were tearing them up, and I was just following your lead. You were terrific...I've never been so proud of you!"

"Proud of me? What does that mean? I hate this war for all kinds of reasons and my parents are blind and my brother is a brat, but you...you obviously don't know a thing about me! Oh...the room is ssswirling..." she sank onto the bed, her head falling across the rumpled clothes in my case. I sat down next to her, pulled her up and put my arms around her. Her head fell onto my shoulder. I rubbed her back.

"Hey, wake up," I jostled her arm. "You've just had a little too much to drink. We both have...it's all going to be okay."

"Oh God...what did I say?" she mumbled, then her head popped up, eyes following a trajectory along the spinning pink walls until she found me. "You...you called him a murderer! What if he hesitates for one split second...because of you? He'll be killed. And I...I'm the one who brought you here!"

She pulled away and started to pace again, hugging and slapping herself as if she were trying to keep warm in the frigid night. "Janet, please. Okay, I'm sorry. It got out of hand...the last thing in the world I would want is to hurt you. I hoped you'd feel like I was joining you in your fight. Speaking out in public. On your side at last!"

She kept pacing, waving her hands, her shouts alternating rhythmically with a whining tone. "Oh God! What have I done? That fight is in Berkeley, not here in my family's living room.

You of all people should have understood that!" She'd stopped and sucked in a breath, then stared vacantly at my knees. "That was about you down there, wasn't it? About your draft situation. Admit it," she challenged. "Not about Matt and certainly not about me."

I wasn't ready to be contrite. I replied hotly, "Well, I thought if it was about my avoiding the draft, it was about us."

Several deep breaths later, when she spoke again, her tone had lowered an octave and frozen solid, as if an entirely different girl were speaking. "And of course, caring about me as you do, that was why you were going to leave the country. Sneak out without even telling me..."

"I was waiting!" I cut her off. I swallowed hard and my eyes slid down to the crimson carpet, guilty as charged. When I raised my eyes, Janet was standing there, scowling and breathing as if she'd just run the mile. "I'm sorry, okay? I chickened out. I know I should have told you."

"Told me? What about asked me? Talked to me...Draft dodger! What a terrible idea," she cried. "You'd never ever be able to come home." She shut the suitcase with a flourish. Taking in the whole roomful of air in one breath, she shouted, "Why you... you... cowardly, self-righteous, self-absorbed, insensitive, cretinous, cowardly, SMALL... you...you...you're mean!" Her pitch had regained its octave. "...God, you asshole, son-of-a-bitch, bastard, mother-fucking piece of shit...!" She went on like that for a full minute. I'd ceased to breathe and was unconsciously backing away from her.

The instinct to run was overwhelming. From her, from this house, from the war—run for my life. Without a word, I grabbed my suitcase in an automatic movement and before I knew it, I was on the back stairs, creeping past the maids' rooms and out the kitchen door.

My landlord and good buddy Neil Strand had agreed to take care of Dork while I was down in L.A. with Janet, then visiting Cora for a couple of days. Neil was a poet and sometime grad student, who owned a big, two-story house, its land, and our adjacent cottages, thanks to a grandparental legacy. Significantly, he also possessed a 4F deferment, thanks to a congenital heart condition—the kind you get checked twice a year then forget about, except during wartime. What surely he did not possess was his roommate and main squeeze, Joanna Larkin, a lively person with a mind of her own. Together they occupied the second cottage in back of the big house, preferring their privacy to living with student renters, even though their floor plan was only slightly larger than mine.

I'd never known a couple who had rejected legal formalities on principle. Joanna and Neil preferred to live together without tying the knot, not trusting nor believing in the marital ties that had ended in divorce court for both sets of their parents, as for mine. With all the crap we had in common, and despite their ownership of my humble abode, these two had become my closest friends at Cal. It had begun in the days when I lived in the big house and asked Neil about renting the cottage that finally became mine only this year. Their unswerving warm welcome and their status as graduate students—the fact that they seemed older and wiser—encouraged me to drop in nearly every day to shoot the bull. Didn't hurt that they encouraged me to help myself to Joanna's delicious smörgåsbord, the heaps of Swedish hors d'oeuvres, mostly fishy, that she always seemed to have on hand. Both Neil and Joanna were of recent Scandinavian descent, curly-white-blondes with ruddy faces. Joanna had learned to assemble the delicacies from her paternal grandmother. Neil considered them a staple, like bread and wine.

In some ways, if I was lucky enough to get my ticket, I was going to miss my friends—and my cottage—almost as much as Janet Magill. After years cooped up in the apartment with Cora, the home I had made for myself was like an extra prize in the Cracker Jack box of UC Berkeley. Only Janet knew the inflated value I placed on my cottage. I was brooding over some of the big and little personal revelations between Janet and me and the complete debacle I'd left behind in LA, as I headed for Neil and Joanna's to retrieve Dork. My possible international flight, double entendre intended, was weighing heavily on my mind. I decided to introduce one catastrophe at a time. So I told my buddy about the intended request from Dad for a one-way ticket next June. I asked him if he would be willing to take care of Dork for an indefinite period of time.

"Where'ya going?" Neil asked.

"I've got the whole world to choose from, with the exception of Ecuador and Vietnam."

"Stockholm is nice in June."

"Stockholm will be a cold bitch by September," Joanna chimed in. She had begun her listening from inside the living room but had gradually worked her way out onto the porch, her blond frizz lit up in the afternoon sun. With an arm wrapped tightly around Neil's waist, her mournful expression felt like an assault.

"Maybe Paris. If I can get the funds, I'd like it to be Paris."

"Ah yes," said Neil, "it's the Francophile thing. Lingua franca. The culture of those in the know. French phrases, French wines, French artists, and my favorite—French seductions."

I shrugged my shoulders. "So shoot me. I like believing that the French are all wise, witty and très sensual."

"And Jeanette," said Neil, aping a terrible French accent. "Zat woman has a petite t'ing about France, mais non?"

I snickered, and hung my head. How to tell them about Janet Magill?

Neil went on, a sappy grin beneath his luminous blue eyes. "Follow her to her dreams, my friend, only if you sleep and dream together."

"Never mind," Joanna said. "She's very young yet, in more ways than one. How did she react when you told her about your plans?"

"Well...I...actually, I'm still hoping grad school will keep me safe. And then, with her brother leaving and all..."

"You mean you haven't told her yet?" Joanna dropped her arm from Neil and put her hands on her hips like a scolding housefrau. "Talk to her about it, Aaron. Dammit...what's with men?"

"Don't be so bossy, Joanna," Neil said. "Let the lad do as he pleases."

"Actually, I told her in L.A.," I sang out, forcing a smile. "Only it didn't exactly come out like I'd intended. She's pissed off." They each came across with varying degrees of disbelief and sympathy. Neil pulled me inside the cottage, and we parked ourselves around the kitchen table. With as much wit as I could muster, I pushed the story out through my lumped up throat, recounting the highlights of the Beverly Hills fiasco.

Like the good friend he was, Neil was somber, reflecting my feelings more than my flippant air. "I'm sorry, buddy."

"I've come up with a plan that might lure her back," I said.

"A plan? Really?" Joanna's head drew back. "You mean a straightforward conversation, right? Because that's what I'd..."

"A special gift," I said. "Something French." Joanna's eyes narrowed and Neil's head wagged.

"Listen to me, Aaron," Joanna said. "Trust is about the most important thing you've got going in any relationship. Loyalty and trust."

"I can't figure how I'd get that into a conversation. I've already tried explaining...say, I've got to get on home, settle in." I'd had enough of Joanna's Dear Abby impersonation for now. I stood up. "I'll have to think about all this. Thanks for taking care of Dork."

"Of course." "Sure." "We'll talk more later..." With that, I lifted my bird in his cage and fled to the shelter of my cottage.

On Monday morning, off I went to a San Francisco store that catered to arcane tastes in music. I found what I was looking for, an album by Serge Reggiani, the rage of female Paris. I decided to go the whole nine yards and bought some wrapping paper covered with fleur-de-lis. The F bus back over the bridge, the hike home, the gift wrap, the apologetic note. By then it was nightfall. I walked my peace offering down the hill to Freeborn Hall and dropped it at the front desk, wondering when I'd get my response.

FIVE

A LONELY WEEK back in Berkeley included my New Year's Eve date at the Villa Freeborn —a paperback of The Count of Monte Cristo by Alexandre Dumas. The French-English dictionary sat primly by my side like a chaperone for the evening. After a while, I picked up my guitar and started to strum, but set it down again because the sound of my high, tinny voice made me shudder. So I put on my new Beatles' album and raised my hands above my head and clapped and danced around the miniscule dorm room singing "La-laaa-the-magical-mystery-tour." Pretty soon, I was just howling "is-coming-to-take-you-away" over and over again to the moon outside my window, perched like a fat dove over the bay. I needed a dove and voilà! There it was!

After several choruses, Margaret Brenner came down the hall and told me to knock it off, she was trying to sleep. So reluctantly, I went back to Dumas.

The Count was just the kind of book I loved. Romantic and exciting. It kept me mesmerized the rest of the evening except for the five hundred and eighty-five times my mind strayed to Aaron Becker, then to my own embarrassing, drunken folly—all those people gathered in our living room with their plastic eyes, like those plastic bayonets on Mother's buffet, aimed right at me.

On Monday evening, Aaron left an album of French songs for me at the dorm desk. How pathetic! Some pittance to remind me what we used to share, when life was as mellow and soothing as a sip of French cognac. I was furious that he couldn't even come see me, didn't have the nerve. That would have given me what I'd fantasized about every single day since Matt's party: the opportunity to reject him again. For making a big mess even bigger. For not trusting me enough to discuss his plans. For ruining everything between us! When I saw the album, I realized that I had wanted Gene Kelly and Leslie Caron, dancing along the banks of the Seine, but all Aaron could offer me was Daddy Long Legs. Fred Astaire protecting Leslie Caron like she was an ignorant little kid.

On my way back to Freeborn Hall the next afternoon, I balanced a sheaf of leaflets on my books and clutched at one after another. I had just had my first real conversation with an antiwar protestor. I felt relieved, exhilarated and exhausted. I'd returned to Ludwig's Fountain to find Todd, the boy who was so nice the day I first learned about Matt last October. Radical or not, he was as easy to talk to as I remembered. He had no sense of humor, of course, but I wasn't in the mood to laugh anyway. I pictured Aaron's derisive smirk. What a relief that I would not have to tell Aaron about my frustrations and new hopes!

When I arrived at my dorm room, Barbara sat writing at her desk. She ignored me, as usual. I stood behind her, took a deep breath, and floated one of the leaflets down to cover her pen hand. She stared at the sheet without moving, then turned to me in slow motion. "This is it," she said quietly. "Everything's going to change now."

"Yes, the leaflet and a conversation I had in the Plaza today make sense. This outrageous new twist might stand a chance of being effective. The Yippies...Youth International Party. Jerry Rubin and Abbie Hoffman."

"They're right, you know. No one is ever going to listen to us. So let's just screw it all. Get crazy. Go crazy. Kennedy is supporting the war and Johnson, can you believe it? He just declared victory is around the corner. What does that mean? After the whole country is flattened?"

As Barbara stood up, her eyes landed on my new political button. The big red peace symbol looked like it was painted in drippy blood. I'd felt rather brave when I accepted it from Todd and put it right on, without hesitation. "I like your button," Barbara said. "Where did you get it?"

"A guy in Sproul Plaza gave it to me, along with the leaflet and some other information."

Barbara reached both her hands toward me and squeezing my arms, her yellow-brown eyes gazing straight into mine. "I can hardly believe it...but I'm glad. I saw you out there on the Plaza today and I was hoping. But I saw you with Todd. I figured he'd have a better chance with you."

"A chance with me? You mean to persuade me?" Barbara let go of my arms and beamed at me in a friendly way, not a trace of scorn on her lips.

"It's just that certain types of women respond better to men than to other women. You don't respect yourself much, so you don't respect other women either."

"I respect myself..."

"All I know is, I don't know whether your brother being drafted finally put a dent in your veneer or you're not such a dunce after all, but I'm thrilled that you're going to be one of us."

"Now wait a minute, Barbara. I can't be one of you!" I shouted, trying to firm up my voice. How could anybody ever take me seriously with this child's voice?

Barbara was patient while I caught my breath, then nodded encouragingly. I continued, trying to speak rapidly before the ideas evaporated. "This just means I agree that students haven't stopped the war because nobody's listening to them. And that we have to make them listen. I like this idea of insane comic relief, the 'Politics of Ecstasy.' And they say that's going to drive the older generation crazy enough to end the war!" I hooted in triumph, as if it had already happened. "And I believe it. I love it! I'm so damned sick of doing what everyone else wants. My parents, my boyfriend...ex-boyfriend," I stumbled, "and professors, newspapers, even you and your radicals! I want to be free and I hate hate hate this war!"

I sat down heavily onto the corner of my bed. I was going hoarse and my heart was pounding. I felt as though I'd just climbed a mountain and realized I wasn't ever going to get back down again.

"But you've made up your mind. You believe what we're doing is on the right track?"

"I have made up my mind," I whined. "But shit, no matter what I think, I can't even talk rationally to you about it. Yes, I can wash off my makeup and trade in my sweaters for ponchos and leather vests and I will! But how can I possibly influence anything?"

Barbara had let me shout and whine and now she sat down next to me. "Janet, I'm not asking you to protest and give speeches and argue publicly. But if you believe that these new Yippie tactics can turn things around, at least help us with the practical aspects of letting the government know that we're still out here. And that we're changing. That we've freed ourselves."

I hesitated, searching the room as if war protestor instructions were inscribed inside my open sweater drawer. "Well...what do I do?" I asked.

Barbara was ready with her answer. "What good does it do to establish your personal freedom if nobody knows it? Come to our meetings. Just be there. And when we're in public, just stand there with us. Show yourself. That's all you have to do. Dress however you want and sing a song with the rest of us if it feels good to you. Todd will be there. He's a special friend of mine. And lots of others will be there, too."

I nodded. "Todd's your boyfriend?"

"Comrade in arms. And sometime lay." I have no idea what I looked like at this announcement, but Barbara cracked up.

"I'm trying to decide if you're more disappointed or shocked. Don't worry. I'm willing to share."

"Christ, Barbara. I'm not a baby. And I'm not interested in Todd that way. He's all yours." She shrugged her shoulders and squeezed my arm again as if to steady me. "Suit yourself, friend. I just wanted you know that with me, freedom means freedom."

We broke into smiles, then laughter, and in the end I gave one whoop of surprise. A normal college dorm room, at last, with two chummy roommates!

"Say, are you hungry?" Barbara broke the spell. "You want to join us for dinner? Meet some of the others?"

There was no longer any reason to hold back and every reason to go. "Yes, I do. But wait. I want to wash this crap off my face and put on my blue jeans."

"So, get ready, and then we'll be on our way."

"Won't they all make fun of my sudden transformation?" I asked.

"Janet, friend, I don't even think they're going to recognize you."

Once I had followed Barbara to the SDS office and let my intentions be known, relief swept over me as if McNamara himself had written to thank me for my efforts on behalf of our soldiers. For a day or two, I indulged my own irrationality. All the antiwar groups working together, I thought, might bring Matt home early.

Whatever the outcome of the protests, at least I was beyond Aaron's pontificating. I attended meetings, worked in the SDS office, listened to student and faculty speakers and viewed underground films. But I understood that showing up at protests was my most important function. Just showing up. Every few days, Barbara gave a pep talk to remind the group that our presence on the front lines was a patriotic act.

A week into my new life, Barbara's SDS group scheduled a protest outside the Fairmont Hotel in San Francisco. Secretary of State Dean Rusk would be there defending his indefensible strategies before big shot supporters from the local Commonwealth Club and the World Affairs Council. It was Todd who explained that Rusk had been a liberal all his life and had intended his bombing the shit out of Vietnam to convince the North to back off. All he wanted was to get Johnson back on

"The Great Society" track, with the Democratic agenda of justice and equality for all. Nice concept, Todd assured the group, but it wasn't going to happen without a little help from the antiwar movement. With Rusk blindly backing the president's pursuit of total victory in Vietnam, they would show up in San Francisco to remind him that Johnson's Democratic establishment supporters wouldn't be the only voters next November.

As Todd wrapped up, I decided to make the Rusk protest my debut appearance at an antiwar demonstration.

When our group climbed aboard the F bus from Berkeley, I slid in by a window. Barbara surprised me by taking the aisle seat right next to me. "What a turnout! Aren't you stoked?" she bellowed. I pumped myself up with as much juice as I could muster. "I'm excited," I replied. My tone sounded hollow and hesitant compared to hers. She smiled sympathetically and squeezed my arm, but quickly turned her attention to friends across the aisle.

I hadn't lied, not exactly. I was excited but also anxious. I huddled quietly in my corner, staring out the window. The engine roared as we accelerated over the Bay Bridge, and all around me, my new Yippie acquaintances chattered softly, talking about everything from war news and the evening's plans to their grades and music. I perked up when I heard a guy behind me talking about the recent Stop the Draft Week defense fund concert at Fillmore Auditorium. Phil Ochs had played, and I had wanted to go. He and Dylan were the only two acoustic musicians I was interested in these days. But didn't I need a date for a big crazy event like that? Feeling sulky, I comforted myself with the certainty that Aaron probably wouldn't have been interested in that concert anyway.

The volume in the bus was picking up. Comrades were admiring each other's tee-shirts and sweatshirts, silkscreened with protest slogans or psychedelic designs. Barbara noticed my new rainbow tie-dye sweatshirt. "Yours is perfect," she said, "especially with a button that drips and dribbles peace."

I laughed at her weird description. "Thanks. And you had a great idea about the sweaters underneath." She beamed. Especially cashmere, I mused. Nice and warm without the bulk, so I didn't have to hide my new tie-dye with my old brown car coat.

THE BERKELEY GIRL

Barbara had taken to wearing a kind of tan, fringed cowgirl pants. Tonight she wore them with a matching vest embroidered all over with little colored flowers. That must be new, I realized, and that must be the foul animal smell drifting my way. I was relieved when, within minutes, someone had lit up a cigarette and smoke had replaced Borden cow dung and softened the air. I suddenly wished someone had a joint to share. If I had a drag, I reflected, maybe it would calm the incessant jittery stings that had taken over my limbs and held a grip on my heart. But I knew no one would be stupid enough to smoke dope on a public bus. I thought longingly about Aaron's finest, always stashed in his kitchen drawer with the Lipton's. Why had I never asked anyone where to get my hands on the stuff for myself? Everyone just seemed to magically bring it out of a pocket or drawer. But this wasn't the time to bring it up, to make my utter ineptitude into the brunt of jokes. I glared out my window at the deepening night sky.

In the distance, the lights of the city glittered like gold and diamonds, reminding me of the people in all their dressy finery who would soon be walking into the Fairmont to hear our Secretary of State. I knew those people. They were just like Mother and Daddy and their friends, the same people who lauded Matt at his farewell party the night I humiliated myself in a drunken stupor. A slow burning sensation filled my stomach. That was the last time I spoke to Aaron. No, screamed at him would be more accurate. Tears clogged my throat. What if Aaron left the country and I never ever saw him again? I shook my head and shoulders violently, as if the motion could be as effective as a great big drag of pot.

Before long, both the guys and the girls began to tie back their long locks and to remove and stash necklaces and bracelets, preparing for action. I followed their lead. With the San Francisco Transbay Terminal just minutes away, the girls began to pull protest signs off the upper shelves with slogans I couldn't read in the dark. Barbara reached up and fetched ours. Hers was the usual "Make Love, Not War," but mine said what was in my heart: "Bring our troops home NOW!"

Suddenly, from toward the back, I heard a loud report of laughter as sharp as the firing of a gun and a raspy "Far out!" The hilarity came from two guys. As city lights flickered through the interior, I could see one wielding a red brick and the other a soft balloon. They were playing at slapping the one against the other. Todd stood up in his seat and shouted above the commotion. "Quit it, you morons. If it breaks, that crap will be all over us and the bus! Save it for the pigs." I was amazed when they instantly obeyed, stashing their hilarity with the "crap."

My heart had begun to race at the sight of the brick. What had happened to MLK's commitment to nonviolence? Were we willing to fight and possibly injure cops or even innocent bystanders? And what was with the balloons? "Hey, Barbara," I asked, trying to sound cool. "What good are water balloons?"

"Water? Oh no, not water. We're going to mess up those pretty Academy Award frocks and tuxes," she said. "The balloons are filled with animal blood—just don't ask the source—and some paint mixed in to give them the full horror of sticky, bright bloody red. Nice touch, don't you agree?" She must have seen my own horror-struck face before she turned away. Or maybe that's why she turned away. For about five full seconds, I didn't care what she thought of me. Nausea rose through my whole system and the Fritos and Coke I'd eaten for supper were about to come up onto my new sweatshirt. That's what I had been smelling! I stared out the window at Mission Street, swallowed hard and fought the tears forming in my eyes. Then it hit me that Barbara understood what we were up against. We had to make a statement, not just about our own dissatisfaction with politics as usual, but about war and death! Before I could analyze and rationalize my way completely back to a calm stomach, I was following Barbara and my comrades out the doors into the Terminal.

Our group set out immediately, heading across Mission Street, up Market and then Nob Hill. As we strode along, we were joined by many others going in the same direction. No singing, hardly any talking. We hadn't much time to make it to the hotel before the grandees.

Soon our small band stood on the street, walking forward amid the chants of hundreds of strangers. Most of my new acquaintances were lost in the larger crowd, and I kept my eyes glued to Barbara's bright hair and Todd's high head. As the pace of the chant quickened, they pushed their way forward as if they wanted to leave me behind. I heard the repeated "Hell no...we won't go," tried to open my mouth, but I couldn't match the rhythm.

Gradually, we slowed down, and then, several limo lengths from the hotel entrance, I could just barely make out Huey Newton up ahead when someone pointed him out. The famous Black Panther stood up on a low wall. Guys were setting fire to their draft cards and a cacophonous whoop flew up with the ashes. I imagined Matt up there burning his card, wished it with all my heart, but the stinging smell of smoke, breath, and overheated bodies made me want to shut down all my senses. I felt desperate to close my eyes and pretend like I wasn't there. A new chant took over. "Hey, hey LBJ, how many kids have you killed today?" I conjured defiance and fury, forcing myself to remember the anger that had brought me here. I lifted my face to the dark sky, mouth-breathed, and counted to ten backwards.

Then, steeling myself, I lowered my chin, eyes open. I spotted the police squads just as the first bloody balloon struck one of the stone columns over the elegant porch of the Fairmont Hotel. Relief swept over me when I realized that the protestors were deliberately aiming away from the dinner guests, who were rushing through a police line into the lobby.

Another missile splotched the facade, followed by the shattering of glass. Now the protesters were throwing glass bottles along with their bricks and balloons, but not for long. The whole troop of policemen charged the front and began clubbing people with their sticks. Those cops were all big guys, every one of them, their features hidden by the smoky plastic visors of their helmets. The smell of mace drifted meagerly back, stinging my throat and eyes, but the source was far away, at the front of the crowd. Squished and craning, I saw a club landing with all a cop's might on some poor guy's head, then thrashing at his head and shoulders over and over again until he went down. The cops seemed furious, out of control, like no one was giving orders and they were attacking on their own. I heard the screams and my limbs put me in automatic retreat. Picket still raised way above me, I rotated and began to squeeze through slivers of space. Everyone around me was headed in the same direction, away from the police.

The pigs had succeeded in dispersing us! Overcome by rage and shame, I tried again to push toward the action. I focused on people nearest the hotel, squinting in the smoky night. There was Barbara's flaming bubble of hair. A moment later, a police club came down on it as if it had been an irresistible target. I only discerned one rather restrained stroke, but her head disappeared from view. Was she knocked out? Would she be trampled underfoot? I was screaming but could not hear myself scream, pushing toward her but carried along backwards by a tide of fear. My picket fell from my grip and I turned away one final time, giving in to the inevitable. Then I pushed and kicked and elbowed my fleeing comrades until I achieved space and path enough to run full throttle out of there and all the way back to the Transbay Terminal on Mission Street. I arrived, thoroughly ashamed of myself. And there was Barbara, standing in the ticket line! I caught my breath and nearly lost my legs.

Barbara was laughing at me. "Hey, they didn't catch you either! You're as pale as a ghost!"

"Really? I feel hot from running," I said, wiping city soot from the corners of my eyes. "I thought you'd be in jail by now."

"Todd may be. They banged my head..." she rubbed at the spot where the clubber had caught her, "...and I ducked and crawled under the crowd. Sometimes it helps to be a shrimp. My leathers are shot to hell. But my philosophy is that if you can escape, it's not a bad tactic to run away. We don't want to seem too eager for jail, like it's a publicity stunt, or the public won't get that I'm just an earnest, beleaguered college student."

"Which you are! Are you okay? Do you need me to get you to a hospital?"

She chuckled, then rubbed again. "Ow. Thanks but no thanks. But I'll be glad to be home with an icepack."

"Why didn't you ever tell me your philosophy before? I started to go back..."

"Hey, you act as if I can predict the scene. But you know those cops are fucking dangerous. No use even trying to rescue people who are grabbed. I've tried that in the past. Tonight I would've gotten my skull broken."

I pondered my instant of insanity, trying to return through that panicked throng. My next question came out almost like an apology. "So, you were afraid? Like me?"

"Why...of course," Barbara said, looking somewhat bewildered. She had reached the front of the line. I handed her a five-dollar bill. "Here. Can you get me a ticket?" She hesitated, her hand poised in the air between us, as if my money might be counterfeit.

As soon as she had our tickets in hand, she began to admonish me. "Listen Janet, you take this whole thing too seriously. I mean it. Go ahead and be scared, but it can be fun, too, if you relax and see it as a big party. Better yet, as a big sass of the authorities. Man, we're driving them to the wall!"

I offered a weak smile. "Yes. I guess so. Are you sorry you recruited me?"

"A body is a body. And for the record, I didn't recruit you. You volunteered, remember?"

"Of course. I didn't mean you..."

"...Of course you didn't." She patted me on the arm. "Say, you're doing a great job, roommate. Think of it this way: it's not courage if you're not afraid. Your first week and already you were out here with us. That's courage."

A grateful "thanks" extinguished the gulf between us. "Now let's get home." She glanced around, smiling and waving to people I didn't recognize. She behaved so much like a political candidate that I had to stifle a laugh. "Man, am I ever beat," she said, rolling her eyes at me. I followed her to the crowd of Berkeley students already waiting in line for the F bus, trying not to dwell anymore on what might have happened, or what could very well happen at the next protest.

The following afternoon, I sat on my dorm room bed tweezing splinters from my hands. How ludicrous it had been to carry our signs on pickets made of cheap wood!

Barbara was right, of course. I was way too serious about the fight and repelled by the crowds to have any fun with my new career as a radical. My feelings about the demonstration came in Malibu-sized waves that I couldn't control. I threw the tweezers down on the pile of newspapers littering the bed and studied the leaden bay out the window. As long as I was going to spend my day obsessed, it was a relief to be all alone. Incredibly, Barbara had gone to class.

I blew out a big, noisy breath, and picked up the New York Times and the Berkeley Barb, comparing two opposing views. About 400 or 700 demonstrators had been at the Fairmont, depending on the politics of the reporter. But everyone seemed to agree that the Cal contingent showed well. Around 60 people had been arrested. Many others were hurt far more severely than my roommate.

When I read that it was clear the police had planned ahead of time to inflict grave injury, I had to stop myself from shouting: We threw bottles, bricks and blood, for heaven's sake! What did we expect? That they'd let us damage private property and endanger lives? The Berkeley Barb accused the authorities of intentionally busting up our protest to prevent free speech by anyone who disagreed with Rusk and the Johnson administration. But where, I wondered, did free speech begin and end?

The cops weren't defense, the Barb declared, they were offense. This was no longer our group's performance for the cameras, as Barbara had touted and Aaron had presumed. Last night had been the enemy's performance, Rusk's and Johnson's political strategy of clubbing to kill, willing to kill, to silence. So why did Barbara's group decide to play into their hands? Give them fuel to toss into their fire? These arguments always brought me, keening with frustration, around to Aaron's brand of inaction.

I was trying to judge for myself, but it wasn't easy. Every time I had what I considered a logical reaction, or even an Aaron cynical moment, I thought of Matt and innocent Vietnamese people, and yes, Aaron's dilemma too, and my insides churned like I'd swallowed a quart of Mazola. Then, with clenched fists and tears, I imagined myself breaking down hotel walls and police barriers, even the White House itself, with more than weapons that shatter and splatter.

Was there no one in the world to still this seesaw of logic and emotion? Feeling as isolated as ever, I reached for the San Francisco Chronicle to read more quotes from the dinner speech by the architect of my family's destruction. According to Rusk, Vietnam's war should not be called a civil war when it only contained "civil war elements." What kind of hocus pocus was that? People were dying just the same, and one of them might be someone I cared about.

Resigning myself to the best of the bad choices available to me, I went back to plucking splinters from my hands. I knew I'd be following Barbara wherever she might lead me, and I vowed to spend more for a better brand of picket from now on.

Beyond my demonstration anxiety, in the week following the protest action, I became disheartened by the way Barbara's male cohorts in the leadership swooped down on my donated labor like a colony of seagulls pecking at a small fish. I was working as a kind of secretary, running petitions and leaflets off on the mimeograph machine, answering phones, hanging posters and assembling picket signs. Although I noticed immediately that most of the girls in the group were there with boyfriends and had similar low-status jobs, I hung around the guys, hoping for more substantive assignments or at least for a stimulating conversation. I practiced on the sly—writing and drawing for leaflets and posters. Barbara caught me sketching on a clipboard in the room one evening.

"There are lots of talented people doing that work," she said. "Maybe you should be doing homework so you don't flunk out."

"You should talk. You hardly ever crack a book."

"I get by. But I don't waste my time."

"How will I know if I have talent or not if I don't develop it?"

Barbara sighed and sat on the bed next to me. "Janet, you're new. Let's just say it takes a while to develop the trust of the group. You have to pay your dues."

"Well, I'm doing whatever they tell me to do, aren't I?"

"Yes," she nodded. "You've been great. Just don't push all your ideas on every guy who'll give you the time of day."

Only a moron wouldn't recognize that Barbara jealously guarded her position as the only female on the steering committee. But I decided that I must be annoying some of the guys, and she was just being helpful. Besides, what strengths could I contribute, really? For now, the new kid in class would do a lot of listening, complete menial assignments, and try to fit in.

Even with our antics, most Americans still didn't get it: in a Gallup poll published right after New Year's, only 45 percent believed that it was a mistake to have gotten involved in Vietnam. And I understood that only a fraction of those would want to swallow their American pride to get out immediately. How could we actually lose a war?

But by the end of another week, my enthusiasm picked back up when 5000 women marched and sang in a Washington, D.C. protest just as the second session of the 90th Congress opened. We crowded around the Berkeley Barb at the SDS headquarters. The march renewed my confidence that Aaron was wrong in his stubborn insistence on our counter-productivity. The action was lead by 87-year-old Jeanette Rankin, the first female member of Congress. I thought about Mother and suddenly I understood and resented how my timidity was genetic. Jeanette Rankin proved that you didn't have to be a radical—a nymphomaniac with dirty hair—to be against the war.

SIX

JANUARY, THEN FEBRUARY, and still no word from Janet. It was as if I'd shoved that Serge Reggiani album into a trash can. The girl had lowered a gigantic terrarium glass over the Berkeley campus, and I was standing on the outside. I had my lab rat buddies, then my new classes and labs. And my groovy ornithology course with Ames, adaptations and systematics of bird species...but I felt alone. And it took me by surprise. I hadn't anticipated what such a long split from Janet would feel like.

Eventually, I gave in to the notion that true lust and self-torture are synonymous concepts. Since France was a place that Janet and I had talked about incessantly, I devised a cherished scene to jazz up my solitude. In my fantasy, Janet and I were touring France on a Eurail pass, watching quaint villages whiz by from an upper bunk between sessions of passionate lovemaking. Then, we were returning to a humbled and forgiving U.S. of A., the war was over, declared a debacle by one and all. Her parents welcomed us into their vast living room, sat us down with Cokes in tall frosty glasses and listened awestruck to our tales of adventure in the birthplace of la liberté.

Despite Neil's skepticism, I couldn't let go of the hope—the belief that Janet and I shared—that France meant beauty and a way of knowing what to do. Savoir faire.

Gigi, Vincente Minelli's Hollywood version of Colette's confection, was the big film when Janet was nine and I was twelve. Maurice Chevalier displayed an insider perspective regarding life and love, appealing naturally to two gawky, outsider preteens. Much later, when Janet and I met again and carried on our long-distance romance, Beverly Hills to Berkeley, we would swap novels—my Hugo's Les Miserables for her Hemingway's A Moveable Feast. At her house during vacations, we'd sip our pilfered cognac, her mother's display book reproductions of Matisse and Braques stretched across our two laps.

Unfortunately, news from the front was no vacation travelogue. Politics and the urge to maintain power being what they are, I could see why Johnson had publicly pitted himself against the youthful "communist doves." Our president persisted with his war policy, ignoring advice from Asian scholars and his own ranking government officials. Never mind that Matthew Magill and I were working on Boy Scout merit badges the year this war began. Johnson had convinced most people that it would be over soon, and that's all most Americans, including myself, really cared about.

But what I could not understand was how Johnson dared to stick to his story after January 30, 1968, the Vietnamese lunar New Year—the Tet. The North's aggressive military push, dubbed the Tet Offensive, spattered our TV screens with blood for weeks. So much for the North Vietnamese being beaten down and the imminent end of the war. They weren't going to give up until our military might had destroyed their entire country and everyone in it. Jesus, did they hate Americans.

After the Tet, it didn't take long for news to leak that within weeks, President Johnson would announce limitations on graduate school deferments. The draft numbers for the year ahead blew my mind. They'd shot up from an estimate of 40,000 to 150,000. My stream of luck had run dry.

Trying not to panic, I wrote my Dad a short note to ask if he'd received my request for funds. I didn't repeat the whole pitch. He hadn't written me a word since that mid-October plea, and since our usual pattern was an exchange every month give-or-take, I had begun to worry that he was pissed at me. Although he had escaped combat in the 40's, he had not escaped service. He had always talked big and sounded happy about his good fortune, denigrated the regimented parts of Navy life, and in general given me cause to assume that he wouldn't want his son to be drafted. Now for the first time, I wasn't sure if he would agree with my politics. I considered, then rejected, bringing up the subject with Cora.

Every day I searched my mailbox for a reply from Dad or a note from Janet. Meanwhile, I clung to my choice of Paris as my refuge and began to formulate my plans. And all the time that I was reading up on housing, work permits and graduate programs, I tried to accept the reality: that this best and only full proof option would change my life entirely. By Valentine's Day, nothing from Dad, and from Janet, not even a word of thanks for the cool Reggiani album.

The sun was shining and cherry blossoms prematurely filled Berkeley's cold, clear air with their seductive scent when I spotted Janet on Telegraph Avenue. She was rushing along with her arms full of books and the yard-long scroll of a poster in one hand, and she had, unmistakably, adopted the garb of a dispossessed generation. Her pink and purple tie-dyed shirt peeked through the top of a navy blue knitted poncho, and the original sweater-and-skirt girl was kneading the droopy cuffs of her Levi's jeans with the heels of thick-soled sandals. Much to my amazement, she had let the long, wavy locks that I'd loved to stroke go frizzy, now a sputtering froth that splashed her thin, elegant shoulders. Her skin was rosy from the cold weather and she had put on a little weight. Damn if she didn't look incredible.

As she was about to pass me, I ventured, "Did you receive the record album?" I managed my most non-accusatory tone.

"Yes. Thank you." Then she continued speaking without taking a breath, as if she'd been waiting with the question for weeks. "Have you heard from your Dad? A check for the ticket?"

I stood there mute, sifting through all those clever, fantasized dialogues about the land of liberté and lumière. Finally, in a tone more breathless than I'd expected, I replied, "Not yet. I can't decide if it worries me more that he hasn't sent the check, or that he hasn't answered at all."

"He's probably just deciding."

"Hmm, yes...well...there are many months to go before June," I said, lightly.

She nodded, then jerked her head away, her attention fleeing on past me, up Telegraph Avenue towards the noon crowd at Sproul Plaza. "Not long enough for us to end this insanity though," she said.

"Us? Oh yeah, I see you've got a peace badge. Kind of gory, but..." I considered my choice of word carefully, "...unique."

"You like it?" She stuck her thumb under it and tugged it out.

"Yeah, I actually do," I lied. "But I guess this means you've joined the dreamers beating swords and plowshares against brick walls?"

"Don't be such a cynic, Aaron." The strains of Jimi Hendrix' new album were crashing out of a record store just ahead. I recognized the cut from Experienced, even though I hated the sound. Everyone I knew, including Joanna and Neil, was listening to this plugged-in stuff.

Janet bounced with the rhythm, chin propelled forward and moving like a piston. "I've gotten away from folk, even Dylan," she told me, her brows raised defiantly. "I'm into Hendrix now. And for something softer, Buffalo Springfield and the Doors."

"Don't you play your acoustic anymore?"

"No time."

"Too bad, you're so good..." We stood, listening, and all the time I pondered the insanity of discussing our musical tastes when all I wanted to do was talk her into going out with me again.

"Of course, I wouldn't expect you to groove on the hard stuff," she frowned, "but it fits my mood." Then she spun on her heel and stomped off, elbowing her way through the crowd, knowing full well that I'd follow her. "I just feel angry," she was saying. I pushed to keep up with her. "Really furious, you know? And besides, this music turns me on."

"Suit yourself." I puffed as I drew up beside her. "But I'll stick with acoustics. Peter, Paul and Mary... Remember playing their stuff together? Leavin' on a Jet Plane...?

Her eyes bugged out at me, then she snickered. Very un-Janet-like. "No, I don't remember two months ago," she said sarcastically. She slowed down. "I'm just past that now, Aaron. Especially Leavin' on a Jet Plane."

Silenced by the musical reference to the war, to Matthew, we pushed on, side by side, eyes straight ahead. When I finally took a peek, Janet's gorgeous eyes glowed like street lamps on a gloomy day. My already confused mental state was rapidly deteriorating into a physical direction that threatened some embarrassment. You just couldn't scrutinize a chick like Janet Magill for too long without repercussions.

She faced me head on, "You're like a grouchy old man, Aaron. The music you like says it all. Always bitching about the war from your rocking chair. But I know you do care about ending the war. Even if you're not willing to help."

"Are you trying to goad me into it?"

"You'll do what you want," she snapped.

"It's not as if the work I'm doing in biochem won't be useful to humanity. You used to feel that way too..."

"I never said it wouldn't. I just hope there's a humanity left to benefit." She pumped up the tight roll of butcher paper tucked under her arm and started off toward the campus. "I'm on my way to a meeting right now with this poster...it's for a rally tomorrow night."

"By the way, how's Matthew doing?" I blurted out, raising my hand to her sleeve. She turned back toward me.

"You care?"

"I care. Yes, well, of course I care about him. And you...um...I know you're worried." I sighed and shook my head, unable to continue because of a peculiar tightness in my chest. I glanced down at the street, at store windows, awkwardly avoiding my intense desire to reach for her. People shuffled by. When I finally looked up, she was smiling at me like a cat who has cornered a mouse.

"A shy and stammering Aaron," she said. "That's something new. Since for one reason or another, you care, Matt is fine. The Tet didn't get him."

"Good! Hey, that's great. Whew! That's just great. Listen, Janet, about the party—guilt by reason of insanity. I'm sorry I blew my mouth off like that, and you had every right..."

Janet cut me off. "Enough about the party! It's just that if you put doubt in Matt's mind for one moment...I just can't forgive that."

"But he wasn't listening, Janet! He was basking in glory and he was drinking scotch and Jesus, so was I!"

"Oh God," she cried, "I was so drunk." Reluctantly then, she began to cackle a bit, shaking her head, and finally hooting until we were both putting out big, cleansing, hysterical belly laughs. Tears welled up in our eyes. She coughed and breathed herself into composure. I opened my mouth to speak but her hand clamped down over it. "What happened there was all about my family," she said roughly. "The war and my family." Suddenly she moved her slender white fingers onto my cheek and narrowed her eyes on me. "Stay safe from the war, Aaron. Listen, I've got to go now. See you."

She broke into a run across Bancroft Avenue. Suddenly, my legs were moving and I was shouting, "Hey, Janet, hold on!" as she disappeared into the Sproul Plaza crowd. I finally caught up with her as she reached the steps to the Lower Plaza.

"Hey, wait," I rasped, "Can I see the poster?" She began to tug at the thick rubber band and unfurl her artwork. On it, a black man in uniform, obviously defending our country in the jungles of Vietnam, stared into space with slightly crossed eyes. Clearly, she'd had a problem making the eyes. Beneath the image was bold, colorful calligraphy: Why us? Why anyone? Janet was smiling. "I made that slogan up myself. Like it?"

"You're pretty good at this. It's...convincing. But is this a civil rights rally or anti-war?"

"It's Huey Newton's birthday party and they're using the occasion for SNCC and the Panthers to merge. Civil rights and the war are connected. Who do you think is fighting this war, anyway?"

I cracked a crooked smile. "A quarter of a million blacks plus your whiter-than-Squaw-Valley-in-December brother? We can't lose."

Her lips curved briefly then settled into a grim, tentative expression. "That's a rotten thing, to bring Matt into it, but well...you'd make a terrific radical. You'd get along with my comrades much better than I do."

"Pas moi, mademoiselle," I quipped, trying to keep it light. She swallowed hard and I realized how ridiculous it was that the two of us stood there with identical lumps in our throats. Then, with as much of my old bravado as I could muster, I made an offer. "But if you ever want to get together and talk about it, I'll be happy to lighten the whole thing up with a little of my unique Becker perspective. I mean, there's no reason we can't be friends, is there?"

She nodded slowly. Rolled up her poster, nervously. "Well, okay." She looked at me as if I'd proposed that she munch her poster for a snack. "But I've got activities, homework..."

"No expectations." My palms flew up. "We'll just keep in touch. Have lunch once in a while."

She blew out an enormous quantity of air, perusing the entire Lower Plaza before finally smiling my way at last. "I'm glad I ran into you," she said.

"Yeah, me too." I grinned like a damned fool, but was already worrying. I had a shitload of sympathy for what drove the radicals, honestly. Didn't I stand by the edge of the proverbial cliff, waiting for June to see if I'd jump or the government would push me? But how long would it be until Janet, as naïve and impulsive as she was, went off her own ragged cliff?

We heard the bells of the Campanile ringing, as if on cue. She ran down the steps, her poster bobbing above her head like a drum majorette's baton. "I'll call you," I shouted. I turned, wobbling unsteadily toward the arch of Sather Gate. I thought about how the word friendship comes in all kinds of guises, and wondered how I was going to make it through my biochem class with my wits about me, now that Janet Magill was back in my life.

SEVEN

SIX WEEKS AFTER MY "AWAKENING," as Barbara liked to call it, and two days after the Huey Newton rally, Aaron dropped onto his sheepskin rug and I settled in half a room away from him on a chair by the kitchenette. Aaron's beloved cottage was filled with the glow of late afternoon sun, but I kept to the shadows.

If I had been embarrassed and disgusted with myself after Matt's party, at least I could blame the green Hungarian wine and Daddy's scotch. My part in that fiasco was actually rien—a dry, blown leaf to Fontainebleu—compared with how I felt confessing how royally I had screwed up by attending the SNCC-Panthers merge. Folding my arms across my chest, I searched for a way to tell Aaron Becker what had happened to my illustrious career as a radical.

He began, his tone all chipper. "You said you had to see me right away?"

I squirmed in my seat, swiping at my long wisps of hair to get them out of my eyes. The aquarium motor hummed and Dork pecked at seed. "Well...they snapped my picture."

"Who snapped your picture?"

"Photographers. The newspapers."

"At a demonstration?" Aaron prodded.

"At Huey Newton's birthday party." I tried without much success to keep the warble out of my voice. "I'm in trouble. Daddy's golf partner's wife saw my picture."

"Oh shit..."

"Just my tiny head, no bigger than the Lincoln on a penny. In the newspaper photograph of the Big Bad Negro rally. She told her husband, who told Daddy."

"Shit, Janet..."

"Stop saying that!" I shouted. "I don't want to hear about how you warned me about radicals. How you're smarter than I am for staying out of it and all that self-righteous crap."

"Well, dammit, I am smarter and I did warn you," Aaron shouted back, flapping his arms like his stupid bird. He had come across the room and was standing above me. "Anyway, where does it get you?" he continued. "Or the blacks going to war, for that matter? And why do you have to be the one...?"

I looked up at him. The tower of his height over me just made me feel all the more defiant. "Shut up, Aaron! I don't need a lecture."

He was taking deep breaths, but I could see he couldn't calm himself. When he spoke, his throat sounded as dry and cold as the skin of a hissing snake. "So now what? What about consequences?"

"Mother and Daddy are insisting that if I don't leave the turmoil of Berkeley until Matt comes home, that they will absolutely, no question about it, lose their minds."

Aaron leaned forward, as if he needed to hear again what he'd already known I would say. "Leaving Berkeley...? Can they make you leave?"

Now I started to whine, out of control. "You should have heard them. Mother on one extension. Daddy on the other. It was a horrendous phone call."

"I understand what happened only too goddamn well," he spat out. "Your radical roommate has leftist parents. You don't. You should have known better than to follow her into the fray."

I avoided his eyes but watched him get up. He crossed the room and kicked sideways at a neat stack of papers on the floor. They scattered all over and he just left them where they lay. He moved to the hi fi.

"The Beatles," he growled, taking the album out of its cover. "The Fool on the Hill. Doesn't that seem appropriate?"

"Jesus, Aaron! You were talking about running away. So now we'll both be gone, because of the war."

"You heard then? About Johnson's limitation on deferments for grad students?"

"Yes, just this morning. I'm sorry, Aaron, truly. What a mess this all is. I was trying to help. Didn't though."

"You did a bit too much, I'd say."

"I was a terrible radical," I mumbled. He perked up, cocked his head. Inquisitive. I sighed, then pouted, "I guess you're the one person I can confess to. I never did fit in with my so-called comrades. Barbara was nice to me, but she was the only girl they respected, and she wanted to keep it that way. Her guy friends put me to work as their secretary and gofer. When I tried to add my ideas to the discussion, they cut me off and I ended up tongue-tied—or as harsh as the Wicked Witch of Oz if I managed to speak over them. That poster for the Newton party was the first creative contribution I'd made. And only because I forced it on them."

Suddenly I felt exhausted. I'd had two sleepless nights, the night of the rally and the next, after my parents' call, dreading this confrontation. My shoulders sagged, curling forward over the kitchen floor. "Could I please have a cup of coffee?" I asked. Without saying a word, Aaron wheeled himself around into the kitchenette and put on the kettle. He spooned out the Nescafé and stood silently for what seemed like an eternity until the kettle finally whistled and he poured the coffee. He added cream and sugar the way he knows I like it, then dragged a saucer under the cup and a napkin under that. I moved up over it, slurping carefully, smiling despite the situation. "A saucer and napkin, Aaron? You're so weird sometimes..."

"I figured the exile could use a little civility," he snapped, not sounding at all civil.

"Exile. I guess that's what it is, isn't it?"

"Damn right!" My eyes steadied on the coffee cup, my hand shaking as I stirred. I stifled a sob. A few seconds passed, then I felt Aaron's hand on my shoulder. I gulped the coffee and set the cup and saucer down and raised my hand to his. "I've always liked the way you kept the place neat and paid attention to the way you live," I said. "You're not a slob..."

"I'll be honest, Janet," he interrupted my conciliatory speech. "I know I have to dredge some sincere empathy up from my shredded guts or you'll walk right out of here and I'll never see you again. And I couldn't stand that."

"Please don't look so tragic," I pleaded.

"Maybe you'd be happier if I whistled Leavin' on a Jet Plane." I groaned. He sat down close to me and covered my hand with his. His breath grew shallow and his voice low and constricted. "Goddammit, Janet. The main reason that I tried to make my cottage a home was so that I could plant you in it in some satisfying way. But the war just pisses on everything."

71

"Yes it does," I said, taking a deep breath and blowing it out slowly. "But we may beat it yet. There's one part I haven't told you."

His eyes shot open, catching on mine. Then, with a quick shift, he deadpanned, "You're smiling, Janet. Do you know you were just crying, and now you're smiling?"

"I'm not crazy, Aaron. But...I'm not going home. I told my parents that I might as well travel and make use of my time." I paused for effect. "I chose Paris, of course."

A glow from deep inside spread across his features. "Whoaaa," he breathed. Then he tugged at my hand and guided me to the bay window seat.

"Daddy wasn't happy," I continued, "because Johnson asked Americans not to travel abroad—something about the economy. But I went on about studying history and art and architecture and becoming fluent in French. Mother was on my side. She badgered Daddy about Paris teaching me a little 'refinement'—like a finishing school. Finally, two against one. I'm taking a leave of absence. I'll be in Paris by March."

Aaron's hand settled on mine again and I felt its warmth sear through me. "You might have guessed that when I wrote to my dad in Ecuador, I asked specifically for a ticket to Paris. I actually didn't know how I was going to do it without you."

I wrapped my arms around him and he kissed me and we held on tight. "I would be kind of excited about it," I whispered in his ear, "if it weren't for Matt. I'm always worrying about Matt." Aaron squeezed me even tighter, then backed away, listening intently. "And then there's the feeling that I'm deserting the antiwar effort and that my parents are taking complete and utter control of my life as if I were five years old. And just as the protests are totally heating up all over the world because of the Tet Offensive. More reporters telling the truth and hunger strikes and tens of thousands at each demonstration." I sighed and my arms collapsed into my lap.

"Maybe it's for the best, Janet. You'll be safer in Paris...people here have gone crazy. Huey Newton was involved in a murder. Explosions at draft and ROTC facilities. I can't believe you would get involved in the violence."

"They finally found something to pin on him," I snapped. "They've wanted to put Huey away since the Panthers were founded."

"That's one version," Aaron said quietly. There was nothing quiet about the way Aaron's attitude ignited all my old resentments. His parental side made me want to scream. I shoved him away. All the memories came flooding back. My need to reject, disappoint and frustrate both of us. My desperate need to save Matt.

"Well, now I'll be safe in Paris. You should write a thank you note to my folks."

He managed a weary smile. "Guess I can't suppress that grouchy old man persona."

Suddenly, it felt as if all my intense desire on Matt's behalf had been kicked out of me. My mood swung yet again, and I sighed, working my way up to admitting the truth. "You're right. I hated the violence, and I've seen enough of it to know I don't belong in those situations. My best-conceived hope is that I'll learn and grow up in Paris so that someday I can contribute to worldwide peace and justice."

"I'd love to be with you on that life's journey," Aaron whispered. His loving protection settled over me like a roof in a storm. Outside was personal freedom. I wasn't ready for it, couldn't handle it. We faced each other, his dark eyes searching mine. I struggled to accept Aaron as I wanted him to accept me.

Then without conscious thought, we were holding on and kissing, aggravating the juicy sensations that I'd been trying for so long to avoid. My fingers circulated from his head to his neck. I started to reach under his sweatshirt for his warm skin, forgetting about everything except for the need beating in my whole body.

"I've missed you so much," he whispered.

"Me, too," I mumbled, wishing he'd stop talking, keep kissing, move his hands around...

But he went on yakking. "You've got a lot more guts than I do, Janet. I'm supposed to be the brave one. I just want you to stay safe. I'm still hoping for some sort of happily-ever-after for the two of us." He pulled away again, sank back into one cushion and hugged another.

"I guess I know you by now," I said. "You're the Boy Scout, the 'safety first' guy. Bad timing, though. You might have gotten your way with me just now."

"If it wasn't the right time before, it's certainly not now," he said. His voice was laden with bitterness.

We stared at each other for a moment. "So, what now?" I asked. "You're saying we're back to just friends?"

"Fact is, ol' friend, I'm a little irritable because I can't count on anything in this fucking lunatic world. And if you're counting on me, you should know that right now I have absolutely no way to get my hands on a fucking plane ticket."

I felt as if Aaron had thrown a stone directly at my head. Suddenly, as if that projectile opened up my brain to light and air, I understood the irony. Unfathomable! My father sending me to Paris for refinement, while Aaron has had to beg for his life. Then more light streamed in, filled with dust motes. Aaron was afraid of the unknown, a cautious guy, unwilling to take risks, here or anywhere. Now he was forced out with no immediate way to earn a living and no hope for return, ever. And I weighed the sheer quantity of pure muck that must fill Aaron up on a daily basis. No wonder he didn't want to make love for the first time right now! We were about to leave each other, maybe forever. And we were both desperately afraid.

I curled up against Aaron's big cushion, our hands twisted together like a homely braid. I had only simple, true words to comfort him. "I will miss you, Aaron. Right now you're my best friend in the world. I don't quite know what I want from my life. But I know that I want you safe, just like you want me safe. And I want you with me. Do you...want to be in Paris with me?"

"Hell, what do you think?" He swung around and pulled me to him. Then I relaxed in his arms and we held each other for a few moments. The bells of the Campanile rang like an exclamation mark, completing the drama of our troubled months together at Cal. "I want you to write me all the details of your new life," he told me, "and I promise you letter for letter. I'll let you know my plans as soon as I've got them."

"Will you walk me down the hill?" I asked. Aaron rose and pulled me to my feet. He grabbed his jacket and helped me into mine. We stood for a moment at the door, and I scanned his nifty cottage. I would probably never see it again. "I can't believe it," I said. "We're back to a long distance romance like last year. Only this time, it's half a world away with no end in sight. We never seem to progress."

"Progress or regress?" Aaron whispered. "But count on it, Janet, the earth moves, even if we can't perceive the motion or its direction."

≈PART TWO≈
Paris, France

EIGHT

WITHIN A WEEK, I was back in Beverly Hills, entangled with Mother in preparations for the trip abroad. First there were her endless lists. With these in hand, she led me by the nose on shopping excursions full of phony exchanges—her cheer for my gratitude. Then we organized and re-organized, packed and re-packed.

All this had nearly driven me to the brink when the question about the Kodak calmed me down. Daddy offered me a new Instamatic, but I disappointed my parents with a big fat lie. "I don't enjoy taking pictures," I declared. Until that moment I hadn't realized that a tourist toting a camera to Paris was supposed to leave some day and need reminders of the holiday. But what I wanted was to make Paris my home. No, our home, Aaron's and mine. I was sick of Ameri-chaos. In France, maybe we would find some sense of purpose and a good life.

Without so much as asking, Mother made a series of long-distance telephone calls beginning with the admissions office at the University of Paris. She assumed that I would want to be at the University's famous liberal arts facility, the Sorbonne. As things turned out, one doesn't just call up and tell the Sorbonne you're on your way. It was way too late to be admitted for the spring. I comforted Mother by assuring her that my French wasn't good enough anyway, and that perhaps I could enter the following September.

Mother's phone calls led to a connection with Madame Marie-Claire Bouleaux, who had boarded students for several years. She wrote Mother a letter in complicated French (I translated, using my dictionary), assuring her that I would be welcomed into a family-type setting in which I would enjoy both physical comfort and emotional warmth. For once, Mother and I breathed our sighs of relief together. It seemed that I had found a safe, welcoming home in Paris.

Less than a month after leaving Berkeley, I arrived in the Paris of our dreams, Aaron's and mine. I had flown halfway around the world by myself and was dazed from lack of sleep. Watching the taxicab drive away, I pulled my luggage up close, then gawked at the Mansard roofs and baroque facades lining the street—just as beautiful as in the pictures we had admired in my art and French classes. 95 Boulevard de Port-Royal. This was the place. I congratulated myself for having made it to the front door of my new home. It was just after 11:00 a.m. on a bright day, but the nip of Paris in early March penetrated my meager tie-dyed shirt and knitted poncho. I shivered and squelched a sneeze. The air was fouled with exhaust, noisy with the overlapping squeals of an erratic flow of traffic, and smelled faintly of burning sugar. But I beamed at the screeches, engines, brakes and horns as if they were a brash and sassy band brought out to welcome me. More George Gershwin than New York City.

Dragging my suitcase and guitar across the broad sidewalk, I scanned the multistoried building and wondered if there could be a mailbox list. I had no idea which of the apartments above belonged to Madame Bouleaux. Just then, a woman emerged from the archway under the curlicues of the 95, an empty shopping sack dangling from her arm.

"Pardon, Madame, je suis Americaine," I said in my best, carefully-executed accent.

"Oui, bien sûr," the woman sneered. Yes, of course you are.

"I need help finding the family I am supposed to stay with," I continued, now stumbling amidst the grammatical wasteland of my B minus in fall quarter's French class. "This is the address, but I don't know which apartment. The name is Madame Marie-Claire Bouleaux. Do you know her?"

The woman parted her lips slightly and jammed her eyelids up toward her bushy crescent brows to signal recognition of the dilemma. "I am Margot Chabert, Madame Bouleaux's daughter," she said, speaking with deliberate clarity, "and you cannot find the apartment because we have no apartment. You will follow me, please." She walked swiftly back through the archway, not stopping to wait for me as I lifted my backpack over my shoulder and dragged my heavy suitcase and guitar into the foyer. Margot was holding a door open at the other side of the passage while I stopped to gaze at the elaborate ceiling. The arch was carved in a majestic diamond-patterned faux relief from its peak to the wainscoting on both sides. To my right and left were stairways to the apartments above. I grabbed up my burden again and followed her through the second door.

We emerged into a sunlit courtyard, and it was as if we had fallen down the rabbit hole and found ourselves in Alice's Wonderland. Suddenly, the world was quiet and smelled of the freshness of growing things. Once again, I pulled up to gape and catch my breath.

A stone walkway went down the middle of rectangular patches of struggling grass and all around the edge of the courtyard. I recognized the same ash and plane trees that we have in California, their pruned stumps sprinkled with early blooms. Birds high above were singing a more pleasant greeting than the one out on the street. Flanking the courtyard were six identical houses, each three stories high, whitewashed and embellished by forest-green shutters and matching window frames and front doors. Shadows from the trees played against the brilliant sunlight, which poured in from overhead onto the house facades.

Margot turned to me. Where her bobbed, dried-out brown hair reflected the sun's rays, there were blotches of dull gray instead of the silvery sheen I would have expected. She attempted a smile which turned sour as soon as it appeared, as if her lips, like the feet of Chinese women, had been bound in her childhood. Then much to my relief, Margot began to speak in English. "This is where you will stay," she said. "My mother, Madame Bouleaux, owns these three," her arm swept across to her right, "where her family and our guests live. All of the houses are very old, so you will have to make allowances.

Americans sometimes have difficulty making allowances." Her eyes grazed mine, then hastened to dart away. At that, she launched into a long explanation in her strangely-accented English, which sounded as if she were chewing the insides of her cheeks. I listened closely, struggling not only to understand, but to lodge her speech in my memory.

The entire family had moved to Paris from Alsace in 1940. Three of Madame Bouleaux's four grown children lived with her. Margot lived in the first house with her son and daughter and cooked for the student boarders. That was where I would take my meals. Her brother Frederic, in the middle house with "maman," was still a student, in his last year of electrical engineering studies. Her sister Hélène and her husband, Jean-Louis, were in the third house with their two daughters. "There are student boarders living with the family in the second and third houses, and you have a room in the third house with the girls," she concluded.

Margot's explanations were delivered in a flat, dull tone, in what must have been a frequently delivered introduction for newcomers. With an attempt at sincerity, I thanked Margot for speaking English to me and asked, "Where did you learn to speak English so well?"

"In Alabama," Margot replied. "I studied there for a year when I was just out of the lycée. You know? The high school." I nodded, trying to keep myself from smiling at what I recognized now as a deep Alabama drawl folded into Margot's French accent.

My landlady trudged on ahead of me and mounted the steps of the third house. I had begun to move forward with my cargo when Margot turned. "Leave your things here in the courtyard," she said, "and my brother Frederic will pull them up to your room later."

Inside the third house, a moment passed before my eyes adjusted to the darkness of the foyer. The musty air held the smell of woods from furniture and wall paneling, filling my nostrils with the age of the house as if I could sniff my way through history.

"All three houses are alike," Margot was saying, "except, of course, for the furniture. All of these are antiques. They are worth a lot of money, so please be careful how you treat them.

They are my mother's. I know you come from a good family and that you will understand."

"Oui, I understand. I will be careful. They belong to Madame Bouleaux."

Margot returned her best sour smile. With that, she tromped up the stairs, turning on lights as she went. Trailing by a few steps, I listened to her warning that the lights would go off automatically after 15 seconds. If the climber did not reach the next level in time, she would be left in the dark. I must be especially careful between the second and third levels. Then, incredibly, Margot smiled her first smile of genuine pleasure. "This is a modern invention for saving electricity," she said, adding as if speaking to herself, "Merveilleux!" Wonderful!

We stopped on the second floor, where my landlady showed me the two rooms, the separate toilette and salle de bain. "That's convenient in a house with many people," I noted. "Was this house built for boarders?"

"Of course not! This house was built over one hundred years ago by merchants of comfortable means. You will find all the baths are separate from the toilets in France. It is not civilized to have them in the same room as they do in your country."

Margot went on to instruct me in the use of the flushing mechanism on the toilet and to list the rules: Do not fill the tub too high. Do not use it early in the morning or late at night. Too noisy. Do not drop towels on the floor. You must try to use them for a week. How would I remember all these rules? There was no shower, only a bath, and Margot suggested that most boarders liked to take their baths in the middle of the day when it was warmest because there was no hot water. "Too expensive to heat the water," she said. "And anyway, it's not healthy. Much better for the constitution to take cold baths. You must arrange the time with the others in this house."

I squelched a shudder at the thought of cold baths, then smiled politely. "Who are the others?" I asked.

"My sister Hélène's family lives here on the first two floors. The children are very small, so do not be alarmed if you hear them crying sometimes. On the third floor, where you will live, are Elizabeth Prior, a British girl, and Gabi Souris, a Swiss girl. You will meet them all at dinner."

"Your brother lives in the second house, the middle house?" I asked.

"Yes, with my mother and two other boys—students."

"And your family lives in the first house," I said, just to confirm what I recalled from Margot's monologue in the courtyard. Margot's active eyes froze on mine and she responded with stilted calm, "I live in the first house with Cecile and Laurent, my children. I am a widow."

"Oh, I'm sorry! Was your husband a soldier?" I asked, indexing through my recollection of France's historical entanglements with Germany, Indochina, Algeria.

"You are the first American boarder we have had in a while," Margot said coldly. "I forget how you Americans are inquisitive." It came out "in-quaaay-za-teef," a French word, but sounding more Alabaman. This time I wasn't in the least tempted to laugh at her accent.

"I'm sorry...it's true...vous avez raison..." Suddenly, I went from being a tired but exhilarated and self-confident, cosmopolitan traveler with a fresh start—back, way back, to being a shy, tongue-tied American with a little girl's voice.

Margot stared down her nose at the carpet, but raised her brows imperiously. "My husband was killed in an accident."

"I'm sorry. I didn't want to...to..."

"No harm, no harm." Margot dismissed my apology with a wave of her hand. She turned to mount to the final floor. There we entered a sunny, sweet room, its walls covered with vertically striped wallpaper, the palest lime alternating with creamy white, climbing to a simple dado of Roman wreaths a few inches below the ceiling. Over the wallpaper hung four etchings of Parisian architecture, two on each side of the room and all very much like the facade of 95 Boulevard de Port-Royal. I was charmed out of my gloom. I took a deep breath and stood up straight, determined not to let Margot's sour puss destroy my euphoria.

"Que c'est joli!" I exclaimed. How pretty! I looked around wide-eyed at my new quarters, unable to believe my good fortune. To live in such a place! There was an antique armoire on one wall, along with a case full of leather-bound books; opposite this were the bed and nightstand in a recess with a slanted ceiling. Just outside the sleeping nook, near the foot of the bed, was a sink with separate spigots for hot and cold water and a rubber plug on a chain attached to the hot water tap. A towel rack above the sink held two fresh towels, folded so that indecipherable cursive initials were centered on the visible side. In the middle of the room, a sturdy writing table was grouped with a torchière and two straight-backed chairs. A fresh vase of pink and white tulips had been placed on the table to welcome me. One of the shuttered windows opened out onto the courtyard.

"Please keep the door shut when the windows are open," Margot instructed. "If you like the cold, that is your affair, but we do not heat the houses. No noise after nine o'clock at night. You don't want to wake the children who sleep beneath you."

My landlady gave me another few seconds to absorb these rules and to look around the room. When she started up again, her tone had softened. "I can see that you are pleased with your room," she said. "That is excellent. We want to make you feel welcome here. Alors, Jeanette, starting right now, we will speak only French. All of the people in our houses except our small children speak English. And we will all be patient while you learn."

"Does Madame Bouleaux know how to speak English, too?" I asked.

Margot drew herself up straight with her arms folded in front of her. "I already told you that we all do. When I want to make sure you understand, I will speak privately with you in English. But otherwise, our language is French."

Margot left me to rest, telling me that Frederic Bouleaux would be up with my luggage and that the midday dinner would be served at one o'clock. She would send someone in an hour to wake me up and to accompany me to the first house.

Alone in my new room, I wondered at circumstances that were so beautiful and richly appointed in superficial ways, yet so impractical for living. Cold water baths! No heat! All those rules...and the kitchen two houses away.

There was a knock on my door. Frederic entered, a short, narrow-shouldered man with a hang-dog expression and a shock of fair hair falling over his eyes. He wouldn't be bad looking, I thought, if he stood up straight and put some energy into acting one bit friendly. He nodded and lifted the suitcase up onto the table, then strode across to the armoire, opening one of the doors with a flourish. "Voila!" he said. "Alors." Here it is, and so.... With that, he backed out of the room, closing the door. Tears of relief and exhaustion came to my eyes. I dropped to the edge of the bed and let myself cry, slowly at first, then in great stifled sobs. Seeking comfort, I pictured Aaron, sitting on his sheepskin rug with the fire blazing, reading a book about bird organs or some such thing. I rolled over and stretched out, calming down. Then Matt entered my mind uninvited, tiptoeing through jungle trees, his heart beating heavily, alert to enemies with unpronounceable names. Shaking my head as if it could scramble this dark kaleidoscope, I rose to move toward the window, but paused at the polished table top. I ran my fingers slowly over its caramel-colored surface, knowing that I would write many letters to many different people in this perfect setting.

Wrapped in my poncho, I sunk back down onto the bed. The ache of many hours of travel pressed my arms and legs into the clean-smelling layers beneath. I thought about my mistaken expectations of this Parisian "family": one stucco house in the suburbs of Paris, Madame Bouleaux as a wife with one nuclear family, and I the boarder who fit in like a daughter. Why had I expected Paris to be Beverly Hills? Despite my nervous desire to find sanctuary in my new home, I sighed contentedly at all the fascinating cultural differences. How amused Aaron would be, reading my letters in his far away Berkeley cottage, when I confessed to the discrepancy between my bourgeois expectations and the reality of the situation!

I thought back to one of my last conversations with Aaron. Since he had asked for details, we had agreed that I should write him a kind of "diary" through my letters. Would he please save them, I had asked, and bring them to me when he joined me in Paris? How I wanted to begin my first letter this instant, but I simply couldn't move! For just a moment, I imagined myself back in the airplane, high enough for a view of the planet, with the European land mass on one side and the West Coast of North America on the other. I measured the distance between, and taking stock of how far I had come from the other side of the sphere, I fell fast asleep.

There was a loud knock on my door and a gentle voice urged me to wake. "Oh, never mind, I'll just skip dinner," I mumbled, half asleep. Another knock, even more insistent. "Go away, I'll eat later," I shouted in English.

The door opened. "Oh la! You must eat now. You must not to sleep more." She reached out to grab my two hands and tugged me gently until I was sitting up on the edge of my bed. "I am Gabi Souris," she said. "I am sent to bring you to dîner." Gabi. I remembered that she was my neighbor in this house. I smiled at her wonderful English, and she returned it. She was a ginger-haired girl, short and busty, with long, airy bangs falling onto her forehead, two thick pigtails in back and two huge, ginger-colored eyes. She seemed an absolute pixie. For an instant, I thought she might be just my age, but then I guessed that she was probably well into her twenties.

"My name is Janet Magill. I'm sorry to give you so much trouble."

She shrugged, still smiling. "Only, you must eat dîner with everyone here." Gabi stood up, her hands on hips. I started to drag myself from the bed. Gabi walked over to the sink, speaking in a bright voice. "Why you do not splash your face so you can wake up?"

I turned from the sink to my tormentor's lightly freckled face. "Hot water?" I inquired hopefully, pointing to the "H" on the spigot. I remembered Margot's diatribe on the bath: Too expensive to heat the water.

"Ha! Not in this house. That is a false tap," she laughed merrily and shook her head so I would be sure to understand.

I splashed my face and arms with the cold water and shivered, then seeing that I'd doused my poncho, I squeezed at the soaked yarn tips while wiping my hands dry. Feeling embarrassed, I turned and shrugged my shoulders sheepishly.

"We are supposed to speak French," I instructed my messenger.

"You are still asleep in your brain. Anyway, you will speak French enough at the table. Please do not think that every French person is as stingy as Madame Bouleaux! She is so cheap, you know?"

"Oh, I wasn't making any judgments!"

"I am part Swiss, but even my French part is not that cheap. And Frederic is not cheap. You met Frederic?"

"Yes. He brought my things upstairs. He didn't say two words to me though."

"He is sick of boarders. We come and go, he says, and he has seen so many in his life, coming and going. He does not like to bother."

"But Margot is not like that. She was very friendly. She even told me all about the family."

"Oh la! She makes that speech to every new boarder."

"Yes, I guessed that. But still..."

"Yes, she is friendly. She is lonely," Gabi said, raising her hand to twist one pigtail. She surveyed the room, stopping her perusal at my suitcase, where her gloom suddenly transformed into cunning. "Did you think Frederic was handsome?"

"Well, attractive. Not my type though."

"That is good. Because Madame Bouleaux will not have him making love to boarders. It is forbidden!"

"You tried?" I asked, giving this little sprite of a girl a wry smile.

"Hush! You bad girl! I would be put on the street for imagining such things!"

"But what if Frederic liked one of us? Is he to remain at home with his mama forever?"

"What a shame when parents are the masters of their adult children." Gabi's head swung side to side. "Poor Frederic, poor little boy." And she repeated "petit-petit-petit garcon," laughing and clicking her tongue against her teeth. My head moved side to side in automatic response, reflecting upon my own sad saga of parental masters. Gabi declared, "Do you know that Frederic is twenty-seven years old?"

I was amazed. He looked far younger. "I should try to get him interested in me just to break Mme Bouleaux's spell."

"Do you not suppose I am trying this?" Now she raised her hands to her ears and held her head between them. "Poor Frederic. Caught between, in the vise, is that how you say that?" But Gabi had stopped laughing. "I am not squeezing him. I am doing nothing wrong. It is her. Madame Bouleaux. She is wrong, do you not agree?"

"It is not my family and I am new here, Gabi, but I do agree, yes."

Gabi lowered her hands with a sigh. "I will not tell anyone about our conversation, do not worry. And you will not either, n'est-ce pas?

"C'est vrai," I agreed.

"And now it is time to meet this crowd of people. We go." She winked at me and led the way downstairs.

NINE

GABI RUSHED AHEAD of me into Madame Bouleaux's first house and on through the entryway to greet her friends. I hung back, lingering in the protective cover of a darkened foyer identical to the one in the third house. No one was paying any attention to me, so, feeling quite invisible, I began to peek inside. What I saw resembled a stage set more than a living room. The furniture consisted of a divan fit for a languishing Camille, a loveseat, several chairs and as many impracticably tiny footstools, not more than a few inches off the ground and arranged in a circle. All were upholstered with well-worn brocade silks in shades of russet to gold. Our hostesses had strategically placed mahogany tables with small round tops among the chairs. The same warm-toned stripes and florals that I saw on stuffed furniture covered large sections of walls and dressed the casement window that faced the courtyard. Along each of the other walls, two incredible pieces of furniture caught my eye: a sideboard, its top glistening with inlaid stones and its cabinet doors carved in sinuous abstractions, and a vitrine, filled with china and bric-a-brac from other centuries, other civilizations.

Jean Magill from posh Beverly Hills, I thought, you've been outdone.

Old words popped into my head, like parlor, drawing room and my favorite, the French word salon. Where late nineteenth century poets and painters gathered. Mallarmé, Baudelaire, the Nabi painters and in this century, Picasso, Hemingway and their patroness, the eccentric poet Gertrude Stein.

Filling every chair, flopped onto the low stools and standing or leaning over them was a mix of people babbling in rapid, incomprehensible French. Future Picassos? Future

Hemingways? There was no television. Not even a radio or a record player in the room. Only the grace and visual richness of traditional French forms and people excited to be talking to one another.

Finally Gabi turned and came over to where I stood, pulling me out of the shadows. Then the seated ones stood and everyone talked at once. I heard "Jeanette" and saw tentative smiles and nods and over and over again, "Jeanette."

Where the fourth wall of the salon would have been was the broad opening to the dining area, and just then, Margot Chabert stuck her head into the salon from that direction, shouting over the crowd, "Enfin. Gabi has brought her at last. Come in. We can eat."

People took their places around the large rectangular dining table. The seats seemed assigned, as if it were a classroom. I was placed next to Margot at the end of the table near yet another antique, a china cabinet. We were opposite a casement window identical to the one in the salon, but here the drapes were opened to the brightness of the courtyard.

Margot began to instruct me on proper use of the knife and fork. "The fork is held with the left hand," she said, demonstrating with her fork perpendicular to her empty plate. Her knife crossed it, poised in her right hand. "Not switched back and forth like the Americans." One of the boys said something that I thought included the word "politic" and everyone laughed. I beamed, wanting them to know I could take a tease, whatever it was.

Then there was the custom of saving the cloth napkin after each meal in the matching pocket provided. "Fold it and put it in the pocket," Margot said, "and at the end of the meal I will put it away in the drawer." Margot handed me a ballpoint pen and a small piece of paper. I wrote my name on the paper, which she then slipped into the pocket's clear plastic slot. "We will give you a clean one at the end of each week."

I wanted to be accommodating, to say something like, "Vive la différence!" But I had to ask, "What if it gets very dirty?" Margot's lips grew tight and she narrowed her eyes. "It lasts a week if you are careful, but of course, we keep a few extra napkins if you have an accident."

While Margot made her explanations, the company was helping themselves to bread, butter, and radishes. They sliced these plump red roots and layered them atop their buttered bread, which they tore from the crackling, fresh baguettes, each about two feet long, one for each two places set at the table. I began to do as my neighbors: tear, butter, slice, layer, take a bite. The delicious sweet-and-bitter of butter and radish made me hungry for the first time since the plane. And the fabled bread! Soft and moist on the inside, its crisp crust flaked onto the white tablecloth in front of each person like part of the place settings.

As we ate, people began to introduce themselves, speaking with exaggerated clarity. "I am Le Grand Laurent," pronounced a boy from across the table, "and I love the Americans, especially American girls. My parents live in Alsace, and I live in Paris to attend the Lycée." His broad grin seemed glued down in the middle of his rosy, dimpled cheeks. Although he was as tall as a man, his face was the frank, open face of a much-loved child.

"What do you study, Laurent?" I asked, unable to bring myself to the use "Le Grand." I knew I'd burst out laughing and hurt his feelings.

"I study mathematics, physics, and chemistry, and I excel in all three subjects."

"As you can see, a boy of many fine qualities," Margot cut in. "Brilliant, handsome, and conceited too." Everyone laughed, politely.

"We've heard that one before," whispered the girl seated to my left.

"French, Elizabeth. You must speak French," shouted Margot.

"I did speak French," the girl protested.

"Then why whisper?" Laurent teased.

"Because I was telling her you are 16 years old and not to take your flirting seriously." At this, the laughter around the table was genuine.

"Well, Elizabeth, since you are only 15 years old, who are you to tell her about the ways of the world?" Laurent shoved a piece of buttered bread into his mouth.

"Elizabeth, Laurent, stop now. Elizabeth, introduce yourself to Jeanette."

"Elizabeth Prior," she said, reaching to shake my hand. "From Kent, Great Britain. I attend L'Alliance Française, where I am in the fifth level."

Elizabeth appeared more sophisticated than any teenager I had ever known. Her straight blond hair was perfectly trimmed and fell upon her shoulders in a graceful semi-circle. She wore a powder-blue wool suit, the short-jacketed, straight-skirted kind that I might have bought with my mother at Saks in Beverly Hills to wear to church. The mauve tint of her pink lipstick was obviously selected with the suit in mind. She was telling me that if I decided to study at her school, we could walk to class together. "My goal is to study the history of French art, which I adore, and to be fluent in French," she continued. "After this month, I will also help Margot take care of the children. I will be au pair. Do you know what that is?"

"Au pair?" I repeated, then automatically said in English, "A mother's helper?"

"Pas en anglais, s'il vous plaît!" came a sharp report from the gray-haired, square-shouldered woman sitting to Margot's right. No English, please! Without a doubt, she was the Madame Marie-Claire Bouleaux who had written the effusive letter to Mother.

"Excusez moi," Elizabeth and I both spoke at once, then smiled at each other. "Oui, c'est ça," said Elizabeth. That's right.

The formidable matriarch set down her knife and bread, bowing her head in a brief, formal greeting. "I am Madame Bouleaux, your hostess." She spoke her name in two distinct syllables. Boo – low. "I have entrusted your care to my daughter, Margot. Welcome to Paris, Jeanette."

"Merci, Madame Bouleaux."

Rumblings of conversation had begun around the table, having nothing to do with the introductions. I took advantage of the moment to relax my concentration and take a few more bites of the radish hors d'oeuvre. I had noticed that Elizabeth kept straining her voice in an odd, deliberate way to lower it and keep it at the back of her throat. She released it like a fisherman controlling his line, in a moderately successful effort, I thought, to appear more mature and somewhat strait-laced. But now, I heard one of the other boarders using words that I knew translated as "damn" and "shit," and a vivid blush spread over Elizabeth's face. Yes, strait-laced, I'd call it, just as I had been not so long ago.

"The blasphemer is Bérnard." Margot was clearly annoyed as she introduced him as a 20-year-old French literature student from Nice. Bérnard fidgeted in his chair, his short, wiry body in constant motion. Dark, wavy, uncombed hair grew out from the sides of his cheeks. I wondered if he even realized he had sworn in front of several small children! He nodded dutifully in my direction, but didn't speak to me. Just as well. When he spoke to others, his French was so rapid that the words all slurred together and I couldn't distinguish a single one. At the end of each short slur was a little clipped accentuation. Short sentences, I observed, for someone with so much to say, as if he were out of breath from spilling it all. I was definitely going to steer clear of Bérnard.

Next to Elizabeth, Margot told me, sat Le Petit Laurent. He was her own plump, rosy-cheeked four-year-old boy who was, although they were no relation, a miniature version of Le Grand. He had been chatting incessantly to himself, wiggling in his seat and poking Elizabeth for this and that all through the conversation. Margot's five-year-old, Cecile, whose short dark hair seemed cut with a kitchen knife, said nothing and kept her eyes on her plate. I thought she must surely be from a different family than Le Petit Laurent, maybe from a different planet.

While a bowl of soft-boiled eggs was passed around the table, I realized that I would have liked to sit with Gabi and Madame Bouleaux's grown son Frederic, whom I had met up in my room. They seemed to be happily chatting away together on the other side of the table, as were Bérnard and Le Grand Laurent. Another self-contained group was the family of Madame Bouleaux's eldest daughter. As the main course was served, some species of flaky, buttery fish, this daughter waved at me with a cheerful "Bonjour, Jeanette. Je suis Hélène." I waved back, wondering if I would remember any of these names by the end of the meal. She explained that her family usually dined on their own first floor, but that on special occasions, they joined the others at Margot's table. Today, I was the special occasion.

Pointing her finger at the two children sitting to her side, she pronounced their names as Jeanette and Lili. These lovely girls of six and four had identical blond hair, clear-skinned faces and home-sewn tunics, like different sizes of the same package on a grocery store shelf. Their father, Jean-Louis, sat between them, a plump, scraggly-bearded man, helping the pale, delicate creatures to the fish, while stroking their fair hair and talking to them in pleasant, soothing undertones.

Hélène's expression was kind, more natural and relaxed than Margot's, although like her younger sister, she seemed prematurely aged. The Bouleaux women wore no make-up and their pastel sweater sets and strands of tiny pearls brought to mind old photos of Mother in the 1940s. Hélène's hair was pulled up in a bun just like that of her square-jawed, straight-backed mother. Hélène said quietly, "Welcome to Paris, Jeanette. Welcome to my house." I remembered only then that it was Hélène's house where I would be sleeping.

Once a real conversation got going, with more than one person around the table speaking at a time, I could follow some general concepts, but not the details. I kept my attention on the meal. There were six separate courses: following the radishes, eggs, and fish, we ate cauliflower with melted cheese sauce, a mixed green salad, and finally, three kinds of cheese passed on a board, along with more bread and fresh fruit. With every course, the wine and water circulated, and I marveled at the amount of wine consumed by people who would, presumably, be returning to their studies and to work.

Margot informed me matter-of-factly that in a few days I would be sick to my stomach. "Everyone that comes from America is sick here. It lasts a few days and then all will be well. We don't refrigerate everything like the Americans. Your body will adjust."

"Microbes," said Le Grand Laurent, grimacing playfully before the incessant smile returned to his face.

"Germs, ach, germs!" Bérnard bellowed in English before the others could silence him.

I squelched a giggle and returned the conversation to French. "Alors, before I become ill, I want to enjoy myself. This is all very delicious." Margot's lips curled up briefly. She offered me the return visit of the cheese board, which I promptly accepted.

After the midday dinner, the entire party went into the salon to sit and talk. What followed was nearly an hour of conversation, right in the middle of the afternoon of a workday, which I was amazed to learn was the after-dinner rule and not the exception made for my arrival. Most of the students sat on the footstools, while I was offered a place between Margot and Elizabeth on the upholstered chairs. Everyone sipped from cups of rich black coffee. As the cups emptied and were refilled, I tried to follow phrases that moved rapidly from books to art to politics and back to art again. Here with la famille, my usual inability to find the right words in a crowd of people was exacerbated to the point of nonsense. Just as at the dinner table, by the time I had thought of a sentence I wanted to say, the conversation had gone on without me. But here, when I did open my mouth to speak, someone was always there to focus and listen, nodding and smiling patiently until I finished. I sipped my coffee to cover my embarrassment and worried that their patience would turn off like the hot water—too costly— when I failed to keep up with their French for more than an afternoon.

Margot lifted one leg so that it crossed the other almost at a right angle and leaned forward in attack mode. Pulling a blue cigarette pack from her pocket, she scratched at its cellophane with her stubby fingernail. I recognized the legendary Gaulois. "Are you understanding us?" she asked.

I nodded. "Some things. Not the details, only the themes."

"Don't be discouraged," she said, poking a cigarette between her lips. It wiggled as she spoke through it, lighting up. I hoped she wasn't going to blow the smoke into my face. "The average American speaks English at a rate of about 150 words per minute." Her cigarette nodded up and down as if confirming her explanation. "But the average French person's rate is 350 words per minute. So, we know we must slow down for you at first." The smoke wafted out over the crowded room. Elizabeth coughed into her fist.

The Brit was talking to most of the group, reliving her visit to the Jeu de Paume the previous afternoon and enthusiastically extolling Monet's water lilies. She sat stiff-backed, knees together in her little powder-blue suit and low heels, her smooth hair unruffled even after half the day. Elizabeth proceeded to teach them all a thing or two about the development of French Impressionism.

Here was the Paris I had dreamed of, exactly how I had expected it to be! A stimulating group of people, who were eager to help me adapt. Here I was in the City of Light, in an elegant salon, listening to a civilized conversation. Was it too good to be true? Was that Aaron's voice inside my brain, being cynical as usual, ruining my good time?

I had drifted off. When I forced my attention back to what was being said, Bérnard was complaining that Elizabeth was learning more by visiting museums than he did in his courses at the Sorbonne. He spoke more clearly than he had at dinner, forcing little snippets of sentences out between his tight, narrow cheeks. Classrooms were crowded. Professors demanded rote memorization. Offered stale, outdated material. The university was the greatest disappointment of his life.

As I watched Bérnard list his frustrations, I pictured him out on Sproul Plaza, shouting and foisting a leaflet into my hands. Matt's angry grimace at his farewell party and my whole botched attempt to help end the war flashed through my mind. I felt a blush rise to my face. I decided then and there that I could not discuss my brother or Aaron or the war with this family. This was a world away from Berkeley, whatever this student's complaints about his education—and just as well.

Bérnard rose to his knees and declared, "Perhaps I had better skip my lessons. Go to the Jeu de Paume. Perhaps the Louvre. That way I will not lose my enthusiasm for learning."

Gabi tried to reason with Bérnard. "Studying always combines both positive and negative," she said. "Cooking has always been a joy, but not the mathematics!" She turned to me, her chin tipped up proudly, "I am studying for my certificate in French cooking at Le Cordon Bleu." Changing her tone again, she exclaimed to Bérnard, "It is boring to memorize so much! For example...the complicated measurements for feeding various numbers of people..."

"At least," Bérnard cut her off, "you have real teachers there with which to exchange a word. Not simply the tiny figure, far off at his podium. Delivering his automatic lecture."

He had turned to me and was speaking for my benefit. "No discussion possible. No challenges welcome. Incredible! Three thousand people in one class. One large exam at the end of the year." By now, Bérnard was waving his arms and shouting again, "And if a student fails, he must repeat the entire year!"

If I caught most of this recitation, I assumed it was because Bérnard wanted me to. I tried to compare Bérnard's Sorbonne with anything I had ever known as "school." A shockwave ran through me—I had my own hopes for the French university. But then, I considered the source. Perhaps he was exaggerating.

"Calm down, Bérnard. Your shouting won't solve anything," Margot bellowed, uncrossing her leg to lean even farther forward. I thought she might bump onto the carpet at any moment, but her cigarette was resting in an ashtray and her two hands, rough and reddened from her household duties, were locked onto her knees.

Bérnard sat down on a low stool and I felt a tension that I hadn't been aware of go out of my body. Margot might be a bit crass, but it was just as well she was there to referee. Bérnard quieted down and repeated to Gabi that her choice of school was heureux. Fortunate. Margot lazed once again on her chair cushion and puffed on her Gaulois.

Oh yes, Gabi agreed, all in all she was satisfied with the course at the cooking school, and she was eager to begin patisserie after the holiday in April. With what recipe would the instructor begin, Margot wanted to know?

As she explained to Margot that they would begin with the perfect pâte brisée—the flaky dough that can be shaped into any form imaginable—Gabi glanced repeatedly toward where Frederic sat. The little man alternated his gaze between Gabi and the floor between his legs.

Meanwhile, in the guise of instructing Le Grand Laurent this time, Bérnard was blaming the poor educational system on the French government. I had been observing details—hands, words, faces and every expression—as if I were a detective searching for clues. I was tiring of the effort required to understand anything at all, but what was worse, hearing the words "socialiste" and "système" and "gouvernement" stiffened my muscles and stirred the meal in my stomach.

Just as I renewed my efforts to follow what they were saying, a chubby, jet-black cat dashed across my feet, through the room and out into the foyer. With a great scraping of chairs and shouting and pushing, the four children scurried out from under the dining room table where they had been playing "fortress," and four-year-old Lili was in tears. Le Petit Laurent was halfway to the foyer after the cat.

Madame Bouleaux had risen from her seat. The sound that shot from her throat was like the sharp report of a pistol. "Arretez mes enfants!" The children stopped and faced her from where they stood.

Everyone was talking at once. Elizabeth leaned close to me and whispered into my ear in English, "They say Laurent stuck a fork in the cat until she bled. It was an experiment. He wanted to see what would happen," she giggled. I winced.

Madame listened to the explanations and eyed Margot. Four-year-old Laurent, the culprit, had run to the side of Margot's chair and was staring up at his grandmother defiantly. Margot stuck her two fingers with a quick, sharp poke into Laurent's ribs and he yelped and jumped away. "And how do you feel if I stick you with a fork?" Margot asked her son. All eyes were on the little boy, who had begun to look a little less sure of himself. "Did you hurt Yao-Yao or not?" she shouted.

"Ouiaaa!" he wailed.

"And what will you say to Yao-Yao when you see her?"

"Excuse-moi Yao-Yao!" he shouted, a military reposte.

Madame Bouleaux announced that it was time for naps. Margot rose to hold Laurent, now sobbing, more from shame and fatigue than pain. I was marveling that Madame Bouleaux could brake four wild children with a quick shout, when I felt a cold hand wrapping itself around mine. I gazed down into the gray-blue eyes of the most beautiful child I had ever seen.

"Say your name," commanded the child. As she spoke, a healthy blush became so prominent against the pale skin on her cheekbones that I thought that Hélène must have rouged her for a school play. One of her two front teeth was missing, the other was loose.

"Je m'appele Janet," I pronounced the name in English. Then, recognizing what the child was after, I said, "En Français, je m'appele Jeanette."

The little Jeanette peeked at her grandmother for reassurance. Sweetly, she instructed me, "Then you are La Grande Jeanette and I am La Petite Jeanette."

"Yes, I guess that's true," I said. "And what is this?" I felt a bump and a stroke of warm fur against my leg.

La Petite Jeanette lifted the injured cat, who had returned to the scene and slid between us. "This is my cat, Yao-Yao."

"That's a good name. It rhymes with 'meow-meow.' That's the word we use in America for the way cats talk."

"Yao-Yao is 'yogurt,'" Hélène translated into English. "That is a crazy name for a black cat, but the children just began calling her that, so we all call her that now."

"She's my cat, too," said Lili, now holding her mother's hand and staring at us with dry, heavy-lidded eyes. La Petite Jeanette tightened her embrace of the cat and frowned at her sister. She petted Yao-Yao on the white spot of fur under his chin.

I turned to La Petite Jeanette and petted the top of the cat's head. "Perhaps you named the cat for the one piece of white fur...?" I pointed at the white spot on the cat's neck. Everyone laughed, and I realized that I had been engaging easily in the conversation.

"Will you play with me after school sometimes, La Petite Jeanette?" I asked.

"After my nap," said the little girl, in a serious, grown-up tone.

The children were whisked off to their beds and the others went separate ways to work, study, and rest. As we left the salon, Elizabeth told me that they would talk again that night after supper. The sheer quantity of conversation astounded me. People listening and responding. Surely I would improve my language skills in no time!

TEN

AFTER THE INTENSE CONCENTRATION, I was ready for another nap. But on the way back to the third house, Elizabeth convinced me that I ought to force myself to stay awake, to align my internal clock with French time. She asked me if I would like to take a walk with her, and eager to get out and see some of the city, I readily agreed.

Back in the foyer of our house, I waited for Elizabeth to use the facilities. Jean-Louis's round form appeared, leaning up against the doorjamb of the darkened salon. The house was quiet, his family already tucked into their beds. I nodded in greeting.

"You know," he said, his tone almost drowsy, "you are a very pretty young woman. There are a lot of wolves in Paris. Perhaps you need a protector, an older man..." his voice drifted off. Without shame, he let his eyes dribble down to my legs, then sucked them back up again, skipping nothing. I hurried to wrap myself in my coat, holding my breath, unable to come up with any smart rebuff. "You understand what I say, n'est-ce pas?"

"No, I don't understand," I lied. I was disgusted by his devouring eyes and amazed that this was the same man who had played the doting father at the dinner table. I put my hands in my pockets and avoided his stare, trying to stay cool.

He clicked his tongue like a scolding father. The smile in the center of his whiskered mouth had flattened into a wicked grin. "Quelle dommage! Perhaps I will be able to make you understand soon, when you learn French." His voice had grown thick and gruff. I was forced to step back as he brushed past me, but stopped at the foyer table and picked up a polished brass trumpet. Mon passe-temps," he said. His hobby. "I forgot to put it away. Margot mentioned that you brought a guitar with you," he rasped. "Perhaps some time we can make music together."

"Trumpet and guitar? Not a good combination," I responded, a little too swiftly.

He frowned. "I suspect you understand me after all."

Elizabeth was coming down the stairs. I wrapped my two mittened hands around her coat sleeve and pulled her quickly outside.

"Don't you find it creepy that we live in the house with Jean-Louis?" I whispered.

"What!?" she blurted out, obviously shocked.

"He was making lewd suggestions in the foyer..."

She laughed. "Chubby Daddy Jean-Louis? You've got a lively imagination, Jeanette." Then I realized that I didn't know Elizabeth any better than Jean-Louis. I let go of her arm and stuck my hands in my pockets. Bérnard was obnoxious, no doubt about it, and there were Gabi's gripes, and now Jean-Louis. I didn't know any of them, really, or whom to trust. I shivered as the afternoon breeze whistled through the garden. After all, I reassured myself, Madame Bouleaux would protect me. And surely Margot, tough old workhorse that she seemed, would not let anything dastardly befall me.

We exited through the archway onto Port-Royal and down the busy street toward Boul' Mich'. That's what Elizabeth told me was the slang term for the street virtually "owned" by the Sorbonne students, the Boulevard Saint-Michel. The thrill of being in a place about which I had read and dreamed nearly took my breath away. I took in the scene: Rive Gauche, the Left Bank, teeming with people, mostly young and in pairs. Many carried guitars or sketchpads or books. In the outdoor cafés where so many philosophies had been born, students spoke animatedly with their hands flying above their luscious cakes, coffee cups or wineglasses. Shops and street vendors also catered to students. The booksellers offered as many books on the sidewalk as inside the shops, and as many used books as new. We passed the imposing facade of the University of Paris, Mother's beloved Sorbonne campus, and in about twenty minutes, reached the bank of the Seine. There we strolled down the quai toward the Petit Pont, where dry-mouthed, hot in the cold wind, I gazed at Notre Dame Cathedral. Its enormous, weighty blocks heroically drove toward heaven, filling the pearl-gray sky.

"Oh God, Paris is every bit as wonderful as we thought it would be," I said, dancing round and round with my two arms raised above my head. I was smiling and squinting into the late afternoon sun, feeling full to bursting.

"We? Who's we?" Elizabeth asked.

"Aaron Becker. My friend back in Berkeley."

"Is he your beau?"

It helped to laugh at the old-fashioned word. I hesitated, struggling to affect a casual, offhanded tone. "No, well...not at the moment. But he's a friend and he knows lots about Paris and..." I took a breath and finished quietly, "he's my very best friend. That's all."

"That's nice," Elizabeth nodded. "I wish I had a friend like that."

"Have you made friends with the other students here? How about the people with the Bouleaux family?"

Elizabeth turned her face to the river. "You will think I'm a silly child when I tell you."

"I doubt it. You're the most grown-up teenager I've ever met."

Elizabeth winced. "I hate that word. 'Teenager.' It puts one in a box."

"I'm sorry. You're right. Anyway, technically, I'm a teenager for more than another year, so don't worry about it."

Elizabeth put her hands up on the retaining wall, then pulled them away and brushed her hands off. "Ugh. That's so filthy."

"Elizabeth, I do get the feeling you're trying to tell me something," I said, making no attempt to hide my amusement.

"All right. Well, back at home in Kent, I do have gentlemen callers."

"Gentlemen callers?" I repeated. "That's more hilarious than 'beau'!"

"I suppose you Americans call them 'dates.' To me, a date is a series of digits on your calendar or perhaps an Arab fruit. Learning French is difficult enough. I refuse to learn American English, so you'll have to adjust to..."

"Okay, okay. I'm sorry. I don't mind learning British, if that's what you want. Please, do go on," I said with a bit of a British inflection in my voice.

"You do that rather well," she said. "I should think you'll learn French very quickly." She began to walk away from the river, back toward home. I pulled up alongside her. A breeze blew and I felt exhilarated, but when I glanced at Elizabeth, her shoulders drooped and her expression had softened once again. "As I was saying, I do have gentlemen callers at home but I've never met anyone like Laurent de Cirey. He's the brightest boy I've ever known."

I couldn't help but chuckle. This Laurent, though probably six feet tall, had appeared uncomfortable with his own awkward shape. He attempted a brave swagger, extending this bravado to the slur of his words, so that I rarely caught his meaning the first time around. When I asked, though, he politely repeated himself. He was anxious to please and so, I thought, a perfect match for this pretty but stuffy Brit.

Elizabeth's long face made me turn serious, fast. "I want him to like me," she said, "but it seems as if everything I say comes out wrong. He teases me all the time. Of course, he could be trying to get my attention. He may like me too, but I don't know how to...to..."

"Flirt?"

"What!? That's so cheap. I'm not a flirt."

"Flirting isn't cheap. It's letting the boy know that you like him that way. Romantically. Then he has to take it from there. If you don't flirt, you'll never know if he likes you too."

"I kept hoping things would just click between us without my doing anything. Maybe you're right. Should I tell him I like him and see what he says?"

I laughed. "Boy, you just go right from the freezer to the oven like a TV dinner, don't you? C'mon. I'm cold. Let's walk faster." We began to thread our way back up Boul' Mich'. I explained to Elizabeth how to use subtle signs to let Laurent know how she felt without embarrassing herself with an outright pronouncement. "Use your eyes," I advised, "and your smile. Watch Gabi. She's a master."

"Oh là là!" said Elizabeth with an exaggerated imitation of the French exclamation. "I wouldn't dare to watch Gabi. She absolutely despises me. I suppose she hates all the British. But then, too, I fouled it up when I first came to the house. I spoke out of turn."

Now I suppressed my laugh. "This doesn't by any chance have anything to do with Gabi and Frederic, does it?"

"What? How do you know about Gabi and Frederic?" she countered.

"Gabi told me..."

"What a bloody packet! And she shouted at me that the British are a bunch of gossips! Evidently, she doesn't mind gossiping about herself. What did she tell you?"

"Just that she resents Madame Bouleaux's control over her son. I got the distinct impression that Madame Bouleaux would forbid any romance between them, and Frederic would never cross maman." Suddenly, I felt guilty again. "I must admit, Elizabeth, I feel a little strange talking about the personal lives of these people. After all, I'm a stranger here."

"Well, if I were you, I would want to know what was going on between the people under my own roof."

"And I can see that you're the person to go to when I want information." Elizabeth nodded earnestly, completely missing my sarcastic tone. We resumed our walk and were almost back to our Port-Royal archway when Elizabeth stopped again.

"I daresay Gabi's right about hiding her hanky-panky with Frederic from the family," she declared. "But believe me, there's nothing of Gabi's feelings hidden from Frederic."

"She didn't sound like...I mean, how can you be so sure?"

"Because Gabi is having an affair with Frederic. They're romping up there in the third house right next to my room!" Elizabeth turned from me, her petite nose in the air, and disappeared under the archway at 95 before I could ask any more questions.

I stood there absorbing the possibility that the omnipotent Madame did not, evidently, control all of them—and surely not Jean-Louis. I followed quickly after Elizabeth, more anxious than ever to rest and think—and to lock my bedroom door behind me.

ELEVEN

ON THE SIXTH DAY after my arrival, letters from home and from Vietnam perked me up. The Tet Offensive was over. Matt had been ordered out of the jungle and behind the wheel of a delivery truck. Mother and Daddy sounded more relaxed. Aaron wrote how he thought about me all times of the day and night, which thrilled me even though I'd known it. For the rest, he wrote about trips to tide pools and speeches by Eugene McCarthy and Bobby Kennedy. Maybe Bobby would save America, I thought, but that was certain to be too late for Aaron.

My return letter was honest, if not complete. I decided to make light of the "old letch," Jean-Louis, not wanting Aaron to worry about me. I described the profusion of characters in our household, adding that I was determined to be cautious and self-reliant until I could learn which of my new friends to trust.

Despite my brave assertion, I felt like I was staring at a fogged-up windshield, squinting to see the demarcations and solid surfaces right in front of me. Paris was not Berkeley, I kept reminding myself, and I didn't have to watch for goblins in the road. Perhaps no goblins, but my first impressions of the people I'd met so far, even the most sympathique of the household, like Gabi, Elizabeth and Le Grand Laurent, didn't lay down right, as if there were potholes lurking beneath the visibly smooth surface of the road.

If the spoken language, with its frustrating speed of delivery and mysterious syntactical twists, kept me from any real understanding of my new acquaintances, my limited reading ability was equally frustrating. Aaron's second letter had referred briefly to an "explosion" of worldwide anti-Vietnam War protests.

After breakfast one morning, I tried to make my way through an article in Le Monde. Elizabeth Prior was peeking over my shoulder in the foyer while I read a laundry list of nations where people were protesting—Italy, Germany, Spain, United Kingdom, even Brazil and Japan. I groaned, positively longing for more information. "This paper might as well be written in Swahili!" I complained.

"You ought to get the English language Herald Tribune from the kiosk at the Métro," Elizabeth said. "Just don't let Margot or Madame Bouleaux see you reading it." Then Elizabeth asked a question that I could hardly believe I hadn't asked myself. "But aren't you going to study formally, at a school?" As my embarrassment subsided, she encouraged me to begin French language classes where she studied, the center for government-sponsored French language learning, L'Alliance Française.

So it was that just as my first week had passed, I let the 15-year-old guide me across the Latin Quarter to the Boulevard Raspail, to an old school building as elegant as the French language itself. I gawked at the six stories, with their smooth ochre surfaces above a first story of rusticated stone, the arched and sculpted doorways and windows, and balconies with iron grillwork. Elizabeth lead me through the iron-spike fence and the patio garden, under an archway and into the main office. There, with her help, I filled out the papers and registered for the first month. L'Alliance permitted its students to register for a month at a time, $12 American for a class that met for two and a half hours every morning.

A secretary wrote out a proper receipt for my money, and after a few minutes of conversation, gave me the third degré book to take along with me. I liked the fact that they were called degrés, or "levels," not "grades" as in an American elementary school. I spent much of the time over the next few days up in my room, memorizing pages of new vocabulary, so that I might fit into the third degré, already in progress.

One afternoon in the salon, Madame Bouleaux pulled her chair up to mine and began to tell me about her antiques. I loved all of the beautiful things in the room and was attracted by Madame's enthusiasm. Struggling to follow the details, I thought I had heard her attribute the inlaid cabinet to "1760, the reign of Louis Quinze." 1760! I was thrilled, truly. I tried to show my emotions by opening my eyes wide in surprise, then alternating admiration with amazement as she set more pieces into context. Finally I mustered a cordial voice. "All of America is so new. These things seem very special to me."

"If you like," Madame said, "you may come with us when we go to our vacation house on l'Île de Ré for a week at Pâques."

"Pâques?" I repeated, glancing at Elizabeth.

"Easter," Elizabeth mouthed the word. I turned back to Madame. "L'Île de Ré is in the Atlantic?"

"C'est ça. Off the coast of La Rochelle. There you will see our nineteenth century antiques," said Madame Bouleaux, smiling proudly. And then, in a voice I took as sly, she said, "And there you will talk to the children all day and improve your French language skills!"

How kind to invite me to join them on their vacation—and surely those beautiful children would teach me without even knowing it!

"My youngest daughter, Suzanne, lives there with her family," Madame continued. "Perhaps Margot has told you?"

"No," I shook my head. Madame nodded at Elizabeth, who began to tell me, in French I could understand, about l'Île de Ré, Suzanne, her baby daughter Michelle and her husband Jean-Luc, an architect who built vacation houses on l'Île. Among these, Madame owned two houses, a third under construction. l'Île was an island of farmland surrounded by beach. It would be too cold to swim at Pâques, but in the summer when visitors came to bronzé in the sun, the tiny village would swell from 400 people to 10,000.

Madame and Margot had been listening to Elizabeth. Now Margot interjected, "French people have different values than Americans, you understand? We will invest in a vacation home with the same money that Americans spend on airplanes and hotels. We believe in property. Investment. And we believe in the importance of a close family." She smiled, tight-lipped, turning to maman for an instant of approval. "At l'Île de Ré, the entire family can be together for all the holidays, including the long August vacation." I was trying to figure out how those values were so awfully different from Americans. Leave it to Margot to throw a bit of negativity into what should have felt friendly, like a spoonful of bacterial culture souring a cup of fresh milk.

As I tried to better understand the alliances I might make, I was delighted—no, relieved—that Port-Royal was far, far away from both Rodeo Drive and Telegraph Avenue. I admired la famille, even the rough Margot, for their intelligence and good will. I was relieved to see that since our one conversation, Jean-Louis was steering clear of me. I began to make an effort to spend time with Hélène and her lovely little daughters.

So I took it agreeably when Madame Bouleaux came up to my room and asked me for all of the money for my stay through the end of August. Six months in advance, at $200 a month. "We need some guarantee that the room will be filled for the semester and the summer. You want it guaranteed that it will be available for you, n'est'ce pas?"

Madame Bouleaux smiled pleasantly and patted and smoothed the fabric coverlet on the back of the chair at my writing table. I considered the marvelous room. I had thought it rather expensive for Paris, where the dollar was worth so much more than the franc, but my mother had told me, "They will do your housework, cooking, and even laundry, and why go to Paris to wash dishes when you can be visiting sights and making new friends?" Two hundred dollars for each month of such royal treatment and delicious meals seemed like a bargain. And anyway, Matt would not be back from Vietnam for another nine months.

When I telephoned home to explain the situation, both Mother and Daddy picked up the extensions. Mother gushed that the check was as good as in the mail. Daddy was suspicious.

"The usual way to pay rent is by the month. Ask her if you can sign a contract for the rest. That should guarantee you the room and them their payment."

"But Daddy," I said, failing to curb the whine in my voice, 'how would I even know what was printed in the contract? My French isn't very good yet..."

"She has a point, Marsh. They might try to cheat her."

"You be careful, Janet," Daddy said. "A new Gallup poll came out and General de Gaulle's popularity in the U.S. has sunk to a new low. Some are even calling for a boycott of French products and travel, I might add. That would teach those damn greedy French."

Takes one to know one, I thought. "Daddy, what can go wrong? You said you wanted me here until Matt gets home..." My voice drifted off and hit what felt like an electric wire fence blocking the connection.

Then Mother spoke. "Marsh dear, Janet is happy and learning and safe. Imagine the thrill of living in Paris in a nice atmosphere, away from war and the bad element at college."

"There was nothing bad about my friends at college! They were just trying..."

"Do you want to stay there or not!" Mother shouted into the line. Then, quickly, "Marsh, for heaven's sake, is it the five months' interest that's bothering you?"

"I don't know what is bothering me. It's just not regular, that's all. And yes, they've got our interest." Mother and I both groaned at the same time. "Okay, okay," Daddy surrendered. "You go ahead, Jean. Write her a check."

I went the next day to the American Express office to pick up the check my mother wired. She had included a little extra—a bit of ointment smoothed over yesterday's blows? So that afternoon, I went to the Prisunic to buy a sweater and pairs of wool slacks and cotton ones for later in the spring. Even the children in French schools wore slacks, and I decided that sticking with my American Levis was like branding Old Glory on my forehead. Pleased with my "new look," I stopped on my way home to buy fresh red and pink tulips at a corner stand—for my room, for Elizabeth, and for Margot and Hélène, which seemed the best way to express gratitude for the help of new friends.

"Thank you, Jeanette!" Elizabeth took the flowers with both hands and held them up by the window, admiring their colors in the sunlight. I handed her a vase from the top of her armoire. She filled it at her sink.

"Is there an occasion?" she asked.

"Just that I've given six months rent to Madame Bouleaux, so I'm staying. I feel more part of the family now. I brought some for Margot and Hélène, too." I sighed. "I do feel so lucky to be here, among an intellectual family like this—well-educated and interested in so many things. Not bourgeois and narrow like my own family." Elizabeth's eyes opened wide and she hooted. "Did I say something funny?"

"Can't you tell how absolutely bourgeois this family is? Why, every move they make revolves around money. Like the large sum they've just collected from you. They are bourgeois, Jeanette, and not very well-educated at all."

I felt heat rise to my face. "I thought...well, I thought the advance sounded like a reasonable request. And all those salon conversations. Their appreciation for the arts, their awareness about politics and even science. And the antiques, the vacation houses. Aren't they in the French upper class?"

Shaking her head, the Brit rose to splash her face at the cold tap, dried it hastily, then sat down next to me where I waited on the bed. "Look. They have antiques because all they wear is thin, shabby 20-year-old sweaters with strands of fake pearls. And they have all these houses because they stick together under Madame Bouleaux's frugal thumb. Every spare cent goes into the land and building materials. Those are French middle class values. The petite bourgeoisie. It's the property they're after, every time. When Suzanne, Madame's baby, married an architect, they all pitched in and built those island homes with their own hands. Plumbing, electricity, the whole job."

I chuckled at the image of Margot laying bricks and Madame Bouleaux tinkering with the plumbing. "Yes, I can see that. I can see it in their hands, all red and rough."

"Heavens, there's nothing wrong with the middle class," Elizabeth conceded. "At least they're respectable."

"Well, I'm not a snob," I said. I rose and began to pace the floor. "Wealth isn't my issue. It's the values. I was hoping for something different. To disassociate the Bouleaux of Paris from the Magills of Beverly Hills. All America is bourgeois. Television is bourgeois. I wanted to believe that I'd found something different here."

"Ha! I'm afraid not!" Elizabeth cried out. "What else can you be but bourgeois to an extreme when you are a widow with four children? That's how Madame was left in 1948. She had to take care of them all. Her husband was killed in French Indochina."

"Indochina! That was Vietnam." I shuddered. "Oh, don't tell me that..." Unhappy thoughts of Matt washed over me, but I forced myself back into the present moment.

"I can barely keep all the wars straight," Elizabeth continued. "These days, Madame Bouleaux only talks about World War II. That's how my parents met her. When my father was over here during the war. I've heard their stories for years. I know that later, when Monsieur Bouleaux was killed, Hélène was the eldest, just fourteen, and next was Margot, who was eight. Madame had little formal education. It must have been quite a struggle. But as you can see, she did very well with her emphasis on material things. She does love her antiques, and she did want her children to be educated."

"Well, those things are admirable values, at least."

"They still run a nice house, don't they?"

Another noisy sigh escaped from me, then a groan. "Everything's so complicated. I've been gaining confidence. Now I'm back to mistrusting all of my impressions..."

"Be patient. When your French gets better, you'll get everything straight."

Once I began to study at L'Alliance, Elizabeth Prior and I shared the walks to and from school everyday. I loved our route through the Latin Quarter, across the luminescent Luxembourg Gardens and up Boulevard de Port-Royal. As we strolled, our eyes were drawn up and around at the beauty of Paris in the early spring. Elizabeth remarked upon the brilliance of Baroque architecture, and how every building resembled a monument, at once imposing and graceful.

We became friends. Sometimes she was as overdrawn as a character from a Dickens novel. She used words like 'dotty' and 'bloody' so much that I had to stifle my desire to laugh throughout our conversations. Soon I began to feel a strange yearning for those little white gloves that Elizabeth coveted, peering into a shop on the Champs Elysées. We began touring museums and sights together, gossiping in English and reading guidebooks in French, trying against the odds to use the French language.

We may have been mutually obsessed with the beauty of Paris, but each of us had other, more pressing fixations. Hardly a minute went by when I wasn't dreaming about Aaron Becker, sharing Paris with him in my fantasies and trying to keep my mind off the memory of his body—heated, hungry and tangible. It helped me to sympathize with Elizabeth, who never let an hour go by without mentioning Laurent, bemoaning her lack of progress with him. "I only see him in rooms full of other people," Elizabeth complained, "and that is not a romantic setting."

I tried to devise a plan for her, enjoying the prospect of playing Cupid. Finally, I suggested that she think of a question for him about something that required a complicated answer. "Then pull him into a corner," I said. "Perhaps back into the dining room after people leave, like Gabi does with Frederic."

"Gabi again! Oh well, alright. But then what shall I do? Flirt with my eyes?"

"Yes! And your voice! And if you get any signals back, it's time to tell him how nice it is to finally have a meaningful conversation with him without the teasing. Just be honest. And don't forget to be a good listener, too."

Several afternoons a week, Elizabeth and I traded off first choice of activities, one day visiting L'Etoile and the Arc de Triomphe, even though Elizabeth had seen them many times before, the next day exploring the Greek and Roman antiquities at the Louvre, Elizabeth's choice. Then one day into the third week, Le Grand Laurent joined us on an afternoon excursion to the Musée d'Art Moderne. I hadn't noticed the salon tête-a-tête I'd suggested, but they stood before the Fauves—the early-century "Wild Beasts"—holding hands, their flushed faces rivaling the vibrant colors on the canvases. They were definitely a couple.

"I got him after everyone had cleared out," Elizabeth explained up in my room that evening. "I heard him tell Bérnard he needed to ring up his dad, so I followed him to the foyer and before he could place the call, I queried him about sights in his region. I told him I was planning to travel to the countryside. We sat on the stairs. And then everything happened just like you said it would. You're like an advice columnist, Jeanette!"

I thought in a self-congratulatory way about how much more sophisticated I was with Aaron, even while still in high school. Remembering and comparing gave me an empty feeling in the pit of my stomach. It helped to realize that every bit I learned now and every friend I made would help Aaron adjust when he arrived. Laurent would be my first French friend. Young, but smart as any Berkeley student and agréable. Aaron would take to him despite his youth. I said a little prayer for the high schoolers' happiness.

That night, I lay in bed comforting myself with a long, complex, sexy crescendo of an imagined conversation with

Aaron. Then counting the days until June, hoping that would put me to sleep, I realized that back in Berkeley, winter quarter was coming to a close. Aaron would be down in L.A. with his mother for spring break. For the first time, it occurred to me that he had said nothing about his father's funding of his "escape" to France. Surely he would have written me if he had the check in hand.

That could only mean one of two things: either his father had not responded at all, or he had refused. Eyes wide open, I felt my heart began to race. Why, nothing had changed! Aaron hadn't learned anything from our devastating break-up this year! If he were in trouble—no, if we were in trouble—why didn't he share his worry, frustration, his anger at the powers that would keep us apart? Was he proud? Too proud to show me that he wasn't always in control, with a clever comeback? I scowled at the ceiling above my little bed nook. Even Elizabeth and Le Grand Laurent now spoke to one another more frankly than Aaron and I! Sleep was useless. I pulled myself up and spent the next half hour writing a letter—partly the funny one I had been composing about Elizabeth and "le Grand"—and then at the end, I added a P.S. "By the way, what news from your dad?" That seemed casual enough. Sealing the aerogram, I suddenly felt defeated and exhausted. I climbed back into bed, and assuring myself that he would reply directly to my direct question, fell sound asleep.

TWELVE

THE THIRD DEGRÉ CLASS at L'Alliance Française turned out to be just right for me. The teacher was an old, old man, wrinkled and white-haired, but funny and very lively. There was only one other American in my class of eighteen. The rest of the students, from what I could gather, were Yugoslavs, Germans, Italians, Dutch, Spanish, Czechs, and Poles. The American woman seemed years older, and she hadn't approached me at all. One day, I gathered my courage and walked right up to introduce myself in English.

"Claire Caplan with a 'C,'" she told me with a warm smile. Claire was what Mother used to call "pleasantly plump," a cheerful young woman, whose only makeup was bright red lipstick. I thought she must be in her late twenties, but soon discovered she was just out of college. "A graduation gift from my parents," she said of her stay in Paris. "I start teaching next Fall in Waltham, so I'll be here until then."

"Near Boston?" I asked, but already knew the answer from her familiar Kennedy accent.

"Just outside Boston, where my parents live...say..." she interrupted herself, starting to walk away. "We're missing the fun," her voice rang out. "Let's get down to the café."

"What café?" I asked.

"There's a café in the next building. C'mon. I'll introduce you around."

We threaded through the crush of people on the stairs. "So what do you do?" she asked.

"What do you mean?"

"I mean, I'm a teacher, or will be. How about you?"

Blushing, I gave my usual inadequate reply: "I don't know yet."

She burst out happily, "I'll be teaching third grade. I'm very excited about it. That's an important year. The kids learn to write cursive and multiply and divide."

"That's wonderful," I said. "I've thought of a teaching career. But I want to see what else is out there first."

"My mother always said teaching is the best job for a woman. So that after she gets married and has her own children, she can be off during school vacations and summers. I guess I'm very practical, like my mother."

I eyed Claire, her red sweater clinging to her flabby bust. Its scarlet matched her brash lipstick and contrasted with her pasty, blemished cheeks. She was such an energetic and self-confident person. She made me believe absolutely that her vision of herself as a wife, mother, and teacher would all come true.

Elizabeth was waiting for me outside the school's giant front door. I introduced her to my classmate. "Claire's taking me to the café," I began, but Elizabeth cut me off with a wave of her hand. "Sorry, no thank you," she said firmly. "You two have fun and I'll just run along home. Ta ta!" and she was gone.

Claire shrugged her shoulders. "C'mon. You're going to love it."

There were tables outside, but they were empty and the building was shuttered up. I surmised that was why I'd never paid much attention to the café from the sidewalk. Inside, the ambiance was cozy and animated. I followed along behind Claire to a long Formica countertop. We ordered coffee and cake and carried our snacks off to a table near the corner of the large, bustling space. A man came by and raised the shutter on one window, rousing dust and letting in light, but not much air. Now I saw lots of familiar faces from my class. Why hadn't Elizabeth ever told me about the café? I wondered.

True to her word, Claire began to introduce me to friends, jumping up momentarily from our table and dragging me along, then grabbing arms and pulling people over to join us. I loved her enthusiasm. It seemed to infect everyone around her, and soon several people were crowded around our small table.

Most predominant was Irena, from Poland, who spoke no English at all. She was a tall woman, around thirty, with round, pretty cheeks, sparkling blue eyes and dull brown hair. "I've been in Paris a whole year," she said, pushing her stringy hair out of her face in order to talk. "I live with my aunt who came here after the war. She's a smart woman, and we get along fine. If it weren't for her, I'd be back in Lodz with my parents. And Poland is no place for a person with ambition and ideas. Poland is no place for me!" she boasted.

Irena's French was wonderfully fluent, but slow and careful as she sought to communicate with the rest of us. I sensed right away that here was another strong personality, like Claire's.

Most of the people around me were in their early to mid-twenties. Irena's friend Charlotta, from Dresden, Germany, seemed to be just a little older than I. "Stunning," was the first thing I thought when Irena introduced us. Charlotta was dressed quite well, almost too well for a morning in school, and as diminutive as Irena was lofty. Her short-cropped auburn hair set off her emerald green cashmere turtleneck. It was odd to see her chatting with Irena and Claire. She seemed as eager as I was to practice her French with someone who was more advanced.

Charlotta was flirting with a dark-complexioned young man in a long-sleeved white shirt and dress slacks. He sat between the two of us. After a few moments, he shifted his focus away from her, pulling his chair uncomfortably close to mine and smiling at me, smooth and sweet as a milkshake. "I am Philippe," he said in perfect English.

"Parle Français seulement a cette table, s'il vous plait," I said crisply, asking him to please speak French at this table.

"I'm from Jordan, so it is easier for me to speak English if I want to get to know you." His large brown eyes grew wide with expectation.

"No good. I'm sorry, but I must practice my French skills," I replied in French. I found myself returning his smile with a strange feeling of nostalgia. It had been a long time since I'd met anyone with whom it was worth flirting. Philippe was complying, speaking in French more broken than my own and sipping his coffee, nodding and smiling at my terse replies. I was trying to listen and respond, all the while fighting the feeling that I wished Aaron was sitting there instead of Philippe. I caught myself staring at his substantial biceps and returned my attention to my coffee cup. I wanted to wrap my hands around the muscular bulge and squeeze.

Suddenly, I was furious, my anger making the coffee burble in my stomach. I still didn't know if Aaron would ever be here. Would it cross his mind that romance might be part of my Parisian adventure? Would he date other girls back in Berkeley? Then suddenly, Philippe was asking me out to a dancing club that Saturday night.

Thrilled by the prospect of a real date, I deliberately defied Aaron Becker. "Yes. Okay. Merveilleux! That will be fun!" I was instantly elated that Philippe had made his move, and that I had made mine. But a few seconds later when we stood up to say goodbye, his height was quickly condensed into his upper body. My eyes descended at least five full inches to meet his, and I squirmed at the thought of dancing with Philippe. He saw the problem too, of course, but graciously arranged our meeting. Then he shouted a hearty au revoir to everyone and made a quick exit.

The very next day at the café, Charlotta brought a friend of hers to the table and introduced him as Teodor. It was Charlotta who pulled in the chairs and commanded, "Teodor, you sit there, next to Jeanette." I had dragged Elizabeth with me, but without her saying so, I could see why she had avoided this crowd before. Here, she seemed no older and perhaps younger than her fifteen years. I placed her to my left side. Claire was sitting on the other side of her, and they began to re-introduce themselves. I turned my attention to the inescapable presence to my right.

Teodor was a square-faced boy—no, a man—with a bold, broad body to match. The first thing I thought as he initiated a handshake and asked politely, "Comment allez vouz, mademoiselle?" was that he was the tallest man I had ever seen. There would be no question of standing up to receive any small surprises. I looked around for Philippe, hoping that he wouldn't show up but feeling sure that if he did, Charlotta would re-establish her claim on him.

Teodor spoke with maturity and assurance, in what sounded to me like excellent French. In quiet tones, he asked me what degré I was in and if I liked my class. I had to strain to hear him in the noisy café crowd.

I answered as directly as I could, and then he was telling me his own favorable impressions of L'Alliance. A few strands of his thick, brown hair hung over his forehead and a few pale freckles budded on his fair-skinned cheeks. I liked the worn tweed sports jacket that he wore over his plain white button-down shirt. He reminded me of an aspiring college professor. All he was missing was the pipe. Suddenly, a Tinkerbell-sized egg cracked open in my chest and her wings fluttered over my heart.

"I wonder if you could do me a favor," Teodor was saying. "I collect stamps, and in my country, we do not get the chance to find American stamps. Could you bring me the stamps you receive from your friends in the United States?"

"And...what country are you from?" I asked. Teodor searched the café and his eyes settled briefly on a heavy-set man, sitting alone on this cold day at an outdoor table, beyond the café's open jalousie. This man tipped his seat so that its back chair legs edged perilously close to the soft, wet earth in a garden plot. He returned Teodor's steady gaze.

"Czech. I am Czech," said Teodor, turning to peer down at me. I forced a smile, gripped uncomfortably by those insistent gray eyes and feeling anxious about the stranger. I assured him I would bring him some stamps.

When I reached the house after school, I realized I would have few stamps to offer Teodor. Most of my correspondents sent pre-stamped aerograms, but I had saved two letters in their envelopes, one from Mother, one from Barbara Borovsky.

The next day, I brought those two stamps to the L'Alliance café. Teodor seemed delighted. He guided me to our own separate table, apart from the others. At first, we exchanged the kind of basic information that puts people at ease with one another. I had searched my memory for what I knew about his country and it was precious little. It had been a republic before the war. Now it was communist. That was all I knew.

Teodor was telling me about his school in Prague when Irena came over to our table. "Have you heard the news?" she asked.

"What news?" we responded together.

"About Nanterre? They are protesting, like at Berkeley. Your American friend mentioned that you went to the Berkeley university. I thought you would want to know."

Involuntarily, I groaned. Just as in the political discussions at the boardinghouse, I could sense a flood of emotions blocking my concentration on the language. I turned to Teodor, hoping he would help me out. But he merely lifted his cup and hid his face behind it.

Irena continued, too engrossed by events to notice our reactions. "The students there have occupied the salle des professeurs. They want to make a big statement. They defend the famous Berkeley concept of free speech."

I was still struggling to catch her meaning, but when I heard what I was sure translated into "faculty lounge," I had to stifle a laugh. The Free Speech Movement sit-in had been a take-over of Sproul Hall, the university's central administrative building. But of course! The pathetic little faculty lounge was intended as a respectable attempt to honor the original action! I wiped the smirk from my face.

"They began with twenty, last January," Irena rambled on, but slowing now so that we could understand. "Now there are hundreds. Lots of different groups. They think separately but strike together. That's from Lenin, you know?"

"Strength in numbers," Teodor said. His eyes had risen from his coffee. Suddenly, he was listening intently. "What is the main group?"

"They call themselves the enragés, from the French Revolution."

"What is that?" I asked.

"It means people that are angry," Teodor explained.

"Why are they angry?"

"Nanterrrrre," Irena rolled her r's and paused dramatically. "Such a horrrrrible place to study. A cheap Parisian suburb. Overcrowded and dreary. All the students want is to hold meetings on campus! Talk about mixing sexes in the dormitories, educational reform, imperialism, capitalism, socialism. Just to discuss and learn. They want basic rights! Free speech!"

My head swam with all these causes, but I bristled to realize that they lacked what every American took for granted.

"What a pity!" Teo said. "So similar to my country."

"Oui, my friend. And why, may I ask, do you not wear a beard and Texasski like so many other liberated Prague students?"

"What is that? Texasski?" I asked.

"You know Levis jeans pants? Like in state of Texas, to show love for American democracy." He turned back to Irena. "Our tormentor, President Novotný, resigned from the presidency. Now Dubček has full control. But I have no beard and Texasski because I am not liberated from mon père, who is a good communist. He must pay for my travel. We agreed to my boring style," he concluded wryly.

"Ah, I understand the problem. I apologize, my friend. Now, about Nanterre..."

"Alors, merci, Irena," I cut in. Suddenly, I'd had enough of student unrest. I wanted this big Czech for myself. "It's good you told us." I turned back to Teodor and our eyes met.

"That is all you have to say?" asked Irena, surprised. "I can see you are busy with more important things." She eyed us both, more with amusement than annoyance. Teodor set his cup back down and snickered, then covered his mouth to cough. "Have a nice time, little one," Irena said, patting me on the shoulder and glancing over at Teodor. She walked away, returning to Claire, Charlotta, and the others.

Our conversation proceeded through the maze of our mutual inadequacies with French. Teodor was just one degré up from mine at the school. His speech was slow and delivered in a kind of cadence. Periodically, he turned toward the same mysterious, black-eyed heavyset figure, who sat outside the café as he had the day before. Now that the stranger's face was more familiar, I noticed his ill-matched clothes—blue slacks with a brown striped sports coat. I wanted to ignore this menacing presence, but my eyes followed Teodor's whenever he turned in that direction.

After a while, we sat in silence, unspoken questions just beyond our ability to ask. I placed my hand strategically on top of the little table and expected Teodor to take hold of it, but he kept his giant hands folded together a few inches away from mine.

He was staring at our fingertips as if he were making a huge decision when we both noticed Elizabeth, standing at the gate to the café patio, signaling that it was time to go. I flashed a big smile at Teodor and told him how much I had enjoyed our conversation. He tapped the tabletop nervously. "Alors, au revoir," he uttered politely. I was puzzled that our café pleasantries had not resulted in the big Czech man asking me for a date. And I was disappointed.

As Elizabeth and I walked home from school, I told her about Teodor and the mysterious older man who watched him from beyond the café. Once again, Elizabeth knew something about European people.

"Can't you guess about him?" She stopped in the middle of the sidewalk. "Oh, you Americans are so naïve." She enjoyed a sneer. An elderly man glared as he was forced to walk around us. I put my hand on Elizabeth's arm and guided her under the canvas overhang of an electrical repair shop.

"Tell me..."

"Well," she lowered her voice, "In all Iron Curtain countries, but especially in Czechoslovakia, informers fill police dossiers with information about their citizens. Every Eastern European studying in a free world country has a spy. Some spies even have spies."

I stood aghast with my mouth open. When I caught my breath, I asked, "Do they all know about this...?" I hesitated. "Surveillance?"

"Some do and some don't. And some know their spies quite well," she answered with authority. She rounded her shoulders and peered inside the glass door of the repair shop as if she expected to see someone standing inside, taking notes on our conversation.

"Jeez. This is nuts." I shook my head to clear it all away. "We'd better go. We'll be late for dinner." We passed through Luxembourg Gardens, down the alley of towering boxed topiary and around the fountain as big as a pond. I didn't know if I believed everything that Elizabeth told me, or if the man outside the café was Teodor's spy, but the discussion had stirred something sympathetic in me. Sympathy for Teodor and for Czechs. As we fought the wind whipping the shallow water in the fountain, I noticed that even on this raw day there were parents and children outdoors. The sight provided a poignant contrast to the scene with Teodor and his spy. I decided to share my apprehension with Elizabeth.

"If only that spy or whoever he is weren't so creepy-looking. It may not be fair to make the association, but he reminds me of a gangster in movies from the 1930s. One of the bad guys. His face is pitted with acne and his clothes are mismatched. He blows big puffs of smoke from his cigarette, like fire from a dragon's mouth."

"A far cry from Teodor," Elizabeth responded. "They don't seem to belong together. That's why I think I'm right with my spy theory."

When we reached the outer door to our building, I hesitated. "Elizabeth...I wanted to talk to you about my date with Philippe Saturday night. He mentioned that his hobby is wrestling, and I wasn't quite sure what kind of wrestling he meant. Any chance you and Laurent could come with me that night?"

"Sorry, no. We're going to a dance at his school. Maybe one of the others." She turned and walked ahead of me into the building.

On the designated Saturday, while Elizabeth selected her wardrobe for the dance and primped herself in the bathroom, I knocked on Gabi's door to find her reading, lying on the bed with a textbook about the chemistry of food ingredients. She was in a restless, sassy mood.

"I want you to come in and save me from this book. And I want you to leave me alone so I can try to understand it."

"So, what should I do?" I laughed.

"Come in, of course." She stretched noisily. Rising from the bed, she asked, "So how are you doing in that school of yours?"

"You hear the results. What do you think?"

"Your French is better." She sat down next to me at her writing table. "But it is good you are going to l'Île de Ré with the family for Pâques. You will speak French there all day long and spend a lot of time with the children. You will return much improved."

"Oh, I hope so! I hate to leave Paris, but if it will improve my French..."

"Yes. Definitely. Anyway, no one will be here to keep you company. Everyone is going there or to their own families. I'll be home with maman, studying the whole time." She pouted.

"Gabi. I have a favor to ask of you. One of the boys from school asked me for a date tonight. He's very nice, but not my type. I shouldn't have said yes, but at the time I just thought it would be fun to get out on a Saturday night. His name is Philippe. He's from Jordan..."

"Oh làaa," I knew that meant trouble. "A middle eastern boy, an Arab...and you are going out just the two of you? Where is he taking you?"

"To a dancing club."

"Oh làaa," she repeated.

"Gabi, you're not prejudiced against Arabs, are you? I mean, he's very modern."

"Never mind, modern. Just watch out for him. Don't let him get you into a dark corner."

"Exactly. I was worrying about that. He mentioned that his hobby is wrestling. He's small, but built..." I put my hands on my shoulders and pulled them outward in a mock exaggeration of Philippe's muscles. "So I wanted to ask if you and Frederic would come with me as chaperones."

Gabi had narrowed her eyes at my mention of Frederic's name and was on her feet before I could finish my sentence.

"What makes you think...?" she screeched, then stopped short and went over to shut the door tight. She lowered her voice to a hoarse whisper, "What makes you think that Frederic takes me out?"

"Well, I just thought..."

"You've been talking to that English girl. You walk to school with her."

"No. Well, a little. But you said..."

"I said that I like him. Not that we go out together. That girl has been gossiping again. The two of you, talking about me in your language!" she concluded, as if the greatest travesty was that we had been doing the gossiping in the English tongue. "There is nothing between Frederic and me, and we can't come with you because we don't go dancing together." She pronounced the word dancing as if she meant an activity much more extreme. "Now please get out of my room. I have work to do." She flopped back down on her bed and lifted her textbook.

With a lump in my throat, I shut the door behind me and paused in the dark hallway, taking some deep breaths to regain control. I wasn't sure whether I was more upset with Gabi, with Elizabeth, or with myself. The subject of Frederic and Gabi had not come up since the day I arrived in Paris, and since I saw them so obviously communing in the salon and at dinner, I felt they must at least go out together. Now I had lost a friend and worse, I was stuck for an evening alone with Philippe.

I knocked on Elizabeth's door and pleaded with her. "If you finish at the dance, couldn't you come by then, just to walk me home? We'll be at Le Riverside, a dancing club on Saint Germain." I didn't want to tell her about what had happened in Gabi's room. I would never tell her. I just wanted her help.

Reluctantly, she agreed. "Anyway, I'll try," she said. "After all, I do owe you something for this special evening with Laurent."

THIRTEEN

WE GATHERED DOWNSTAIRS around 7:30, and Elizabeth explained to Laurent about meeting me after the dance. It was to protect me, she said, from the young man I was going out with for the first time, who was a "professional wrestler."

We walked down to the Métro station together and they took their train in one direction and I took mine in another. Ascending from the Métro at Odéon, I walked quickly with what I hoped was an air of self-confidence along Saint Germain. I was alone in the noisy crowd headed for cafés, restaurants and clubs on a Saturday night. Philippe, thank heaven, was standing outside Le Riverside when I arrived. He greeted me warmly, bouncing up onto his toes to kiss me on both cheeks. My rib cage tensed. If he plasters his face against my chest during a slow dance, I thought, I'll just have to be rude.

Putting his hand around my arm, Philippe steered me into the club, but before we could find a seat, he pulled me to the large, crowded dance floor. We danced fast, the throng moving in unison to a poor rendition of an old Beatles' hit. "She was just 17," came the words in English. Above were abstract rows of garish, neon lights that lit the room at infrequent intervals. Everyone on the floor was dancing together, boys with boys, girls with girls, many in lines with boys and girls together. My eyes drifted over the heads of hair bobbing up and down, shining under pins of light that shot across the dance floor. Suddenly it felt great to be dancing again. Then I settled into the beat and forgot there was anyone in the room but my own body pushing steadily and amiably against the sound. The Beatles were followed by something I didn't recognize. Our feet accelerated to the pace of another strong drummer.

Then the safety of the fast set ended. Just as the slow, dreamy music separated the crowd into couples, Philippe excused himself to go to the restroom. I sat down in an empty chair at a table near the dance floor. I looked around and shivered. Couples were making out in every dark corner and rubbing up against each other under the gaudy lights. The place was just plain sleazy. I was a long way from the senior prom at the Coconut Grove or even Kips in Berkeley. Instinctively, I crossed my arms in front of my body.

After several minutes, two young Frenchmen with identical faces approached my chair. "Voulez-vous danser?" They spoke simultaneously, as if they had rehearsed it. Each had heavy sideburns and shocks of long brown hair pulled sideways. They wore duplicate leather bomber jackets, and even their sweat patterns were identical in the glare of the lights. But at least, I observed, they were tall.

"How do I choose?" I was trying not to laugh, turning from one to the other.

"I was here first," said one brother.

"It doesn't matter," said the second brother. "The girl should choose."

I giggled, fighting a nervous twitch in my upper lip. "What if I don't want to dance with either of you?"

They stood there silently, glaring at one another. "This is your fault," said the first brother. "If you hadn't followed me, she would have danced with me."

"You don't own this club or the girls in it," said the second brother, defiantly pushing the first away. The first shoved back, scowling.

"Excusez mois," came a familiar, composed voice. There behind the angry twins stood Teodor the Czech, towering over them. "This lady is my friend," he said, "and I want to dance with her. Do either of you have a problem with that?" I was smiling perhaps a little too gleefully as I rose and inched in toward Teodor's side. The two glared up at him but backed off, one going to the right and the other to the left.

Confidently, Teodor touched my shoulder and turned me around. His chin was cleanly shaved and beneath it, he wore a dark turtleneck under his tweed sports jacket from school. There was that Tinkerbell again, with her wings fluttering around my heart like signal flags in a fresh breeze.

"I'm sorry to intrude," he said, "but I could see there would be trouble. I was watching from across the room."

I thanked him sincerely for my rescue. We were being crowded out by dancers. He waved over to the left of the dance floor, and I followed his gesturing hand. A moment later, we arrived at the table of the dark, mysterious stranger Elizabeth had claimed was Teodor's spy. "My friend and I are having a drink and listening to the music."

"But you said you'd dance with me!" I protested. "And you'd better do it, or the *jumeaux ennuyeux* will return." Teodor laughed and I felt myself beaming. I had wanted to say Trouble Twins, but the French for *troublesome twins* had sounded great and *almost* rhymed. Teodor was shaking his head and smiling. "You are a funny girl, Jeanette. Come, let's dance."

It was just in time, because the music was still slow and Philippe was on his way across the floor from the restroom. He spotted us and turned on his leather soles and headed straight for another, shorter girl with frosted blond hair and a big nose.

A feeling of relief bubbled up through me. I glanced over at Philippe. He waved and I waved back. Such an understanding guy, that Philippe. Teodor noticed Philippe, my reaction, everything. He chuckled knowingly, and then I felt his strong arms come full around me. "Mmm, already?" I said. "In America, we call this étreinte ours." A bear hug dance.

"I like that expression, but I suspect the French don't know it." He drew me even closer.

"You can leave me after this dance, if you want to. I don't think the brothers will return."

"I can't do that," said Teodor. "It wouldn't be polite to leave a lady by herself."

"Very gallant of you," I said. "But I don't want to cause you any discomfort."

"Do I seem uncomfortable?" He pulled me so close that his eyes were no longer visible. I shut mine, settled into his broad chest, and felt as if I were sinking down into it. Over the speakers came 'Love is Blue,' but not the Paul Mauriat version. Bleu, bleu, l'amour est bleu, I heard. Blue love, kisses in a shadow.

After a few moments, I backed away just enough to see into his eyes and asked, "What is your whole name?"

"Teodor Pelnar, from Prague, at your service. Please call me Teo, by the way."

"And I am Janet Magill, from California, at your service," I gave a little curtsy.

"Jeanette." He bowed, one hand on his abdomen, one behind his back. A second later, we were back in a tight embrace.

"I love this song," I said, dreamily. "It's a beautiful melody."

Teo whispered in my ear, "I'm very glad to see you here tonight, Jeanette."

"I'm glad too. Why didn't you ask me yourself? I would have come with you."

"I know. I knew that. But you are a special girl..." his voice drifted off and he pulled me tighter, so that I couldn't back away again to talk.

When the dance ended, Teo took my hand and guided me to a table where we were alone in a dark corner. He ordered a beer for himself and a glass of red wine for me. "We are both lucky to be able to travel, aren't we?"

"Do many in your country get to study abroad?"

"This is the first year Czechs are permitted to travel abroad! Did you not know this? Now suddenly, perhaps hundreds of thousands. I am one of many prisonniers released!"

My breath left me when he uttered prisonniers with such intensity. I stared at him wide-eyed and mute, picturing bars pulled back like licorice sticks and birds held to the light, taking off with a great flutter of wings.

Teo continued, more subdued now. "But Jeanette, I am surprised by how few Americans I have met at L'Alliance Française. Perhaps all the Americans show up in the summer?"

"Yes. That's right." I replied. "Or they are on more formal college programs."

"Then, why are you not on one of these programs?"

I stared down into my wineglass while one song ended, another began. Gently, he took my hand and I faced him again. His eyes were wide open, patient. "Because my parents sent me here to get me away from the demonstrations in Berkeley," I told him softly, "while my brother is in Vietnam." Teo's eyes narrowed in recognition of the place names: Berkeley, Vietnam. He nodded, but said nothing. Shyly, I lowered my eyes again and mumbled, "I'm sorry." To him, and to people far away. Involuntary thoughts skidded over the icy road of my useless career as a radical, my humiliating exile, and my dread of bad news from Vietnam. I had not wanted to mention anything about my American life to my French family. Why had I spoken of these circumstances to this stranger? The music flared up as if a log had just been thrown on a fire.

When I glanced up, still embarrassed, Teo's broad face had sagged with sadness. He was staring at me. I wanted desperately to know what he was thinking. Teo leaned forward, put his face next to my ear and whispered, "That is an evil place, Vietnam." He used the word mauvais, but I knew he meant evil, not just bad, when he added, "dépravé."

"Très dépravé," I repeated back into his ear, but he went right on. "And there is an evil place in my country as well. That evil place is in the hearts of those who would keep us from being free and at peace...ach..." Teo pulled back, then shrugged his shoulders, obviously abashed.

My eyes had grown large and were wet with the desire to hear more. He stared intensely at my face, his own rigid with tension. Then he pulled me close again and went on in an even more passionate whisper. "The young in both of our countries are struggling. The old ones want us to need them. But we know how to live our lives. We don't need them anymore."

Whether it was the wine or Teo's words, I began to feel crushed by the weight of the world. Tears filled my eyes. That week, since I'd met Teo, I'd been reading every piece I could find about Czechoslovakia in the Paris edition of the New York Herald. I had been learning about the new air of liberation in Teo's country, and about the brave support of that direction from the new Czech president, Alexander Dubček. "But what about Dubček ...?" I began again.

"Ah yes. Dubček." He ran his fingers nervously up and down the sides of his mug, making thick, wet tracks in the frost until it was dripping and clear. Again, he reached out for me, and this time I scraped my chair closer to make it easier for him. He kissed my wet eyelids, my cheek, ran his hands up and down my spine. I put my arms around Teo's broad shoulders and hugged as he blew hot words into my ear. "Dubček's heart is one of ours," he told me, "but Dubček's vision is narrow, his process is always proper and practical. He is put in to lead us by the old ones who know they have already lost. They must give us something, so they give us Dubček. It is like giving a slice when we want the whole loaf. I am hungry, Jeanette..."

He nibbled at my ear. His forehead went down and pressed hard against the crown of my shoulder. The blade smarted, but I didn't move except to rub my fingers in circles on his back. "For now," he said, "the crumbs. We wait like mice in the corner, hoarding our crumbs."

Then, as suddenly as he had guided me off the dance floor, he pulled me to my feet and across to the spy's table. Up close, he looked even fatter and more fearsome, with his dark, disheveled hair and mismatched clothes. Teo introduced him as Miroslav, his friend from Bratislava, in Slovakia. They exchanged a few words in a language that bore no resemblance to anything I had ever heard before. Teo began to speak in French about the American and British bands he had heard. He asked lots of questions, and I dredged my memory for answers and for vocabulary. Miroslav watched the dancers and did not join the conversation. He seemed more than aloof. To me, he seemed rude and menacing.

When a slow number came on, we pushed our way back into the crowd and just then, I spotted Elizabeth dancing with Laurent across the floor. "There are my friends," I said, guiding our dance over to where they stood.

"This is not Philippe," Elizabeth said to Laurent, without even greeting us first. "He's the one over there with that blond girl."

Laurent's head jutted back as he appraised the five-foot-two of Philippe's dancing physique. "That was your wrestler?" Laurent asked, sneering first at me, then at Elizabeth.

"Small but strong," I replied. "Seriously, I did not want to be alone with him!"

"Well, it doesn't appear that will be your problem now," Elizabeth said. "Hello, Teodor-from-school. This is my friend, Laurent."

They shook hands and Teo danced me away. "I want to say things to you, Jeanette." Once again, he spoke in an urgent, secretive tone. "That man I am with is a friend of my family. He is here at the request of my parents, to watch me. To make sure I don't get into trouble."

"Then, he is your spy," I blurted out.

"Well, not exactly..."

"It's okay, I know all about it."

I reached my hand out to tap Elizabeth's shoulder as she glided by with Laurent. "You were right!" I whispered, pointing and nodding in the direction of the dark stranger.

Teo grabbed my arm and folded his big hand over my pointing finger. "That's not polite, is it?" he pleaded. "Even in America, n'est-ce pas?" He put both his arms around me and kissed me on the lips. It was a comfortable kiss, unrushed but not passionate, as if we had known each other for a long time. "Please, you will be courteous to my friend?"

I nodded. "Yes, of course, but why is he so silent?"

He answered smoothly, "He speaks no English. And he speaks almost no French."

I smiled, still feeling his kiss. Then we were back in our bear hug, moving to the slow, heavy beat of the music.

A while later, out of the corner of my eye, I watched Philippe leave, chatting steadily as he walked alongside the little blond girl with the big nose. I noticed the dance floor was emptying out. "Do you have a safe way home?" Teo asked.

"I'll walk with Laurent and Elizabeth."

"Of course. That is why they came. To protect you." He laughed. "It is good, because we don't live in the same direction." His hands were around me and he was rubbing the center of my back. "Now, I must...see you again."

"I leave with my French family on Tuesday for Easter," I said. "They have a vacation house on l'Île de Ré, an island off the Atlantic coast. I'll be gone until April tenth."

He whispered, more steadily this time, "I hope to see you when you return."

"Yes, when I return," I said. "And I'll be practicing my French."

"Then I will be surprised at how well we can talk together." He leaned in to kiss me gently on the lips and something slid into my hand. "Call me after Pâques," he whispered. I closed my fist over what Teo had placed in it, and said goodnight.

Thrilling, that's what it was, Elizabeth told me as we walked home. "You'll never know if he is Teo's spy, will you?" she asked, leaning across Laurent to speak in breathless English as if he weren't there.

"He is, Elizabeth. I can guarantee it."

"Why are you so sure? Did Teo say something? I can't believe he would risk that."

"Not in so many words. He never said 'spy.' But I'll tell you something else. When Teo kissed me goodnight outside Le Riverside, he slipped me 50 centimes and a card with his number. Just slipped it into my hand. And he whispered to call him when I return from l'Île de Ré. His breath in my ear made me shiver. I've never in my life ended an evening like that!"

"Let's see the card," Elizabeth said. I took it out of my little purse and held it under the yellow glare of a street lamp. "Oh my...Place Pigalle! He lives in one of those horrid little flea-traps up in the Pigalle." She shuddered. "The red light district."

"Dammit. But he's so nice," I cried. "His French is so good, and he's polite, and he...he collects stamps!"

"He must be from an upper crust family," Elizabeth said, conspiratorially. "Maybe with important government connections. Perhaps that is why our corpulent friend has nothing better to do than to follow poor Teo! I can't imagine why he lives in the Pigalle. We certainly have a story to anticipate when we return from holidays."

"Okay, enough. This is not fair," Laurent said, switching the conversation to his native tongue. "I am going to die of curiosity soon, and then who will escort you girls home?"

We began to repeat our entire conversation in French, taking Laurent into our confidence, and all the way home on the Métro, we talked about Teo and Miroslav and intrigue in countries behind the Iron Curtain.

That night, lying quietly in bed, just remembering Teodor Pelnar at Le Riverside made my heart surge and my cheeks sizzle. I could almost feel him holding me close and touching me, his breath grazing my ear as he whispered passionately about his very real political anxieties. I hadn't the foggiest notion whether he was pretending to seduce me so that Miroslav wouldn't know what treason he was passing along to me—or whether he was sharing his politics in order to seduce me. After all, everyone has this idea about Berkeley and its politics. Whatever game he was playing, he was winning. Both of his seductions, physical and political, had left my head spinning. I wanted more—to touch more and to know more about his country.

I felt shreds of guilt. At the moment Teo's cup seemed brimming with a rich, fragrant wine, while Aaron's seemed empty, washed and dried. Briefly, I tried to conjure the yearning for Aaron that I felt I should have, but cutting into this effort was the sharp imprint of Irena at L'Alliance, excited over the trouble among French university students. Would Aaron want to go from Berkeley's frying pan into a Paris on fire? And then, my friend in Ameri-chaos had not said a word about his father in the letter I had received just this afternoon. I felt shut out by his patter about school assignments and "counterproductive" antiwar demonstrations.

Hurt once again by Monsieur Becker, I rose from my tangled sheets and took up my pen. I might as well try to establish a modicum of honesty between us. My long letter was that of a true friend, and nothing more—about school, Phillipe, Le Riverside, and Teodor Pelnar. I did leave out most of the details, except for my political sympathies. I'd let Aaron use his imagination. Satisfied that I had done the right thing, I crawled back into bed and fell sound asleep.

When I awoke on Sunday, I lay in bed waiting to dress for midday dinner and thought only about Teodor, how I might grow close to him and learn everything I could about his life.

FOURTEEN

I WAS TRYING not to feel superstitious about the departure date. We were scheduled to leave for l'Île de Ré the next morning, April Fools. In the salon after dinner, La Petite Jeanette walked right up to me and presented me with two pictures. "For you." Her voice was soft but not a bit shy. I had been drawing pictures for her in the salon since the first week, with my lovely little friend doing me the favor of translating my images into French. Now there was one picture of Le Poisson d'Avril, a fish symbolizing April Fool's Day, and another of Bateaux sur l'Île de Ré, boats off the beach at the island. Gratefully, I admired the pictures, trying to point out features that were especially nice so that La Petite might believe in my appreciation of her artwork, as one artist to another. She giggled and pumped her hands into the padded arm of my chair, pushing her feet off the carpet over and over again as we spoke.

Finally, sister Lili climbed onto my lap, and together they taught me all the words to a French song I thought I knew: Sur le Pont d'Avignon. I had only heard the chorus before. Madame Bouleaux sat in her chair, tapping her big clumsy hands together in rhythm. The children jumped up and forming a circle with Cecile, they demonstrated a little dance. I was utterly charmed. They told me I must join them so that we could bow to each other, two and two. "Tomorrow, I'll bring my guitar," I promised. "Perhaps Le Petit Laurent will dance the fourth part while I play the dancing song." They all clapped and squealed, asking if I would teach them to play guitar. "And can we learn American songs?" Cecile asked shyly.

I had been restricting my music to my room, comforting myself with the tunes that Aaron and I used to play, a bunch of familiar folk rock and some Beatles thrown in for good measure. I kept my door shut and my voice low. Sometimes I went off on strumming and picking tangents and didn't sing at all. Now I was holding two little hands, laughing and singing loudly, "Sur le pont, d'Avignon, on y danse tous en rond..."

Our sweet dance was just ending when Frederic burst into the room. He spoke loudly for Frederic, and so rapidly that all I could understand was *le président* and Johnson. I knew it was important news from home. "What is it? What's happening?" I asked.

Margot was listening from the dining room where she sat smoking and talking with Hélène and Jean-Louis. When they heard Frederic's news, they stood in a row along the divide between the dining room and the salon, Margot translating into English: "President Johnson has announced he will not run for *président* in the next election." I felt my breath catch. Despite the distractions, Matt had been haunting my dreams, making two similar appearances in Parisian scenes dressed in battle fatigues, then both times blown up horribly by bursting clouds of fire. Something dripped down into my throat and I began to cough.

"Frederic, is this an April Fool?" Madame Bouleaux demanded. "It's not until tomorrow!" She turned to me. "Some fools take this holiday quite seriously in France."

"No, no, maman!" Frederic protested. "It's the truth. It was on the car radio. Jeanette, why do you cry? Are you sad? Do you like President Johnson?"

Out came one last cough and I began to laugh at Frederic's mistake. "Pas du tout!" I shouted. "This is such a surprise! Do you see what this means?" They were all shaking their heads, bewildered. "The American students have finally been heard! Johnson knows we do not like his war. Oh, thank God... No! I do not like President Johnson!"

Now they all circled around me, the American in the room. La famille, the students. Even Gabi, who appeared to be my friend again. Both she and Elizabeth came and put their arms around my shoulders, one on each side of me. Though I was crying, I had to stifle a laugh. Elizabeth was sweet to comfort me, but I knew she did not understand anything about American politics. I wondered about Gabi.

"So this is excellent," Bérnard was saying. "The Vietnam War will be over." Voices swirled around me, "At last!" "What a wasteful war!" "Oh, those Americans...!" "Indochine." "Historic!" "Marvelous!"

"Not so fast," I raised my voice above the din. "Oh, I do want to believe it!" I felt the tears rising inside me again. "But I'm afraid it's not going to happen that way." They all quieted down, their eyes on the "expert." "Some other president may want to end it. That's what I'm hoping. But I'm sorry to say, it will be a long time..."

"...but don't most Americans want the war to end immediately?" Bérnard interrupted. "We read about protests. And the Tet Offensive last January? The turning point! All over Europe, the students marched to support those in America!"

I moaned. "Most students want the war to end. But not the older voters, not if it means losing the war. The objective is still a government of South Vietnam that is independent and democratic. There will be negotiations."

"But that will take years," whined Le Grand Laurent. "And meanwhile, they will fight."

"There may even be more fighting," I said, crushing the hope of my audience. I stared at the floor, trying to imagine what this would mean for Matt, for my parents...and then, too, for Aaron! Guilt swept over me as I wondered how my politically tuned-in friend was taking this news. I shook off an image of Teo on Saturday night.

People were mumbling softly, expecting more from me. I felt a completely new sensation sweep through me. Suddenly, it was as if Barbara Borovsky's group of protesters, my parents, and even Aaron had never existed. None of those people thought I had a brain in my head! But here they respected my opinion, asked for my opinion!! I continued, "The Americans will want to do as much damage as they can, to prove to the North Vietnamese that they must give up."

"Zut merde! That is just the same as before!"

"Bérnard, don't swear!" Margot shouted.

Bérnard peeked at me sheepishly, shrugging his shoulders. I said, "Not quite the same as before, but the war is not over."

"But surely, you don't want Vietnam to be communist, do you Jeanette?" Margot asked.

Thoughts of Teodor Pelnar re-entered my brain as soon as I heard the word "communist." Sooner or later, Teo would ask the same question, in the same tone. Before I could formulate an answer, Bérnard called out, "Here we go again...the dance of de Gaulle and the Bouleaux family..." He signaled Laurent and the two began to drift toward the door with Elizabeth trailing behind. I thought about leaving, but I had woven the net around myself.

"Whatever your opinion of Charles de Gaulle, the communists are worse!" Jean-Louis imposed his opinion as if Margot had not asked me the question.

"I like our President de Gaulle," Madame Bouleaux added. "He has been one of the greatest leaders of France."

"He's been wonderful, maman," Hélène said, "but he is getting old..."

Margot broke in, "Alors...!" She clicked her tongue and waved off her mother and sister, "Communism can never take hold in France. But you see, Jeanette, we are still afraid of it. You Americans can't know what it is like to be so close to a huge, powerful communist country like the Soviet Union. Look what they've done in Central Europe. Criminals!"

"Terrible..." "Powerful..." "So close..." I heard several of them agree.

"We Americans worry more about China," I said. "Most Americans want to win in Vietnam because they think China is behind it..."

The conversation was still pitching chaotically around the salon when Madame Bouleaux held up her hand. "It's a terrible war. Indochine is no place for Europeans or Americans." Her voice was heavy with sadness. For a moment, it was so quiet that I could hear the clock ticking from the dining room.

≈PART THREE≈
Berkeley

FIFTEEN

PHRASES, SENTENCES, and whole thought patterns from Janet Magill's letter had begun to appear in my biology texts. My self-proclaimed best friend had begun by describing an evening out with a short guy from the Near East, but then suddenly she was talking about a big fellow named Teodor. This one danced with her and then taught her about the politics of his fragile Communist nation. "Czechoslovakia." The mythic-sounding, tongue-crunching word was superimposed over reliable printer's ink by the wounded synapses in my brain. Now there was a nation with real problems, Janet claimed, not ones manufactured to bolster the military industrial complex. Or like those of the French students with their strident complaints. Were these the fruitcake ravings of a naïve and vulnerable girl, or what?

In biochem lab on the first Thursday morning in April, stubborn images from Janet's letters shrank to fit within the slides of enzymatic substances I had prepared for the microscope. A small café table smelling like decades of cheap wine. A big creep holding Janet's hand. Whispered insurrectionary slogans. The liquid seeping from her enraptured gaze. Somehow over it all, the word "chump" and "sucker" kept appearing on those laboratory slides in letters black as beetles. Her, I wondered, or me?

I didn't know whether to feel more angry, betrayed, or frightened, but I settled on "scary damn shit" when I shared my angst with my buddy Neil Strand. By the time I got to the lab that morning, it had occurred to me that it was all my own fault. Janet's best-friend-in-the-whole-world crap was a product of my failure to make it with her when I'd had the chance. Not to mention my more recent and far less tolerable failure to secure necessary funds for a ticket to join her.

Next to me was my lab partner, the petite, mousy brain with whom I was lucky enough to be paired. Her name was Sheila Delgado and she held every conceivable academic scholarship: for future scientists, for women, for people with Hispanic surnames, and of course, for future women scientists with Hispanic surnames. I felt proud to be in the human race knowing that Sheila had all this loot, because she was going to discover something amazing some day.

Without knowing what she was up against, she helped me focus on the task at hand. Sheila and I were good partners, probably the best in the class. We labored side by side, shielded from chemicals by identical oilcloth aprons and gray rubber gloves. We had passed a couple of hours together, calibrating the test tubes and cloches, making our meticulous notations, paying strict attention to business. When we were pretty far into the period and the experiment, a spooky thing happened. Very disorienting. Sheila looked up from the little grids in her lab book, interrupting my concentration.

"Becker, is there a problem?"

"With this equation? No..."

"I mean, you seem sad today. Distracted. Is there something bothering you?"

I sighed and cleared my throat. "Do you want a laundry list?"

"Is it the draft?"

"Yes. You might say that."

"Oh." She turned back to the grids.

Well, that was certainly productive, I thought, returning to my own calculations. Seconds later, a cold brown hand, not much bigger than a child's, was placed tentatively on mine. My muscles stiffened as if she'd poured a tray of ice down my shirt. Sheila Delgado's brown eyes, as mousy as her hair, were positively luminescent. "I'm sorry," she said. "If there's anything I can do to make you feel better..."

In my trade, luminescence is defined as any giving off of light caused by the absorption of radiant or corpuscular energy. I sensed the energy being sucked out of me and absorbed by this snippet of a woman, and there was no resisting it. I felt my left eyebrow and the left side of my lip tugged up skeptically. I waited for clarification.

Her hand traveled up my lab coat sleeve—but underneath the sleeve. I could feel her fingers inching up my skin, getting warmer as they rose. "Actually, I'm sure you can help," I said. I chased her hand under my own sleeve and brought it out under the fluorescents, giving it a squeeze. I checked to make sure the professor was busy elsewhere, then rubbed my finger between each of hers, slowly, one at a time. "I've never quite appreciated the scope of your powers, Delgado. We'll just have to arrange a time and place, or else I'm liable to pounce on you and make everyone in class forget to watch their projects."

"Including us," she said, drawing away. She squinted up at me. "My place. It's the women's co-op on Piedmont. Four o'clock would work out."

My lab partner proved to be as focused about sex as she was about her academic goals. We met up in her room in the Co-op where she exchanged hours of household duties in payment for her room. Four in the afternoon was the time she was able to cull for us from her calendar, not an ideal time for romance. That was fine by me. I wasn't in this for the romance.

The clinical way Sheila undressed, folding each piece of clothing neatly into its proper place, reminded me just a little too much of myself—the tidy me I was before the guest of honor was due to show up at my cottage. Once down on the bed, however, Sheila undulated as expertly as a streetwalker, leaving no body part unafflicted. She was all over me, and I must admit I enjoyed the experience, alternately observing the whole thing as if I were across the room in a chair taking notes, then forcing my mind back on the bed long enough to get my kicks. In between all this mental racing back and forth from the chair to the bed, my heated brain was sweating bullets over Janet Magill, a young lady who, I realized with yet another cerebral sector, was not there to defend herself. Goddamn Janet's tell-all letters and her chatty, affable little heart. My ego being what it is, I was sure she was telling me about this guy, "Teo," as she called him, just to make me jealous.

Picturing Teo the Czech, it took me only a hot second before I fled that mental outpost and pounced on Sheila Delgado with a fierceness she clearly appreciated. But then, at the moment I was getting into her tight little cunt, what weirded me out even more than my own schizo nonsense was my partner's monologue. All the time we were kissing and sweating and working ourselves up to the climax, Sheila kept repeating, "You're a good guy, Becker, a good good guy." Yep. Those were the exact words. A good guy. Over and over again. Was she trying to flatter me or convince herself that she hadn't made a mistake?

We had just finished, and it was one of those times I wished I smoked so I'd know what the hell to do with myself after making it, besides sleep. Sheila didn't want me to sleep because she needed me to regain strength and get out before her roommate came home for dinner.

Anyway, I was lying there, my hand reaching out to pet a spot on her miniature, round ass. Perhaps she felt like I did, wondering what to do or say at this point, not having much in the way of conversation beyond the latest lab assignment or the new equipment our prof had ordered. She turned on the radio and was fiddling with the dial, careening from station to station, when something I heard, some grievous tone they must teach them for emergencies in radio announcership school, made me leap across the bed.

"Wait-don't-change-that!" I belted out. Sheila drew back, as if she knew that blocking the route between me and that broadcast could cost her a wrist bone.

"...is DEAD. The great civil rights leader, winner of the 1964 Nobel Peace Prize, advocated peaceful protest methods in the name of freedom and justice..."

"Martin Luther King...?"

"Shhh...!"

"...assassin's bullet outside the Lorraine Motel in Memphis, Tennessee, where he spoke last night on behalf of the garbage workers..."

"What a way to go..."

"Shut UP!"

"I won't take that personally, asshole!" she shouted back, but kept quiet then. I listened for another minute. I switched off the radio, glaring at Sheila. I was sure that the gory details would be repeated for hours and days to come, ad infinitum.

"Don't you want to find some music?" she asked.

"Didn't you hear what just happened?" I shot back, incredulous.

"Sure. It's too bad." She gave a little high-pitched, rodentlike sigh and rolled smoothly over and off the bed.

The only words that came into my mind were 'fuck her,' but the irony of that particular put-down in this situation made me sit there on the bed, naked and mute, while she selected some neatly-folded underwear from a drawer. Without a backward glance, she headed for the bathroom.

I was dressed and outta there before she emerged. "See you in class, Sheila," I called through the bathroom door. At least at home, Dork would give me a squawk once in a while.

Over the next week, Sheila said so little about the most startling event since President Kennedy's assassination that I wasn't sure whether she would bleed if I pierced her skin.

To my surprise, the reaction in Berkeley was also low-key. On campus, some classes were cancelled, and beyond that, a few Berkeley High School students smashed windows down on Shattuck Avenue. But according to Walter Cronkite, rioting broke out in 125 cities in 29 states, so eventually I surmised that half of the campus must have gone over the bridge to San Francisco to add to the general mayhem there.

Well-practiced at avoiding the fray, I remained chez moi. But still, I mourned, as outraged as the next guy. MLK had been a hero to me all through my teens, and I knew it wasn't just because the whole white liberal sector of the country was taken with him. To me, MLK was part of a particular childhood memory, one of those few intense moments when you know you're in the presence of something that matters to someone who matters to you, in this case, dear ol' Dad.

My father was living with us, just before he wasn't anymore. We were sitting in front of the old Philco together before dinner, watching events unfold in Little Rock, Arkansas. "That could be the Jews, running through a tunnel of hate to the schoolroom door," he said. I remembered that "tunnel of hate" thing. He put one arm around me, drew me to his side, and I heard his gruff whisper, "That could be you, and don't you forget it."

I've speculated in recent years that the whole civil rights revolution inspired my father to clear the path toward his own private revolution and head for Ecuador. I'll never know. But I realized now that I felt as secure with MLK as I had with my father. I'm sure I was one of many who had seen the great black preacher as a safe, non-threatening, acceptable kind of guy who would get white Americans to do what was right. He was leading us, along with his own people, drawing us gracefully away from generations of vile prejudices and behaviors.

So I understood all those rioters and in my anger over his murder, part of me wanted to be out there. I thought maybe if Janet Magill were still around, she would have been across the Bay raising hell. And then there was freaky Sheila who didn't give a damn.

When classes resumed on the Monday after the assassination, it was all I could do to be civil to Sheila in lab. Somehow in my mind she had become associated with the crime itself, which was ridiculous, of course. I tried to get rational about it, but it was tough. Maybe it was a Chicano thing. Chicanos and blacks. I'd have to check that out.

On an evening of televised nationwide chaos, I comforted myself with fantasies of Janet returning from the streets, flushed and gorgeous, smelling like hot asphalt and perspiration. She'd gab on and on about events as if her relating them to me was an affirming part of her participation. Then, of course, the best way for her to calm down would be to rest in my arms. I would comfort her. Feel the sweet wilting of one kind of tension and the mounting of another. I covered Dork's cage and climbed into bed.

My fantasies accelerated. I was jetting across the Atlantic with a hard-on as powerful and destination-bound as a DC-10's, when right over the ocean, Sheila Delgado rose from the waves, her face as frozen as North Atlantic ice, and the plane started to dive. A cold wind rushed in on me: Wasn't I Janet Magill's "Sheila" after all? When Janet was trying her best to play a part in the antiwar movement, did she experience the same twist to the gut with me that I had when I realized Sheila didn't give a shit about MLK?

The truth about the similarities between Sheila and me made me squirm. I got myself out of bed and pulled up my PJ bottoms and paced from the bedroom to the front room and back, lifting Dork's terry to peer into his cage. He was sleeping peacefully, lucky ignorant bird. I resumed my pacing and my deliberation: I wasn't out there on the streets now any more than I'd been then, but, I reasoned, Janet did know I cared about ending the war. I tried to recall precious time we'd spent together in my cottage. So what if my cynicism had been a disappointment to Janet? She'd come back to me, even if only as a friend, and she'd written to me, expected me in France...but Janet knew that I still had no way to France, and she was not here.

It took me seven hours of fitful sleep, and the next day and a half of complaining to Dork that faraway Janet was driving me insane, to realize that I ought not to judge what I did not understand in Sheila Delgado. When I came into lab on Wednesday, I flashed Sheila an apologetic smile. "I'm sorry if I've been a little distant lately."

She shrugged her shoulders. "I know. You've had a lot on your mind."

"So, you want to keep getting together?"

"Sure, but no more radio. I'll borrow a record player from the girl in the next room."

"Never mind. We'll just make our own music."

"Cute, Becker. Real cute. Four o'clock. My place."

"Want to go out to dinner afterwards?" I asked, feeling I owed her that much.

"Naw. No thanks. I've got stuff to do."

SIXTEEN

SIX WEEKS HAD GONE BY since my last plea to Dad. I decided to phone Cora about the lack of communication. I had to be sure Dad hadn't totally rejected what he might perceive as his cowardly and unpatriotic son. And I had to provide Janet with some reason to wait for me.

Just as I was debating the timing of the call, in the week after the MLK assassination, I finally received a reply from Ecuador. It was not the one I'd hoped for. Dad went on about life in the tropics and the financial needs of my extended family there. He told me that they (and he included Juanita in every sentence) felt they'd done right by me (which they had) and that they had been looking forward to my "independence." Then he asked a perfectly logical question: "Why don't you just hitch a ride up to Canada like the rest of the boys who don't want to serve?"

For another couple of weeks, I considered this option, especially while reading equally chatty letters with equally thoughtless questions from Janet Magill.

April 23 was Janet's nineteenth birthday. She'd taken her guitar all the way across the Atlantic with her, so I decided a Byrds songbook would be welcome despite her professed abandonment of our beloved folk rock for screechy acid rock. The note I enclosed with the gift was calculated to bring her eighteenth birthday to mind: I'd flown to L.A. for the occasion. We'd started with a little brandy in my room at Cora's apartment before heading out. I remembered her sipping it like a proper lady, one little taste at a time. As for me, a taste was all I indulged in, always cautious when it came to the mortal danger involved in drinking and driving. The real thrill of the evening was the cruise along Sunset Boulevard in the groovy yellow Mustang convertible her father had bought her for her birthday. She'd asked me to drive so it would "feel like a real date." One hand on the wheel, one arm around my girl, top down. McGuinn's famous   Rickenbacker 12-string guitar diddling the stars over our heads. Janet's hair billowing in the wind. It was a mellow night.

Never mind that I was trying like hell to face reality and tear my mind away from Janet's hold. Everyday when I returned from class, I poked into my mailbox for the latest dispatch from France. I would tear open the letter before taking off my windbreaker or shedding my pack of books. My knees would fill with a toxic gel as I read, forcing me to sit before the stone cold hearth to complete the first perusal.

Neither rain nor sleet, nor Sheila nor science could keep me from my self-inflicted postal route. There was nothing more delicious than the trip from the letterbox to the queen-sized bed: I reveled in the dazzling color of Janet's words, squeezed her cool, thick hair, tasted the Wonder Glow on her cheeks, studied her wide green eyes, found them wanting me, reached for her long legs and for the damp silk between them, felt her grab me where she had never dared, and shoved myself daringly deep inside. I commandeered her Wonder Glow soul along with her body. My childhood friend, my innocent, trusting friend. I chided myself. How much easier it was to feed on her airmail feasts than to deal with what was right in front of me. How comforting to turn away from Sheila's narrow body and pale soul, the bloody war, my bleak prospects and the lonely, frustrating quagmire of my life.

I reached into my Levis pocket and withdrew the day's aerogram from Janet. During the month of April, her letters were written in two distinct tones, as if two different people had decided to share the onion-skin paper to save the cost of an additional stamp. One minute she was racing around like the Ugly American on a whiz-bang tour of sights and museums and la belle Paree—and the next moment she was delivering a sociology lecture on the intricacies of social class, analyzing and criticizing her French family, then without so much as a paragraph indentation, haranguing me with information about the terrible French educational system and how the young rebels wanted to change things.

There was impending rebellion—and there was the Louvre and the gardens and Camembert cheese. And between these two sides of the centime was the edge, flashing romantic, refracted light from the Seine. The name of the edge was Teodor Pelnar.

Even though Janet was not technically my girl, I had my dreams, and I had thought that our dreams were the same. Hope flew around inside me when she wrote questioning me about the money from Dad—but it quickly crash-landed. How could I write about my failure to convince him? Janet's father had sent his son to war, but afforded a luxurious trip to Paris for his baby girl. Perhaps she would not understand a father saying no to such a request. I felt confused, ashamed, and trapped.

Janet's letters weren't the only ones to be read until they frayed. From my Dad's tone, I understood how easy it had been to detach himself from me. Hopefully he hadn't forgotten our close times, hugs and conversations, funny moments and the like that I remembered so clearly from my childhood. But without forgetting, he might just disengage and lose himself in his newly-born existence: in an absorbing new language, beguiling customs, even everyday things like eating, socializing, driving, working...and in the new people in his life. I hung my head low over Janet's aerogram, now grasped in two hands, and the writing blurred. It struck me that like Dad, Janet might become disoriented and ultimately detached from "home"—and from me. I had considered that from Canada I might be able to proceed to France. But that could take months, even years, and I needed to be with Janet Magill before she made some terrible mistake.

Teo the Czech was intensifying that probability. How could I hope to compete with a bonafide victim of rigid, reprehensible dogma and political repression? How could night after night of perfectly decent dinners spoiled by the six o'clock news measure up to the suffering and raw need for freedom so inscrutable to an American, yet so deeply human?

I folded Janet's latest letter carefully, already wondering what tomorrow's mail would bring. As always, I had to admit the sincerity of Janet's letters. Sincere, honest, but most of all conflicted. I pulled myself up and went to clean Dork's cage. And while I was sitting on the john, watching Dork splashing around in the fresh fountain of my tub, I tried to figure out what the hell I could write back to Janet. Even with her access to political discussion among the foreigners at her school, it was clear that Janet had not understood much about the student unrest fomenting in the outskirts of Paris at Nanterre.

In March, before Johnson resigned, Newsweek had covered the Berkeley-style incidents at the grungy, suburban Nanterre campus. Janet understood that students at Nanterre, like the one loud-mouth in her boarding house, were dissatisfied with the status quo in higher education. It seemed incredible to me that she had accepted her French family's simplistic explanation of the unrest: the root of the problem was the educational system and a battle between leftist students and rightist students. A political problem between student groups. And that kind of squabble, she concluded, would soon be resolved by university administrators.

I could have told Janet a few things about Nanterre. That the protest had been against President de Gaulle's government and the denial of basic rights, like freedom of speech and assembly. And what they had wanted to assemble and protest about was her own cause, the war in Vietnam! But I did not want to be the one to explain what the French students were fighting for, because I did not want this to be her fight while I was not there to protect her. Janet did need protection, and primarily from her own impulses.

So what to write? How in hell could I return Janet's excruciating honesty—about her new friends and her enemies, and all the conflicted opinions that seemed to run like mottled threads through the white lace of her dreamlike spring season in Paris? Janet, Teodor, Sheila, et moi? The quadrangle could have been amusing if it wasn't my problem. How could I reply sincerely without it seeming tit-for-tat?

Meanwhile, whatever Janet's delusions, life here on the other side of the world had to go on. Shit! I would wash the bird and make myself a sandwich, even though I was not hungry. Listen to the news I did not want to hear. Study for the future I might never have.

I coaxed Dork back into his cage and wiped the wires down with a clean towel. Then I fed my ward, who I presumed could at least taste his food. I walked into the kitchen to make the requisite sandwich and found myself turning on my heel, winding up back on my window seat, staring through the glass at the approaching night.

And then I decided. Before I answered Janet's letter, I would try to crawl inside her conflict, to envision Paris through her eyes and face her reality head-on. Janet had written diary-style letter after letter in such vivid detail that I could fill in the blanks. My eyes were closed but my brain was setting scene after scene. As soon as one ended, there was another in its place. I saw her re-establishing contact with Teo the Czech on the first day of school after Easter vacation, running away from an ugly spy character straight out of film noir. They spent the afternoon together in a beautiful park surrounded by sensuous sculptures. Nudes...nakedness...

Leaning back against the window seat pillows, I shook my head to erase these images. After Easter, seeing Paris again, and no doubt Teo the Czech, Janet felt sorry that she'd missed any of that precious month in the "City of Light." La famille had evidently disappointed her, but the sights, sounds, history, and art of Paris would not. She wanted to see all of Paris and to experience the city's extremes. One day, dressed up in her polyester suit and heels, some of the hippie frizz brushed out of her hair, she strolled down the Champs-Elysées with her new sidekick, a very straight teenager named Elizabeth, drooling over the trop cher merchandise—expensive gloves and perfume and fashions worthy of her Beverly Hills credentials. Another day, she was back out in her knit poncho and a pair of black Capri pants—nooo...those were what she wore in high school. It must be Levis by now—stripped of her makeup and strolling with Teo the Czech along avenues lined with pink flowering trees, distant relatives of the Berkeley cake sugar outside my bay window. Holding hands, gazing at the Seine, agonizing over all the wonderful books sold from stalls on the riverbank...and there, for only a few centimes, was Colette's Le Blé en Herbe in French...

Le Blé en Herbe? The Budding Wheat?? Screee...ch! The TV documentary running around in my head of 'The Adventures of Janet Magill' came to a halt. Wasn't it Colette who had first advocated free love? The first woman, anyway, or one of the first? And Teodor Pelnar right there with her when she bought the friggin' book! What was she trying to tell me? A conversation between them began to form in my mind and I plucked it right out again like a bee's stinger. After all, I knew better than anyone where my old fashioned girl stood in the debates over the sexual revolution...didn't I? Didn't I?

I rolled over on my side and wiped the sweat from my face with the cool edge of my shirt. I tried to relax, clutching my pillow against my chest with my arms around it. Perhaps I should confront reality one small chunk at a time. I focused on Janet in art museums like the Moderne and L'Orangerie with its two thrilling oval rooms of Monet water lilies. The immensity of the Louvre. The historical sights she enjoyed most of all. She'd loved the tangible reality of Musée Carnavalet: that Robespierre's whiskers had actually dropped into this shaving basin, Napoleon's hands slipped into these diminutive leather gloves.

What else...? The death mask of Voltaire...Louis XIV's tea service. Wigged heads. Spinning wheels. I was beginning to get sleepy. The hodge-podge was there, floating above my head like proverbial sheep, comforting me with their sheer ordinariness: clocks, shoes, porcelain...

I was just drifting off when another distinct image of Janet made me groan out loud and throw the pillow at the wall. She had written that the conversations among students at her French school were beginning to corroborate the obnoxious Bérnard's diatribes about the students' plight. Perhaps, after all, he might be more trustworthy than she had at first assumed. So, what if Janet started to sympathize with the students, giving in to her natural inclination to side with the underdog? Yes! Okay, I thought, so there was something I could write her: maybe Bérnard was as dangerous as he appeared. Suspect everyone!

My nocturnal imaginings took me to the kitchen for a drink of water. Dork slept the peace of the ignorant under his terry cloth. The aquarium motor rasped in the quiet night like a large European city. I sipped and imagined Janet greeting Teo the Czech after her French class, talking to him about Bérnard and the Sorbonne. It was a conversation I could only guess about, but I could hear Janet's pleading tone. She would say, "I let my parents drive me away from doing my part in Berkeley, and now the issues have followed me to Paris. I'm so ashamed of myself." She would take hold of Teodor's thick, woolly sleeve and squeeze the material in her two hands just to relieve her tension. Then, softly, "I'm sorry..." She would let go of the sleeve and smooth out the wrinkles.

Teodor is responding, "That's okay. You need to grab on to something."

Janet continues, her baby whine gathering grease as it rolls on: "I have a friend in California. His name is Aaron Becker. And he never wants to get involved in any kind of cause. Why doesn't he feel comfortable enough to stand up for things he believes in like other people do? Why don't I?" Teo the Czech wants to protect Janet, takes my side. "But you are not even sure why the French students are protesting. That's what you said, so why would you participate?"

"So why don't I know?" Janet whines. Teodor starts to speak but she interrupts. "No, wait. I'll tell you! I don't know because I don't want to know. I want everything to be perfect in France. That's not very nice of me, is it? And Bérnard, in my house. I could find out from him if I wanted to. But instead of asking him, I've been avoiding him as if he carried a contagious disease, trying to convince myself I detest him."

"So, now you will talk with Bérnard?" Teodor is concerned.

Janet lets go of one of those high-pitched little-girl giggles. "Don't worry, he's not ever going to be competition for you, Teodor." Flirty. Phony. Not Janet. No...

Janet takes a deep breath and lays her head on Teodor's shoulder. He strokes her hair and after a while, he asks, "So, this friend of yours in California, he is a coward?" She lifts her head, pondering.

"Not a coward, just completely cynical and self-interested. What Aaron lacks is compassion. If you have no compassion, you only watch out for yourself. Not just for your own safety, but your own plans and goals, like finishing the school year so you can get a job if the war doesn't kill you first..."

"...or like finishing the beautiful trip to Paris that you started to take in the spring?" Teodor's voice is soft and sympathetic. Then he asks the obvious question, "Was he your lover?"

Tears have begun to fill Janet's eyes. "No, just my friend. We write each other letters."

Teodor draws away. He notices the red rimming Janet's eyes. "So he is not such a bad person?"

"Oh no. He's smart and fun to be with...," she hesitates, wants to explain exactly how she feels, "...and trustworthy, most of the time. I mean, well, we've known each other since we were children."

"And he was never your lover?"

"No," Janet insists. "Why do you ask that again?"

Teodor shrugs his shoulders and drops his eyelids, as if he is dismissing the whole subject. But he answers her. "Maybe you miss him."

Okay...this was definitely getting freaky. Awake the whole fucking night and barely able to move my body to class. I crept along Prospect Road, books feeling like barbells in my achy arms. Shutting my eyelids in a game to see how far I could walk before I'd run into something. Open, close, open. A peace poster in a second-story window. Close, open. Brown-shingle cottages with wild, scraggly roses blooming out front. Close, open. Channing Way to the Circle. Close, open. The "Fee Gee" house. Phi Gamma. Didn't Janet go to a party there once with some of the dorm girls? Something about a beer keg leaking all over the floor...sloshing through beer for a dance and a half before she lit out of there. Wisely, she'd fled up Channing to my place and arrived smelling like a sailor on payday. Janet, again. Sex, politics, war, France, America. And Janet, again. Everything roiled around in my brain as if I'd been up the whole night drinking. If there had been anything in my stomach at all, I would have puked right there on the Fee Gee steps. Not like it hadn't ever happened before, I thought, and the sick humor of it cheered me for an instant.

Trudging along Piedmont, I passed other frat houses, two-story mammoths I'd scrupulously avoided through the years. I wasn't the only one these days. Many of the big monster houses were empty now that Cal students had begun to feel foolish playing drunken children's games with a war hanging over their heads.

Close, open. I'd made it to Bancroft Avenue. It was a morning as dappled and dripping as any other in April. I leaned against the wall in front of I-House to catch my breath. International House. Its buff tower loomed over the campus, cautioning us to pay attention to what was beyond our borders. I wondered if any Southeast Asian students were living there. Any Vietnamese.

I started to move on down the hill. A black guy with a beret was there at the corner of Bancroft and College. A Black Panther. They'd had a bad week...there were headlines. "Hey," was all he said, shoving a leaflet into my hand. I nodded, bestowed a hearty "thanks," an involuntary reflex. Smoothed it and pretended to read.

Pretending, I saw something in capital letters about the recent alliance between the Peace and Freedom Party and the Black Panthers. Good for them, I thought. In my heart I wished them well, but I was way too tired to fret about it. Then, I noticed the bold print "Free Huey" like two menacing eyes. Huey Newton—wasn't he the cause célèbre who had sent Janet packing? My good will curdled like yesterday's cheese sandwich in my stomach. I crumpled the damn thing to a wad, using both hands until I was tossing it back and forth, my books tucked under my arm. I walked past Boalt Law and the ugly new architecture school. And just as I was about to toss the leaflet into a can, there came Sheila Delgado. Her eyes narrowed and the corners of her mouth turned up in an obligatory slant. That was the extent of her greeting: surprise at seeing me there, a tight-lipped smile and an edgy "Hi Becker." A gracious good morning to you, too, I thought.

Then she saw the leaflet. "What you got there?" I smoothed it out, saw a string of dates. I flashed back to her stiffer-than-tits-in-winter reaction to MLK's murder and I wanted to convince her that I was into this stuff. I wanted her to believe that civil rights and the war were important to me, and more meaningful than screwing her could ever be. I read from the leaflet, knowing she had wanted a summary, not a recitation, but I read. Loudly, defiantly. Every word:

"Noon rally today. Support Stop the Draft Week. Events planned for April 22nd to 26th. Get over your doubts! Stop the Draft Week: Monday, April 22 – Free Huey & Oakland 7 rally, noon. Features Fred Halstead, Socialist Workers Party presidential candidate. Tuesday, April 23 – Rally and march to Oakland Induction Center and Alameda County Courthouse to visit Huey. Free Huey! Wednesday activities pending what happens Tues..."

"Okay, I get it...I get it..." she grabbed the paper menace out of my hands and tossed it without a scrunch into the nearby can.

"You had no right to trash that, you know. That was my property."

"What's your problem, Becker? You were about to throw it away..."

"So that was my prerogative."

"Well there's your colored guy back there...go get another one." We glanced up in the direction of College and could see where the Panther was accosting other Whiteys with his stack of leaflets. I laughed bitterly. Shook my head. "What is your problem, Sheila?"

"I just don't get what the Negroes have to do with ending the war. Seems like it's all getting messed up together."

"Okay, that's an easy one," I was trying to be patient. "The blacks are most of the people fighting this war, and they're second-class citizens here and deserve equal rights. It all fits together and besides, the same people that are for the blacks are against the war."

"But they're trying to make a war here themselves, with their uniforms and this killer in jail and trying to say he didn't kill anyone."

"They're just defending themselves! I mean, I don't condone violence of any kind, but you have to admire the Panthers for sticking up for themselves."

"Because of the King assassination?"

"That...and...didn't you see what happened this month right here in Berkeley?

"What...?"

"For Christ sake, don't you read the papers?" I realized I was shouting, people passing were staring at me. I lowered my voice along with my gesticulating hands. "The Oakland police ambushed a group of Black Panthers, shot Eldridge Cleaver in the leg and hit a 17-year-old Panther rookie. He died."

"But I don't get it...they're doing it to themselves. The cops don't like these guys to walk around with guns."

"But that's just half the problem. They don't want them to organize. Hell, they don't even like their free food program or health clinic. Is that objectionable, too?"

"No, they've got some good stuff going. But that paramilitary stuff is the problem. It's illegal. I mean, isn't that enough to incite the cops?"

"I'm no lawyer, but I know it doesn't matter to the Panthers." I sidestepped the question. "Nothing's going to stop them. And now they've got all these culture heroes. Eldridge, Bobby Seale, and Huey." I stopped short, a tinge of pride straightening me up. "Christ, Sheila...let's just say I count myself with the student majority, silently siding with the underdog."

"I'm sick of hearing about the Negroes and all their problems."

"What in hell have you got against blacks?" I was shouting again.

"Not a thing. Just don't care about them one way or another. Nothing against them or wetbacks either, though they're the worst. Nothing against WASPS like you either."

"I'm not a WASP!"

"What are you, Irish?"

"No..." I squeezed my eyes shut, then relaxed them, pressed my index fingers against the lids. A stinging hit my eyes and my gut simultaneously, and Janet, my black-haired Irish, was there. I turned away from Sheila and took a deep breath and blew it out, then opened my eyes. "Let's get to class, or we'll be late."

We walked silently across Faculty Glade, side by side, not touching like real lovers. Forcing my feet forward, my breath to steady, I noticed the sky was coated now with a layer of gray. And the grass with a layer of dew that made it seem slick and hazardous. The old dead sycamore at the bottom of the Glade, its branches like claws—menacing. The spring-heavy flow of Strawberry Creek—threatening. Finally, we reached the hill up to LeConte Hall, appearing as a steep cliff, impossible to scale. Our lab class awaited us. I stopped on the far side of the bridge. "You go ahead. I'll catch up to you in a minute."

"Becker, tell me. What are you?"

"I'm a jerk."

"No, I mean. You're not White-Anglo-Saxon-Protestant?"

"Well, kind of...."

"Just because I'm Chicana, you don't want to admit it?"

"I'm a mutt. WASP mom and kike dad. But Dad's been out of the picture for a long time, so I'm a WASP by default..."

"Complicated, aren't you..." she said sarcastically, her eyes narrowing again.

I moaned. "Sheila, just go. I'll see you up there."

"Okay, okay. Don't be late..." She left me in peace.

I sat on the top step of the bridge, my head in my hands with just enough space between my fingers to see my legs sprawled downward onto the sunlit stone. Janet and I had stood on this bridge when she had visited me during her senior year of high school. Kissed in the moonlight. We had both been so optimistic about the future then...idealistic, confident...even arrogant. How I'd loved the university that night, and science, Janet, and the whole fucking world.

SEVENTEEN

ONCE AGAIN, I had put off writing a reply to Dad. When I returned to my cottage after class, I thought about my all-night bout with Janet's apparition and the acknowledged imperative. I must proceed directly to France. I didn't want to lose Janet until I was definitely sure I had. And I couldn't let myself believe she wasn't still in love with me. An additional motivation, as if I needed one, was that I didn't want to lose her, emotionally or physically, to another revolution. So before I rested, I drafted a letter to Dad with a new playing card in the deck, a card I'd been turning over in my hand for quite a few days. I had run the idea by Neil Strand, and he thought it might just do the trick.

Dad,

I have to admit that I was relieved to hear from you. My worst fear was that you hadn't written because you'd lost respect for me and my politics.

> At this point, I am writing to suggest another possibility for my future. There are lots of reasons NOT to go to Canada. There is quite a crowd of American guys headed for Canada—and this year, they're all recent college graduates with little work experience. Jobs there are scarce. So, what I'm proposing is that you send me the ticket to France as a <u>loan</u>. If I can re-establish myself, brush up on the language and get a job, I will happily live in one of those famous garrets (I hear life is cheap there) and pay you back with interest.
>
> You might recall that French is my second-best language and you know I'm a quick study. A bilingual scientist might be a valued commodity in

Paris. Also, you might recall that Paris is a favorite destination of my girlfriend, Janet Magill. As a matter of fact, she's there already, getting to know people and paving the way for me. So this is no pipe dream.

Since you served your country honorably in a war that, among other things, saved the Jewish people from complete annihilation, I want to add some final words about my personal abhorrence for this particular war. You have to understand that I don't want to leave merely because I'm frightened (which I admit I am) or that I don't want to kill, especially young people and people I don't know (which I don't), or that I don't want to kill anonymously and get used to it, or worse, come to like the sensation (back to fears). It's just that I feel that the U.S. is not threatened and that the war is ill-conceived and morally wrong. I feel confident that I can contribute more to society, to the field of biochemistry, and to the enterprise of respectable citizenship wherever I land than I can to securing the American borders from a jungle a million miles from home.

Please reply as soon as possible, since time is growing short.

Your son, Aaron

I included particulars about dollars and cents this time, itemizing the most conservative budget I thought would suffice. Then, as beat as I was, I dragged myself out to the post box, then down to Sproul Hall steps for the rally I'd read about on that Sheila-repelling leaflet. I stood up close, forced myself to stand there for twenty minutes while the crowd gathered, the shrieking microphones were adjusted, and guys like my leaflet-passing friend from Bancroft and College spoke enthusiastically about their protest plans. There were a few hundred in the Plaza and as many more passing through. The main events were scheduled for the following week and the message today was easily absorbed: Get over your doubts and be with us! So mulling that over, I went down to the Lair for a quick burger, then over to my favorite grassy knoll by the side of the library, flopped down, and fell asleep.

When I awoke, it was five o'clock. The Campanile bells were ringing high up over my head—One More River to Cross, a campus favorite. Suddenly, I had an overwhelming desire for hearth and home. A safe haven and friends. There was only one place to find all that together. So I trudged back up the hill toward Joanna Larkin and Neil Strand's cottage, knowing full well that I couldn't spend another night freaking out, or I'd be seriously behind in my classes.

My landlord and his lady shouted their "Come ins" simultaneously, so I knew I hadn't interrupted anything private. Even before I dropped my books on their kitchen table, I started in with my day. "I got an earful at the noon rally today. Maybe we ought to get out there next week. The Spring Mobilization against the war. Stop the Draft Week. Show the wishy-washy liberals that we mean business. What d'you think?"

"You, my friend? And even more absurd, me?" Neil was cooking something with beans that smelled disgusting, and he was not going to stop stirring for our conversation. I stood apart, keeping my distance after peering briefly into the big pot. "It's going to flop, like the draft card turn-in a couple of weeks ago. What's the point?" he asked. "What's going to be different?"

"This is an international effort against the war and racism. Both."

Joanna was listening from behind Joyce's Ulysses. She set her rocker in motion and pushed her petite nose up over the top of the volume. "Most people hope Johnson's resignation and now the Paris peace talks will do the trick."

"That's just the problem. Nobody's demonstrating anymore because they want to believe it's all over. But I'm skeptical, aren't you?"

"I'm skeptical a-plenty," said Neil, "but why don't we give it a chance?"

"So you don't think this new Stop the Draft Week will have any effect?"

"We don't need an effect. It's happening," Neil replied, dropping the top on the pot with a flourish. "It may not be soon, but it'll happen...and believe me, it's the wishy-washy liberals that'll do it, not the juveniles. Wanna stay for supper?"

I crunched my nose. "Thanks, but no thanks..."

"Aaron, sit down," Joanna ordered. Obediently, I dropped into a chair. "Listen," she said, "These guys doing Stop the Draft Week are still radicals who are in for deeper stakes. They're not just anti-Vietnam and pro-civil rights, but anti-imperialism and anti-capitalism and anti-America-as-we-know-it. You're just adding fuel to their fire. We want to separate the end of the war from all that—or it's never going to happen."

"Well...what you say makes sense...but then why...?"

"I'll tell you what kind of fuel I'm gonna add," Neil cut me off. He grinned and scratched his curly yellow hair to the scalp. "I'm goin' out on strike and use the time to catch up on all the shitwork I've got to do around here to maintain this posh establishment."

"Not a bad idea," said Joanna. "And I'm sure we won't be the only ones."

"You mean you'd skip class but not attend the rally?"

"You got it. And can you give us one good reason why not?"

I couldn't, except scruples. And the very definite opinions of a certain studious Chicana. Sheila would never approve any excuse for skipping class. But I found myself saying, "Because at some point, it all gets to be too much. I mean, I get angry. The MLK thing got to me. And now this Panther murder."

"Not like you to approach events so illogically," Joanna said, rocking in her chair exactly like the elderly grandparent that Janet accused me of being. "Treat it like a science project."

"Don't think I haven't been analyzing it," I responded with a casual shrug of the shoulders. I didn't want to completely spill my guts with Neil smirking there in the kitchenette, a ridiculous flowered apron wrapped around his waist. But I continued, "Look. MLK was a man who advocated peaceful protest, working within the system, doing the right thing by America. If he had been assassinated because he was growing an Afro and standing in front of a public building with heavy artillery, a beret and dark glasses, I would have hated it, but could have understood it. But he was a preacher with a wife and kids, trying to make it a better America. And they offed him. So where does that leave the rest of the blacks? In a big way, I've been asking myself, where does that leave any of us? Where does that leave me? I just don't know..."

"Ah, now that's the ol' Becker we've grown to know and love," Neil said. "And where does that leave you...?

My stomach flipped over and I swallowed hard. "So now I'm a selfish son-of-a-bitch?" I shot back. My nighttime terrors about Janet's accusations returned. About lacking compassion—like Sheila Delgado.

"Calm down, there." Neil said. "And now hear this: that was not an insult. A compliment, my friend, is when your buddy tells you you're using your head."

"It may be time to use another part of my anatomy—my guts."

"Jeez, I'm glad you didn't use 'heart.' It's so passé..."

"Honey, for heaven's sake," Joanna stood up, "can't you see how dead serious Aaron is?" She dropped Ulysses behind her onto the rocker." This is no joke," I faced Neil. "Maybe you can laugh because your ass isn't on the line. But everyone I know, myself included, is fighting for their lives and the future of this country. I may not be as selfish as you and Janet Magill think I am..."

"Hey, wait a minute! Just because I'm 4F..."

"Janet...? How did she get into this?" Joanna blinked and stepped closer.

I stood there panting, staring at the dime store salt shaker on the table, feeling resentful of them, of Janet, of everyone who thought they understood me and didn't. How could they, when I didn't understand myself?

"Ah, another fool by heavenly compulsion," Joanna pronounced wisely. "Never thought you'd be one, Aaron."

"What's that?"

"Shakespeare. William the Bard. Let me quote it for you: 'This is the excellent foppery of the world, that, when we are sick in fortune, often the surfeit of our own behavior, we make guilty of our disasters the sun, the moon, and the stars: as if we were villains by necessity; fools by heavenly compulsion.'"

I caught my breath and straightened my shoulders. "It's not just a foolish personal thing..." I cut myself off. There was nothing more to say. No way was I going to open up the can of worms about Janet's letters with these logical thinkers. "Never mind, just forget it." I tried to flatten the bitterness in my voice. They stared and said, "Okay, right. Of course," and I couldn't figure what the hell they were thinking. I peeked at my wristwatch, sighed and stood up, grabbing my stuff. "Anyway, if I don't hit the books I'm gonna fry in class tomorrow. I'll see you later." And I was outta there.

That night and in the nights that followed, I thought about everything Neil and Joanna had said and I still didn't know where I stood. One day I was ready to pin a Stop the Draft Week flyer to my wall and the next to rip down all the flyers on campus. But after a couple of days back in my routine—attending class and lab, washing my beakers, hitting the books and meeting Sheila at the co-op—I was convinced that my own personal draft issue was separate from all this rabble rousing. I began avoiding the Plaza. I had no lack of compassion for those who suffered—but was the desire not to be among them so reprehensible a crime? Some shit about the war or civil rights had come down nearly every day this spring. It didn't take much brain power to realize that my obsession with Janet had made me vulnerable to events, and that events—the rolling catastrophes—were what had left me so defenseless against Janet.

Stop the Draft Week went by in a blur. On Friday, April 26, the day of the "International Strike against the war, the draft, and racism," I ran into picket lines way up the hill next to the Greek Theatre. They must have planned to block every single entrance to campus. Were they afraid we were going to forget what was going on, or what? From my perch in the laboratory, I could see the edges of the noon rally. At one o'clock, I came down to slip through Faculty Glade and ran smack into a gathering crowd. They were setting up for a rally in the open space between Kroeber and Boalt Halls. Anthropology and Law. How appropriate, I mused. The patio was thick with bodies and more were on their way. Students and faculty, climbing the hill from Sproul and streaming from the doors of Boalt Law.

"Shit! What the...?"

"The mics are on campus property in Sproul Plaza," said a cheerful voice to my left, "so they moved them here. On the sidewalk. Technically, it's safe ground." The person speaking to me looked familiar, a suntanned dude with blue eyes that didn't seem to belong on that face. A neat, clean white shirt and crisp new Levis. "How'ya doing, Aaron?"

"About like everyone else, I expect." Still couldn't place him. Some class?

"Ever hear from Janet Magill?" Now I remembered. A guy who knew her from Beverly High. She'd always called him a "Beverly Hills snob." "Like my brother," she once said, "only more studious." I'd met him a couple of times, at her senior prom and once up here. Jim? Jer...? Yeah, that was it...

"I hear from her all the time," I said. "We're still friends."

"I hear she went loco after her brother was drafted. I imagine that's what my little sister would do, too. She's fifteen, but those radicals are getting them early these days."

"'Those radicals'? What are you doing here if you believe that antiwar activists are such lunatics?"

Jerry beamed confidently, "I'm becoming a lunatic in my own best interests. But I'm not letting it change me or my plans."

"Have you got a full-proof plan, then? I mean, I could use one myself these days. I'm due to graduate in a few weeks. Expecting a draft notice any day now."

"If I had a plan you could steal I wouldn't let you in on it, would I? But you can't steal it because my old man has connections with the Coast Guard. He's in the reserve and that's where I'm going when I graduate."

"Good for you," I smiled as graciously as I could, "and my old man has connections with a bank vault," I fibbed. "My fortune cookie tells me there's an extended journey in my future, and it's not to Asia."

He whistled. "That's no good for me. Conflicts with my plans. I'm a political science major..."

"So...?"

"So I can't run for office from Canada, now can I?" The sun glinted from his substantial front teeth. Then, without waiting for my reply, he turned away to face the podium.

The mics were set up and they were ready to roll. The speaker, a young man all dressed up in a blue business suit, blasted us in an angry voice: "The Academic Senate has proclaimed that classes are to be held today so students have a choice. If they're so concerrrrned about our right to make choices, why in hell aren't they concerned about the choice we can NOT make to live or to die...?!"

The crowd began to yell, quieting between phrases as if they'd been rehearsing all morning: "...to kill or not to kill..." "...to fight or not to fight..." "...to be free or to be in prison..."

By now the crowd, including Beverly Hills Jerry, was wild with the desire to squash the speaker's painful words with their shouts and screams and whistles and claps and hoots and fists swiping the air. I stood there, wondering why I wasn't shouting with them, no longer able to see the speaker because of the tears in my eyes. I glanced at Jerry—my fellow-draft dodger, no matter the difference in our methods or the life-wrenching outcome. And there he was, unafraid, shouting support with the rabble. How dangerous could it be to stay to the end, to stand firm for my oft-stated convictions? Why was I mute, when this enraged, disembodied voice from the podium was speaking straight to me? For me? My fists were opening and closing and I heard myself groan. An angry, dumb noise catching in my throat became a cough, as if fumes from my personal internal combustion engine had backed up into my carburetor. I gave one last cough into my hand. Then, I raised my face and fist to the podium and bellowed with all my might.

EIGHTEEN

IN THE WANING DAYS of April, my forays to the mailbox in search of letters from Janet and Dad began to include the expectation that I'd find my mother's annual handwritten note. The formal note, which Cora always inscribed on creamy, elaborately bordered stationery in a hand sweating flourishes and curlicues, would announce the "surprise"—her intention to visit Berkeley on Mother's Day.

I realized somewhat mournfully that this Mother's Day would be our last. Since the May holiday was the only time during the prior three years I'd been at Cal that Cora had visited—and since she offered it as a gift to herself each year, pulling out all the stops on finances—I looked forward to it. The tradition required certain formalities: the picnic, the dress-up night out in San Francisco, the brunch. And it always began, not with a phone call, but with the handwritten note.

With April flying by and no note appearing, I began to worry about Cora as I walked down the brick path toward the mailbox each day. She and I talked a couple of times a month on the phone, but wouldn't it be stepping on unholy ground to mention the surprise before I received the note? One evening, practically mid-sentence, I shut my biochem text with a noisy slam that jolted Dork. He let out a frenzied squawk.

"I wonder if she knows about my plans," I confided aloud to my parakeet. "But how could she?" I ransacked my memory, unable to come up with a slip about my impending draft evasion. Conversations between my mother and me about the war had always faded quickly to a kind of auditory vanishing point, as if Vietnam was so far away and my potential for state-sponsored travel there so vague that the two concepts met on the horizon line and cancelled each other out. There had been no easy way to tell her about the letter to Dad, the lack of viable options, the anticipated departure.

Suddenly, it hit me for the first time: I might not see my mother again for quite a while. I swallowed hard, surprised by the surge of emotion. I'd reconciled to leaving my cottage, my friends, Cal and my studies, even my parakeet—always buoyed by the possibility of joining Janet Magill. But I hadn't even tried to find a way to break the news to Cora. Telling her had been, I realized now, too terrible to contemplate. I'd made the mistake of keeping my plans from Janet and now again. Shit! What a fuckup! I jumped to my feet and stood by Dork's cage, poking my finger through the wires to give him a nibble.

"Time to find out what the story is, old friend."

Cora's voice on the line was untypically cool. "I was wondering if you'd noticed," was all she said. Silence, as my mind collided head-on with my inability to tell her that I intended to dodge the draft.

"You're angry," I stated flatly.

"Keep thinking, hot shot." Her voice, low as a man's from years of smoking, exuded the kind of flirtatious lilt, even in this mood, that could only come from a woman. I cleared my throat, preparing to grovel.

"Okay, so I screwed up. I apologize. I should have told you."

"Mmmm?" was all she said. Another pause. "Told me...? You should have told me and invited me. After all, this is an exciting time in your life."

"Exciting...?"

"Your graduation. Didn't you know I'd want to share it?"

I was struggling to comprehend the noun in that sentence. "Graduation?"

She sighed. "Yes! What else? It's getting late, hon. Don't you agree? For me to make plane reservations, the hotel, all that?"

"Mom, you've got to be kidding. I'm not going to... Listen, a Cal graduation is huge. It's a sham." I could feel my voice cracking, my face red hot with relief, guilt, and embarrassment. She didn't know—it was the goddamned graduation ceremony that had steamed her.

"What...a sham? What are you talking about?" she was shouting hoarsely into the receiver. "You don't want to graduate?"

I laughed, couldn't help myself. "Let me explain. I don't have to go through the ceremony to get my degree. I am going to graduate. But to sit there in Greek Theatre under the broiling sun in a sucker's costume listening to long speeches with thousands of fellow-grads who are total strangers... The only person I know graduating is Raymond Chan and I'll be in the "B" section and he'll be in "C"—IF he goes, which I doubt. Do you actually expect me to go through a thing like that?"

"So, you don't want me at your graduation?" she sounded hurt, even meek—not a tone I'd heard often from Cora Becker.

"This has nothing to do with you. I just don't want to do it. The ceremony is a meaningless convention. Do you understand?"

"Okay, okay. And yes, I understand. I guess. I'm disappointed. After all, you're the first in the family, and I wanted to share the glory."

"I'm sorry, but that's the way it is," I cut her off before she wound herself up with her arguments. Then, with all the sticky damn charm I could muster I asked, "We can still have our Mother's Day, can't we? I was waiting for the handwritten note."

"Not much of a surprise now, hon, but I guess it wasn't after the first year."

"I was delightfully surprised every year," I reassured her.

"Okay...I can send one. In fact, I will. I just thought I'd be there for graduation instead of Mother's Day this year. Only enough moola to do one trip up right."

"Yeah, I know. But we'll have a better time just the two of us. You'll see. Mom?"

"Yes, Aaron?"

"I've enjoyed it, the Mother's Day thing. I'm sad that it'll be our last year."

"Doesn't have to be, hon," she said brightly. "Whatever you do next, there's still Mother's Day."

"Mom?" Here it came, I had to do it. She wasn't saying anything. Now was my chance. "I'm not going to Vietnam."

A noisy exhalation filled the line. "Well, thank goodness! I mean, I'm relieved. Of course, I didn't mean I'd be able to pop over there for Mother's Day," she chuckled. "I didn't know how you were going to get out of it, but somehow I always figured you would. You're such a smart boy...but now that I know for sure, well, I'm relieved."

"Don't you want to know how I'm getting out of it?" I said, picturing again the landscape of my life, the perspective, the thick mist on the horizon, the vanishing point.

Silence on the line. "Mom?"

"Sure..."

"I'm leaving the country. Going to Europe. Evading the draft."

Silence again, while she absorbed what I'd told her. Then tearfully, "Oh, Aaron. Is that the only way?"

"Your smart boy hasn't been able to figure anything else out," I said. "Nothing else is foolproof except going to prison."

"But does it have to be foolproof? I mean, maybe one of your professors could stick up for you. Or maybe you've got flat feet." She sounded wistful.

"No flat feet, and profs aren't senators. They've got less pull than rich guys. Anyway, everyone knows profs are a bunch of overgrown antiwar troublemakers."

"Well, they're right. The professors, I mean."

"Cora! Hell, you're a stinking liberal? Wow! Good for you!"

"I don't know about politics, Aaron. But no war is worth the price. I said it in the last war, the Korean thing, and it's certainly not worth your life. It's ridiculous, taking my son—and such a smart boy."

"Go get'em, Ma..."

"Enough of my speechifying."

I swallowed hard. How I'd like to prod her into more speechifying! "I like to hear your opinions. We've never talked much about the news. I wasn't even sure if you knew there was a war."

Her hands-on-hips voice bustled through the line, "I may not be a doctor of philosophy, Aaron, but I'm not a complete dunce."

"So, you must know about the antiwar protests. What do you make of those?"

She sighed. "Well, the whole world's gone crazy. War at the college isn't worth it either. You're not involved in anything dangerous, are you, Aaron? Don't be foolish..."

"Not involved, don't worry. I was just asking."

"And I was just being a mom to my grown-up boy. Say, Aaron, why go off to Europe? Why not just hop to Canada? It's a lot closer."

"That's true," I replied, "a lot of the guys go to Canada. I might end up there, but you know I've always had a thing for Europe..."

She sighed. "Of course. What's the matter with me? Janet's over there, right?"

"Enough about that, okay, Mom?" I begged. "Not much to say about that right now..."

"Oh!" she huffed, amused. "Well then...okay! Not another word, I swear!"

"So, I'm outta here," I reaffirmed. "Mother's Day may be our last hurrah for a while."

"Well, I'll miss you, but I've missed you before. When you went away to college. I always say, kids've gotta live their own lives. As long as you live it. None of this Vietnam stuff."

"But too far away for Mother's Day." I circled back.

"Oh, you never know," she was cooing again. "Maybe I can get your father to help me visit you. It's not out of the question. He's a good guy at heart, just screwed up."

"So far, Dad won't even spring for my ticket. But we're still in touch. I'm hoping he'll change his mind."

"You talked to him?" she screeched like Dork into the phone.

"I wrote him."

"Why would you write to him and never even let me know?" she whispered. "And he never let me know. Never said a thing. Never wrote..." Then, in a louder, firmer voice, she added, "I suppose you assumed this was man territory, because it was about war."

"Don't be upset...it just happened. I got nervous, wrote, he wrote back, and still in progress. I meant to tell you..."

"Do you know I care about your future? You need to include me..."

"I apologize. I promise after this..."

"How does he sound?" she cut me off, then after a pause to catch her breath, asked in a softer tone, "How's Ecuador? How's the SS?" Showed no class, her calling my father's wife Juanita the "SS" for "Saucy Spic"—but not for me to criticize.

"He's fine. He seemed to agree with you. Canada is good enough."

"Yes, well, that's something." She sighed and added, "Anyway, it's your father who should have told me."

"No," I said, repentant. "I should have told you. I messed up."

She cleared her throat, as if she'd been trying not to cry. "Well, then. We'll make the most of the time you're still here."

"I'll be checking my mailbox for a handwritten note."

"You'll see something soon. But if you change your mind about graduation...I don't know. Maybe I can come twice."

"I won't change my mind. Sorry, not a chance."

"Well, okay. This is gonna be a first-class trip, then."

"It always is, Mom."

My draft notice arrived. I was to report mid-June to the Oakland Induction Center, the site of so many well-publicized rallies and vicious protests. I had never stood on that unholy ground. My ultimate protest would be that I would never sanctify it with my presence.

That afternoon, I hoisted a pack and headed up to the pastoral meadows of Tilden Park. In my pack, I carried a cheese sandwich, an apple, a little bag of Sugar Smacks, my binoculars, and an air letter pad and pen. More than news about the note from Uncle Sam, I needed to share my momentary aberration at the rally on Bancroft Avenue—as brief and meager as my rebel status was to be—with the girl who had willed it from the other side of the globe. A fat oak tree served as my anchor as I listened to the wind whip through the branches above me and thought about what a beautiful day it had turned out to be. The sun brought clarity to the twigs on the treetops. Irrationally, I hoped that putting my confusion about the two of us into words would cause an answer to appear clear as daylight before my eyes.

Dear Janet,

Today, I'm up in Tilden, taking time out to answer your letters with more than my usual quick note. Please know that your amazing words have my complete attention.

Enough going on here to curl your hair (that is, if you hadn't already taken care of that by yourself—ha!). Most people in Berkeley are still staying out of the protests despite the blows, the Tet, the King assassination, the local racial violence, the national riots. What a sweet spring this has turned out to be! I sense that you still are frustrated with my inaction. It may surprise you to know that I've attended a couple of rallies and although I hated every moment of them, found myself shouting and raising my fist with the best of them. Guess after a while it's just too frustrating keeping all this angst inside me, grieving for myself and our nation only to a chartreuse, caged avis, a captive audience if ever there was one.

Since it sounds like you are encountering your share of activists in Paris, please remember what we all gain by weighing options and acting logically. Safety may not sound very glamorous to you, but no matter how just the cause may seem, if you stay safe, you will live to be in the generation with power and can do better. As you observe, experience, even participate—as you listen and learn—watch out behind you. Stay safe, Janet.

And as I trust your ability to judge character (after all, you once befriended me), so I trust Teodor Pelnar will treat you with the respect you deserve.

Your friend and confidante, Aaron

P.S. The notice from Uncle Sam was in my mailbox this morning. No check from Dad yet. Negotiation still in progress. It may have to be Canada first, France later.

I squirmed against my tree, feeling a lump the size of a rat's skull calcifying in my chest. As always, I played the entertaining friend, the concerned mentor, but I'd written from my heart. All I knew was, despite my best efforts at logic, I still wanted Janet Magill. To be with her. Despite my cynicism, I knew I needed someone to hold up the candle of hope in the dark lunatic ward of the world. At Cal, Janet's all-purpose passion for humanity had become focused on the war and the blacks. Would they now be usurped by French causes? Czech causes?

The last sentence about the Czech sounded too accepting of their relationship, whatever it might be. Angrily, I scratched it out. Then I had to copy over the last half-sheet, skipping a few pages in the air letter pad in case Janet had taken to reading the imprints left by the pressure of the pen. I reinstated the P.S., which seemed to make more sense without the words about the Czech. I began to nibble at my cheese sandwich, staring sideways at what I'd written to Janet, but the fossil blockage in my chest made eating impossible. Throwing the sandwich, pen, and pad in my pack, I left the solid oak and took off at a run, hoping to get lost for a while on Tilden's wooded paths.

≈ PART FOUR ≈
France

NINETEEN

TWO SHORT WHISTLE BLASTS marked each village passed by the express train from Paris to La Rochelle. As we whizzed through the countryside, Margot Chabert sat up straighter than usual, like a potentate surveying the blurry landscape, her idle arms resting at her sides, her chin tucked into her brown faux turtleneck. It was Elizabeth Prior who spread the sauce mayonnaise on the soft bread and folded it into half boiled ham sandwiches for La Petite Jeanette, sister Lili and cousin Cecile. It was she who navigated the aisle outside our cabin to help Lili and Cecile in the toilet stall. And when they returned, it was Elizabeth whose lap became a target pillow for three bored, weary heads, making deals and jockeying for two spots. La Petite Jeanette finally conceded that my lap would be as comfortable as Elizabeth's and cuddled up on me.

Margot had made it clear that as a paying guest, I did not have to help with the children during the Easter vacation trip. Madame seemed pleased that I would improve my French language by playing with the youngsters. Margot preferred me to "relax" with her and learn from our conversations. I remembered that Gabi had called her "lonely" on my first day in

Paris, and for that reason, my sympathy went out to our landlady.

But that morning, as we prepared for our journey, I had heard Margot bark at Elizabeth, "This is my vacation, but make no mistake. It will not be yours. The children will be your responsibility, along with cleaning and helping with meals."

As I saw it, Elizabeth had gone from being a friend to a servant girl overnight. Her parents insisted that if she wanted to stay in France, she had to do so as an au pair, working for la famille instead of paying for her board. I understood that she had to help out, but why was it necessary to be so Cinderella-harsh? I could not help imagining Margot's attitude toward me if I were suddenly unable to pay.

Fine, soft strands of La Petite's hair scattered on my lap and invited my fingers. I glanced up just as Sovereign Margot wrenched her eyes away from us and out the window. Resentment overran my sympathy for her. Was it some snooty adherence to class distinction or just simple jealousy of my friendship with Elizabeth that I recognized in her antagonism? In that instant, I resolved to spend my time on l'Île helping to lighten Elizabeth's load.

Margot excused herself to use the facilities. I whispered, "Elizabeth." She turned to me drowsily. "It must be so different for you, being au pair."

Elizabeth shrugged her shoulders. "The girls are sweet." She gazed at the two peaceful pink faces. "I'm only worried about Le Petit Laurent...and, well, Le Grand."

"What...why...? Because you'll miss him over Pâques?"

She gave a histrionic sigh, noisy as a horse's whinny. "That, and because I don't know how he'll regard me now that I'm a hired girl."

"WHAT!?"

"Shh..." she frowned at me. Cecile stirred and she petted moist, blunt-cut hair away from the child's face. Le Petite rolled over, her eyes met mine briefly, unseeing, then shut again.

"Why?" I mouthed the words.

"Did you know that Laurent is from Alsace, just like the Bouleaux?" she said dreamily.

I shook my head. "So what?"

"You know he's Laurent de Cirey? Nobility. An only son. A handsome, brilliant future baron. So, you see..."

"But Laurent's not like that at all!" I protested in a husky whisper. "Not a snob. Notice how he sticks up for Bérnard – and what is he?"

Elizabeth's face brightened. "I never thought of that. But... I thought you didn't approve of Bérnard," she said.

I stared at her bugged-eyed, horrified to realize that I hadn't done a better job of masking my antipathy. "Oh no! But not because of class." I sighed. "This whole European nobility thing is so superficial. I don't disapprove of Bérnard. It's just that I've had my fill of political rants in Berkeley, and he is so obsessively political."

"Laurent thinks he's quite intelligent," Elizabeth said.

I sighed. "I'm sure he is. But about you and Laurent..."

Just then, Margot reentered the cabin, reclaimed her throne and made a racket coughing and clearing her throat. She announced that it was time for milk and cookies. Three little heads bobbed up. Margot brought out the sweets and began cooing right along with the rest of us over the magnificent scenery of the chateau countryside. I began to cheer up, reflecting on our new, evenhanded generation.

After five and a half hours, at last we were nearing La Rochelle, a bustling port town on the Atlantic Coast. From there, we dragged our luggage on and off a bus, a ferry, then another bus before we pulled up by the side of the road in the village of Les Portes en Ré. Apparently, Hélène and Jean-Louis had wanted a vacation from their daughters. They were working a few extra days in Paris before going off to Jean-Louis's parents for Pâques. I had been relieved to hear it. Mme. Bouleaux had come ahead to l'Île de Ré with Le Petit Laurent and now, here she was, cheerfully greeting us on the doorstep of our vacation house.

From the moment I entered, all royal treatment for the paying guest was focused on me. After Mme. Bouleaux's effusive greeting and a very British tea service with cheese scones, she showed me to my own room. In true family style, I was to sleep in a carved four-poster, covered by a goose feather mattress and a white embroidered bedspread. And I was to vacation surrounded by finery from a storybook world: paintings, carvings, an enamel clock in working order, and leather-bound books on cherry wood shelves. I fussed over each and every object, but inside me, I cringed. What was I to do with their solicitousness but accept it graciously? I felt a little like they'd crowned me Jeanette de California. If I'd had a real crown, I would have pulled it down to hide my face.

That evening, Madame's "baby," Suzanne, came over for a brief time with her own baby, one-year-old Michelle. Although Suzanne spoke in rapid-fire, breathless French that I could not understand, she turned out to be the only snappy dresser of the clan. With her chunky body and pretty round face, she resembled Madame more than any of the others, and I imagined that Madame had once looked exactly like Suzanne, with a different hairstyle. Jean-Luc, the architect, a slight young man with a well-manicured appearance and crew cut, visited only long enough to exchange greetings and escort his family home, a few doors away.

We awoke to a chilly and gray morning, and it was then that I first noticed that the house had a washing machine and all other modern conveniences—but no central heating. The entire house was heated by a small fireplace in the family room, a stone hearth that reminded me of the one at Aaron Becker's cottage. The family room adjoined the dining area and the kitchen beyond it—Jean-Luc's plan had been to make the whole downstairs into what was essentially one large room. The fire blazed all day long and we settled in front of it.

Despite the lure of the books upstairs and Margot's assignment of childcare to Elizabeth, playing with the children at the hearth became my principal diversion. I hadn't brought my guitar, but I sang them songs en anglais, explaining the words en français and letting them embellish. In their sweet, guarded voices, they began to sing more of their French kindergarten songs, repeating phrases so that Elizabeth and I could join in. Each day, in the same gloomy weather, we sang the same songs, drew pictures, tripped over new words and phrases, and took short walks to a nearby beach, where there was nothing to do except stand in the freezing wind and stare at the monotony of the sea.

Then, on the fourth day of vacances, the sun came out. Margot told me that sometime during the day we could expect a visit from a family for whom Jean-Luc was designing a house. While Jean-Luc and Mme. Bouleaux chatted about the project and the baby napped, Elizabeth announced that she and I were taking the children for a walk in the sun.

"How long will you be?" Margot asked, eyeing us from the door to the kitchen.

"Oh, sorry," said Elizabeth. "Do you need help?"

Margot sighed. "Never mind." But instead of turning back to her tasks, she fastened her eyes on mine. I knew I should remain with her or perhaps ask her to come along. I hesitated. How I relished time out of the house, away from la famille, to frolic with the children and enjoy the relief of a little English conversation with Elizabeth!

Suddenly, Laurent and Lili were demanding help with the zippers on their windbreakers, and their au pair had only two hands. I turned away from Margot's stare to help. La Petite Jeanette and Cecile were loudly bragging that they could fasten their own jackets. Rough words ensued. Then the sliding glass door opened to the fresh air, bringing sudden smiles all around. I grabbed my car coat and ran off after them without a word or a backward glance.

Our delightful crew tramped energetically for nearly two miles across the island: Lili and La Petite Jeanette just in front of us, Cecile and Le Petit Laurent taking the lead. We followed their short legs patiently through village after tiny village, skirting the salt ponds and farms in between. In the villages, there were one- and two-story houses like the Bouleaux's being constructed everywhere. No wonder architect Jean-Luc had moved to l'Île de Ré!

When we swung around to the beach back near the house, a most fantastic sight awaited us: the tide had gone out! Shedding our shoes, we dashed down the beach and into the briny muck, slowing down where the ground softened. The beach seemed to go on forever, for miles—a long, broad uninhabited beach. I was sure there was no such place in all of California. "Our beach is called le Conch," Mme. Bouleaux had told me by the fireside one evening. She had sounded proud, using the possessive form. "It is five miles long. The Americans made a movie here about D-Day, not in Normandy where the invasion actually took place.

Too many tourists and cars there now. So they made it here...do you know this film?"

"Yes, I saw it a few years ago," I had replied. "It was called The Longest Day." I did not want to mention that my high school friends and I had joked that The Longest Day should have been called The Longest Movie. Boring.

Le Conch, however, was anything but boring. I ran ahead of the rest, whooping and spreading my arms like wings. What a marvelous expansive feeling, breathing warm, clear air for the first time in days. I stooped to examine tiny crabs scurrying in the sand, and tromping along, discovered live limpets, scallops, and even a black and white stripped conch, its pointed crown attended by a court of a dozen tiny barbs. I called to the children, who had begun to chase each other, full of squeals and giggles. They each touched the conch gingerly. "They've got intuitive respect for its artistry and its life, haven't they?" I asked Elizabeth.

She smiled. "Rather more like they're intrigued by something new, I'd say."

With all my pent-up energy, I hauled my arm back and lobbed the conch back toward a distant tide. "Back into nature!" I bellowed. Behind me I heard laughter, but all I felt was release and joy. Gazing out to sea, I imagined Teodor Pelnar's big frame rising over the horizon. It would have been so much fun to have him there now, running with me, holding my hand. What footprints he would make! I laughed right out loud at this, then at myself. How impossible it had been to put thoughts of Teo aside, even for a few days. He kept rushing headlong into my mind with all the speed and vitality of a sparkling ocean wave.

Nearly two hours after we left, we returned to the house. The family had been joined by the people I guessed to be Jean-Luc's clients, a middle-aged businessman and his two college-aged daughters. We entered through the glass doors, laughing and raining gritty sand down on the hardwood floors. "Faites attention!" shouted Mme. Bouleaux. Elizabeth and I immediately began apologizing and directing the children back out on the porch until we could brush the sand away. When we re-entered, a cleaner and more subdued group, I saw that the college girls were twins, both tall, about my height, sharp in their coordinated pants and tops. Their hair fell in soft waves over their shoulders, the way mine had before I had changed my style. They had keen, intelligent eyes, and right away, I yearned to know them.

But Margot had raised her hands to her hips and was frowning at me. Not at Elizabeth, but at me! Staring me down, right in front of the new college girls. She took her eyes off of me long enough to direct Elizabeth upstairs and into the showers with the children. Then her searing gaze returned, this time accompanied by pursed lips and an uncomfortable silence. "You, too," she barked.

I could feel the heat rising to my face. Hastily, I excused myself, and went up to await my turn for a rinse. Presentable at last, I could have joined the group downstairs. Instead, I found myself sinking down into my feather bed. That soft bed symbolized my life, and I imagined Mme. Bouleaux sleeping on a hard flat board barely raised from the floor. Like one of those nap boards we had lain upon in kindergarten. Our bones were supple then, and we would fall asleep peacefully. I pictured the bright hearth downstairs with friends and family gathered around it and I not one of them. They had not even introduced me to the two college-aged girls.

As I calmed down, I grew sleepy, the aftereffect of wind and sun on the beach. In my mind, there was the jolly hearth downstairs, and then another. Aaron's cottage seemed cozier to me now, the scratchy sheepskin rug more comfortable. I would write to him later in the day, but for now, I comforted myself with the thought that he missed me as much as I missed him. Suddenly Teo seemed like a very mysterious person, like a character in a paperback thriller, and although just hours away by train, he felt more distant than Aaron. I fell asleep picturing the little brown-shingle cottage, the small, firelit room, the green parakeet in his cage, and a dear one as familiar as the sky.

That night, we had Swiss Fondue for dinner, all gathered round a large oval table and dunking our bread into a tureen of melted cheese spiked with wine. It was Madame Bouleaux who had eventually introduced me to the Sorbonne students, Bernadette and Brigitte, explaining that they were twins. Non-identical, I surmised. Brigitte had a thinner face and sadder eyes and a smaller mouth than Bernadette, as if she had been squished into the corner of the womb by her sister. She studied philosophy and Bernadette economics.

These were the first real college girls I had met since coming to France, and I was eager to befriend them. Clearly, Margot had other plans. After dinner, we sat with our coffees as we had in the Paris salon. But every time I spoke, Margot sneered at me like I was the stupidest person in the world, then interrupted me.

If she had wanted to be with me so badly, I thought, why hadn't she just invited herself on our hike? I knew the answer was that she had wanted time away from the children, and had wanted me to herself. Now, feeling confused and controlled, I wondered if I hadn't made a mistake, resisting Margot at every turn.

The conversation swung around from the topic of student life to the topic of students in England and the United States. Margot had been in Alabama at a tiny woman's college for one year, about 12 years before, and she thus considered herself an authority on every inch of my homeland. She pressed forward and spoke in a serious, confiding tone, informing the others, who had never been across the Atlantic, that the U.S. was riddled with crime and covered with cement. No parks, no farms. It was a film noir version of my country, but Margot's coup de grace was her blanket description of its young people: they were alienated from their parents, she said, like James Dean.

A more balanced opinion ran around and around in my head, bringing in the most recent cause for youthful alienation, the war in Vietnam, but I could not even formulate the words properly in English, let alone in French. When I did manage to break in, I shook my head vigorously, "Non, non, non! Ce n'est pas vrai!" I raised my voice to its most ridiculous soprano. "That's not true! Well, not exactly..."

But when it came to opinions, Margot would not allow herself to be contradicted. Her voice enlarged in correlation to mine, and she conveniently reverted to 350 words per minute. They all laughed and glanced my way with pleasant expressions. I laughed at the joke on myself that I did not understand. I shrugged my shoulders and sat back in my chair. I could only hope that they all knew Margot's description was just a big fib.

That night in bed, I relived the evening's humiliation over and over again. Someday, I thought, my French would be adequate to the task of self-defense. Then sadly, I had to accept my own limitations. Someday I would be more confident of my French, certainly, but defending myself in any language was never going to come naturally to me.

The next morning, the company would be gone. I understood perfectly well that I would never see them again. Margot had made sure of that with her ridicule. I had to defend myself, at least to try! Not in a group. That would always be impossible. But perhaps I could speak directly to Margot. I would watch for my chance. What should I say to her? I fell asleep with a dozen awkward conversations buzzing in my brain.

TWENTY

MME. BOULEAUX LEFT for Paris on Friday morning after breakfast to attend to some household business. Elizabeth was upstairs reading to the children. Margot was engrossed in a paperback. I switched on the radio in the family room, hoping that Margot would not complain about the noise.

I had been listening to the news everyday since our arrival on the island but had missed the day before. I needed to hear the news. Before we got to the island, the Herald Tribune and Aaron Becker were my conduits to world news and commentary, both usually received after events had gone stale. There was no Herald Tribune on l'Île, so I was thankful for the radio. I had asked Margot to translate reports from Paris, Monte Carlo, Luxembourg, or Brussels, but eventually I discovered BBC. Now I was sitting by myself when the newscaster's tone became even more solemn than the usual stiff solemnity of the British reporters. He informed his audience that Martin Luther King, Jr. had been assassinated in Memphis, Tennessee.

I felt as if my chest cavity had opened up and was bleeding onto the hardwood floor. Margot had set her book aside. Together, we listened as the reporter described the shooting, which had taken place "our time," a whole day before. Dr. King was in Memphis to lead a march of striking sanitation workers. The station played portions of a wonderful speech he had given just the night before he died. "I've been to the mountaintop," he said. How far from the pinnacle the mighty had to fall, I thought. He was only 39 years old.

I didn't even realize I was crying until the news ended. Margot brought me a cup of coffee, evidently able to forgive in a crisis. We went to sit by the hearth. I didn't have the strength to go upstairs where the au pair was tending to the children, and it distressed me to realize that Elizabeth might not understand the significance of this event. I was so grateful when Margot began to speak that I didn't even notice that her words were in English. "I am stunned. I did not know violence in America had come to this. The killing of such a man."

"He was a great leader," I said. "I can hardly believe it, even after the assassination of President Kennedy."

"Oh yes, that was terrible. But this is worse. This is racisme. And a sample of how things have gotten out of hand in America."

The conversation of the night before flashed through my mind and I was struck by how intensely I despised this woman's self-righteousness. It was only when I found my own voice that I realized we were speaking in English.

"Margot, I don't mean to be rude," I began, aware that rude was just how I sounded, "but I wanted to ask you why, last night, you led those people to believe America was such an uninhabitable place? After all, Americans are flesh and blood, just like French people. We have farms for food and parks for our children. Borden Cows and the Yosemite, for heaven's sake! And we manage to walk the streets without getting shot in the back."

Margot wore the sour, nasty smile that I had come to expect. "It is closer to the truth than you would like to believe."

"Lies. You were lying." My voice was steady, my eyes leveled on her.

She hesitated a moment. Took a sip of her coffee. "You are upset."

"I am upset at more than King's death." I continued to glower at her. I wanted an apology. I should have known better.

She cleared her throat. "And anyway," she shrugged her shoulders, turning away from me toward the mild glow of the fire, "I don't blame you for the racism in your country."

I sighed. "Margot, I'd like you to understand. Europeans don't know what it's like having this great mixture of people living in one country. Getting along together. Working toward the best for everyone. Negroes aren't the only minority. We have Mexicans. And Chinese. And Jews. We have a successful community of Jews..."

"Yes, we do know what it's like to live with many different people!" she interrupted. "You speak to me, a European, about Jews...the poor Jews and the poor Negroes..." She clicked her tongue.

"But, what happened to the Jews, that's history now. And every day things are getting better for the Blacks in America."

She looked at me skeptically. I began to cry. "They will get better, no matter this senseless, horrible, violent act!" Margot was waiting patiently for me to calm myself, dab my eyes and blow my nose. But before she could comfort me, I dredged up my anger at her once again. "And don't talk to me about racisme. There's plenty of class prejudice and racism right in your own house, Margot. I'm surprised that France doesn't have a Ku Klux Klan for Algerians!"

"Yes, of course," she whispered huskily. "For the French, there are the Algerians. Even I am prejudiced against the Algerians. But you Americans think you are better than the French. Or else, why does a rich American girl come here and behave like a servant girl? Impolitely ignore her hostesses who have treated her with kindness? Everyone here must obey the rules of our society. I suspect that you did not obey all the rules in America. But you must do it here in France."

I swallowed hard to keep myself steady. Margot was bossy and boring and...bourgeois. I tried to understand what I had done that was so bad besides not offering an invitation to our little beach party. It wasn't as if I refused to converse with her! She didn't like me helping Elizabeth with her chores, now that Elizabeth was her personal drudge. And she liked to be boss. Here on l'Île, especially with Madame gone, Margot was boss.

I answered her, "You are trying to enforce French rules that I suspect are just your own, like all the many house rules you have so carefully explained. I have to learn the French rules and decide which ones I want to follow. French society is so different..."

"What do you mean, 'which ones I want to follow'?" she came back at me. "You simply pick the ones you please? Like going to a dance club with a boy from the Middle East..." Her lips were clutched tightly in disgust. "Those boys are dangerous. You thought so too, or you wouldn't have asked Elizabeth and Laurent..."

"So you want to screen my dates now?"

She calmed herself with a sip of coffee and sighed wearily. "I merely want to advise you. As you say, customs are different here. Sip your coffee. It will get cold."

Dutifully, I sipped, then stared at her for a beat before speaking. "Like prejudice against any kind of dark skin is okay. Algeria, Lebanon...that's your custom?"

"These dark skins cause trouble in France. We are not prejudiced for no good reason. We leave that for the Americans, who murder their Negroes."

"Merde!"

"So now, you use foul language. I am beginning to see why your parents sent you away."

I gasped and shouted, "I did NOT leave the United States because I swore or went out with boys my parents didn't like." I breathed hard and hesitated, but finally spit it out: "They wanted me here while my brother is in Vietnam!"

Now it was Margot's turn to gasp. Her hand went to her chest with a grating intake of air. She stared at me. Was I a different species from the moment before? "Oh là!" she breathed, "You never told us!"

Slumping back down on the sofa, I begged, "It's not something I like to talk about."

Margot clucked her tongue several times against the roof of her mouth. "War. My mother's war. Your war. Indochine. It's all the same. What a frightful business. Is your brother...how is he doing?"

"He's doing better now that the Tet Offensive has ended. You know...?"

"Yes, yes. Bien sûr. I am glad to hear that." Her heavy brows curled with honest pity. Her tongue clicked in sympathy. "MLK, Vietnam...mon dieu..." Click cluck.

I forced my eyes away from her face and stared into the fire. The smoldering coals calmed and mesmerized me. "Martin

Luther King..." I said nostalgically, as if remembering someone I knew and loved from a distant, romantic past. "I still can't believe it." I had no idea what more to say and considered going upstairs after all. Before I made my move, Margot broke the silence.

"I hope the sunshine stays for our Pâques," she said, absently. I noticed another sunny day outside the glass doors to the garden. "I remember when Laurent was alive," Margot continued, "it always seemed to rain on Pâques. But then, we had no children to do eggs for in those days, so it didn't matter as much."

"Laurent was your husband?"

"Yes. And now we have a surfeit of Laurents around here." She gazed into her coffee cup as if searching for a cure to the disease of loneliness. She set her cup down gently. "We can never plan our lives." She had reverted to French, speaking slowly, clearly. "Cecile was nine months old when the accident occurred. Imagine, chopping a tree down on top of your own head. How could he do that, people asked, a boy raised on a farm? It was a terrible thing to happen...and, I was pregnant with Le Petit Laurent. He has never had a father."

Her voice was aimless and faraway, not at all like the crisp, matter-of-fact voice I was now so accustomed to hearing. I was amazed that she was sharing her secrets with me, but not flattered. It was tit for tat from a pitiful woman. She lit her Gaulois, took a puff and leaned back, crossing her leg awkwardly, the oafish pose I had come to expect. "Do you want to talk about Vietnam?" she asked, her eyes narrowed to slits in her face.

I shook my head. "And please don't tell the others."

"Maman?"

"No, not even her."

"Well, as you wish." She paused, the corner of her mouth raised in annoyance.

As much as I had sought French friends, and Margot had wanted a friend in me, I asked myself now how I could be close to the bigoted, bourgeois, supercilious, and controlling Margot? I considered her tone every time she referred to my "upper class" family, and felt that was her primary motivation where I was concerned. What a shame...it might have worked out for both of us, ha! if only one of us had been a completely different person!

Then I remembered that since Berkeley, really, I had sought to determine my own values. By the time I arrived in France, I thought I had some answers, and had high hopes that I'd find my beliefs and values reflected and confirmed by the French. In many ways, they had come through. But in others, and especially in Margot and Madame's generation, certainly not.

I tipped up my chin as if to fend off yet another blow, then forcing a smile as sarcastic as Margot's, I rose from the sofa. "I would like to stay and talk, but Elizabeth works very hard for a girl her age, don't you agree? I want to go give her a hand."

Upstairs, Elizabeth was reading picture books in French to the children, doing fine on her own, so I shut my door on la famille and eyed the pink onion skin stationary, matching envelopes, aerograms, and pens scattered on the antique desk. With determination, I sat down to clear space and smooth a curling sheet. Mme. Bouleaux would return from Paris with letters from Matt and Mother. I also expected a letter from Aaron with at least some response to my honesty about Teodor Pelnar, not to mention yet another direct question about his plans. As I took pen in hand, I realized that the yearning I had always felt when writing Aaron was simply not present. There was only anger: at Aaron, at Margot, at a world that could kill a bonafide hero.

For now, I would write Aaron because he was the one person to whom I could fling all the new impressions and frustrations of the moment. Cataloguing all I'd learned about the family and myself here on the island, and remembering the hope I felt on the train after my talk with Elizabeth about Laurent and Bérnard. I felt stronger now than when I'd arrived in France. The mix of unsympathetic and insincere voices I'd endured had allowed me to distinguish my own. After venting about the rift with Margot, I summed up my latest philosophy for Aaron.

I'll try not to hate the Magills or the Bouleaux for being what they are, but I have no respect for either bunch. From now on, I will observe their lives as if I were doing cultural research for a class—The Worldwide Culture of a Tired Civilization. The

Bouleaux cannot "represent" my dream of France any more than my parents can represent my dream of what America should be. I'm not sure what I want out of life, but I am sure that as yet I have no role models.

The fairness in my words surprised and pleased me. They felt just right. Then I wrote Aaron about hearing of King's assassination on BBC. How difficult it was to be so far away when tragedy struck! Such trite sentiments, and nothing compared to how I felt, but what else was there to say? At least Margot had shared my grief about King. I lay there conjuring some sympathy for her, but feeling sorrier for myself. And sorry for King and his family and for the whole U.S. of A., which would have to suffer through the loss of another great leader.

On Saturday, Mme. Bouleaux returned from Paris. We were all gathered around the fireplace after breakfast, reading and playing with the children, when Madame swept into the room as if pushed from behind by a furious breeze. "Margot, come. Now!"

The two retired to the kitchen. Elizabeth, without even glancing at the others, tiptoed ostentatiously to the kitchen door to listen to their conversation. She needn't have bothered to position herself as an eavesdropper. The only thing that was keeping me from understanding every word was the rapidity of angry thrusts of language. I could tell that something horrendous had happened in Paris, and that it had to do with Frederic and Gabi.

Through the weeks in Paris, I had picked up that the family thought Gabi Souris was going to do very well as a professional cook, maybe even as a genuine chef in a respectable restaurant. Margot occasionally consulted with Gabi about the cooking she did for the household. More importantly, everyone recognized that Gabi was a serious student. Upstairs in the third house, Gabi had related to me more than once that she was raised by her mother, because her father was some string of words that sounded for all the world like "alcoholic, no-good, wife-beating son-of-a-bitch." Gabi had absorbed life's lessons early. She had no intention of ever becoming financially dependent on her husband, who might also turn out to be an alcoholic lout after he knew he had her trapped. So, after passing the first baccalaureate exam, Gabi worked, lived with her mother, saved her money, and was accepted to the famous Parisian cooking school, Le Cordon Bleu.

With all her pre-professional pride, however, I had assumed from my first encounter with Gabi that her primary goal was to be a wife, specifically, the wife and mother of Mme. Bouleaux's relatively well-fixed, respectable, sober, eminently presentable and docile son, Frederic Bouleaux. Despite Gabi's harsh rejection of my assumptions, I still believed that to be her goal.

Just a couple of minutes went by and the two women emerged from the kitchen. Without so much as a "bonjour," Madame went upstairs to her room and closed the door. As Margot took her place among the others before the hearth, she actually beamed, nodding with satisfaction, as if she'd just polished off a dozen stolen cookies.

"It won't be long," she said to Suzanne, Elizabeth, and me, peeking at us with a high-pitched chuckle, "before we have a wedding in the family." Immediately, we jumped all over Margot's announcement, pressing for details. The children all talked at once, not to be left out of the general clamor.

Margot held up her hands, achieving quiet with a clap. "It seems that Maman went home to take care of the household accounts and found Gabi there with Frederic. The little guttersnipe was supposed to be at home with her mother on vacation, but she told her mother she was with us at l'Île de Ré! She and Frederic have been living in sin all week in the middle house. What a party they've been having!"

"I can just imagine the absolute scene Mme. Bouleaux made!" Elizabeth said, breathlessly. She sounded somewhat indignant and very British, even in French.

"Yes, we can all imagine." Margot sniggered gleefully. "There is finally a woman who will have first place in Frederic's heart, and it's killing her."

"Does Frederic want to marry her? I mean, does he love her?" Elizabeth asked.

"But of course!" Margot said. "But he was never going to ask her to be his wife because he was never going to have the nerve to tell Maman. Gabi is perfect for Frederic. It had to be a woman as strong as Maman, and young and beautiful too. Anyway, I am quite relieved. He is close to 30 years old."

"But does she accept that they will be married?" I asked.

Margot sat back and sighed with deep satisfaction. "That, indeed, is the best part. Maman is trapped by our code of morality. Now that she has caught them in their sin, they must get married. But the truth is—and Maman is not ready to admit this—she knows that Gabi will be a wonderful wife for Frederic. We will all enjoy having her in the family."

When Madame had entered the house, she had tossed a wad of mail onto the dining room table before hustling Margot into the kitchen. There it sat while the family drama played itself out. While Elizabeth eavesdropped, I quickly rifled through the stack. There were several for me, and after things settled down, I retreated to my room to read, filled with joy and foreboding.

I went to Matt's first, but as soon as I could see he was fine, I shoved Mother's aside for later and ripped open Aaron's with a quick stroke that destroyed the envelope and bit into the stationery. The message said absolutely nothing in answer to my question. I threw it furiously across the room and rolled over to bury my sobs in my pillow. I remembered for the umteenth time how frustrated and angry Aaron had grown when I'd asked him about coming to France that last visit to his cottage. I tried to erase my disappointment with thoughts of Teodor Pelnar. Teo waited for me in Paris right now. Then, knowing that his attractiveness and accessibility were indeed of some comfort, made me start crying all over again.

The evening before Pâques, all the women of the house except Mme. Bouleaux, who was still sulking in her bedroom, were in the kitchen, boiling and coloring eggs. I joined them, getting into the holiday spirit despite the occasional bitter awareness of how wonderful it would be to have a trustworthy, sweet, and safe Easter bunny be the center of your world. There were three dozen eggs, tinted with red, blue, green, orange, and purple dye, and patterned with designs painted in red and pink nail polish. Elizabeth and I cut out little bunny-caps for some of the eggs. At midnight, church bells chimed and the voices of villagers returning from services filled the narrow streets. The family had chosen not to attend, which was just as well from my point of view, but Margot explained defensively, "We will go when the children are older."

Sunday morning, Mme. Bouleaux appeared, never mentioning the Parisian dynamite. She assembled the children and away they marched to Suzanne and Jean-Luc's house, while Margot, Elizabeth and I headed for Pré Nouveau, a nearby piece of land once covered with chicken houses. Jean-Luc had installed a large woodshed on the property where they kept the wood for all of the family fireplaces, and next to it, there was the foundation of a house that would become the last of the family trio of vacation homes.

All this was adjacent to a large, overgrown lawn with a sprawling oak tree in the center. We hid the eggs, scattering most of them in the tall grass. Then along came Mme. Bouleaux, Suzanne, Jean-Luc and the brood. All five children hunted for the eggs, little Michelle receiving a large portion of help from the grown-ups.

I was enchanted with Mme. Bouleaux's antics. She seemed a different person than the irate mother from the stormy scene of the previous day. Sitting beneath the tree, keeper of the basket where all the children deposited the eggs as they found them, her game was to throw the eggs back into the tall grass when little eyes were turned away, so the hunt went on and on. Besides the decorated boiled eggs, we had hidden handfuls of chocolate eggs, rabbits and ducks, so that it was almost an hour later when the excited children plopped on the grass next to Grandmère Lapin and gave up, begging for food. We all traipsed back to the house, where we feasted on the eggs and on cold chicken and vegetables with homemade sauce mayonnaise.

And sitting there, eating and talking and laughing, I realized how much of the conversation I understood. It had been a wonderful day, the day of Christ's resurrection. My status in the family no longer mattered to me as much as my determination to walk the line between protocol and my independent spirit. I pushed my chair back noisily from the table and began to follow Elizabeth's lead, picking up dishes and carrying them to the kitchen. I was only trying to emulate Dr. King, I thought, fighting to free all those maids so that they could get out of my mother's kitchen and go home to their own families, or perhaps to universities. I would not be a spoiled, rich American girl, even if that was who they wanted me to be. I put some cups back on the sideboard and grabbed a rag right out of Elizabeth's hand and would have washed the dishes in the sink, but Margot came in and pulled the rag away and handed me a dish of butter.

"In the refrigerator," was all she said. So I accepted the dish, excited by her change of attitude, permitting the served, the paying customer, to play servant. I opened the refrigerator door and there, staring me in the face, was the head of the freshly-killed chicken upon which we had just dined—black, congealed blood smeared on its golden feathers, eyes opened stiffly, its beak sharp and spread as if it were killed mid-squawk. Margot was staring at me with a vicious grin. "Americans like their meals wrapped in plastic, without blood, n'est-ce pas?"

Without a word, I turned back toward the fridge with my eyes wide open, and set the butter dish next to the severed head.

TWENTY-ONE

WHEN CLASS FINALLY ENDED on the first day back after vacation, I raced downstairs ahead of Claire Caplan. Her laughter rang behind me in the stairwell. "You're sure in a hurry! Hey, wait for me!"

I stopped in my tracks at the café door, out of breath, my heart pounding more from excitement than from the run. Claire bumped into me from behind. I felt her head peering around me. "What in the world...?" she whispered.

Le Café de L'Alliance had been transformed by its customers. Shutters closed for the winter were now fully open to the patio, light pouring in over the one single table surrounded by all the people and chairs in the room.

Claire and I entered cautiously, bought coffees, and took seats at the edge of the circle. Dissonant voices struggled to be heard over one another. I grasped familiar words: "Sorbonne" and "sexual revolution." "Educational reform" and "new kingdom of the imagination." The slogans and political messages grew more repetitive, the tone more ferocious, just like some of Bernard's salon diatribes.

As I sipped my coffee, the crescendo positively decimated the longing I'd had back in Berkeley for Parisian justice and liberté. Was the price of justice and liberté always going to be one continual, frightening battle after another? My mind shut down. I recognized the myth of Paris slipping from my grasp like the myth of college life had last fall. I wanted nothing more than to hang onto that myth, yet how could I? I felt terribly ashamed. I searched the crowd of faces. Where was my new boyfriend?

When I couldn't spot Teo, I noticed that Claire was listening to Irena, the Polish woman who seemed to know so much about current events. I forced myself to pay attention. Irena's French seemed slower to me after two weeks on the l'Île de Ré, though I knew my rate of comprehension had merely speeded up.

"I have identified with the students at Nanterre," she was saying, "because I am going to be part of the system when I complete my studies at L'Alliance." Hadn't Irena said something once before about a confrontation between students and administration at the Nanterre campus? Now she was proclaiming loudly, "...if something isn't done by them, then we, all of us together, we will change it..."

Clearly, there was a lot of sympathy for the Nanterre students. Many cheered Irena's declaration. But her German pal challenged her. "And who is this we, you speak of?" Charlotta said. Nervously, she crimped her auburn hair. "The dissenting students have such a variety of issues and ideas! Tired-out Communists, extreme Maoists, Trotskyites, Gaullists, anarchists and even nihilists. Left against right, and both against the middle. They all want to dominate..."

"Don't be so negative, Charlotta." Irena tossed her stringy hair back and curled her lips contemptuously. "They will unite around the cause," she continued, her eyes gathering in the larger audience. "They must unite to make progress...and they will." Voices from the crowd hummed as if they were the Greek chorus behind Irena's starring role. I was watching Charlotta as she mumbled the words "Keeping order is important..." She had bravely challenged her older, more assertive friend, but her words were swallowed up in the crowd's refrain. Then the two bent back down over a thick newspaper—the slight German girl and the big brash Pole, an odd pairing of opposites in every way.

Elizabeth laid a tentative hand on my shoulder. I wondered how long she'd been standing there at the back door, afraid to enter until the assembly settled down. She whispered three distinct words in my ear, "I'm not staying."

I turned to her with a nod. "Okay. I'll see you back home." The Brit mumbled "sorry..." and began to walk away. I caught her by the sleeve and pulled her close again. "Will you please tell Margot I won't be making it home for dinner today?" Quickly agreeing, she hurried out.

Just when my thoughts had turned once again to Teo, there he was—big, solid, fair and fair-featured—pulling a seat up right next to mine, balancing his food expertly on his lap. I squirmed closer to him. Then silently, formally, he extended his hand to me for a gentlemanly handshake. It was not what I had expected of our reunion. Teo's broad mouth wolfed down cake as if he'd seen me at the café every day for these two weeks.

I fiddled with my coffee cup, listened to the talk of "revolution." Suddenly I noticed that Teo was staring at me coldly. His demeanor spun me off-guard more than the new, fervent café rhetoric. I steadied my eyes on his face. "I want to go for a walk," I said, "and not home." I stood up, nearly tipping my chair over. Teo caught it, held it awkwardly at an angle. "Do you feel like walking just now?" I asked him as casually as I could. He rose alongside me and followed hesitantly. I gave Claire a perfunctory wave, "See you tomorrow."

So the two of us turned our backs on the revolution, slipping out the back door and circling around onto the patio. There was Miroslav, leaning back precariously in his chair, as usual. I smiled politely, but Teo did not even acknowledge him as we passed. As soon as we reached the sidewalk, I said very matter-of-factly, "I'm glad you still want to be friends."

"I'm glad too. I wasn't sure of you. You never called me."

I halted, caught my breath. "I'm sorry, but I am not accustomed to calling boys." I reached into my purse. "Here are the fifty centimes you gave me for the call."   He pushed my hand away. "Never mind. Keep it."

"Don't be angry. You asked me to call but you didn't wait to hear an answer from me. I've been expecting to see you here, at the school."

"Okay, okay. I won't be angry. Anyway, your French is truly much better. That is good. It will make our friendship easier. But I want you to call me sometimes. It will make me feel like you want to see me."

I laughed out loud and shook my head in bewilderment. Then, as if my radar switch had been flipped on, I peered around uneasily, wondering if Miroslav was following along after us. Teo did the same and sure enough, the dark hulk was rising from his place among the patio plantings. I sighed. "This is ridiculous..."

"Yes, ridiculous. And outrageous. We would have more freedom in my country now than this fellow gives me." Teo took my hand and we walked quickly away from the café. Then we were running. "Never mind about him," Teo shouted across the space between us. "Today, you will be with me only. I have a special, beautiful place I'd like to show you. Come."

What Teo had in mind required a Métro ride. His guidance through the maze of escalators, directions, and destinations was swift and sure—a far cry from my own navigational skills. I had always found myself pausing before maps or accosting strangers or ticket-sellers with questions. With a sense of relief that took me by surprise, I relaxed and let Teo take control. Underground, he kept a tight grip on my hand, pulling me into a run again as the pneumatique entered the station. Instead of entering the nearest car, we raced full throttle along the track. With a great leg-stretching, heart-stopping leap, we were inside the first car, right behind the engine. There were no seats, so we had to hold tight to the leather grips, sucking in deep gulps of the stale air, laughing noiselessly against the clatter of metal on tracks, swaying toward each other and away. We knew without a word that the point of our run was escape and that we had succeeded.

"So where are we going?" I finally asked.

"To an old kingdom of the imagination."

I laughed too loudly, as if laughing were the only way to express the pent up joy at being with Teo once again.

"Just what is the 'new kingdom of the imagination'? I don't understand what these revolutionaries are talking about most of the time."

"It's something they believe is being kept from them," Teo explained.

"Are they right?"

"No one hands you that kingdom wrapped up in a package like a gift."

"A gift from God...?" I shouted over the train's clatter.

Teo shrugged his free shoulder. "I don't believe it, but perhaps you do."

Hand in hand, we rose from the depths of the Métro to enter a large garden in a quiet arrondisement. In the middle of the garden was an old townhouse in the style of the chateaux. At the front gate, a sign of recent addition: Musée Rodin. "Auguste Rodin," Teo said. "Do you know of him?"

"Of course!" I replied. But in searching my memory for information beyond an image of the famous sculpture, The Kiss, I came up empty.

"The sun will be bright for only a little while longer. Let us see the garden first."

The Rodin Museum garden was a microcosm of springtime in Paris, the path meandering among tiny, dripping yellow-green leaves with white and purple flowers that seemed to radiate with the light of Monet's impressionist water lilies. And along the path, just a little larger than life-sized, were Rodin's bronze nudes with their uneven, impressionistic surfaces. Suddenly, in the shadows of an alcove, I spotted The Kiss. A little cry emerged from high in my throat, filtering up from the sudden sting between my legs.

"It's like we are intruding on their privacy," Teo said, speaking softly as if to avoid disturbing them. We approached the passionate couple. I was mesmerized, so much so that I barely noticed when Teo's hand came around my shoulders.

"I can feel the artist's fingers on the bronze when I see the bodies," I said.

"The artist's hands dug into the clay. The bronze came later, out of the clay model."

"You know about art?" I asked, still staring at the sensuous bronze, now aware of his pale gray eyes on my face, his warm hand holding me firmly to his side.

"I know more about music. I play violin, but my violin is back in Prague," he said sadly. "Here in Paris, I learn about art."

"I know more about music, too," I responded. "I play guitar and piano."

"Ah, yes, so many of American youth play guitar."

"I brought it here. Perhaps sometime I'll play for you."

"I would like that very much," he said, suddenly devouring my face, my eyes. Then the kiss came, the real kiss, the one I had been waiting for, and his mouth still tasted like the bitter-sweet of heavily sugared coffee. His thick, muscled arms came around me as if to replicate Rodin's forested lovers. Without finishing the kiss, I went for a second, which became part of the first and breathed its way into a third. Just one, long, deep, sweet kiss.

Teo lifted his head to his full height. Six-foot-five? Six-foot-six? Keeping both his arms around me, he crushed me to his chest, moaning contentedly with a great sigh, as if he had just passed through the Métro door and it had shut securely, leaving out the "other," all the others that might intrude into our private retreat.

Then Teo raised my hand to his lips for a bit of gallantry, a knight's kiss that unexpectedly shot through me. My body tensed around the sweet wound and I gazed at him wordlessly, prettily, wanting to wound him back.

I let myself be led through the rest of the garden, into the beautiful old Hôtel Biron, now the indoor museum. There were other artists' sculptures there. Teo was eager to share his favorites: a Don Quixote by O. Zadkine and a small room devoted to the abstract sculpture of someone named Slavkos. But the best were the Rodins and Teo saved the best of these for last. Balzac was an overpowering, wise giant, whose expression changed at every angle. "If Rodin were alive today," Teo remarked, "he would probably create a de Gaulle just like that."

"Yes, perhaps that is why there is a de Gaulle," I said. "What I mean is, maybe Rodin created the possibility of a de Gaulle in this century."

"Does an artist have such power?"

I stared at the majestic form, cocking my head to the side. "No, no. Perhaps not," I finally answered. "Perhaps the idea was there already. An archétype? Is that what they call it? Before Rodin, in kings like Louis XIV or dictators like Napoleon. Those men weren't gods, but the French people needed gods. They magnified their heroes until Rodin came along and made Balzac." I laughed sheepishly. "Do you understand me?"

Teo was taking in my every word. "You know a lot about ideas and philosophy," he replied. I smiled up at him, pleased at his praise, but his face was rigid and solemn. He sighed, facing the amazing Balzac. "And so," he continued, "from this archetype, actually a powerful literary genius, now we are back to the kings and dictators with de Gaulle." His voice had descended into a deeper, more menacing timbre. His grip on my hand had tightened until my blood no longer circulated. I kept it there, willing to suffer. "But soon de Gaulle will be history, like Louis Quatorze and Napoléon. I wish so much that the new Balzac, whoever he may be, will be an artist, a creative young person leading France from the streets of Paris or in the courtyard of the Sorbonne."

I understood Teo's words, but the politics bewildered me. "I'm afraid I've lost track of the situation here," I told him. "It is difficult for me, not just with the language but with all these confusing issues. I had no idea that some French people consider de Gaulle a dictator. I was so hopeful that France would be the ideal. You know, 'liberté, egalité, fraternité...'"

We stepped out the back door of the Hôtel into the garden, faded now from green to gray. There was a cold stone bench just big enough for the two of us. He motioned for me to sit and squeezed in next to me, sighing wearily. "Even two centuries ago, that was only a fond dream of poets, Jeanette. If only the Balzacs and Victor Hugos would float their fine ideas down to earth long enough for them to stick!"

"Do you agree with Irena, then. That we should support the overthrow of de Gaulle?"

"Yes, I do. Perhaps the new Balzac is on his podium at Nanterre." Teo laughed bitterly. "But for different reasons than you, Jeanette, I cannot participate. I can only mumble to myself and now to you that I wish the students success. I do hope they do not go toward communism, for their sake. Many students think they will like communism. They will not like it. Pas du tout."

Teo sounded sincere, but I had no bright ideas left for a reply. I was glad when he took advantage of my silence to wrap both of his thick arms around me. Muscled arms that would have been daunting if they had belonged to a less gentle soul than Teodor Pelnar.

At the boarding house after vacation, Gabi Souris had greeted me with kisses and hugs. She backed away and proffered a sheepish smile. "You knew all along, didn't you?" and I accepted that as an appropriate apology. We were agréable again. Gabi was happily preparing both for exams and for a wedding. The house fairly reeked with perspiration and spring flowers.

Elizabeth, also "in love," was occupied most of the time with her au pair job, but still came out with me occasionally when Margot temporarily unlocked her shackles. As important as l'Île de Ré had been to my French—not to mention my social enlightenment—I was sorry I'd missed a single day touring the City of Light.

Most afternoons, it was Teo who would go touring with me. He came by for me after midday dinner, offered polite greetings, and off we would go. I was relieved that the household seemed to accept my well-bred Czech boyfriend as a frequent visitor.

The historical sights were my special passion. Teo stood patiently while I read passages in my English guidebook, then listened as attentively as a star pupil when I translated the best for him. Sometimes Elizabeth or Claire would join us. Teo liked Claire because she was a "no-nonsense girl." Often too, when Teo and Claire had other plans or simply tired of my frenetic touring, I went alone and was content.

But like background music to the drama on stage came my gradual awareness, throughout April, that every sight and every conversation had a double meaning. There were more heated discussions in the café after school, occasional street demonstrations for a myriad of confusing causes, and talk around the dining room table about "leftists" and "rightists."

One beautiful Sunday in April, I was in the courtyard, all dressed up for church and pulling on my coat and knitted gloves. I was not very religious in the ritual sense, but I was excited about participating in a mass at Nôtre-Dame de Paris—something that I wanted to do that I could actually enjoy writing home about. Part tourist, part Catholic, I was headed for the mother of all cathedrals.

Then I caught sight of Jean-Louis approaching the house. I stepped aside, trying my best to ignore him.

"No need to move for me," he said. "I'll just walk around you." I didn't answer, busying myself with buttoning my coat. He stayed where he was. We were alone in the courtyard. "Don't you talk to me?" he asked. "That's very rude, you know?" I ignored his belligerent tone of voice, finishing with my coat, then stood stock still, not daring to move, staring at my pumps, my heart in my throat. "Say something!" he shouted, shaking my sleeve as if he expected it to rattle.

That's when Bérnard, as disheveled as ever, walked out of the first house. Immediately I feared—no, expected—what? Snide laughter? The two of them ganging up on me...? Where was feisty Margot when I needed her? I imagined the landlady running after the two ogres with a broom held like a battering ram...but no, no Margot. Only the troublemaker.

Bérnard stopped in his tracks, sized up the situation. "Where are you off to, Jeanette?" he asked in a more normal, conversational tone than I had ever heard from him. I couldn't answer him. Jean-Louis still had hold of my sleeve. Bérnard strolled over, placed his hand on top of Jean-Louis', and smiling calmly at the older man, shook his head reprovingly and clucked his tongue against his teeth. Jean-Louis' hand dropped to his side, his cheeks enflamed. He shrugged. "I was...I was just teasing." He turned toward his house, mumbling to himself, "...ce n'est pas drôle..." And he was gone.

"No, not funny," Bérnard said. He observed me. "Are you all right?"

I released a giant breath into the cold spring air. "Oui, thanks to you, Bérnard."

"You've heard of the wolf in sheep's clothing?" Bérnard asked. I cocked my head, puzzled by the question. "Well, Jean-Louis," he continued, "he is the sheep in wolf's clothing." With a curt au revoir, he walked quickly through the courtyard, disappearing under the arch.   I had plenty of time to ponder Bérnard's rescue on my way across town to Nôtre-Dame. I still didn't like Bérnard, but at least I was sure now that he wasn't as dangerous as he appeared. I stretched my legs as I walked, beginning to relax, feeling thrilled to be on my own, smiling to myself and swinging my arms. Despite the unusual cold spell, I was warmed by the sun bolting in and out of rain clouds like a coy, capricious child.

When I entered the timeless, holy site, I found it filled with organ and choir music and thousands of people. Unable to imagine praying in that crunch, I resigned myself to the role of tourist, yielding to the joys of observation and to chords bouncing resiliently off stained glass.

Outside, after the mass, about a hundred erstwhile soldiers from World War II and the Indochinese and Algerian Wars were standing at attention, each in full dress uniform, holding a flag of France. The next mass was to be special, in honor of them. I lingered, staring into the faces of the shriveled men and women who were living their lives through to the end. I felt my heart dragged down by the waste of those, like Monsieur Bouleaux, who weren't there.

A large, classroom-sized crowd of students with angry, windblown hair marched toward the veterans. Intuitively, I knew what was going to happen as soon as I noticed that hair. The placards they carried scolded, "Make Love, Not War," "War is the Product of Little Imagination," "De Gaulle=Lord of War," "Did God Die So We Can Die And Die Again?" As the peaceful march approached the front of the Cathedral, the placards bounced in slow motion, glinting in the freshness of the morning sun. I discerned anger and defiance in the faces of the young, and fear and defiance in the faces of the old. And I knew, because I had seen it all in California, that I would hear the whistle blow, see the police move closer. The instinct to flee began in my stomach, traveled to my toes, propelling me to turn away and after an instant, to run. I ran all the way to the Métro until I was deep under the ground in the dim tunnel, waiting for a train to a transitory home.

That night, I wrote to Aaron Becker at last how creeped out I was by Jean-Louis and how Bérnard, the highly strung radical in our midst, came to my rescue as the phony, fat letch tried to get my attention in quite a nasty way. Then about the pending student unrest and the antiwar demonstration at the cathedral ceremony for war heroes. In fact, I had begun to write more frequently to Aaron. As I grew closer to Teo, my anger and expectation diminished. Aaron still didn't feel exactly like "just a friend," but he was a good friend and a touchstone. Writing to him provided a way to record events and to make sense of them.

Paris was not in a celebratory mood. I had decided not to tell anyone about my nineteenth birthday, not even Teo. But Aaron had remembered, sending a Byrds songbook with all our old favorites. His note assured me that he remembered I had rejected acoustic music, but since I'd toted my guitar across the Atlantic, he hoped I might enjoy playing these songs. He reminded me that we had been together for my eighteenth birthday, bringing all the details into sharp focus. For one whole day, he seemed closer to me than he had in a long while, until after supper, when I wondered if friendship seemed the only lasting result of all that we had shared.

Two days later, I received the letter I had waited for so eagerly. A typical Aaron letter, newsy and preachy. But then in his oddball way, he used the P.S. to tell me that he had been drafted. "No check from Dad yet," he wrote. I could just hear his phony cheer. "Negotiation still in progress. It may have to be Canada, France later." That was all. I felt sick to my stomach, more for Aaron than for myself. Now my fear about his silences were confirmed. Not only would he be broke at graduation, I was absolutely sure that he was waffling about joining me at all. If protests erupted in France, why would he leave one nation under student siege for another?

As I reread the letter, I expected my own tears, but none came. I was worried about Aaron, but I knew that he would find a way to a safe haven, even if it had to be Canada. My yearning for him had been replaced with pity, nostalgia, and a mixture of annoyance and amusement. He had instructed me more than once to stay safe. I couldn't fault Aaron for being concerned about me, but I still bristled at his overprotective harangues.

With a thrill, I realized that the one I wanted now was Teo. In the days ahead, I left my new boyfriend out of my letters to Berkeley, but as if on automatic pilot, my "diary" was written and sent, and return letters anticipated.

TWENTY-TWO

L'ABBAYE WAS A NIGHTCLUB near Saint-Germain-des-Prés, a cross between an American coffee house and a French dive. A score of round tables, their tops shining in the harsh light like black vinyl record albums, surrounded a dingy dance floor where two couples clung and swayed to a scratchy pastiche of the Rolling Stones. Elizabeth and Laurent had joined us, their own decision this time. Our foursome pulled chairs up around one of the disks. I winced at the sight of our faces, ghoulish beneath the sharp, blue lights.

A waitress about my age, dressed in a sweater and slacks so tight they seemed about to split, served us strong, sugary coffees. Just after our first sips, Laurent took Elizabeth's hand without a word and led her to the dance floor. I noticed their movements as they awkwardly found their pose and rhythm. Two shiny blonde heads tinted fluorescent blue-green, coming together from across the natural boundary of the English Channel. They fit together perfectly. "Why did you bring these youngsters with you?" asked Teo. "Do you still need their protection?"

"They asked me what I was doing tonight and I told them. They invited themselves. It's probably difficult for them to get away from Margot and Mme. Bouleaux. So now I'm their chaperone. Anyway, then I have someone to escort me home. You don't have to go all the way up to Port-Royal and then back across town..."

"But this isn't really a dance place," Teo interrupted. "A singer will come on soon and they will have to sit with us. He sings American folk songs in French. I thought you would like to listen to this." He squeezed my hand. "Très intéresant...he is an American nègre who lives in Paris. This is his own club. I understand he doesn't like us to clap our hands. Instead, we snap our fingers at the end of the song." He snapped the fingers on both his hands, then again. When I didn't respond, he quickly sobered, trying to explain. "I see you are so sad these days, because of all the trouble. I wanted to cheer you up."

"I am sad, Teo. Paris has not turned out to be...Paris. But please, don't give up on me."

"Give up on you?" He made a dull whistling sound, pushing the air out between his teeth and his pursed lips. "Nonsense! We are more than that to each other now, n'est-ce pas?" He peeked at the door of L'Abbaye. Then, his words spilled out, "Chérie, I also wanted to bring you here because I need to talk to you about something important. Miroslav will be here, but he will not sit with us." Teo leaned toward me until our eyes, lips, hands were all drawn together, but even so, his voice was so low that I had to strain to hear him. "Jeanette, would you do something for me? For my country?"

I lurched away from our huddle, "For your country? What do you mean? What can I possibly do?"

"You can be *un leurre*," he said. I searched my vocabulary for the word and came up empty. "An excuse, a deception," he continued impatiently. A decoy, then. I nodded and he blew out a dramatic breath. He looked French when he puckered his lips that way, as French as Laurent.

Then, with quiet intensity, Teo explained how he had been watching for an opportunity to get completely away from Miroslav and meet with a Czech émigré living in Paris. He called this man the 'Prestup,' which meant 'connection' in Czech. This connection guy was a newspaper editor whose anti-Communist sheet, known as a 'samizdat,' was published in Paris and widely circulated among Czech and Slovak émigrés. The Prestup had been sentenced in absentia to fourteen years in Czech prison by the Communist government. The charges were subversive activity and espionage.

"I must meet him," Teo said, his grip on my hands beginning to hurt. "He is a genuine hero, Jeanette." I wiggled my fingers and he sat up straight, let them go.

"This is okay...," I said, taking Teo's hands lightly in my own again. I didn't need to question his motives. Not after all he had said about his anti-Communist sympathies. But I asked, "Why do you see an opportunity to meet him now?"

"Because, don't you see? We are alone here. Miroslav waits outside the door because he has respect for our romantic affair."

I smiled uneasily. "And because he doesn't want to pay the entrance?"

Teo snorted, then continued. "Bien sûr. But...I have been preparing Miroslav for several days now. You see, I know you are a good girl, Jeanette, and I would never take advantage of your innocence. You know that, don't you? But I told Miroslav that I am desperate to have sex with you and that I would ask you today to come with me to a hotel." As he spoke, his eyes met mine unflinchingly, the words falling from his lips as if he had been rehearsing the speech as often as he had rehearsed his lies to Miroslav. Only this was different, because I knew absolutely that what Teo told me was the truth, and that I would be safe with him wherever he took me.

I was nodding, indicating understanding and assent. "If I wait up late enough," Teo continued, "eventually he will think we have had our fun and are fast asleep. Then he will leave to get sleep himself, and I can sneak out to find the Prestup. I have gone to great trouble to arrange a secret meeting."

I squeezed the big hands. What could I say that would be neither too timid nor too eager? I felt him waiting now. I told him, "I feel honored to be asked to help you and your country." He smiled, then checked the door of L'Abbaye. His eyes returned to mine and he signaled for me to go on. "I have been reading more about your country, Teo. The young against the old, just like here, just like everywhere. In Nanterre, Prague, and Berkeley too, we are a disenfranchised class. Perhaps none of us can hope to stay out of it."

Teo squeezed my hand hard, so hard that I jumped at the pain and stopped talking at once. "I'm sorry, Jeanette," he whispered. "Miroslav has just poked his head inside the door. We will have time to talk more when we meet." His mouth twisted into an exaggerated grin. "Anyway..." he let go of me, "...here come your friends, and here is the singer."

Elizabeth and Laurent accompanied me home, which was the main reason I had wanted them along. There was no doubt about the passion I felt for Teo, but how should I respond to him? I plotted to avoid winding up in his Pigalle studio by default. In the back of my mind, I always held thoughts of our inevitable separation.

The Métro had stopped running. The beautiful Saint-Germain-des-Prés arrondissement slept peacefully, its shops and galleries closed, its residents sequestered behind darkened windows. "I love to walk at night," I told my companions. "We've got the whole city to ourselves."

"We can use the air after all that horrid cigarette smoke," Elizabeth said.

My companions strolled off to the side of me. Laurent had his arm lodged comfortably around Elizabeth's back. I wondered if they had been seeing each other up in one of their rooms at the Bouleaux. Was I, after all, the odd-girl out where my virginity was concerned? Being the 'last virgin of my generation' had never troubled me before, but there had never been a Teodor Pelnar in my life before. With Aaron, at least, I had always thought I could expect a future.

I was not completely naïve. I knew that what Teo wanted, although he'd never call it that, was 'free love.' Aaron, too...and he'd certainly never call it that. I snickered grimly. Nothing, I thought, was for free.

I did a two-step to catch up to Elizabeth and Laurent, now arm-in-arm and chatting quietly. When you're in high school, I thought, it makes sense not to assume a permanent relationship. At what point did that become a requirement for sex, or even desirable? I was frightened for all the reasons I had always been frightened—of pregnancy, of an irreversible involvement, of not enough involvement, and most of all, of the physical act itself, wrenching me away from the storybook illusion of love's tenderness.

But now, with Teo and so far from the familiarity of home, I questioned the sense of my fears and my values. And now I'd agreed to spend the night with a guy in a hotel room. Yet I trusted him, perhaps more than I trusted myself.

I was mulling all this over with no distraction greater than the turmoil in my own mind when the three of us turned up toward Boul' Mich' and my thoughts drifted from Teo to some gossip I had heard after school. "Let's take the side streets home," I said. "I heard there was trouble at the University this afternoon. Who knows what's going on there by now."

"What kind of trouble?" asked Elizabeth.

"They closed down Nanterre. The whole campus. The administration was afraid of warring factions," I said.

"They think we are fools!" said Laurent. "That was just their excuse."

"It seems the rightists did make some kind of overt threats," I said. "So the leftist groups came over here to the Sorbonne courtyard. They considered it a safe place to meet."

"Aren't you curious about what happened?" asked Laurent.

"Well...yes. But I'm not interested in getting trapped. Besides, I'm exhausted. And I've got a lot on my mind." I thought again about Teo's request.

"Come on, Laurent," Elizabeth said, wrapping both her hands around his arm. "You know we're right." Laurent grumbled something in rapid French but allowed Elizabeth to lead him onto the Rue de l'Odéon. It was after 1:00 a.m. and the air smelled fresh and damp. Our shoes scraped audibly over rough cobblestones. An eerie orange glow from the street lamps bounced off the ancient stone walls across Place de l'Odéon. I examined the Théâtre building, hoping for some sign of authority, as if its pillars and pediment could advise us like the Oracle in Greece. Laurent linked one arm in mine, the other in Elizabeth's. We held ourselves close to him as we moved forward.

"Écoute!" Laurent halted suddenly. Listen. We stood motionless, shouts and jarring impacts of metal and stone reaching us from some distance to the east.

"What's going on?"

"It sounds like a mob in the streets," said Laurent. "Like a riot. Perhaps the students from Nanterre who have come to Paris! We must go see..." He shook off our arms, ran ahead and then back to us again.

"What in the world are you talking about?" Elizabeth cried. "Let's run...home, if there's going to be trouble!" Elizabeth stumbled over her French words.

"I'm not going to run away," Laurent shouted. "Are you crazy? At least, I want to watch what they're doing..."

"Quiet, you two," I cut him off. "Which direction is the noise coming from?" Laurent's tall frame hunched forward, his hands fled to his pockets, his anger was dispensed in quick, short breaths. The noises were growing, now sounding as if they were coming from all around us. We began to hear voices. Boys and girls barked angry retorts to a collective war cry, which then rose in a frantic crescendo, quashing distinct words.

"Which way to go?" asked Elizabeth, grabbing at Laurent's arm again. Her boyfriend's eyes were flashing, his head twisting at each new concussive sound. "This will bring us home," he said, his voice surly. He broke away from Elizabeth and began to head down the Rue Racine, toward the Boul' Mich'. I followed him, not seeing any options, talking nervously out loud to myself in English. "Why do I get the feeling that this is definitely not the right way?"

By now Elizabeth was gripping my arm. We followed Laurent, who turned right at the corner on the Rue Monsieur le Prince. For a moment I felt easier to be heading south again, but the street ran on a diagonal, right back toward the noise.

Less than a block ahead we recognized a transformed Boulevard Saint-Michel. There, under the orange lamplight, stood hundreds of shiny-helmeted policemen with rifles and ready bayonets. "And we complain about sticks and tear-gas!" I whined. "My God! How can they...?"

"Let's get out of here!" shouted Elizabeth.

"No. Wait!" Laurent exhorted.

"Laurent!! Janet?"

Laurent ran toward the Boulevard. I called after him, then followed—moving forward one step at a time, involuntarily, as if in a trance. Laurent crouched behind a garbage can. When I'd run from Nôtre-Dame, I remembered, I had been in the middle of the crowd, the police moving in. Here, at this distance, we were safe, and I was suddenly mesmerized by a desire to witness, as if through a one-way mirror. A house-length back from Laurent, I stood upright just under a lamp. Half a block away, perpendicular to my line of vision, I could see a neat row of police backing up with their shields raised. Students were throwing stones and glass bottles, shouting "De Gaulle, assassin," "Death to bourgeois police." Then a strong, steady, white light poured onto the Boulevard, dissolving the warm orange glow from the street lamps, blinding the students and giving clear sight to the black-helmeted police. I was vaguely aware that it had begun to drizzle.

Laurent turned toward me and called out, bravado whipped oddly into his plea. "Are you coming, Jeanette?"

"Janet, no!" Elizabeth called from behind. "He's insane!"

The girl was panicky, but I couldn't tear my eyes away from the scene. I watched as cars parked on the street were upended and piles of paving stones were torn from the streets with pneumatic drills. Barricades were growing, eight, then ten feet high, and some of the students behind them wore motorcycle helmets and skin-diver goggles. Then I watched as Laurent ran into the fray, stealthily as a cat, and disappeared behind an overturned car.

"Janet, please! Let's get out of here!" Elizabeth shouted in terror from behind me. It was an urgent appeal from a frightened child and a friend, but when I turned, I saw Elizabeth Prior, dressed to the teeth in the same dowdy high fashion that Jean Magill had spent hours gathering for her daughter on Beverly Drive. I saw Elizabeth Prior with her large, teary blue eyes, her sad, lipsticked mouth, and her long, straight, blond hair curled slightly at the ends with rollers pinned in at night. I saw Elizabeth, but I heard my mother whine, "Janet, please!"

My lips curled, and I felt their corners stiffen into an odd, dreamy smile. "I can smell the tear gas. They use that here too," I said in a voice I knew Elizabeth could not hear. I moved forward again, searching for Laurent, but that was an excuse. I could not leave just yet.

A moment later, the police troops opened the nozzles of a dozen high-powered fire hoses. Students ran, fell. I heard frightened screams, then groans. Ambulance sirens. My eyes shut tight, then opened wide again. Troops were attacking with sticks and rifle butts. It was as if I'd been falling through a nightmarish darkness, then had forced myself awake in the instant before I hit the ground. What was I doing here in this frenzy that was not my own? Following a high school boy into a mob of strangers, and into violence far worse than anything I'd ever seen at home?

Backing down the narrow street, I reached up to plug my ears, then grabbed Elizabeth's arm. The two of us began to run. A fine spray washed my brown car coat and left it shining in the glare of the headlights. Confused, I wondered if the police hoses were spraying us, or the muddled, moonless sky.

Within minutes, we'd reached the safety of the Luxembourg Garden gate, but we didn't slow down. The rain was coming harder now. "I wish I had my umbrella," Elizabeth bellowed as we ran. I laughed nervously at first, then hooted at the image of Elizabeth sprinting like Mary Poppins with an umbrella opened over her head. She pulled a lifeless scrap of blue silk out of her coat pocket. "See, all I have is the bloody cover to my travel umbrella. Never the umbrella when you need it."

Still running, I drew my hands from my pockets and held aloft my own limp umbrella cover. "Look, just look at this!" I shrieked, laughing hysterically, out of control, and she had to laugh too. We ran full throttle along the iron spike fence, then homeward down Port-Royal—two foreigners, whooping like fun-loving tourists, just as the mythical holiday came to an end.

TWENTY-THREE

MY PLACE AT MARGOT'S big, oval dining table had been moved near the open casement window to make room for all sixteen of Mme. Bouleaux's children, grandchildren, and student boarders. The sun streamed in just ahead of the delightful Parisian spring breeze, warming my back and brightening the animated faces around the room. Clusters of French words rose and fell like diatonic scales played by a whole roomful of pianos. I listened, my eyes racing from one voice to the next, amazed by their excitement over the student demonstrations of the previous evening. In my memory, American adults reacted to student activity with only one of two attitudes: haughty distain or disinterest. Now for the sake of student politics, all these people were ignoring the most delicious paté on baguettes I had ever tasted—and everyone was talking at once.

"It is not safe for the children in the Latin Quarter. They cannot even walk to school," Hélène complained. "They might as well shut it down like the Sorbonne."

"The students will shut the schools down if the damn government doesn't let the Sorbonne reopen!" Bérnard said, his two fists grinding into Margot's white tablecloth.

"We'll shut the whole country down, won't we, Bérnard?" said Le Grand Laurent, bouncing up in his seat. The square of white gauze on his forehead shone like a badge of honor above his pink cheeks.

"Be careful, Laurent," warned Hélène. "Next time it won't be a mere scratch..."

"It's not just a scratch..." Laurent protested loudly. "That bastard flic..." I caught the word, had heard it before. Were the flics just the "cops"? Or was that word used more like "pigs," at home?

"Be quiet, Laurent! Sit down! I told you what your parents said. It is home to Alsace with you if you get involved again!" Margot frowned sternly at Laurent, who sat down with an exasperated sigh.

Pushing up the sleeves of her thin, shabby cardigan, Margot began filling plates with aromatic ragôut chasseur and string beans—the perfectly manicured haricots verts. I could have eaten a whole plate of the thin, crunchy vegetable. Next to Margot sat her square-faced mother, who was patting a stray hair back into place. "Mes petits enfants, s'il vous plaît," Mme. Bouleaux pronounced one French syllable at a time, "let us discuss this calmly. I remember just ten years ago, during the Algerian War..."

"The issues are different now!" They interrupted her, all jumping into the mayhem again. "The students from Nanterre had a right to organize!" "Organize yes, but not get violent." "Do you want your children to suffer from an antiquated education?" "But, the police..." "The students know nothing about life..."

"I agree," Elizabeth chimed in, sneaking a frightened, sideways glance at Laurent. "That is, I think I agree." Silent stares.

Then Laurent shouted, "How can you agree with that, you traitor? You are either a traitor or an idiot!" Cecile and Lili had started to cry. More noise than tears.

"Shh, shhh! Laurent, Elizabeth doesn't understand what is going on," Margot said, conciliatory. Simultaneously, Mme. Bouleaux chastised, "Hush Laurent! You wild boy." She tapped on her goblet with the side of her fork, straightened her shoulders like General de Gaulle himself, and commanded "Attention! Écoute!" It was she who had called all three households together to discuss a grave situation. She had instructed Margot to prepare an especially nourishing dinner for the negotiation table.

Now Mme. Bouleaux explained, in slow, patient French, her version of the events that had resulted in the riots. The core of Nanterre students were not radicals, she declared. But they were stuck out on that drab, isolated suburban campus without even the distraction of the Latin Quarter to relieve their tension. First, the rector of Nanterre had closed the campus to avoid trouble from a handful of protesters, and then when they moved into Paris, the rector of the Sorbonne had done the same. Never in history had the doors of the university been closed! Imagine! And along with the police came the Compagnies Républicaines de Sécurité. They are part of the French army. How ridiculous! The army to fight students!

Madame concluded, "I want you to know, Bérnard, that I agree it is despicable that the government used this violence on the students."

"Good for you, Madame. And I'm not saying the communists have all the answers. But that fascist old man, de Gaulle. He has none. Not for my generation."

"He's boring us into an early grave...!" shouted Laurent.

Jean-Louis interrupted loudly, "You two may be bored, but you're well-fed. Be content, my young friends. You are a spoiled generation."

"You must listen to Jean-Louis, Bérnard and Laurent," said Hélène. "You have never had to worry about necessities. Or to fight a war."

"Pardonez-moi, madame," said Jean-Louis, "but I don't need you to fight my battles against this radical and his high school pal. And President de Gaulle..."

"President de Gaulle..." It was Gabi who broke in this time. I didn't think I had ever seen her this angry. "Did you see the newspaper this morning? They called the students 'madmen' and accused them, one and all, of being vandals. That's an obvious attempt by the government, which controls the news, to paint all the students with one brush, n'est-ce pas? And to isolate them, to silence them."

I suddenly realized that I had been listening so hard to their debate that my fingers were cramping around my fork. My assessment of my new famille deepened a notch. Gabi seemed heroic. And Jean-Louis's dismissal of the gentle Hélène was nasty. Jean-le loup-Louis was a pitiful excuse for a man. I took a bite of stew. The meat was tender but I was chewing with great difficulty. Listening.

"The great General will survive this little street brawl," Jean-Louis was saying. "And do you know why? Because he is for France first, and most Frenchmen know that. We trust him. That's why."

"Bravo!" Margot and Madame both chimed in.

"Well, you should trust him," shouted Bérnard. "Trust him to do nothing. For the workers! The students! If we were free, we could come up with solutions. Imagine solutions..."

"You talk to me, a family man, about freedom?"

Madame's goblet rang out again. She struck until she had regained command of the assembled, then issued her orders. "Jean-Louis, bring the radio and place it on the table next to me. Let us listen to the news broadcast while we eat. We need to keep informed. And to eat our dinner! Afterwards, Margot, we will make a marketing list. Stocking up would be the sensible thing to do."

"Incroyable!" I burst out, speaking for the first time since I had taken my seat. All eyes focused on me, the American college girl. "This is incredible!" I was saying. "My God, I love it! You people actually care about the situation!" I took a breath, leaned forward and tried unsuccessfully to tame my enthusiastic expression. They stared at me inquisitively, all except Jean-Louis, who rose as commanded to get the radio.

"You see," I began to explain, "in Berkeley, we have demonstrations like these all the time and no one ever 'stocks up.' American families watch the television news and to them, these events are a game. They don't take anything the students say or do seriously!"

A whole roomful of knives and forks were poised above plates of steamy Gallic stew. I was amazed at how easily the words came, now that I was the cynosure of the discussion. "In America," I told my rapt audience, "the students' issues are life and death. We have a fine educational system, that's true, but what good is it to the boy who is fighting in Vietnam? Or to the black girl in my mother's kitchen, while I am in a classroom?"

"But Janet," Margot interjected, "you must admit that you benefit from things as they are. You must have some loyalty to your family. You are from the upper class."

"My parents are!" My cheeks sizzled. I felt my shoulders go stiff. "I am a student and students are an ignored and despised class. As far as the politicians are concerned, we are invisible. But when the class struggle has been won, I hope none of us will have a class!"

"Communiste!"

"Well, no...socialist! Yes, I'm a socialist." A tangible easing of tension passed among the company. Breaths were taken. A bite or two of dinner. My fork remained at bay. "You can't understand," I continued. "You don't have the war here. Or the race problem. In Berkeley, hundreds of us attended rallies against the war and to support black power. My parents sent me to Paris to get me away from civil rights and anti-war activities in Berkeley..."

"Oh là làa!"

"Oh merde!"

"I detest violence!" I shouted over them. "It makes me sick..."

"But you knew the cause was important. So you did it. You went with them," Bérnard prodded.

"To protest police brutality against the blacks, to protest the huge numbers of blacks fighting the war," I paused, catching my breath. More words came, "And to protest the stubbornness of the government, refusing to allow the university to teach us the truth about the war my own brother is fighting!"

I paused to dab at the tears that had formed in the corners of my eyes. Heard a murmur go around the table. Margot had kept her word. They didn't know about Matt off fighting in Vietnam—not until now.

"I am very sorry to hear this about your brother, Jeanette," Madame said. Many around the table nodded, eyes focused on mine. Madame cleared her throat, "We did not know about this," she continued, "but...you say the university does not teach about the war? You have free press in the United States, n'est-ce pas?"

"We read what government agencies want us to read. And when other voices are heard, those who have gone to Vietnam to see for themselves, there are arranged television responses. They are laughed at or called propagandists. But if you read the articles, as I did, you know they can't have invented what they have seen. Oh yes, we can get an academic degree more easily than a French student. But we hear more lies than truth!"

They had been quiet, struggling to understand my monologue, which was more passionate than grammatical. Now, however, Laurent asked the question that I was sure was on everyone's mind. "Why did you leave your university if you were busy with your comrades, protesting these evils?"

I felt the heat of a blush erupting on my face. "I didn't feel like I was deserting the antiwar movement. I know that's what you feel, Laurent. And you Bérnard. But I had no choice. It was Paris or home to my parents. At least here, I thought I would be putting my time to good use. And with my brother in Vietnam, I did want to give my parents some peace of mind and to enjoy some peace myself. None of us expected what's going on here now!"

"You should have researched the politics of France. Then you would have anticipated it," Bérnard said wryly.

The torrent began again, and to me it was as fresh as the spring breeze. "Don't events prove...?"   "America..." "socialism..." "liberty..." "Va te faire foutre!"

"Bérnard, please, the children..."

I sat in the welcome sunlight listening to three generations argue about politics, a fourth quiet, listening. This was something I had never experienced before. I was remembering why I had chosen France. Mother had thought the French would teach me some degree of refinement. Aaron always referred to France as the "Land of Liberty" and Paris as the "City of Light." What I had wanted was to spend time in a country devoted not only to art and culture, but also to liberty and truth. "Liberty on the Barricades" by Eugene Delacroix was my favorite French painting. Mother preferred Matisse.

Mme. Bouleaux' glass rang out once more and Margot clapped her hands. Everyone was quiet. "First, I will give you some information," said the matriarch. "Then, we will listen to the news. Then, we can debate. But everyone must listen to everyone else's opinions. Politely. Eh, Bérnard? No swearing."

"And the information, Maman?" Margot said, as if this cue had been rehearsed.

"The information is this. Although in the family our sympathies may be with the young people, we feel it is our responsibility to keep you all safe. No one will go out to the manifestations. No exceptions!"

Bérnard growled, "And are your sympathies with the students, Madame?"

"We are happy to debate the fine points. But security must come first. You are too young to remember what the chaos and bloodshed of war is like."

"You and your children, Madame. All are safe and fearful. Self-protective. Self-righteous, bored and boring, petit bourgeois."

"Thank you, Bérnard," said Mme. Bouleaux with perfect composure, "it is so nice of you to say so."

Bérnard caught up with Elizabeth and me on our way to the first house after dinner. "Please walk with me," whispered Bérnard.

"I'm going up to rest," I said. He narrowed his eyes on me like he didn't believe me. Just minutes before, I had been as wound up in the discussion as Yao-Yao with a new ball of yarn.

But I wasn't avoiding Bérnard. Events of the night before and the effort of listening and expressing myself had drained me of energy. And the hoop of sympathetic eyes, which had snared me at dinner, now trapped me with desperate thoughts of Matt, off in the jungle with deadly fire all around him. The French had their cause. I had mine. I wanted nothing more than to carry my worries off to my own corner.

Bérnard had not budged. His face achieved a peculiar aura of brooding, as if he was in trouble and resentful that no one around would help. Elizabeth was already inside the foyer, waiting for me with the door open. "Go ahead," I told her. "I'll be up in a little while." I followed Bérnard under the archway and out onto Port-Royal.

"To a café?" Bérnard asked in his usual verbal shorthand.

"No. Let's walk, as you said. I'll fall asleep if I sit down."

His face relaxed as we headed up the broad Boulevard. He said, "I have thought this all along. Now I know. You are the only one at Mme. Bouleaux's who truly understands me."

I suddenly felt alarmed. "Bérnard, you know that Teodor Pelnar and I..."

"Yes, yes, of course," he swatted my assumption away as if it were an irritating insect. "I mean, you are sympathetic."

"What about Laurent?"

"Laurent is worshipping me, like a hero. This is not reality. This is not the understanding of a true progressive youth." He used the words jeunesse progresif, and I accepted that those words united us across the geography of the world.

"And why do you bring this up today?"

"Because I know now why you were on the barricade behind Laurent. Afraid and with the responsibility for Elizabeth. Oh yes! Laurent told me you would have followed him, but there was the girl. Before, I suspected that you were a shallow, spoiled American. Even with your race sympathies. Plenty of rich people in America have race sympathies. But now I am sure...now I know about Vietnam!"

I stopped walking and stared at him like he had just grown whiskers. "What does last night have to do with Vietnam?"

His grin inflated into a mocking laugh and his crooked teeth shone with blotchy yellow nicotine stains. "You know. How it all began. At Nanterre. Why you support the students. We are not going to stop either. And now that the Americans are here..."

"What in the world are you talking about?"

He frowned, puzzled. "We are not understanding each other."

"Vraiment," I said. Truly. I wondered if this conversation could possibly get more absurd. I sighed impatiently. "Listen, Bérnard. What I know about Nanterre doesn't have anything to do with Vietnam. And the Americans are here? Yes, I am an American and I am here..."

"Okay okay. You are more ignorant than I ever supposed."

"I'm not ignorant! I just don't know what's going on half the time. It's the language!"

"Okay, okay," he repeated, calming himself and stroking my shoulder and arm, one, two, three, as if I were a recalcitrant household pet. "Yesterday, the Americans and North Vietnamese agreed to meet in Paris for peace talks."

"Yes, I know. And that's wonderful..."

"But months ago, after the Tet Offensive, the French students acted. Showing sympathy for the Vietnamese. And admiration. There were two groups at Nanterre, both against the war. Comités Vietnam de Base and Comité Vietnam National."

I translated the names of the groups in my head: Basic Committees on Vietnam and National Committee on Vietnam. "Here in France? I had no idea antiwar groups existed here."

"At the University of Paris campus at Nanterre. Cette miette..." he pursed his lips together and spit out the word. "That crumb...of a university the Gaullists toss to the children of workers outside Paris. It's a lousy place. But a friendly place for radicals. Maoists. Trotskyites. Anarchists. They hate your war."

"Not my war!"

"Of course. Sorry. That's why we are talking now. My own little group stood with the CVB and CVN against the war." We had reached the Place Port-Royal and Bérnard hesitated, then turned back toward home instead of heading toward the University. I followed along.

"So, what did these groups do?" I prodded.

"Occupied a salon des faculté at Nanterre. Talked about students and workers' struggle. Talked and talked. How to change the university. Freedom to discuss the issues honestly in class. And better life. Sex in dormitories. Smoking in classrooms. And society. To stop imperialism. All that. But mostly to protest the Vietnam War. To get attention for their feelings. That was March 22."

I was quiet for a long minute as we walked along.

Bérnard could see my turmoil and remained silent. I had heard of the March 22 Movement and its redheaded leader, Dany Cohn-Bendit. Irena had tried to talk to me about it! The students in the café had thrown the date around like a saint's birthday. I had never been able to figure out why a movement was named after a calendar date. Now I understood! This wasn't just a gripe about the terrible educational system or even about free speech. Not merely leftists against rightists either. Mme. Bouleaux had misrepresented the whole affair.

Suddenly, an insignificant pebble dropped into a pond on March 22 seemed to spread its ripples throughout France, Europe, Asia, America, the world. How mistaken I had been to consider their fight as theirs alone! I felt as if the electric current connecting this latest French student revolution with the Vietnam War was flowing through every vein and artery in my body. I could barely breathe. I stared at Bérnard. His back was to the sun, his face obscure. "So...what was last night?" I asked. "More against Vietnam?"

"We tried to meet again at Nanterre. Now we are a large crowd, so bien sûr, no good without loudspeakers. A group had to break into the Dean's office to take loudspeakers. Just to borrow them. Then they closed the whole campus because—so they said!—of threats by a right wing group! We brought the meeting to the courtyard at the Sorbonne." His face twisted with the memory and he hissed through his teeth, "I never thought Rector Roche would dare close the Sorbonne!"

"And your group wouldn't leave, so the police came to enforce the closing?" I asked, conjuring up images of the Berkeley and Oakland police dragging war protesters from sit-ins and teach-ins.

"Oui, c'est ça. But I am quick. They couldn't get us all. By the night, a couple hundred in the courtyard had become thousands on the streets," he finished, proudly.

"So, it all started because of Vietnam. Because of us."

"That's how it started, but now it is more!"

We were nearly home, so I took Bérnard's arm and guided him across the street. We walked silently along the wall separating the sidewalk from the Val de Grâce hospital. I said, "You sound happy that it has started and happy that it will continue."

"Oui. I am socialist, Jeanette," Bérnard said, lifting his wiry frame up just a little straighter. "I belong to a small group of friends. There are many such petits groupes. We are not Maoists or Trotskyites but like those, we want to change everything here in France. And it should be changed. Starting with the University. This is our moment!"

"So, you want to change American policy and change France, too?"

"Non. We don't think we can change America. There we just express our sympathy. But in France, they won't even let us do that. We have no freedom! So we need to change France."

As we re-crossed the street, Bérnard continued to speak, now in soft, soothing tones. "Come with me to a meeting of my group. I will explain things to you if you do not understand. You will make friends. You will see."

We had reached the curlicues of the 95 and the sheltering archway. Bérnard was inviting me to be part of his group. I paused in the half-light, my tears blurring the field of diamond shapes surrounding us. Ashamed, I told him, "I belonged to a group in Berkeley. I'm afraid I wasn't very useful to them."

"But you will be useful!" Bérnard's fingers tightened on my shoulder. "Your brother is in the war. You have been in the Berkeley university. A famous place for freedom. And you have read much...that is what you said at dinner. You have ideas we may not know about. We are a group that believes in listening. And I want you to understand our ideas. Don't you want to?" he pleaded.

I moaned softly, thrilled and anguished and grateful, all at the same time. "Of course," I said. "I will come." I extended my hand to Bérnard. He shook it with a calm, genial nod that felt like a first hello. "When is the meeting?"

TWENTY-FOUR

MY DATE WITH TEO wasn't until eight, but I decided to say nothing to Bérnard about leaving the group early. In the middle of a revolution, I surmised, Saturday was just another night.

Tired as I was, I had a difficult time falling asleep that afternoon and then slept fitfully. When I dragged myself downstairs after my nap, there was a message from Teo canceling our date. He would explain at school on Monday. It had to do with the "street fighting" between the police and students. There was also a letter from Matt. The great American hero, I thought. Waves of resentment passed through me, quickly overridden by waves of guilt. Elizabeth and Laurent stood close by, ignoring me and talking about their own letters. Bérnard had sworn me to secrecy about the meeting. "Not even Elizabeth," he had said. "Especially not Elizabeth."

I excused myself to walk back over to Hélène's deserted salon for the dutiful reading. Once sequestered in the salon, I sat there curled up on a loveseat for a full minute before opening Matt's letter. Then, prepared for yet another boring note from the infamous Southeast Asian Front, I began to read.

> *April 21, 1968*
> *Dear Jan,*
>
> *How are you? I'm fine. How's France? Bet the food is great. The food here stinks. Everything does. Well, this letter won't be as cheerful as all the others I've written, so fasten your seatbelt.*
>
> *I've got a new friend here. Her name is Lue and she thinks I should write this letter to you. I told her all about you.*
>
> *Things have been more peaceful since the Tet Offensive. I got by that one okay, but some of my buddies didn't. Got blown to smithereens. Guys with faces, families, you know what I mean. I dream about those faces, their wiseacre voices. It's a bitch sometimes, but things are getting better.*
>
> *I'll tell you, since the action wound down, I consider myself damn lucky. You know about my assignment as a mechanic and truck driver. But what I never told you is that one of my jobs is to deliver food supplies to an orphanage in the neighborhood. From the start, the Vietnamese kids (notice I don't call them gooks anymore) gave me a boost and I stayed to help feed them. That's when I became friends with Lue. She's been to school in the city before she got married and she takes care of the orphans. She's no babe, probably quite a few years older than me.*
>
> *Lue and I are real tight. The two of us sit in this damn sticky heat with the kids playing all around and we just talk and talk. Lue speaks great English. And she's smart, like you. Her husband and two kids were killed when an American bomb landed on her small village. Now Lue tries to teach the kids here. She loves them all. She says, "I've got long arms." Having Lue as a real friend has been stretching my orders as far as I can get away with, but I figure I can always point to our little "Pocket Guide to Vietnam." Believe it or not, one*

of the "Nine Simple Rules" of our mission is to make
friends among the common people. But it also says that
the Cong will try to turn the Vietnamese people against
us. No one ever told me that the "common" people are
real, flesh and blood, brave, nice people, and that they
are against us from the word go. In the Vietnamese
language, they call this the "American War." Sure,
there are South Vietnamese politicians and such that
want us here, but most people just want to plant their
fields, eat everyday, and live. So, about the pow-wow
over there in Paris, I sure as hell hope it works, the
quicker the better!

Lately, my army buddies and I have begun to use
the phrase FTA: "free the army" or "fuck the army"
('scuse me, Jan). You don't use FTA unless you are sure
of the sympathies of your buddy. So anyway, you get
the picture. I'm trusting you to keep my new opinions to
yourself. Write soon.

Your brother, Matt

Still startled by Matt's words, I noticed the time and forced myself upstairs to get into some warmer clothes. As I was searching for a wool scarf, I came across the big peace button that I had carried with me from California and secreted away in the back of the armoire. I groaned, shaking just a little as I grasped it. I brought it out and opened my hand, then stood for a moment admiring the blood-red symbol with the ragged edges. As I pinned it on my sweater, my resolve toughened until I knew that I was turning a corner here in France, now more surely than I had that afternoon with Todd on Sproul Plaza.

Walking alone in the twilight, checking the address against my pocket map, I reached Bérnard, who stood waiting for me on a quiet street off the bustling Rue Mouffetard. Behind him was a charming, narrow house with navy blue shutters and a gigantic iron knocker on the front door. "Pas mal, n'est-ce pas?" Bérnard said. "Une maison est un héritage heureux." The happy inheritance was, indeed, a real house, squished in between faux-balconied apartments. I counted four stories.

As we entered a crowded living room, Bérnard put his finger up to his lips. The speaker stood on the first, broad step of a staircase, which made a convenient platform. As he spoke, he pounded his right fist down into his left palm, marking the unsteady beat of his words. The angry fist unnerved me. His features were more Algerian than French. But his dusky face reminded me of all the insinuations I'd heard when French bigots spoke about the Algerians, so I wanted to trust him. "We believe in the 'uninterrupted revolution' that Mao Tse-Tung has perpetuated in the Peoples' Republic of China. Whether east to the Soviets or west to the Americans, we find nothing of value. In those societies, all imagination is crushed! And the French Communists? Totalement inutile." Completely useless.

I leaned over to Bérnard and whispered, "I thought you said you weren't a Maoist."

"Shh. Just listen." He led me over to sit by a big, blond girl called Annette who I had seen once or twice before, going off with Bérnard in the evenings. I lost track of the speaker's diatribe. Bérnard squeezed in next to Annette and put his arm across her shoulders. She moved over to accommodate me on one end of a sofa. A beautiful young man with wild golden hair and perfect, Apollonian features, sat on the arm of the other end of the sofa with his hand casually resting on Bérnard's shoulder. I caught myself staring and forced my eyes back across the room.

There were about thirty boys and girls gathered, several of them more dressed up than I would have expected, as if they had just come from jobs. Others wore jeans and tee-shirts, tie-dyed or stained with peace symbols. My eyes threaded through the crowd, searching for the older faces that had always been there in my Berkeley group, lurking in the background, manipulating the young leaders. Not here. Not today. There were only people about my age or into their twenties. Some squirmed in their seats, carrying on side conversations, others appeared restless or angry or bored. But most were earnestly focused on the bearded, brown-skinned speaker. He was talking about how Mao encouraged the young to take action. The old to make way for the future.

How different from my country, I thought, where the young go out to kill and die to preserve the lifestyle of the old.

"But in China today," our instructor's tone suddenly shifted. "Mao has set the people against one another. China is no longer a model for us. The dictator believes that the culture will not change without coercion, bloodshed, and brainwashing. We believe there is a better way!" His fist smacked his open hand. People were calling out for him to continue.

"I will tell you what we do not believe. We do not believe in polemical categories! We need to talk to each other. Freely. We cannot like what everyone says. But we need to have the discussion. Yes! The endless discussion. We need to work together, everyone who cares about France and the future, to figure out what kind of society we want to be. But first, who must we get rid of...?" and the crowd was shouting, "De Gaulle!" Their fists were raised and the speaker asked them, "Who must go?" And again, "De Gaulle!" "And when must he go?" "Maintenant!"

My heart literally skipped a beat. The speaker had rejected catégories polémiques. Yes, without ever knowing it, this is what I had been waiting for. He had spoken against the polemical categories that alienate people and make them cynical and hopeless.

In the shadows by the stairway, I spotted a familiar ginger-colored head. It was Gabi Souris! And by her side, listening intently, and rubbing his palms together with fat, cataleptic fingers, was Mme. Bouleaux's little man, Frederic!

"Bérnard! What are Gabi and Frederic doing here?" I whispered, leaning over Annette's soft arm. Bérnard put his finger up again, and I interpreted: "Silence!" The silence about Frederic and Gabi's participation would have to last far longer than the duration of this meeting, and I knew I could count on the same from them. None of us would benefit by having our landladies' oppose our political activities. I caught Gabi's eye and held my hand up in an abbreviated greeting. She seemed unfazed, copying my signal, and returning my smile with a conspiratorial wink. Clearly, Bérnard had told her I would be there.

People were clapping, turning heads, and talking among themselves. It was hot in the room. I took my arms out of my coat, unbuttoned my cuffs and pushed my shirt sleeves up above my elbows. Reaching down, I let my fingers play over the glossy surface of my peace button. Annette was staring at it. She nodded her approval. I pulled my hand away self-consciously, feeling warmth and color spread from the symbol up into my face.

They were switching speakers. There were isolated shouts, something about a list of demands. Then, the beautiful young Apollo sitting next to Bérnard moved to the base of the stairs.

Bérnard shouted, "Three cheers for Remi Guitry and the rest of the student leaders released from the fascist prisons!" and an exuberant cry went up, deafening in the small space of the living room, then another, and finally the third. Remi stood red-faced and disarmed in front of his comrades. He put his hands up to quiet the group.

"This will only be the beginning," Remi said in an edgy, warning tone. His eyes were glazed with lack of sleep, but his energy and enthusiasm for his subject were revealed with every bounce of his body and jerk of his glowing head. "Our three basic demands—the withdrawal of police, release of all the prisoners, opening of the Sorbonne—these demands are like the overture of a great concert. The real symphony—the fight for the new France—begins on the streets of Paris! Yes, my friends, this is only the introduction..."

"...also like the frame around a painting!" came Annette's grating voice. She grinned mischievously, waving her two large, clumsy hands in the air above the crowd for attention. Several in the crowd laughed, and a bit of the tension was released.

"As usual," said Remi, his eyes rolling upward in his head, "I stand corrected by my elder sister." More snickers from the crowd. They had heard these shenanigans before.

"Okay, okay," Remi continued. "Paris, Berlin, America, this is a revolution of the young against the old, an international revolution. I have spoken to some of the other leaders. Cohn-Bendit from the March 22nd Movement..." Clapping hands from the audience. A sharp, quick whistle from Bérnard. "...and Jacques Sauvageot." This time, boos and catcalls. "Please, please. Sauvageot is one of us. We are all in this together. Now, listen," he quieted them with his hands and his deep blue eyes. "We must hold together in this effort if we are to succeed."

Murmurs of affirmation wafted through the crowd. "Now! We have spoken about basic demands, but we agree that we must take advantage of both the students' mood and popular support from the people of France to bring the young workers into our struggle. We will raise our voices in open, free, imaginative, endless debate! Endless, permanent revolution!" Bérnard's hands were no longer on Annette, but lifted and pounded together in response to Remi's words. His dark eyes shone in his thin, sallow face. Everyone in the crowd was clapping and shouting and talking and laughing. I clapped in wonderment. And Annette waved one little finger back in forth rhythmically as if she were conducting a miniature orchestra. I did not know what to make of her ridiculous smirk.

Bérnard was rising from the sofa, still clapping. Then he was in front of the group, whispering something into Remi's ear. The two of them were glancing back over toward the sofa. Remi pushed both hands into the air and waved them over his head. When his petit groupe was quiet, he announced, "And now I have a special treat. Bérnard has brought his friend, Jeanette, an American student from the Berkeley university."

A brief hum filled the room, then everyone was turning my way, anticipating. I felt the heat rise in my face and glimpsed my hands, knotted tightly in my lap. I shut my eyes. Sweat felt like a flammable liquid. Flames engulfed my hair, singed its roots, and I lifted my eyes and wondered how everyone could remain so calm with my head on fire. What could I possibly say to these people? They wanted a hero from the Berkeley myth, not a girl with une voix aigue, my weak, high-pitched voice, spouting cliches in bad French. They were sitting patiently. They were waiting...

Then I felt Annette's arm come around my shoulders and I heard her soft croaking close to my ear. "Jeanette, écoute. I know I am a crass girl,"—she used the word grossiere, and I knew that she was referring to more than her gross bulk—"but even so, these people, my comrades, they listen to me when I have something honest to say. We will wait for you to find the words. Please, whatever you have to tell us about American students...or just about what is in your heart right now! We want to listen to you."

This was not the sarcastic Annette of a few moments before. Her face was tensed with the earnestness of her message. Then she was smiling kindly, gripping my arm with her generous, fleshy hand.

I gazed around the room. Thirty or more calm but eager expressions, pairs and pairs of attentive eyes, and there was Gabi by the stairs, Frederic by her side. He was inert, expectant, waiting with the rest. But Gabi smiled encouragingly. Then she blew me a kiss, a pixie with scarlet puckered lips and upraised fingers that fluttered my way like small, pale doves. I realized that the space around my head felt cool and that the space in the room was filled with people that were on my side.

I slid up to the edge of the sofa, my hands resting loosely on my knees. "I am...just so happy to be here because...exactly because...you see..." I took a breath and blurted out, "...listening to each other is something they aren't very good at in America."

I paused. They hadn't moved. I continued. "Parents don't listen to children. The government doesn't listen to its people. And even in the student movement, everyone talks, no one listens." Then I was telling them about my parents, my brother in Vietnam, my involvement in the anti-war movement in Berkeley. How the movement wasn't having much impact because of the competition between groups and the overgrown egos within each group. "Never once in my group in Berkeley," I said, "did anyone ever ask me what I thought. I was only a secretary, answering phones, stuffing envelopes. But like any good worker, I had ideas and opinions...and they were...not... listening..." They began to talk among themselves, but soon quieted each other down so that I could continue.

"But here, all ideas are out in the open, on the table. That is what will make your country—my adopted country—grow strong. Being in your group is like a miracle for me, and the second miracle today! This afternoon, I received a letter from my brother in Vietnam...and I was surprised by this letter..."

Before me, bodies that had slumped while I spoke were again pulled to attention. I had stopped—not in response to the motion—but because I realized that perhaps Matt would not want his sister to share his deepest feelings with a group of total strangers on the other side of the world. I put my hand to my side and felt the lump where I had placed the folded air weight paper in my jeans pocket. I had not wanted to leave it behind in my room. I thought I would carry it with me for a day or two, or perhaps for the rest of my life.

Bérnard, still up by Remi's side, spoke to me gently, "Jeanette, please. If you do not want to continue, we will understand. But if you have a current opinion from a soldier in Vietnam, we want to hear. Naturally, we are all concerned..." The eyes in his thin face were a deep, moist brown, needy as a calf's. I sunk my gaze back into them and reached into my pocket. I could hear the paper crinkle in the silence of the room. Carefully, so as not to tear it, I opened my big brother's very special letter and began to read. I read the English and explained in French. And when my little voix aigue began to quiver, I just kept reading and was sure that no one noticed, intent as they were on listening to the words.

TWENTY-FIVE

MAY 5, 1968

> *Dear Aaron,*
> *It's Sunday, thank God. I finally have time to think about everything that's happened in the last 24 hours. So much! Writing to you always helps me to sort things out.*
> *I hope you weren't too worried after my Friday night (okay, early Saturday morning) letter about the street demonstration and police counter-attack. That night was a turning point for the French students and for the country. But yesterday was the turning point for me. I made a discovery about the Parisian student protests and later, I received what we would call a "meaningful" letter from Matt. The connection jolted me like an electric shock.*
> *First, midday dinner with the family was a political discussion. I let it slip about Matt for the first time. Bérnard heard this, and after the meal, we had the most amazing talk. I understand now that the whole French student mess began with their protest against the war in Vietnam! We are all in this international struggle together, all the young people in the world. I'd heard this before, of course, but I didn't absorb the depth of it.*

Standing there on the street with Bérnard, it hit me that their struggle is my struggle!

Then, later in the afternoon, the letter from Matt. I'm sure before I left, I told you that he was stationed at a base outside Saigon during the Tet Offensive. Well, his letters then were in his usual light, cocky tone. Something like, "I've become a varsity sprinter. You learn to listen for the direction of in-coming missiles. Then it's like the crowd roars as you race for cover."

In this new letter, he wrote about it again, more seriously, mourning his buddies who did not make it to shelter in time when those missiles landed. And he wrote about his job as a truck driver, delivering food to an orphanage. Sounds pretty safe, doesn't it? Anyway, at the orphanage, he met an older, educated Vietnamese woman he just calls Lue. Sounds like she's just a good friend, someone easy for him to talk to, but she has changed his point of view about the war. Did you know the Vietnamese call this war the "American War"? Our war, in their country. And the soldiers say FTA—fuck the army. That's what Matt wrote me.

So, that's the amazing part. Matt has turned against the only allegiance he has ever known— the unquestioning loyalty to all things American. He's asked me to keep his new opinions to myself, but I'm going to assume he meant he wasn't ready to share with our parents.

Last night, I went to the meeting of Bérnard's group—they call it a "petit groupe" here (the English say "grouplet"), because there are a lot of little ones instead of big national names like SDS. There, for the first time in my life, I felt that people I respected were listening to me. Thirty or more pairs of eyes, intent on what I was saying about America and Vietnam.

Somehow others manage to commit to activism, as if it were something in the temperature of their blood. But for me, as for you, getting involved in political causes has never been easy. For you it has been skepticism, for me it has been timidity and something more—the historian in my nature that makes me stand back in every situation and observe, not with the Aaron Becker wisecrack forming in my brain, but with a kind of objectivity that separates me from those who are supposed to be my close comrades. Perhaps this time I will have the inner strength to follow through on my convictions.

I do appreciate your concern for my safety and I will do my best to be careful. I was sorry to read that your father has not come through for you, but with this new trouble here, perhaps Canada is the right place for you after all. I write to you from my new home on "Planète Française." I surprise myself by my feeling of reliance on your return letters. Perhaps your ironic sense is the balance to my serious nature, which takes everything to heart.

    Your rebel friend,
    Jeanette

When I arrived in the dining room of the first house Monday morning, Bérnard was waiting for me. Pitchers of steaming hot coffee and chocolate, plates of crusty rolls and pots of butter and jam were set out on the table. Margot was fussing in the kitchen as usual. No one else was around.

"I'm glad you're early," said Bérnard. "I was counting on it."

"I'm anxious to get to school before Teo goes to class." Then, even though I knew Margot could hear nothing we were saying at all, I leaned forward, speaking in a husky, urgent whisper. "I want to tell him about your group."

"Our group. Yours too," he corrected me.

"That's nice. Thanks."

"Today the students will take back the Sorbonne. Are you with us?"

The promise of action in Bérnard's voice tensed every muscle in my body. "Taking back? What do you mean? How can they...?"

"Sheer numbers will crush the police. We'll demand they give it back."

"Oh zut, Bérnard! I want to be there. But I must meet Teo this morning. I promised him tonight..." I broke off mid-sentence, staring over at a stack of porcelain cups balanced three-high. Bérnard's dark face broke into a knowing sneer.

"Well, you're going to miss our group making history. Perhaps you could persuade Teo to join us?"

"No...you don't understand." I sighed deeply, then blurted out my boldfaced lie: "I'm supposed to go on the American Express trip overnight to see chateaux...the Loire Valley. We leave this morning and come back tomorrow afternoon. I've got a reservation I made long ago."

"Yes. Of course," he said. "It's an excellent tour, I hear. And very romantic."

"Romantic? Oh...oh you don't understand anything, but I can't explain...believe me, Bérnard, when I tell you I'll be working for the revolution tonight."

At this, the inverted vees of Bérnard's brows lifted a full inch. Then, he frowned. "Be careful, Jeanette. These Iron Curtain countries don't fool around."

"I told the others that I'm going to tour chateaux with my schoolmate, Claire Caplan," I continued. "You won't say anything...?"

Bérnard stifled a laugh. "What do you think? I gossip with our landladies? Anyway, I'll be very busy out on Boul' Mich'. And don't worry about missing history. Like Remi said, this is only the beginning." He grinned ear to ear, boyishly bouncing toward the table, grabbing a cup. "When you join us again," he said, "the University will be ours."

I laughed out loud, as exhilarated as if I'd just gulped the whole pitcher of coffee. "I've got to go," I said. I chose the biggest roll, gripped the overnight case I had packed and waved goodbye, running out the door just as Elizabeth was walking in with Lili and La Petite Jeanette in tow. The little girls were still rubbing sleep out of their eyes. "I'm just running today, Elizabeth. The Chateaux Country trip, remember? I'll see you tomorrow..."

"Tootaloo. Have a good time," she answered, wiggling her fingers in the air to bid me farewell. She disappeared inside with her two sleepy charges.

I ran all the way up the Rue d'Assas, hoping to catch Teo out in front of L'Alliance. When we had said goodbye Friday night, he had let me know that Monday was the night when he had been informed he might be able to speak with the Prestup. How he arranged the meeting without Miroslav suspecting anything, he never revealed. But if tonight was to be the night, I wanted my alibi to be pinned down. I had spread the word in the house about the trip and telephoned Claire Caplan, who would understand romance, but not revolution.

I approached the familiar ochre building and ran along its façade. There was Teo, just coming down the street from the other direction.

"We need to talk," I said without a greeting, out of breath.

"We're still meeting tonight?" he asked, anxiously.

"Yes. Of course." We sat on the low wall outside the iron-spike fence. I explained briefly about everything that had happened since Friday night. I emphasized the letter from Matt and the Nanterre-Vietnam connection, and told him about the meeting Saturday night and the group's plans for today. All the while, Teo listened intently but kept gazing up toward the school building, then back toward me with wise, kind eyes. "I didn't tell anyone I'd come to Boul' Mich'," I concluded wistfully, "but I do have this day now, since I'm supposed to be leaving town soon. I wish I were invisible!"

Teo stroked my hair, a worried line bisecting his broad face. "Jeanette, you do not know what is going to happen out there this morning. I don't want you to go. Please, just wait for me until after class and we'll spend the afternoon together. Then, we will go to the pension tonight. That is our plan. Your promise to help."

"But Teo, I know you support the students. I even thought we might go together..."

Teo threw his head back, but no laugh came from his lips. It was as if he was asking his godless heaven why this girl was so naïve. His head shook from side to side, first at the angels, then at me. "Cherie, please. The police are in control..."

"But Bérnard..."

"Bérnard?! I thought you did not like that fellow..."

"He's different when you get to know him. I want you to meet him again and start over with him. And to meet his friend Remi, too. Remi's the leader..."

"...okay, I will, ça va, ça va. If you trust them, I will meet them." He was frowning. I kept still, knowing what a surprise my about-face must be for him.

"Cherie," he said, wrapping his hands around my two arms, "I am sure that Bérnard has his hopes. I have the same hopes, believe me. But I don't imagine it will be so easy. And I cannot be there. I would risk being forced out of the country by the French or called home by my parents or my government. That was why I could not even come out to see you Saturday evening. There are many ways my plans can be changed for me. I am sorry."

Probably better than any other girl Teo could have been counting on, I understood perfectly well how one's plans can be changed because of political protest. I'm sure my head was drooping almost to my chest when I said, "I *do* understand. I will go to a café and read my book. Then, where should we meet?"

"Somewhere away from the action, where you will not meet your classmates or your comrades. A busy, commercial place...let's meet at Sévres Babylon, the *Métro* entrance."

I did not want to sightsee or shop, even though Sévres Babylon was a good neighborhood for both. We could not head back toward the *quartier latin*. So, without making a decision, as if we'd planned it all along, Teo and I began to walk slowly, holding hands, in a direction away from the city's center. Minutes crept by, then hours. The dull sun gradually dropped in front of us as we headed west. In halting syllables, we spoke about our families, about Matt, the war, the waste of all war. Cringing in the shadow of L'Ecole Militaire. Crossing the Champs du Mars. Snubbing the Tour Eiffel. Stopping to buy a bag of almonds at a sweet shop.

That was when I began to talk about my life in Berkeley and how I could not go on with school and normal life as a college coed while my brother was in Vietnam.

"That is why I was so happy," I said, "to be part of Bérnard's group. *J'etais ravi.*" Thrilled, was the word I had sought. Teo smiled, tight-lipped.

Sullenly, he asked, "You know their group will be caught up in violence, even if they do not want it?"

"But I already know what I want to tell them when I go to the next meeting!" I pulled myself up straight. "I've seen first-hand the anti-war violence at home. But here, the protesters seem to be listening to each other, and to reason. I want to speak to them about Mahatma Gandhi, about peaceful protest and passive resistance. The ideas that worked so well for Martin Luther King Jr.!"

Teo leaned forward and stared at the sidewalk a moment, then tilted his head back up to me. "Dr. King was assassinated," he said in a deadpan voice.

"King did a lot of good before he died," I grumbled. "His methods were successful in plenty of situations."

Teo shook his head, then tried again. "Even King knew that there must be violence for the television cameras. And now, television has a new technique. Now they put the action on the air almost as it is happening. Do you know about this? It is very powerful. The leaders of groups like yours want to take advantage of this."

I nodded and felt my body slump. "Yes, a friend of mine once said that performance is the central strategy of the radical groups."

"I'm sorry, Jeanette," Teo said. "I know this is what you must do and I'm not arguing with you. I worry that you may find more danger than you expect...but your efforts are no less valuable than my own."

"And you might have added 'no less dangerous,'" I said. He snickered and started to walk along again, pushing the open bag of nuts in my direction. I shook my head, pouted. "But this is so important. Lives are at stake, my own brother..."

He sighed. "I'm sorry, Jeanette," he repeated. "You are a smart woman. Your group is lucky to have you."

"You really think so?"

"Absolutely. Yes. Now, please..." He held out the little bag once again and I took an almond. I laughed and shook my head at my own childish need for Teo's approval.

We reached the Seine along the Quai de Grenelle and conjured a malicious image of Miroslav growing weary behind us. Opposite stood the boring cement rotunda of Radio-France. I had read that de Gaulle himself had inaugurated it just a few years before, no doubt taking credit, I thought wryly, even for modern popular music. I was about to repeat this wisecrack to Teo when, as if mumbling to himself, he said, "My father is in charge of a segment of radio transmitters."

"Mmm...? Oh, I see. That sounds like an important job."

The corner of his lips warped into an angry sneer. "Yes, he is a trusted man. My father is *quite* a good communist."

I took in his tone. "Some students in Paris are sure that communism or at least socialism is the answer. In Berkeley, too. I'm not clear on the politics of it yet, but I believe some people have to give up great wealth so others can live comfortably. I believe in fairness. And democracy, of course. Freedom of speech."

"Well, Jeanette, I don't like to criticize you. So I will suggest: I have come west, you should come east."

"Go ahead and criticize me. But at least socialism is an ideology that wants the best for all people. The foundation of our capitalism is not even survival, but only greed."

"We are not talking about ideology. We are talking about a political regime, run by bureaucrats like my father who do not care about freedom as much as they do about power. That is, perhaps, not so different from your country?"

I was silent for a moment, feeling awareness rising inside me like a wave of nausea. I turned to lean on the wall separating us from the Seine and examined the unforgiving water, brown and brittle in the late afternoon sun. Teo gazed across the river toward Radio-France. Then, he continued in a matter-of-fact tone.

"My father is a minor official for Prague's radio. A bureaucrat. Now, the image of a bureaucrat is of a man sitting at his desk all day, dreaming about his wife or his mistress, twisting a paper clip until it becomes thin and breaks. This is not accurate. He is quite busy, this bureaucrat. He must keep accounts, hire workers and check on equipment maintenance. He writes reports, then he makes proposals, and then, of course, he must call meetings to discuss the proposals. And always the sub-agenda: watch who is in and out of favor, and how do you say it... *manoeuvre* for a good position."

"We say *jockey for position* in English. A jockey is a race horse rider," I explained.

One bitter hoot escaped Teo's lips. "That is quite appropriate. So what does *your* father do at his job? Can we compare them?"

"My father is Vice President of Finance for a very large company. Let's see..." I thought for a moment. I really knew so little about what Daddy did all day. "I guess he keeps accounts, whom to hire, and how much to pay them. And he sometimes talks about what the customers will want to buy. Of course, he attends meetings where he makes reports and they discuss all these things."

"So, that is not so different from a communist bureaucrat! Very like my father's life. But do you see? Here in Paris, I am reading books about economics. The businessman's motivations are to satisfy the customer and to make big money doing it. The bureaucrat must satisfy the Party to advance his own standing."

"That doesn't sound very fair or for the people's benefit. And no free speech either."

Teo put his arm around me and squeezed. "It is not what most young Czechs would choose." He sighed. "We have much to teach each other, *cherie*. But today, we have come a long way. Are you as hungry as I am?"

It was after eight before Teo guided me back in the direction of the Latin Quarter to a small *pension* on Rue du Cherche-Midi. The setting was not as glamorous as the mission. The proprietress made sure we knew the location of the communal toilet. Then she walked us down a narrow hallway lit with bare, low-wattage bulbs placed at infrequent intervals. She left us at the door to our room.

Just inside, we both stood still for a long moment. Then Teo headed for a shaded table lamp between two unmatched chairs. He switched on the light, then removed his tweed sports jacket and settled it neatly on the back of the chair. I could see his white tee-shirt collar beneath his white button-down shirt. "Have a seat, please, Jeanette."

I scanned the sordid room, wondering irrationally if this was going to be an important place I would want to remember. I noticed the maroon and yellow flower buds ranged in vertical lines down the silver-gray wallpaper. Broad, sepia-edged stains spread among the buds like large splotches of fertilizer in a manicured garden. Up against the wall facing us stood an ancient armoire, its doors and sides containing the etched history of the room—carved initials, striations, and curlicues. Back over by the door, mercifully in the shadows, was the rumpled double bed, covered with dull green chintz.

Almost as soon as Teo sat down, he rose again and walked quickly over to the window. Beyond, I presumed, lurked the form of the patient Slovak. Teo had asked the proprietress for a room facing the street and since most preferred rooms above the quiet alley, she granted this request at no extra charge. The window had a yellowing shade and maroon draperies. Teo pulled down the shade. The drapes closed part way and then got stuck. I giggled. "The drapes are maroon," I observed.

"What? The color...?"

"Someone a long time ago actually cared if the drapes matched this floral wallpaper."

"Oh...of course..." Teo ignored my little observation. He waited a moment, then pulled the edge of the shade back less than an inch. "Yes, Miroslav is there," he said, "and he wants me to see him."

As Teo returned to his chair, I jumped up and pulled one of the pillows from the bed to put behind me on the chair. "I might as well get comfortable," I said.

"Could you get the other one for me?" Teo asked. With a force that satisfied, I threw the second pillow across the room. Teo stretched out his long arms to make the catch. I felt jittery, as if there were bugs under the top layer of my skin. All I had to do was sit here. Teo had promised to respect my innocence. The rest was just a meeting between Teo and this "Connection" guy. So why was Tinkerbell working overtime in my chest?

Teo pulled a liter bottle of cola out of a brown paper sack. "Miroslav assumes it's red wine," he said, smiling. "I thought this would indicate to you my good intentions. Sorry, no cups though. We'll have to share from the bottle."

Teo flipped off the bottle cap with a little metal opener. From beyond the draped window, we heard a concussive noise that trailed off, then came again. I dissected the sounds: a car had crashed, skidded, and then its engine had exploded in a burst of flames.

"A car...an explosion on Boul' Mich'," I said, nervously.

"Probably. I expect the battle has been going on all day," was all Teo replied. He made no attempt to remind me of his prediction of that morning.

The table lamp was the only light source in the room. I had brought my volume of Colette, as Teo had warned me there might be many hours to pass while waiting for Miroslav's departure. But the light was dim. Clearly this room was not meant for readers.

Teo took a rough swig of his cola, then flexed and rubbed his lips to settle what was left of the carbonation. I was staring at his face, feeling as if I would enjoy being the cola bottle, with his lips on my own. Teo's eyes rose to meet mine, then lowered again. We began to sip and stare at each other with too-serious eyes that spoke of more than politics and social unrest. There was a personal unrest hovering between us, and we both knew it. I was relieved when a topic occurred to me. "So...tell me. What were you doing exactly one year ago tonight?"

Teo cleared his throat importantly. "Not tonight, perhaps," he began. "But almost a whole year ago was when my family first heard about the Prague writers' conference. Many writers dared to express their desire for greater freedom to write about what they pleased. That was a beginning for us." He spoke in the low, intimate tones he always seemed to use when the subject was his homeland. "But then, last October," he continued, "there was a demonstration at my dormitory at the Prague Technical College. Not planned, you understand. Spontaneous. It was such a little thing, and we protested so meagerly. But the response was swift and brutal."

"What was the issue?"

"The electricity in the dormitories had been failing, over and over again. We were fed up and marched down the street with our candles, playing various musical instruments and shouting, 'We want light,' 'We want to study!' That was all!" Teo protested, one palm raised and his face wide open as if he were asking me to forgive the students.

"Then we were marching past Hradcany Castle, the President's residence. As we began to walk down the steep hill of Nerudova Street, the police came. They shouted vile abuse and we shouted back, then they threw tear gas canisters and began to use clubs."

As if on cue we heard another violent burst off in the distance. Teo went to the window again and clicked his tongue when he spotted his tormentor. When he returned, he stood in front of my chair like a giant wall rising over me. Then he got on his knees and held both my hands. "Were you hurt?" I whispered.

"I ran and reached my room, choking from gas. But my classmates said that the police chased them to their rooms and beat them there. I know it was true. I saw the cuts and bruises with my own eyes."

"What a terrible..." I shook my head, leaned forward to kiss him on the cheek, another closer to his lips, a breathy kiss on my target, then another, full and strong. I lifted myself an inch and tugged on my jeans. Contriving to move on from the tension of the moment, I asked, "Was no one held responsible?"

Teo moved back to his chair, then replied, "The hard line communist government of Novotný did not punish the police. A mistake. For Novotný, an old man like de Gaulle, that was the beginning of the end. Public sympathy was with the students, like in Paris. By January, Alexander Dubček was the new leader of the party and the nation."

"And things have been better since, haven't they?"

Teo leaned forward in his chair, rubbed his hands together. "Oh yes. In fact, I had a letter from my sister, Katya, and then one from my mother. Both about May Day in Prague. This is the traditional workers' holiday, but this year, people were outside carrying signs that read 'Make Love Not War' like in America. They were waving American and Israeli flags...you can't imagine how amazing this is! There were Boy Scouts in uniforms and other groups that were banned before. Dubček spoke, and he was smiling, good-natured. Everything was peaceful."

"Could it get angry, like here in Paris or in America?"

Teo paused. He shrugged his shoulders. "Right now everyone is so happy, so who knows? We still have the Soviets watching us. And...there are still men like the Prestup, who are exiled and persecuted merely for speaking about what they believe."

Suddenly, as if remembering why we were there, he jumped up and ran to the window. He stood there, catching his breath. Then touched at the curtains and the shade, moving them just millimeters in order to get a glimpse of the street, and gave a great, winnowing sigh. "Why in the world is he still there?" he asked, exasperated. "I'll miss my chance."

"Sit down and be patient," I counseled. "He will go soon. Maybe we should stand in front of the shade and kiss, like in the Herman's Hermits song. A stupid little song called 'Two Silhouettes on the Shade." I began to hum.

"That's it!" he interrupted. He slapped the palm of his hand against his forehead. "How stupid can a fellow be! We've had the lamp on all this time. What must he be imagining?!" He walked back to the table and turned out the light, then sat back down on the edge of his chair.

"My derrière is sore," he said. "These chairs are terribly uncomfortable."

"Go lie down on the bed. I promise I won't bother you." I teased.

Teo was smiling back. My eyes had adjusted and I could see his face by the streetlight coming in through the window shade. He said, "No, you go lie down. You must be uncomfortable too. I'll keep watch."

I had no idea what to say. Lying down on the bed might be like taking the safety latch off a loaded gun. And with all my rumination on the subject, I still didn't know. The love I felt for Teo was of no consequence. He would want to return to his country, and I most certainly did not want to go with him there. I would never see him again.

With these thoughts came the clench of anger gripping my insides. I wanted nothing more than a loaded gun in my hand. I would never see Teo again, just like I would never see Aaron again. Suddenly, certain loss didn't seem like an excuse to cling to virginity. To the contrary...

"I will not bother you," Teo reassured me. His tone was grave. "Although you must know you bother me terribly, just sitting there and talking to me. I like talking to you so much, Jeanette. Every word of yours is like a new world to me."

I pulled myself up and that made me yawn.

"Go, cherie. It will be okay."

My body was relieved to settle into the soft, lumpy mattress, but before even a few silent seconds had passed, I opened my eyes to see Teo staring at me.

"Is that why you like me, Teo?" I asked. "Because I am from America and you are curious about us?"

"You know that is not the case," Teo stated simply. "We have become very close, very comfortable with each other. Haven't we?"

"Like friends."

"Like friends, yes. And like people who are beginning to love each other."

"Do you love me, Teo?" I asked, quickly adding, "because I think I love you."

"Yes, sweet Jeanette. *Oui, je t'aime*. But we cannot love. We have only a brief time together."

"You keep saying that," I said. "It scares me."

"I will go back to my country and you to yours."

"Can't you lie next to me and talk to me?" I asked. "We'll keep our clothes on."

He turned away and coughed. "Well...so...is that what you used to do with your Berkeley...your Berkeley *pen pal?*" He enunciated the final phrase in English.

My head popped off the pillow, then I set it back down again. A pang of something approaching nostalgia filled me up, a wafting of warmth and security, like the longed-for smell of waxy crayons and freshly-shaved pencils to a child, long after school has let out and the release of summer has settled into doldrums.

But Aaron would never come to this bloody city, and I did not want to leave another struggle for justice to hide out in frozen Canada. Memories and guilt lodged in the pit of my stomach, suddenly shrunk to the size of a shriveled walnut. Here was Teo, a man in every way, risking everything. There was no life outside this room. "Forget about him, Teo. Come here..."

He crossed the room and lay down next to me and without hesitation, he took me into his arms and pressed his large frame hard against mine, kissing me as passionately as he could. Immediately then, he released me. I was breathless, grasping him with my fingertips, but he fled to the far edge of the little bed. "It feels good to lie down," he said. "But life is difficult enough, and I must see the Prestup. So do me a favor and stay on your side of the bed."

I rolled over to curl up on my side, but held my hand out in back of me. Teo took it. "Teo, we must talk, so you won't fall asleep." He chuckled a little and stroked my hand sensuously. I squeezed to stop the stroking, but he would not stop. We lay side by side, with a tension between us like a magnetized metal partition, and we two, reduced to loose raw shavings. An irresistible cosmic force brought us toward the partition, me first, then Teo, to struggle with each other's clothes, gasping for breath. I pulled his head forward to kiss him open-mouthed as I had so many times before, but then Teo's big hands covered me so thoroughly and quickly that I could not touch him back. I sent my hands fluttering around, chasing after his, scratching, squeezing, stroking...my breasts, my hair, my stomach, my thighs. And then *it* was there, poking painfully into my hip, feeling larger than I had ever dreamed it would. I squeezed my legs together, appalled, wondering why I ever thought I could do

234

this thing, clawed at him, trying to get away, but feeling his legs pull heat and goose bumps from my flesh at the same time.

He wrenched my hand away from his shoulder where it pushed uselessly against that broad plane and forced it down there, on top of it. Panting, I tried to pull my hand away. He said nothing. Firmly guided the hand back under a soft, warm pouch, then ran it up, up...I yanked at my hand but he was ready, caught it midair and pulled it insistently back down, forcing it to stroke. Stroke. Stroke. He kissed me gently.

His lips were Teo's lips. His eyes were filled with liquid patience. And I was stroking, stroking of my own free will. I caught my breath as his fingers went into me and he froze, gazed inquiringly into my eyes. Prodding, probing, his fingers began to move...he parted my legs. Without thought or volition, my legs went around and pulled him in. Fire singed my fresh wound, as I had expected, but I held on, my arms and legs around his back, a horse rider entranced with the sensation of the ride, the rhythms deep inside me, afraid of falling off, wanting to go on forever.

I remembered afterwards my surprise, that all the fuss I had always heard about boiled down to a few short, urgently necessary moments culminating in an instant of delicious pain. I heard the wild creaking of the bed and then my own groan, followed by a brief cry, a high-pitched "oh," sounding as if someone had just given me the punch line to a riddle I had posed for myself long ago.

Then we lay there, Teo's arm in back of my neck, a warm, pungent spittle running out of me onto the bed. I forced myself to ignore the disconcerting dampness. My clothes hung loosely from various parts of my flesh like useless appendages. I shook away at the remains, then I remembered the filthy carpet and irrationally, sat up to arrange them on the nightstand.

Teo was quiet, except for an uneven, labored breathing that told me he was wide awake. I rolled in to place my head on his shoulder. The natural position I had assumed was close to fetal, my arms extended over his belly, my knees bent, warm to my toes. Then I became conscious of the smile plastered onto my face. I heard clicks and beetles from the walls. The buzz of someone's voice below. The swish of tires going by on the wet streets. "Don't fall asleep, Teo," I said, squeezing him around the middle.

He leaned over to kiss me on the forehead, then rose to peek outside the window. "Enfin!" he hissed. "At last! He is gone." Hastily, he gathered his clothes.

"Bon chance, Teo. I know this is what you wanted...."

He sat by me on the edge of the bed. "C'est ça, to see the Prestup...this was the reason we came here, cherie...truly, truly..." I put my hand over his lips and felt them curl up pleasantly. Holding my head between his two big hands, he kissed me ardently, then left me there, lying naked on the bed, and headed out the door.

≈PART FIVE≈
Berkeley

TWENTY-SIX

THE FIRST WEEKEND in May, the Zoology Department at Cal took a trip to the high country of Yosemite and I went along. We hiked through pine forests to still-frozen glacier-carved lakes. Made notes on freshwater fish, dipterians, and other indigenous species. Melted snow for drinking water. Poked our dinner onto sticks and into open flame. Shoved pine needle mattresses under our sleeping bags. Très nice. Peaceful and totally unreal. But at nightfall, staring into the campfire, even in that place, agonized wails from the city far below filled our imaginations and our talk turned to current events.

Not long before the trip, I'd been sitting in Tilden Park writing Janet about staying safe in her foreign environment. What bullshit! Ironic, but bullshit. What the hell could America hope to offer her in the way of protection when she returned? In other letters, I'd been compelled to write her about the riots all over the country that MLK's murder had sparked. And the Huey stuff. And the Oakland Induction Center. There had been so much damn violence in this country since she left—and I had to include the three, count 'em, three underground nuclear tests that month in Nevada—and now there was an occupation of buildings at Columbia University.

Just before the grand weekend with Cora was about to begin, I received another letter from Janet. Her letter was written in the middle of the night—that in itself was enough to alarm me—about a student demonstration run afoul of riot police that she had just witnessed quite by accident. It was dated May 4, 1968.

Oh, terrific...now I could worry about both Matthew and Janet. And it crossed my mind that Jean Magill was not going to have much of a Mother's Day celebration this year. I imagined she'd have her eye on the news from France as well as Vietnam. Newsweek had covered in depth, complete with photos, what had gone on in Paris the night of May 3. The French army had been called out to put down rioting by college students. What Janet had seen that night was far more vicious than anything she had ever witnessed in California. With her increased understanding of the students' issues, she had begun to feel foolish running around touring museums and cathedrals.

At 11:00 p.m., after the books were closed, my imagination looped around the world to Paris itself. Paris as a destination. The prospect of encountering chaos and Teo the Czech on the same cobbled street. Nervously, reluctantly, I reassessed my travel plans. I envisioned the City of Light transformed into a maelstrom of violent physical encounters. Chestnut blossoms floating on the air, wafting above saxophone strains in a menaced, minor key. Spring showers landing as frigid as ice on the splotchy grass of the Luxembourg Gardens, killing old growth. Paris was no place for a guy who held tight to his political cynicism. It wasn't logical to run away from one war, only to seek another. And it wasn't my way to set myself up to be dumped by Janet Magill a second time.

TWENTY-SEVEN

MY MOTHER'S LIFE revolved around the days and weeks when the women who frequented the beauty parlor most wanted to look their best: weekends, holidays, special occasions. Since a Saturday arrival was precluded by the demand for flawless Saturday night fingernails, it was Sunday morning at ten o'clock when Cora's taxi from the Oakland Airport pulled up in front of my cottage. I marched down the brick path, steeling my gut and pasting a massive grin onto my face. I was determined to give her—no us—the best damned celebration ever.

"Hi there, college graduate," she yelled in a voice low and hoarse from the cigarette habit she'd finally kicked the year before. I reached her just as she was paying off the driver. "Here's for you," she smiled and put a bill into the hand out the window.

"Hey...five bucks?"

"This is my holiday, hon," she said as the guy roared away, "and I don't want to hear another word about money until hell freezes over, you hear me?" I laughed and hugged her, making sure to hold onto her an extra few seconds for good measure. She had some kind of thick fur over her shoulders, already too warm for the day. As I drew back to assess her face, I noticed perspiration forming on the little ridge above her bright, waxy lipstick.

"Did you get any of that red crap on me?" I asked, swiping at my cheek.

Call-me-Cora inspected me, pronouncing me clean. "I was careful," she said, "and I blotted. I don't look overdone, do I?"

She pirouetted, so I gave her the once-over: tall, too skinny, tottering on shoe-stilts, the familiar Cleopatra eyes and a crown of gentle, bleached blond curls. She'd called it a chignon when I'd asked her about it years ago. A phony piece of hair that, along with her Saturday night nails, gave her the sophisticated style she prized. On Telegraph Avenue, she would come off like a tiger at a housecat's convention. But she had looked like this my whole life. And that, at least, was some comfort. "You're gorgeous," I said, feeling surprisingly sincere.

First stop was Neil and Joanna's cottage, after dropping her giant suitcase and makeup box in my dwarf living room. "We've been waiting for you, Mrs. Becker," said Jo, uncharacteristically decked out in a dress, hands extended. Cora tugged at Jo's hands and gave her a kiss on the cheek. "Want some coffee?"

"Black, two lumps, and I love your dress." I noticed the summer dress was in a thin, smooth material with little white flowers all over it. Very nature, very Joanna.

"Thanks so much! Spring is my favorite season!" Jo headed for the kitchenette.

Neil emerged from the bedroom and came to stand by Cora. He put his hand in hers for a shake, avoiding the kiss. "How do you do, Mrs. Becker?"

"Not so formal, Mr. Strand. How are you?"

So, we sat over coffee, Cora and my friends, everyone happily chatting about real estate and gardens and food and school. They were all putting on a good show as they had last year, and it was all for me. Don't think I didn't appreciate it.

Neil was waxing poetic about his spring garden. My mind began to wander from the conversation, contemplating the day ahead, our traditional Mother's Day picnic and Cora's pleasure at my preparations. I kept itching to stand up, to get on with it. I forced myself back into Neil's explication of northern California's climate and soil potential.

Finally, it got to be 11:30. I made my move. With promises to visit again the next day, Cora and I left for our traditional picnic—but this year, she was in for a surprise. She stayed with Neil and Jo while I called the cab company for the pre-arranged drop-off and pick-up. Then I put the finishing touches on the feast I'd put together—packing it into brown grocery bags so she couldn't see what was up.

A half hour later, Cora had checked into the best room she could get at the Durant Hotel and changed out of her fancy airplane clothes, into black Capri pants and a plain blue turtleneck. We drove up as usual into the Mother's Day crowds at Tilden Park in the Berkeley Hills. But this time, I instructed the driver to keep going right on through the throng of picnickers until we reached what appeared to be a small fire road. We turned off and Cora got a puzzled expression on her face. "Where does this go? Aren't we going to have a picnic?"

"Of course, but not with that mob. I've been scouting out a better place." I laughed, rubbing my hands together. I loved the mounting suspense.

Five minutes later, we were in a tiny meadow with a fallen log and a soft bed of oak leaves. The sun filtered in over the blue Dacron tablecloth I spread in the sheltered clearing. "Royal blue. Your favorite color," I said.

"Oh, hon, this is special. Not the usual scratchy wool army blanket."

"And not the usual sandwiches and carrot sticks, either," I said, gesturing her to sit at the edge of the cloth. "Madame Becker?"

Hamming it up like a celebrity, she smiled, primped her hair and folded her legs, managing the descent gracefully. I proceeded to unpack the goodies I'd prepared with Joanna's advice and assistance. Fresh cold roast chicken on the bone with a mayonnaise-mustard sauce to dip it in, the way Janet Magill once told me the French do it. Marinated artichoke hearts and mushrooms, paté from a sardine-sized can at three-fifty a pop, San Francisco sour dough bread, and for dessert, two slices of chocolate fudge cake.

We ate and laughed as I told her how I'd managed to find this place and get all the grub together. Never once did she indicate that she felt my fussing over her was out of line. To the contrary, as my narration wound down, I noticed that Cora's body had uncharacteristically slumped and tears were forming in the corners of her eyes. "Oh Aaron," she cried, "This is so...so gourmet. I just love it, dear, and appreciate all the trouble..." she swallowed hard and lifted her torso up, regaining her regal bearing. A big horsy sigh escaped between the two pads of faded and greasy lipstick. "You're one classy fellow, that's all I can say."

My feelings of childish glee gradually settled into relief. I was grateful that all this had gone off without a hitch. She's had this day, I mused, whatever the future might bring. The rest of the weekend would be a snap.

Cora was chattering about her own cooking—such as it was—and Neil's vegetarianism.

"They're looking well," she said. "Whatever they're eating, it agrees with them."

"Jo takes good care of Neil...they take good care of each other," I said wistfully.

Cora cocked her head to one side. Frown lines rippled between her eyes, which fixed absently on a nearby spruce sapling. Perhaps she was listening to the birds trilling above us. I gauged they were too far up to sense our feast. I was about to tell her we didn't have to worry about them, but the birds were evidently not her issue. "I'm glad you've got nice friends," she broke the silence. "You know, I was a little worried about you after your girlfriend left town."

I had no idea what to say. Cora rarely probed, so when she did, I knew she had a purpose. I pulled a limp piece of plastic wrap out of the sack and began to salvage what remained of our feast. Cora cleared her throat. "Well, if you don't want to talk about it. I don't mean to pry..."

"It's okay...it's all okay now. Anyway, we broke up before she left. For now, we're just friends."

"Oh, hon. I'm sorry. I didn't... do you write to each other?"

"Sure."

I began to peel tin foil away from the cake, waiting for Cora to continue. "I hear there could be a bit of trouble there, too," she said. "In France, I mean. Like here. I just wondered if you'd considered that. You said on the phone you were going to Europe."

"I'm not sure where though," I replied casually. I was glad to have the cat out of the bag on this particular line of inquiry.

"Well, you said 'Europe,' and she's in Europe."

I couldn't figure what in hell to reply. I slid two tall, rich slices of cake onto paper plates.

"Is she okay over there?" she asked.

"She's doing fine."

"And her brother, off in the war?"

"He's fine." I took a bite of my cake and let the sweet stuff saturate my tongue. I noticed Cora hadn't taken up her plate yet. This line of questioning should be over with—the smile back on her face. I swallowed the cake, took a sip of lemonade and met her eyes. "I'll be going somewhere in Europe or Canada, but not France. Somewhere safe and peaceful."

"Don't just say that for my sake, hon," the words rushed out of her now. "I don't imagine France could be any worse than Berkeley. I just wanted to make sure you knew about it..."

"I know about it," I cut her off. "I read the papers. And...I decided earlier this week. Not France. Anyplace but France." Cora took a bite of her cake, but there was none of the appreciative "mmm" I'd anticipated. She swallowed the big lump and stared at me like she had at the spruce sapling full of noisy birds. And damned if a disappointed expression didn't drag at her face. It confused me. Was she about to pull a plane ticket out of her purse? Did she expect me to just pop on over there in the middle of a revolution, or what?

Gradually, the chocolate worked its magic, and the good vibes returned. We finished up, both of us drowsy and lost in a comfortable silence. We lay back, staring up at the branches that surrounded our picnic like our own personal fort. I was nearly sedated when I heard my mother's voice asking how soon it would be until the taxi came for us. Glancing at my watch, I mumbled, "About twenty minutes."

Suddenly she was pulling herself up, and staring me down with her Cleopatra eyes wide open. She held out her hand for me to grab. "C'mon. Let's pack up and walk down toward the park. The driver can find us on the road, and it'll be nice to stretch our legs after a big meal."

Sometimes it amazed me how little time I'd spent in San Francisco during my four years at Cal. You could count my trips on two hands, and this was my fourth with Cora. Sunday night was her treat. We'd always ended up at Fisherman's Wharf with the requisite seafood cocktail, followed by overcooked filet of sole or halibut at Alioto's.

"I guess we both had the same idea, you for the picnic, me for the dinner," she told me. We were still in the cab, the blue tablecloth wedged between us. "I decided we should do something special this year, something more, well, elegant. And remember? You promised not a word about the money."

"What the...?"

"I've made reservations at the Blue Fox," she said, matter-of-factly. "Tell your driver to come back for me at seven. We don't want to be late."

"My driver?" I snickered. "My chauffeur. Right." We pulled up to the Durant and I jumped out before the driver could. The hotel entrance was crowded with Mother's Day revelers, hugging their college kids goodbye in the Sunday night rush. I ran around to open Cora's door. "Thanks, sweetheart." She kissed the air by my cheek. "This was absolutely fabulous. No need to see me in..." and she slipped into the crowd and disappeared.

I thanked the guy for his services and paid him off, intending to walk up the hill to my place. "Don't you want me to come by here at seven, like your mother says?" asked the driver.

"Well," I shrugged, "why not?"

The Blue Fox—the name alone had worked its magic. Walking up Durant Avenue, past the eight-story dormitories where Janet once resided, I flashed back to Cora and Janet, chatting like best friends at my mother's modest apartment on the "other side" of the Beverly Hills tracks. They were discussing the most expensive and glamorous restaurant in San Francisco. "Get your folks to take you to the Blue Fox when they visit you at college," Cora had said. "It's famous. All the best people go there."

"Let me write that down," said Janet. She reached inside her cavernous shoulder bag for the notepad she always carried.

Cora laughed, "That's spelled B-L-U..."

"Don't be silly. I know," Janet said, smiling coyly, "like the fur. My papa got me a blue fox jacket for Christmas last year."

"You shouldn't taunt the poor," said Cora. "It's lousy for Johnson's War on Poverty."

"I think it was jack rabbit," she giggled.

Cora laughed amiably, her low throaty laugh. They noticed me at last, standing there with a glass of Coke for Janet. I grinned like a kid with a double scoop of ice cream—Cora and Janet were my double scoop, and I was glad they got along so well.

"Having fun?" I asked as I handed Janet her Coke. She nodded as she began to sip. Her hair was smooth then, fluffy and shiny black. No frizzy radical chic. Her lipstick left a thin, pale pink mark on the glass.

"Make sure the old man springs for a steak," Cora said. "Chateaubriand with Béarnaise sauce." My mother had risen, making some excuse or another, leaving the sofa and the living room to the two of us. Then, Janet and I had shunned the television, preferring instead to smooch or talk. She had listened to all my sage advice about college as if I were her guardian angel.

I crossed College Avenue, trudged up Channing as I had a million times over the past four years. As I reached my street, my cottage, my current but temporary living room, images from those rosy days were replaced by the letdown on Cora's face when I'd made it clear that there would be no tryst for Janet and me in Europe. At least, I consoled myself, she hadn't been around at Matthew's farewell party to witness the angel's fall.

Chateaubriand with Béarnaise sauce—that's what Cora insisted we both order that night, sitting in the plush velveteen seats of the Blue Fox. The waiter came by, a guy about my age. He had a thin, clean-shaven face and sharp, clever eyes. I wondered if he was a Cal or State student. His hair was slicked back with Brylcream and his tux was just a tad too large; my one dark suit was a mite too small.

A quick snapshot of this guy in a tee-shirt and jeans flashed before my eyes and I chuckled at him. He kind of snickered back as he opened our menus for us and I figured he'd made his own picture of me. As we took our seats, I peeked at Cora, dressed to the nines in a pale green dress with flouncy see-through sleeves, and a surge of gratitude hit me. Gratitude feeling like love—or was it the other way around? I remembered how, as a kid and even into high school—Jesus, had I resented having to live with her! "Call me Cora," she'd say when I called her mom. "I'll never catch another man with a kid on board." I'd snicker and do what she said. But I never knew whether to blame her for chasing the old man away or him for running out on us. At the time, she seemed a vain, stupid woman and I figured he couldn't take her anymore. I'd given her a tough time and mysteriously, had felt both justified and guilty.

But upon reaching college, I'd swiftly forgiven—her, my dad, myself. I'd forgotten all about those years and had enjoyed being swallowed up by my life as a Berkeley student.

Only now, sitting here in front of a menu with no prices, did I realize that my forgive-and-forgetfulness had come so easily because she had never blamed me. Her list of rules had been short and clear, enforcement iron-clad. Her favorite line was "...if you want me to keep doing your laundry?" delivered as a question, with a wry smile. She stayed interested, kept the conversation going, but never made a big deal about my big mouth.

I am happy to report that no one asks for your ID at the Blue Fox. At least not the thin guy with the slicked-back hair. Through cocktails, salad, and into the pièce de résistance, Call-me-Cora and I chatted about old friends and relatives, TV and film stars and food, topics my mother could hold forth on with some depth and confidence.

Once, as always when we got together, she asked me to explain my "classwork," as she called it. And as always, I did my best to give a brief, simplified summary of each course and its goals. My embellished descriptions of my professors were her particular favorite, so I lingered on the subject and received appreciative chuckles from my audience. This time, however, as I was winding down, Cora added a new twist:

"Hon, what I really want you to explain is, where does all this take you?"

"Isn't it clear? Science, teaching, research." I paused to scan her face.

"I mean, who do you work for?"

"After I get my Ph.D., if I'm good enough, a major university. But if I'm not good enough, for the big money," I added, seeing her eyes narrow at my glimmer of self-doubt. "I'm sure I'll be snapped up by a private company. I love the biochem and biology stuff, but I've been reassessing. I might try pharmaceuticals. Coming up with new medicines..."

"Cures?" she cut in, her smile a red swatch across the table.

"That's right. Cures."

She took a bite of her steak. "Mmmm. This is scrumptious. If you come up with an important one, we'll be eating like this all the time."

"Well...I don't know how much..."

"...not that money's what you're doing it for," she added quickly. "Of course, humanity, disease...why, it would be wonderful. I just mean the good life would follow."

I sipped my wine, then decided to polish it off and reached for the bottle. Cora rattled on between bites without looking up. "As soon as this war thing ends—and it will, Aaron, mark my words. Those other wars seemed like they'd never go away, but they did. And this one will too. Honestly," she clucked her tongue to her teeth, "slowing down a smart boy like you by making you leave the country. It's immoral, that's what it is..."

"Lots of people have said so."

"Well, I know. And that gives me hope." Cora finally looked over my way. "For heaven's sake, Aaron. Eat your steak before it gets cold."

After our feast, we emerged into the bustling downtown, and Cora breathed in the exhaust as if it were the perfume of the gods. "The air sure smells sweet up here after L.A.," she declared.

"It's not so great these days," I said, "but if you feel like walking..."

"Absolutely. It's a beautiful night, and after all that food..." She laughed heartily.

"It's okay in your high heels?"

"Hon, I've been trudging around on these things all my life. They're part of my anatomy." She laughed again, this time at her own cleverness. I took her arm, curled it around mine in a gentlemanly fashion and off we went.

TWENTY-EIGHT

MONDAY MORNING, I dragged myself out of bed for my six o'clock lab job, but I'd arranged in advance to get off early. I grabbed a Danish at the Terrace before heading up to the Durant, even though I knew Cora expected to take me out to brunch.

There she was, standing by the front door, dressed to kill again, this time in a lavender mini-skirt, white stockings, and a shiny white blouse. Her top half reflected the spring sunlight like a traffic barrier. The spikes of her white sandals left no doubt that if she hadn't been born on stilts, she'd had them surgically grafted to her soles.

She was talking to the doorman, smiling and waving her hands in the air, and I assumed it was her way of flirting. But when I came closer, I discovered she was asking him to make arrangements for her bags and a taxi to the airport later in the day. It hit me then that this day would be it. Who knew when I might see her again? "Morning, hon," Cora said, giving me a bear hug. I bussed her once on each cheek, the French way. She beamed at me.

We started to walk down Durant Avenue toward Telegraph. "Aaron," she said, "how about we vary our usual routine again today? Do you think we could skip the fancy brunch?"

I laughed. "After last night? You kidding? I could skip right on through to dinner," I lied, thanking my lucky stars I'd stopped for the Danish.

"I don't mean not eat," she said, "unless, of course, you don't want to..."

"No, no...I could do with something. But what did you have in mind?"

"Your day," she replied, her eyes lit up with childish glee. "Like back-to-school night when you were a kid. I'd like to see where you go to eat, where you work, your classes, visit your friends, your professors, you know...whatever you would do!"

"Well..." I didn't know who was going to be more bored, her or me, but I said lightly, "Okay, why not? It's your celebration."

"Are you sure? You sound disappointed."

"Do I? Well, it's breaking tradition, but it's a great idea. I'm...I'm flattered that you want to share my day."

So, off we went down Telegraph, her high heels click-clicking on the sidewalk, through swarms of students whose moms had arrived on Saturday and departed last night. Across Bancroft and by the Student Union, I began to explain the 10:30 a.m. dining choices, but I stopped mid-sentence, still feigning a lightness she was bound to see through once again.

"Hey, Mom, I've just got to ask. If you wanted to come on campus, why the get-up? I mean, the heels, shiny blouse, and the skirt..." The "mini-skirt," was what I thought.

She broke into a big smile and I felt the relief of the child who has missed hurting his mother's feelings. "Aaron, this is a u-ni-ver-si-tee," she said, pronouncing the word as if I'd never heard it before. "Universities aren't just for kids... there are tons of very bright men around here. Professors who might like a mature woman like me. Geniuses, even. Who knows whom we might run into?" She blew the 'hoom' right at me as if she were revving up her engine.

We stood there, silent a moment, with me trying to force feelings of revulsion through a quick funnel of reason, into a big tankard of unconditional acceptance. Finally, I said, "Of course, I've seen you dating for years..." my voice petered out. "Don't remember any professors, though."

"Well, I've always liked smart men. I liked your father, God help me, and he was plenty smart."

"No reason you shouldn't. You're smart, too."

"Not educated, though," she said mournfully. "Not refined like your friend, Janet, either. But I know I'm smart enough."

The unexpected mention of Janet shot through my gut and into my groin like it always did. "Janet had her class handed to her on a silver platter," I spat out.

"But she knows it. She's not a snob about it. I admire that." Cora's voice soothed me like a gentle stroke across my forehead.

"I admire that too," I said, quieting down, "but you've invented your own splendid style. I admire that more."

"Why, thank you, Aaron," she said. "What a nice thing to say."

"I mean it."

"Aaron, one more thing. You're a smart man, too, and I've enjoyed your company all your life."

I snickered. "Of course you have. Potty-training me was fabulous."

"Oh, you!" She slapped my arm. "For heaven sakes..." she turned toward the steps down to the Bear's Lair, but pointed to the cafeteria, opposite. "Do you ever go to that one?"

After a mess of greasy bacon and eggs washed down with Sanka, we strolled through campus to my lab, where there was no one to introduce her to except the sophomore who was standing in for me. He was busy washing a nasty acid out of some beakers, so we headed out for a tour of the library. Then, up the Campanile for the view, which we hadn't done since my freshman year. By that time, there was biochem class.

"This one's taught by a bona-fide genius," I said as we headed into a small auditorium. I sat us down at the back, in case Cora wanted to slip out. "His name is Howard Schachman. He's just been elected to the National Academy of Science. It's a great honor. There's always stuff like that happening around Berkeley, though."

"Is he married?" Cora asked with a sly grin.

"How the hell would I know?" I answered, somewhat amused at how bold Call-me-Cora had gotten with me. "But if you want, we can go up after class and ask him."

She sighed dramatically. "That would be ridiculous, of course."

The prof had already taken his place behind the podium, and all eyes were on him. Cora sat through the whole class, which surprised me no end. Through the rapid-fire equations Schachman scribbled on the green board, through my intense note taking, through questions and answers. As I banged my notebook shut, Cora asked, "So, where can we get some coffee around here?"

After a break in the Bear's Lair, it was time for my immunology class with Professor Wofsy. Cora sneaked out of this one after five minutes, whispering that she'd meet me afterwards by the door.

It's a good thing she left. After lecturing for about half the period, Wofsy put down the long wooden stick he always used to point things out on the board. He removed his glasses and wiped his eyes, then started in. "As some of you may know," he began, "I am chairman of Vietnam Commencement, an event that will take place, despite rumors to the contrary, this Friday at noon on Sproul Plaza."

His forty or so students had stopped writing in their notebooks. Someone dropped a pencil and you could hear it land and roll on the slanted cement floor of the lecture hall. "I want to take a few minutes," Wofsy continued, "a few of the precious minutes that you seniors have left to you at this institution, to explain to you why I've accepted this position, and why I believe you should all—even the women—attend this alternative commencement ceremony."

Then he began to rehash the same old stuff about the immorality of the war itself. I listened with half an ear, my mind drifting to Cora, wandering around the campus looking for men. Nice for her to be outdoors, in the sunshine. Any place but here.

My attention snagged on the word "Paris." Wofsy was explaining how nothing positive would happen in Paris unless we, the people, maintained the pressure for peace. The alternative commencement of the best and the brightest in the State of California had the symbolic value blah blah blah... popular sympathy blah blah and more blah.

As his captive audience listened to what they took for gospel, my frustration grew. Hell, I fumed, "popular sympathy" had been against the war for years at Cal. Fighting dragged on and the peace talks were already bogged down on something absurd like the shape of the negotiating table. I'd already made up my mind: protest wasn't for me. So why did I have to listen to this shit? The so-called ceremony would be just another meaningless, grand gesture. Suddenly, I felt completely isolated. Overwhelmed by alienation from both my peers and my mentors.

Emerging from the Life Sciences Building in a foul mood, I blinked in the sunlight and there was Cora, coming at me, beaming as bright as the day. We turned our backs on the LSB. "I don't know how you can stand it," she laughed. "But I guess it helps that you understand what they're talking about."

"Today I knew exactly what he was talking about," I mumbled, "and it wasn't immunology." She stared at me, puzzled. "Forget it," I waved off her silent inquiry. "Are you sorry you chose this kind of day? I'd arranged to get notes and skip class..."

"No, no. I'm not sorry at all! You've been here all these years and I've been curious."

"I do want to skip my afternoon lab. I worked it all out with my lab partner, Sheila. She hates me to skip and it was a chore getting her to see my side of it, so I'd rather not reverse action right now."

"Well, okay. You have a girl lab partner? How interesting."

"She's the best student in the class."

"Then you're a good pair, aren't you?"

We passed under Sather Gate and I rolled my eyes at the broad, clean sky, squinting in the sunlight. "A good pair? Yeah, I guess so...I'm gonna get a newspaper." I headed off to the little boxes up ahead of the gate, returning with a Daily Cal screaming headlines about "Vietnam Commencement." With a certain sense of relief, I permitted the resumption of my rotten mood to be blocked by the knowledge that Neil Strand was coming for us soon in his VW bug. Surely Neil would have something sane to say about this big commencement deal of Wofsy's.

Neil picked us up, as promised, right in front of the Student Union on Bancroft. He whisked us up the hill for the smörgåsbord snack and tea that Jo had prepared. As the meal and the pleasantries wound down, I pushed my chair away from their dinette and reached into my pack. "What do you think of this?" I asked, folding back the Daily Cal to the full-page announcement.

Neil whistled. "I heard about this, but what an ad. Must've cost a fortune."

"Professor Wofsy lectured on the subject half the period. Seems he's the sponsor or chairman or something like that. A bunch of profs probably paid for it."

"What does it say, Neil?" Jo asked, sneaking worried peeks at Cora, who was staring clear-eyed at us over the top of her teacup.

"'Vietnam Commencement, Friday, May 17,'" Neil read with pomp, then continued in a more solemn tone, "'We will assemble in Sproul Plaza Friday at noon. We invite you to join us.' There are two sections here," he paused to explain. "One is a pledge to refuse induction, another a pledge of support for draft resistors. You're supposed to sign one of these, then give consent for release of your name. It asks for all this information...they won't give it to the draft board..."

"No shit..." I laughed nervously. "Sorry, Mom."

Cora waved it off. "I understand." Then Neil spread out the page on the table and we all leaned over it, reading the pledges silently.

Now Cora began to read out loud, "Look at this. 'As long as the United States is involved in this war, I will not serve in the Armed Forces.' Good for them!"

"You're against the war, Mrs. Becker?"

"Yes, I am," she stated firmly. "Now put that thing away so we can finish up. It's almost time for me to go."

As we left Neil and Jo's, Cora told Neil she needed about ten more minutes before her ride down to the Durant. I figured she wanted a private goodbye in my cottage, and I hoped she wouldn't get too mushy.

But she had one more surprise up her sleeve. She closed my front door behind us without a word. As if a pantomime were in progress, I watched in amazement as she slid my pack from my shoulder, fished for the Daily Cal, turned to the big Commencement ad and spread it out on my own tiny dinette. She slammed her hand down with a bang on top of the bold, inch-high letters. Dork woke up with husky squawks and Cora

glared up at him. "Oh, shut up, Tweety! Don't be so delicate..."
Then she turned to me. "Aaron Becker, you should go to this."

"But...I don't go to those things..."

"Never...?"

"Well, I'll admit I've had my episodes of weakness..."

"Why weakness?" she asked.

I laughed, sighed, squirmed, shrugged my shoulders.
"Okay, then. Call it foolhardy courage," I said. "Basically, I tried
it out and decided it wasn't for me. It's a waste of time. And
then...the crowds, the hysteria. I told you I'd never go to
France..."

"...because they've got the same stuff going on," she
interrupted. I could see she was trying to understand my
viewpoint. I certainly wanted to understand hers.

"You said you wanted me to stay safe. Well, I'm not so
sure..."

"But if the damn genius professors are behind it..."

"That's no guarantee!" I hissed. "They're just grownups like
all of you, sending us in to do their dirty work. Another species
of Johnsons and McNamaras making us fight their fucking
war!" I stood breathless, unable to meet my mother's eyes for
what seemed like several lifetimes. When I finally did, she was
calm, just as I remembered her during my childhood temper
tantrums. "I'm sorry. I shouldn't have included you in that
group."

She sighed and touched her fingertips to the page again,
the red of her long nails standing out like bloodstains over
letters designed to provoke. Then, in a gesture of perfectly
irrational tenderness, she ran her hand in a silky movement
down the entire page. "Do you know what happens at the end of
a marriage, Aaron?" she asked.

"Divorce?" I laughed shallowly, playing along.

"Nothing, that's what. You get married and there's this
gorgeous white dress and canapés and cake and the preacher
and the license and the blood test..." she'd stood up straight,
pulled away from the ad on the table. She looked dignified, very
un-Cora. "But at the end, you sign some papers and it's over.
Nothing happens."

"Okay, and so...?" I prompted.

"So there's no real marking of THE END, like the sign on the screen when the movie's over. You feel like there ought to be another goddamned blood test, to see if you're physically ready for such a big change. Or people around to mourn or celebrate with you, depending on how you're taking it. But there's nothing."

I sighed. "I hate to rush you, but what's this got to do..."

"With Vietnam Commencement?" she cut me off. "Because everything's gonna change for you now, Aaron. And you won't go through the real ceremony, so I just wanted...I didn't want you to think I didn't approve. Because I do approve. This is the choice you've made, to let your whole life change because of the war...to stand up against the war and to keep yourself alive. Isn't that choice what this phony ceremony is about? So you belong there, mourning and celebrating with people just like you."

I was struck dumb by her insight. I nodded slowly, comprehending.

Then she grabbed me and we hugged. "Gimme some of that crappy red stuff, right here." I pointed to my cheek, struggling against tears. And I could feel the perfect, warm, red circle burning into my flesh.

TWENTY-NINE

THE DAY AFTER my mother's departure, I found two letters in my mailbox.

The first was the letter I'd anticipated from her ex-husband. I was glad that Dad would never know how anticlimactic his refusal to fund my trip to Europe had turned out to be. In the nicest words he could muster, he told me how proud he was of me that I had achieved the status of college graduate. "First in the family," just as Cora had said. He had missed the opportunity for higher education, he explained for the umteenth time, because of the Great Depression. And now, because of a national tragedy of like proportions, he wanted me to know that he supported my decision to evade. He respected my knowledge of world events, he said, and then he recommended Canada. Wishing me good luck, he added that he'd love to continue corresponding. I was to send him my address in the frozen northland as soon as I was settled.

Although my dodger destination had shifted and my course was set for Canada, my brain still whirred with fear for both Janet and her brother. The second letter was from my ex-girlfriend. The newspapers all week had headlined the big time French student demonstrations. Let's call them what they were: street battles, nearly eclipsing the nightly carnage from Asia. After this letter, I knew there would be little hope of receiving another for some time. Plans were afoot for French postal workers to support the students by striking, and that kind of thing could go on indefinitely. No telling when I would receive the next installment of Janet's saga.

Though I had feared the worst for weeks, her words confirmed what I'd seen coming all along: that she would be seduced into the fray. Two major developments had collided like two benign substances, combustible when combined, igniting Janet's passions and putting a 180-degree spin on her outlook.

First, she heard from her soldier brother, whose patriotism, it seems, was transformed by first-hand experience of the war and a surprising, close friendship with an educated South Vietnamese lady named Lue. I was relieved to hear that Matthew was still breathing, and that he had found himself in a non-combative position was even better news. As astonishing as his political transformation was, his social metamorphosis was even more unbelievable. Matthew Magill? Golden Boy talking his heart out to a mother-figure from the local population? I couldn't picture it.

Just after receiving the letter from Matthew, Janet was amazed to learn what I had been reluctant to write her: that the current French street rebellion began when the government restricted student activities against the Vietnam War.

I could see what the confluence of the two, Matthew's turn against the war and the revelation that the French were fighting "her" battle, might mean to Janet. Auditory fantasies of Janet's gaggle of politically-minded French youth disturbed my sleep. As I sat snug in my brown-shingle cottage, I could hear the high-pitched patter of brave slogans and the swoosh of warm, synthetic fibers as she rushed out the door behind Le Grand Laurent and the incandescent Bérnard, stumbling over cobblestones or bumping into a barricade and breaking her pretty neck.

Was Teo the Czech beginning to grow on me, or what? At least he was not taking part in the revolution. But he was fading out in Janet's letters like one of those characters on TV who dies but hangs around in a transparent ghost body. So they're not really dead. Teodor's new fadeout made him all the more dangerous and most definitely annoying.

My hours of obsession over the new Jeanette had begun to cut into exam season. Riding the two-headed monster had me crazy. I had to get out. I sat in the Caffe Mediterraneum with a cup of coffee, listening to the clatter of dishes in the back and echoes of voices all around me. It was a great place to be comfortably anonymous. Shoving my coffee aside, I scrounged around in my backpack for pen and paper, intending to write a letter, which I wasn't at all sure would ever reach Janet. What could I possibly say to her now, even if I could speak directly with her? That I wanted her to keep herself safe, but why was that, when I had no money and was going to Canada...when I had chickened out and was going to Canada...when I cared so little for her that I was going to Canada.

Perhaps I should write to Matthew now that we agreed about the war. But I couldn't write him without mentioning Janet, and I couldn't betray Janet with either truth or lies. I put my pen down, staring at it as if it were a severed finger.

Suddenly, I stuffed my pen and paper into my pack with a force that rumpled the paper. The mere physical activity of rising from the chair reinforced the thumps in my chest. I left half my coffee in the cup, not at all my custom. Cool and cynical Aaron Becker. The "no sweat" guy, just lost his cool.

On Telegraph Avenue, a kid of about fifteen or sixteen came up and asked me for twenty cents for a phone call. A leftover runaway from the Summer of Love. Why not a dollar for a meal or more for a joint? I gazed down at the sidewalk. His legs were filthy beneath his shorts, his grimy toes wiggling in worn rubber flip-flops. There was some sort of high school insignia on his tee-shirt. "Where're you from?" I asked.

"Paris..." I flinched as I heard the word. He giggled uncontrollably, putting his hand over his mouth. He lowered his hand, still grinning. "That's P-E-R-R-I-S. Perris, California, east of L.A. Ha! Gets 'em everytime!" Two brown eyes strayed in his head like an unmagnetized compass.

I fished in my pocket and came up with two nickels and a penny. "Here's what I've got. Good luck."

Continuing across Bancroft and onto campus, I veered right, deliberately away from my next class. Up the hill near Faculty Glade was a little spot I knew under cover of cedars and spruce where I could usually find solitude. Once again, I dumped my pack and sat with my paper in hand and tried again to decide what I could write Janet. Instead, my thoughts bent backward to the high school beggar on Telly.

Berkeley had changed immeasurably since my freshman year. That fall, we'd had the Free Speech Movement and I'd observed the whole thing with fascination...from a distance. My character was so fully formed, even by then, that I knew what I was after in life and how to separate that from what was going on in the wider world. That character would definitely not have included giving pocket change to a beggar, even a pathetic child. Would absolutely never have skipped class to ruminate on some personal angst. Nor would it have included dumping an opportunity for a decent lay. True, I'd kept on screwing Sheila Delgado twice a week after class...a regular routine now, just like another lab assignment. But day after day, fuck after fuck, I'd tried to figure out how to break up with my mousy little lab partner.

That former Aaron Becker, the one I sorely missed, would never have gone on for months out of sight of a girl and still get this aching, nauseating, cancerous lump in the abdomen just from thinking about her.

I slammed the pen and paper down again and buried my head in my hands. I was so fucking angry. Angry with Berkeley for changing. With the world for all the shit it was serving up these days. With Janet for leaving me with this god-damned feeling inside me. I didn't want it. Didn't want any part of it. So was I just a lunatic for writing her, or what? Why perpetuate the pain? And when I asked myself that, I knew that I'd changed as much as the hamlet of Berkeley over the last four years. And what I had to show for it was a lot of science in my head and a pain in my gut that wasn't there when I started.

I sighed heavily in a futile attempt to blow out the lump, then tucked the wrinkled paper onto my clipboard. If the Vietnamese, the French, the antiwar protestors, genius professors, Robert Kennedy, Eugene McCarthy, Hubert Humphrey, and even Richard Nixon were all caught with their hands tied behind their backs and their brains up their asses, I was one and the same. A guy with two friends in gravest danger, feeling very far away from them both, powerless to help, to influence, even to communicate how much I cared about their safety and their sanity.

I couldn't write to Janet. Even if there were no postal strike, I couldn't have written about how much I cared about her and wished she would just get the hell out of there. Away from Teo the Czech. Away from Bérnard. Away from danger. But I decided I could write to Matt and hell, just write him the truth about myself, how glad I was to hear he was okay, without gloating about the fact that he had seen the light.

I began by letting him know that Janet had written me concerning his change of heart about the war. Then, the words filled the paper as if I'd already written them in my head.

> ...I truly wish I could do something to help. I'm in conflict every day about whether to go to antiwar protests here, whether they do any good. I wonder how you feel about all the demonstrations. I've decided to participate in Vietnam Commencement—my only commencement ceremony—and even to lend my name to the effort. It will be a one-hour ceremony with faculty and student speakers and the band, but instead of receiving diplomas at the end, we'll be taking a pledge, refusing to serve in Vietnam.
>
> Janet's photo in the paper, taken at a rally, seen by your folks, sent her into exile. People have been jailed at mass gatherings from the Free Speech Movement to this year's Oakland Induction Center. And shooting my mouth off at your farewell party was what caused Janet to break up with me. I realize all this, and I wonder if I'm a lunatic for going to Vietnam

*Commencement so close to my "departure"
date.*

*But there she is, over in Paris and still
trying the best way she knows how to fight
against the war, and there you are in Vietnam
and trying to hold on until you can come back,
when I presume you, too, will speak out from
your vantage point of first-hand experience. So
that's it. One way or another, I'm going to
Sproul Plaza on May 17th.*

*I was glad to hear from Janet that you have
this good friend named Lue. Someone to talk
with, be close with, exchange mutual sympathy.
You're both lucky, and I mean it. Anyone who's
given the opportunity for a thing like that and
flubs it up is making a huge mistake. Please
write if you find time. I'd like to hear from you
directly. Your old Boy Scout friend, Aaron*

THIRTY

MY MOTHER'S VISIT, in retrospect, seemed like one big
inquisition with periodic recesses for relaxation and snacks.
Okay, the Blue Fox was one groovy snack and my picnic wasn't
too shabby either, but there was a LOT of her wanting to know
about me in between. She hadn't been this nosy in years, but I
didn't resent her curiosity. It was only a sad kind of surprise—
now that we were not going to see each other again, maybe ever,
she wanted me to make sure she really knew me. Only natural, I
guessed. The questions about Janet seemed beside the point
until I formed a picture in my mind of what my mother had
hoped for, and what she now knew as reality: wherever I would
end up, I was going to be awfully alone.

On Friday morning, May 17th, those little boxes holding
stacks of the Daily Cal were my first stop on campus. I saw right
away that the event was still on. Governor Reagan wanted the
brass to revoke the student organization status of the Campus
Draft Opposition so they couldn't meet on campus property. He
also called for disciplinary action against faculty participants. I

held the paper against the morning breeze and silently took back the venom I'd spewed against the faculty, comparing them to the Feds. Standing up to the ignorance and rigidity of our photogenic governor, the Chancellor had affirmed the rights of both students and faculty to air their views in public. Free Speech again. It was easy to see in hindsight that the FSM debacle in my freshman year, considered to be a sort of final victory, was only the beginning of the protracted Berkeley Free Speech Wars.

I ran up to my lab job, already late. After washing a sink full of equipment and checking on the cultures, I climbed up on my usual stool and continued to read the paper. An item about Czechoslovakia caught my eye. Almost as a reflex, I scrunched up the whole thing and threw it into the waste bin. Did Teo the Czech have to follow me into the lab? Two minutes later, I was straightening it out, reading about Soviet condemnation of the pre-World War II Czech president, Tomas Masaryk, as an "anti-Soviet criminal." The recently uncensored Czech press had reacted, calling this an "insult without parallel," and current Czech president Dubček was trying to protect his back by urging his own press to "avoid extremism and irresponsibility." I wondered if Janet, who seemed to know so much about French politics these days, was also getting an earful about communism from Teo the Czech.

When the sophomore came at noon, I sprinted down to Sproul Plaza where the invocation was already in progress. The crowds were so thick that I couldn't hope to see a thing. As I elbowed my way back around Sather Gate and into a copse of tall cedars, a stranger shoved a sheet with the printed program into my hands. Stuffing it in my jeans pocket, I crossed a bridge over Strawberry Creek and headed for a spot I knew where I could scale the roof of the Terrace.

I arrived at one of the last empty spots on the roof's edge. What I saw down below made it difficult to regain my breath from the climb. There they were, the orderly throng of thousands spread out below. Opposite, a couple of hundred faculty huddled together at the top of Sproul Steps as if they were posing for a class photo. I squinted, trying to pick out Wofsy, but could barely make out the individual faces. There were so many. Cora might have met her single genius in this illustrious gathering.

Participating students, the ones who had signed the pledge to refuse induction, wore gold armbands; the faculty wore blue armbands. The rest of the crowd were spectators—somewhere at an observational post, I presumed, was Neil Strand.

From where I perched, I could observe from a distance, but today I'd determined that I would participate. To my right and left sat a couple of guys I'd never laid eyes on, one with thick horn-rimmed glasses and short hair, the other with a goatee and a green peace sign inked on his cheek. I balanced my pack precariously on my lap, unzipped it and pulled out my own yellow-gold armband. "Can you help...?" I turned to the guy with the glasses. He tied it on. "You should just wear it all the time," chimed in the bearded guy on the other side of me. I squirmed back from the edge a few inches, not feeling any more a part of this crowd than I had with a bare arm. I stared at the soft flesh visible underneath the green circle. "I will..." I mumbled. "I'll wear it from now on, except when I'm hopping the flight outta here."

"Dodging?"

"Yep. That's what the gold means." My heart began to pound. Saying it to this stranger made it more real than ever. I was about to add "maybe" when I heard him say, "Me, too, probably. Haven't decided yet." He turned back to the Sproul steps.

"I'm Aaron," I said, feeling about eight years old. He shoved his right palm across in front of my gut and held it there. "Ethan," he said. I grabbed his hand for a shake.

The orchestra played a solemn march, then speakers from the faculty praised students for courage and patriotism. Profs I didn't recognize presented three special citations to students whose actions had resulted in "enormous personal consequences," which I surmised meant that they were in jail. Daniel Siegel, a Boalt Hall law student, rose to speak. Told us it was a sad day for Berkeley, a sad day for the country. "And a sad day to commence a life," I reacted out loud, but no one around me had heard. They were busy clapping, their polite applause punctuated by a few of the usual noisy affirmations.

"There is something wrong," Siegel continued, "if Joan Baez and Benjamin Spock are called criminals." I clapped along with the crowd, agreeing, yes, dredging up my anger. Then, Siegel announced publicly, staring right into the cameras hovering about, that he would refuse service when he was called up in the summer. I squirmed uncomfortably on my perch.

An older speaker took his place. "There's Sterling Hayden," said the guy with the glasses, poking my arm with his elbow.

"The actor?" He nodded.

"Grandstanding?" I ventured.

"What kind of an asshole...?!" He shot me all four eyes. I grimaced. The throng around me was applauding, letting go with a few brief whistles and plaintive calls.

"Sorry," I said. "I'm sorry."

"Cynical?" asked Ethan, who had been listening.

"A bad old habit," I replied. He smiled and I returned it. Hayden was invoking America's "holy war." "In World War II," he bellowed, "the enemy was fascism. Now we have the same enemy. The occupying force in Vietnam is the U.S.—it's that simple."

I knew the comparison was right and it made me more ashamed than angry. Ashamed to be an American. I felt an irresistible respect for people like Ethan here, who knew how to express his anger on his cheek and on his arm. I had held my burden under my shirt and suffered in isolation. Now I felt the reason for being here, down to my bones. I realized that Janet had attempted to find a community. What she had done made sense. Just to be doing something, anything, made sense.

Evidently, not all protest was noisy and violent. "This is so controlled," I said to Ethan. "The speakers, the crowd, the cops...it's powerful."

"Amazing how much more powerful peace is than violence," Ethan responded. "Let's hope this sends the Feds a message."

No Fed, anywhere, was listening, I thought, still cynical, still realistic. But I considered Ethan and the others lucky to have their illusions. I'd finally spotted Wofsy in his tweeds just as one of my favorites, Phil Ochs, began to sing "I ain't a-marchin' anymore." Ochs strummed artfully on his acoustic and sang with his mouth right over the microphone. I wondered if guys as smart as Wofsy and as talented as Ochs were fooling themselves like Ethan, or were here, like I was, because something was better than nothing.

Perhaps it was the music, familiar and resolute. Or the dignity of the speakers and the solemnity of the graduates. Whatever it was, I knew that despite the crowd of strangers, the repetition and the formalities, that my mother had been right. This commencement was my commencement. I might never go to another antiwar demonstration again—I didn't know—but from this day forth, I would be a Vietnam draft resister.

Ochs stepped aside and someone introduced Professor Schurmann. He would lead the Exchange of Pledges. Hundreds, perhaps thousands of voices spoke in unison, but I could hear my own and it sounded steady. Not eight years old, but adult and far older than twenty-one. Our voices were not angry, but rather, determined, brave, and edged with sadness.

When we finished, a trumpet blast from the Student Union balcony signaled the end of the ceremony. The sound hung in my ears like a wail. Hastily, I wiped the tears that had sprung into the corners of my eyes.

"Wanna get a beer?" asked Ethan, his voice gruff and barely audible. I nodded assent. Then as if to yank the mood out from under us, the band broke out with a peppy tune. We stood up and stretched, surveying the crowd below. They dispersed methodically. You could hear the drumming of footfalls. Thousands of rational, intelligent, and moral human beings. Cal students committing an act that some called treason. I respected them all. And I respected myself.

THIRTY-ONE

METICULOUSLY, I folded back the newspapers and periodicals and laid them out on the floor of my cottage. The Daily Cal was at the foot of my bay window seat. Next to it, the San Francisco Chronicle. The rest stretched ahead of me like a pathway to hell. I sat back down on my bay bench, downing my fourth beer, hoping Sheila Delgado would be on time. I wanted to get this over and done with. I was ready for her. Ready to do what I had to do.

Dropping my arms to my legs and my head between my knees, I skimmed the nearest headline: "Daily Cal, May 20. Vietnam Commencement at Cal... Over 800 sign pledge, 8000 attend..."

I twisted my neck to spot confirmation of what I'd witnessed myself a few weeks before: "Daily Cal, April 29. Results of the 3-hour rally that began on Sproul Hall steps and continued near Boalt Hall ... Rally attendance...approximately 5,000...student population is 27,500. Cause for the disappointing turnout: Johnson's more moderate policy and changes in overall presidential campaign rhetoric..."

My eyes moved across the hearth, crawled along the floor, catching on the banners of the New York Times and U.S. News and World Report tucked around Dork's cage. My parakeet was unusually quiet, but not unobservant. He ignored the itches under his feathers and perched stock still, staring at me. I averted my eyes, resuming the review of my handiwork. Beyond the cage, The Berkeley Barb, Rolling Stone, and the pièce de résistance: over in the kitchenette and extending into my bedroom were seventeen letters on pastel air weight paper or pale blue aerograms from my so-called friend, Janet Magill. There on my floor lay evidence of Janet's awakening before the postal strike.

With all this shit going on—Janet, the war, the world—I'd like to report that Sheila Delgado was providing some kind of solace. Seeing Sheila was only making my frequent letter-reading sessions more confusing. Sheila Straight-A was a decent lay and hotter stuff than Janet had ever been. But still, I'd become every bit as obsessed with figuring out how to let her down as I was with re-connecting to Janet. Over the weeks, I would come up with words or a plan, then chicken out. So we'd meet again, always at the co-op, weekdays at 4:00.

This media layout was Neil's idea and perfectly aligned with his poetic sensibility. He's the one who brought up the subject of Sheila Delgado—it was a clear, spring day in the week following the Vietnam Commencement when we were out in the front yard. I'd been dying to get away from my books when Neil rescued me with his plea for gardening assistance. I was crawling along in front of him with a trowel, digging holes in moist, fragrant earth. He was coming along after me with fistfuls of petunias and marigolds, interspersing the deep velvety purple with the prickly gold. "I'm trying for homage to Cal..." he was explaining.

I shook my head, disbelieving. "You're kidding, right?" He was bending over, patting earth around a stem, not smiling. I sighed. "Well...I might, with a lot of imagination, derive Berkeley's blue and gold from this arrangement. But I didn't know you were into football."

"I'm into the University," he corrected me. "I appreciate what I'm given."

"Mmm, yeah... Shit, I'm going to miss it."

"I'm sure you are. Your girl, too. Sheila...right? You going to see her up in Canada?" I shoved my trowel into the dirt, sat up on my knees.

"Question is, do I want to see Sheila now?"

"You want to break up?"

"There's nothing there, Neil, except a reliable lay. I feel...counterfeit. I'd like to break up, but we're lab partners. I've got to keep things smooth between us." I sighed. Stood up and stretched. Neil rose to stand beside me. Gazed at me sympathetically. "Fact is," I continued, "There's all this stuff going on in the world and her brain is stuck in a metal beaker." Neil snorted. "You can laugh, but...I simply can't talk to the girl."

Neil pondered a minute. "If she thinks you're nuts," he said, "she can't be angry. She'll just feel sorry for you."

"Sheila never feels sorry for anyone."

"So...but she won't want anything to do with you. And that'll be good, right? Unless you're concerned with self-respect..."

I laughed bitterly. "Too late for that."

"This is perfect," he said, rubbing his hands together, little clumps of dirt dropping back into their natural element. "It rings true..."

"I don't know what you're cooking up, but whatever it is, thanks but no thanks, friend. I mean, I'd like to believe you and Jo still have a little respect for me...."

"What I believe, my friend, is that you're normal. Confused, lonely, horny, bright and frustrated and normal. And you don't need this crap. She's obviously not an answer for you."

I couldn't help but see his point. Neil was more than smart: he was wise. He described the idea of a news-obsessive layout as proof of my insanity. As a bonus, he said, the acting out would do me good. But this play-acting wasn't my style. It had taken me half a six-pack to anesthetize myself before I could begin the set design. I took out scissors and paste and ruler. The place smelled like I was back in grade school. As I laid out the new "tiles" on my floor, I began to get into it. Before I knew it, I was on my fourth beer and rather enjoying the whole thing.

Every once in a while I'd get stuck on a headline and have to tear myself away from the article which followed. I tried to intersperse the front covers and mastheads with the articles, move the publications from present to past and topics from west to east across the room. It had taken me an hour, but at last everything was artfully arranged. I took another gulp of the warm beer and considered asking Neil and Joanna over after Sheila's departure. Let them admire my creation. But then I remembered: Joanna didn't know about this, and I wouldn't want to get Neil in the doghouse. Some ideas were just between the two of us. And we wouldn't want to upset Joanna. I snickered.

There was a loud knock at the door and from outside I heard, "Hey Becker, this your place?" Nothing subtle or timid about Sheila, I bristled, remembering the tentative way Janet had always approached the sanctity of my cottage. I tiptoed across the paper carpet and opened the door. "C'mon in."

"The way you talk about this place, I expected a palace," was the first thing she said, not yet noticing my wall-to-wall unwelcome mat.

"It's home," I said, cheerfully. "My home is my castle." She stepped in and her penny loafer scrunched a copy of Newsweek, open to an article about Rudy the Red in Berlin.

Then, Sheila Delgado tuned in. She focused on the careful collage I'd made, folding, cutting, pasting groups of papers together. She walked across to "San Francisco," bent to inspect photo coverage of the weekend march from the Golden Gate Park Panhandle to Civic Center, then on to Berkeley's Stop the Draft Week. Across the state and the nation she tread, bent over double, her eyes two black slits focused on the major events of our day. To sit-ins at Columbia University. To Germany and

Italy and France. With every new segment of the world tour, I heard my own drunken giggle fill the room like the lunatic, high-pitched rat-a-tat-tat of a snare drum.

Her diminutive loafer hung aloft, then landed gingerly among the handwritten letters. I followed right behind her as she ventured forward, feeling my eyes glaze over, wild with glee. The letters. Sheila. My whole body toasting. Rat-a-tat-tat. Crisp and crazy. She bent again and squinted and for the first time, I realized that neither of us had said a word since she started her inspection. Finally, she stood up and spat at me, "Jesus, Becker. You smell like a beer barrel and your girlfriend's letters stink like cheap perfume." In the corner, Dork chirped and stared, now sizing up the new visitor. I winked at him. I felt calm, the heat drained from my face. I smiled—no grinned—ear to ear.

"She's not my girlfriend," I said, "she's my news source in Europe. And there's nothing cheap about her."

"I should have known there was a rich bitch WASP in the picture. Blond and brainless..."

"Wrong again...!" I sang out, slightly out of tune.

"Are you in love with your news source?" she interrupted me, not listening.

The question took me by surprise. Dammit, Neil. And what do I say if she asks me if I'm in love with Janet? I should have challenged my wise-ass friend. But it was too late. My face had evidently fallen into the waste bin where the rest of this shit belonged.

Sheila's arms were up in the air, her hands pushing at the stark reality of the moment. "Okay. Okay. I get it. I'm not going to bother you anymore, Becker..." She was scrunching her way over to the front door, less careful now not to muss the masterpiece. "...but if you're going off the deep end, better do it outside class time, that's all I can say. You know what I'm talking about. Just don't screw with my grades, Becker..." And she was gone.

THIRTY-TWO

I FELT FREE and relaxed. Free of "entangling alliances" and irrationally hopeful. As soon as I was alone again, I'd perused my floor full of facts and screaming headlines, mentally laying the enigma of Sheila's political stoicism side-by-side with my own political paralysis. I could fold them and crease them any way I wanted to, they still looked black-and-white compared to the enchanting air-colors of Janet's letters. It buoyed me more than I'd anticipated that I'd been there for that one hour of the Vietnam Commencement. It was an important step. Important as closure, more important because I had made the choice freely, with a little help from Cora. And I'd felt something there that I hadn't before: purpose to the protest. I longed to write Janet about it but knew my letter would never be delivered. I watched for something from Matthew, who I assumed would be interested in the ceremony.

Surrendering myself to the practical problems was an adequate method of staving off sheer panic. I formulated a plan, a combination of Greyhounds and boot leather to Canada, then work and live on the cheap if I still wanted to settle somewhere over in Europe. I tried to research Canadian housing and job possibilities, from menial or physical labor to the prized private industry laboratories. But concerned about how to live if work was scarce, I tried to save something from my lab checks and considered selling my only luxury possession: Dork, complete with cage. Such a scummy thing to do, but I comforted myself with the theory that someone who paid cash would give him a good home.

Just as June arrived with its usual humid, overcast days— 'muggy' was what Cora always called them—a letter from Matthew Magill showed up in my letterbox. I ripped it open and read it while standing there at the end of the brick path.

Dear Aaron,
Remember when we used to wear our Cub Scout uniforms to school because we thought we looked so fucking sharp in

them? Ha! If I never see these duds again, it will be too soon. Uniforms are uniforms is all I can say. Thanks for your letter. I'm glad Jan wrote you and you wrote me. Letters give us all a boost.

It's good you're going (went already?) to the Vietnam Commencement. What a weird thing. But it's good, knock 'em dead! There's still plenty of shit going on here. They may be talking about peace in France, but it's too noisy for words around my bunk. They can hit you any time. Everyday I see more guts than a butcher. I don't even retch anymore. I just lie awake at night and pray it's not a buddy's guts next time. If it's mine, the prayer is to feel no pain.

Thanks also for your words about Lue. She's no beauty on the outside, no makeup or what you're used to. What I was always on the make for, stateside. But she's a sweet thing, a real beauty on the inside. Keeps me smiling and dealing with it all. A fine lady. And smart. You and Jan would like her. Mom and Dad...ha! That's another story. A story I'm keeping to myself, along with my new politics, so just remember that, okay?

Can't wait to get the hell home. One thing. Keep away from this place. Nothing good's going on over here. Keep the letters coming. I'll write back.

Your old friend, Matthew

I'd been walking up to my cottage door without even realizing it. Now I stood there on the porch, staring at the handwriting until it blurred. I'd never received a letter from Matthew Magill before, but if I could have envisioned one, this was it. It was short and friendly and a little awkward. A messy, scrawling script. I imagined him composing it on a messy, lumpy bunk. Copter blades whirring outside and men's voices, gruff and low, laughing bitterly, swearing. Here was Golden Boy. All American. Just now learning for himself what he is made of. Not so different from me this spring, I mused, only his has been a much tougher way to learn.

Inside, when I re-read the letter, I was amazed that Janet's brother Matt was not hostile to me. Guess that wouldn't have been his style. Mine, but not Matt's. No word about the party last December, either. Perhaps he felt it just as well to forget it.

If I mentioned it and Matt didn't, that must cancel it out from his point of view. So that was one less worry.

Dork chirped from his cage and my head jerked up. I realized with sadness that our impending separation was not far off. What an enormous transformation would befall me in the next thirty days! Yet nothing was settled for my orderly departure. I would be alone in my new country in the frozen north. The days ahead seemed like an airport runway full of ruts and ridges. As best I could, I bumped along through final papers and exam prep, hoping that eventually, steady pressure to the throttle would take me up for a smooth ride.

≈PART SIX≈
Paris

THIRTY-THREE

EVERYTHING ABOUT TEODOR Pelnar was there with me in the shabby room—his slow, kindly way of speaking, his thick fair hair, his muscle, sweat and massive presence—everything except Teo himself. It had been around two in the morning when he had finally left. We assumed that the stupid mistake of leaving the light on so long was what had kept Miroslav at his post. Now the sun was high and bright, and I was just as eager to hear about yesterday's street battle as I was to find out what happened when Teo met his dissident hero. Rushing to bathe and dress, I ran for the Métro. All my answers were waiting for me at L'Alliance Française café.

"Have fun on your Chateaux Country trip?" was all Claire Caplan said when I caught up with her on her way downstairs. We exchanged knowing smiles, but without waiting for an answer, she strode on ahead into the café.

A large group had pulled several tables into a haphazard circle. I scanned the group for Teo, but he was not among the throng. Elizabeth observed from the periphery, so I went to join her. "What's going on?" I whispered.

"Shh. Irena's translating from Action."

"Action?"

"Shh! The revolutionaries' newspaper."

The paper must have sprung up overnight. I was sure no one in Remi's group had mentioned it. All eyes focused on Irena, who sat with one thick thigh pulled up over the other and held the newspaper above her knees. She was reading from its complicated language and translating it into slow, simple French for her listeners. For an instant, I couldn't help feeling a thrill: I heard myself translating Matt's letter to Remi's group. I felt sure that I would be as self-confident as Irena by the time I reached her age. I had guessed that she was nearing 30.

As I listened, my exuberance faded. "...143,000 troops in the streets. This was one of the 'bloodiest days of May.'" Irena threw up her hands dramatically like a Frenchwoman. "How stupid of the French government!" she editorialized. "Did they think they could close the campus and drag students off to prison without a battle? Now everyone is rioting."

Charlotta, sitting next to Irena, turned up her already upturned nose. "The students are temperamental and restless. In other words," she said, sticking a strand of short, hennaed hair into place, "they are French."

"You're telling me Germany has no rebels?" Irena smirked at her friend and all around, laughter burst out at Charlotta's ridiculous insinuation.

I leaned over Elizabeth's shoulder. "Since when are you interested in all this?"

"Since Laurent's involvement has forced me to be interested," she whispered back roughly, "now please let me listen..."

"...just as in the history books," Charlotta was saying. "The French don't know what they want, but whatever it is, they want it passionately. Nothing here ever changes." Several students grumbled in agreement.

Irena waved away the remarks of her opponents. "All the students want is free speech and their university restored to them."

Charlotta kept it going, her voice filled with disdain. "Their university will be in flames before they finish."

Claire and I traded glances, snickering at the repartee. What a pair Irena and Charlotta made! A radical Pole and a conservative German. Each had found in the other a perfect antagonist to heighten the drama of her existence. In back of us, the clattering and hissing of coffee being prepared went on, but the students were ordering in hushed voices. The circle around the discussion grew until the café was entirely filled with listeners.

"Enragés!" Irena declared. "That's what they have called themselves since the incidents at Nanterre." Clearly, she wanted to take control before she lost her audience in haggling with Charlotta. "The symbol is ten fingers outstretched," she held her hands in the air, demonstrating, "and they shout, 'We are a petit groupe, a handful of the enraged.'"

"Why in hell are they so angry?" said a well-dressed boy. He tried to elbow his way toward Irena, but the crowd wouldn't budge. "They should have to live in my country of Grèce for awhile," he shouted. "Then they would appreciate France."

"All of the youth today are angry, everywhere in the world," replied a calm, familiar voice. There! Across the circle surrounding Irena, Teodor Pelnar hunched down in a chair. Now he sat up straighter, cleared his throat and addressed the group, not the Greek boy. "The older generations, both right and left, do not understand how the youth need hope."

"Teo is right!" Irena interjected. The crowd started to talk among themselves. "Is it true? Should we be angry? Should we be marching?"

"Quiet everyone," said Irena. "Teo, carry on, if you wish."

Teo's outburst in the school group was unusual. It was not his way to stand out in a crowd. I searched the edges of the café for Miroslav, but did not see him there. "In every country today," Teo continued, considering each word with deliberate, quiet effort, "that is where the lines are drawn. Young against old. Whether communist or capitalist, the systems are rigid. No one is allowed to discuss anything or to try new ideas. So the future appears to us like the inside of a gray prison cell. That is why young people are enraged."

"It will be the same old thing," snapped the Greek boy. "The police have the greater numbers and weapons. What is the use?"

"He is right," Charlotta said, reading over Irena's shoulder. "Look at this," she stuck her finger into the newspaper, nearly dislodging it from Irena's grip. "Supporting the police were special sections of the regular army and the Compagnies

Républicaines de Sécurité." She stretched her bow lips out in disgust. "The riot troops from the provinces. They're the worst. Everybody knows they are ruthless."

Irena gave out a hoot. "The government knows they are in trouble. They called up the CRS because of the Vietnam War talks here in Paris. Can you imagine? Using this fire power against a bunch of unruly students?" She cleared her throat and resumed her recitation. "'After battling for fourteen hours with the CRS...' here...over 1,000 injured, 400 arrested. It's a miracle nobody was killed."

I sighed in relief, thinking of Bérnard, Remi, Annette and the others.

"That 1,000 was the number injured for both students and police," Charlotta corrected, still peeking over Irena's shoulder.

"Well, the students are still out there, that's what I have heard," said Sandro, a sweet-faced Italian boy standing in back of Charlotta's chair, balancing a plate of cake. "They're living and making love right on the barricades."

I saw Philippe before he spoke. "Well, this is about freedom, isn't it?" he shouted, laughing. "Doesn't that include free love...?"

"Is it really about free love?" Elizabeth asked quietly. "They said it was about freedom of speech and better education."

"It's about changing what we value," I replied. "And that can include free love." This explanation came out so calmly that I was surprised by the clutch of fear that gripped my insides. I looked over toward Teo, intending to catch his eye. He was already smiling at me. I breathed a sigh of relief and beamed back at him.

The crowd around Irena was starting to disperse and Elizabeth had moved off, talking to Claire. Teo had come around the circle and was standing close behind me. A warm rush of happiness filled me up. His thick, light brown hair was ruffled from the nervous hand that he frequently ran through it when he was excited. He gazed down into my eyes, his own filled with concern. "Are you sorry you missed this battle?"

"I'm not sorry at all. I can join them tonight...if they are not all arrested." I shuddered. "Perhaps the police won and it will all be over..."

Teo shook his head. "There are over 150,000 students at the Sorbonne, many more in Paris with the young rebels like Laurent in the lycées. It is far from over."

"Oh là! So many...? I never realized."

"You are so serious!" He laughed, but his eyes sparkled genially. "Let's sit outside on the wall in our favorite place. That is, if you wish?" I nodded, but turned to search for Elizabeth. Her face was right there in front of me.

"So, Janet? Did you have a good time on your trip?"

"Yes, very beautiful country, thank you."

"I want to talk..."

"I'm going to be with Teo a while, Elizabeth. Maybe you should go ahead without me."

"Well, alright, then. Perhaps another time." I was relieved when she backed away.

As soon as Teo and I had reached our little stone wall, I implored, "Please tell me right now. What happened with the Prestup?" Teo smiled down at me and said nothing, just peered into my eyes until I was forced to laugh. "Well Teo the Czech, it seems we fought for two causes last night, free love as well as a free Czechoslovakia."

"I'm glad you are not sorry," Teo said. "I was worried that it was not the right thing."

I sighed and squeezed my fists to check the trembling that had worked its way down from my shoulders. "I don't know about right and wrong anymore."

"Was it...pleasant for you?" For an instant I wondered if he needed my answer for his own self-esteem or to assuage his guilt, but then he grabbed my hair and tugged it gently, his eyes full of genuine concern, his voice soft. "Because it was special for me. I love you, Jeanette."

"Me, too...it was good..." was all I could manage to say. I remembered the instant of knowing, the night before. I could smell his skin from across the bed, even facing in the opposite direction, and my hand had reached out to him...

"Teo," I said firmly, "last night I did what I wanted. I was lucky because it was what you wanted, too."

He pulled me to his chest and as I settled there, all the trembling ceased. Then I remembered. "Teo, the Prestup? You wanted to see this man..."

275

"...and you simply want to know what happened." Teo finished my sentence. "Yes, of course." Teo eyes darted up and down the street and he stroked his chin nervously. "At first, the Prestup...he told me to stay in Paris as long as I could and study. He said what I learn here will help our country when I am an adult. I told him that I consider myself an adult right now and that I would like to help. But he disappointed me. He didn't trust my sincerity."

"At first? Later he asked you to help?"

"Yes..." He licked his lips and took a breath, composing himself. "He's a small man," he continued, "small in stature, which surprised me. He was very gracious and well-mannered. It was like he was trying to protect me. Like a father, not a colleague. I am twenty years old! Why is it that younger men are able to act on what they believe in and I cannot? It is my family..."

"...it's so frustrating!" I interrupted. "It was just like that for me in America. Always so young and powerless. I wanted to do something! But Teo...didn't he tell you anything else? About what is going on in Prague?"

"Yes, that he did!" he replied. Miroslav had taken a seat where he could just manage to see us from across the street. Teo gave me a gentle squeeze with those tremendous arms. "Do you mind if I whisper in your ear and kiss you from time to time? Just to keep up the romantic ruse, of course."

"You'd better do a little of that right now," I agreed. "It's been too long."

Teo leaned into the back of my ear and began to kiss gently. "Slowly and cautiously," he whispered, "Dubček is making changes. Now that he leads the Czech Communist Party, they have instituted his Action Program. Thousands of people now feel like they are part of a...a...trust of brains...there must be a better expression in French..."

He had used confiance des cerveaux. I nodded. "Yes, yes. Go on."

"Czech freedom appears to be escalating. I told you about my sister's letters. But even Katya did not tell me that after the May Day celebration, Dubček was called to Moscow."

"And you didn't even know about it?" I tried to draw back but he held me firmly.

"No!" I felt his breath singe my ear. "The Prestup's opinion is that if the old hard-liners feel politically threatened, the Soviets will come to their aid."

"What does that mean?"

Teo shrugged his big shoulders miserably. "Would they attack? Shoot at us? I can't imagine it. I would just hate to see things go back to being the way they were before this year. There are moments, cherie, when I wish so much I could be home right now, even if it meant leaving you." He pulled away from me. When he spoke again, his voice emanated from some shadowed part of him that I longed to touch. "After a while, the Prestup did gain some trust in me. When I do go home, he wants me to take something across the border for him. A packet of money."

"But is that safe? And why do they need money...?"

Teo sighed wearily and shook his head.

"My Jeanette... please understand. I have watched my father and his friends all my life. It has bred distrust in me of the Russians and even of some Czechs. I ask, what do the Russians say when they sit down to discuss the Czech situation? A country in their bloc that allows a person to carry a pro-American placard and go home to his wife and children? I said this to the Prestup, and he seemed to share my fears. But he repeated that I should stay in Paris as long as possible."

"So, we're in the same situation. I must stay here to learn and prepare for the future while my comrades in Berkeley fight now to drag history over to our side. At least I have the opportunity to help here..."

"Yes..." He gave a great sigh, then met my eyes. "I must admit something. I do not like to see you out on the streets with the French students, even though I support their cause. It was the army last night," Teo implored. "They have real weapons. I am afraid for you..."

I put my fingers over his lips, "I'm going tonight, Teo. I'm going home for dinner now, and then to rest. Then I'll join my comrades. I am afraid, like you. But I let them force me to run away from Berkeley. Now the whole mess has followed me here to France. God is trying to tell me something. I'm supposed to be doing this."

"Of course, I cannot tell you what to do... You are sweet, Jeanette, but too intelligent to be so naïve."

"It's what I believe!" I burst out. Teo offered me the friendly tilt of his head. I laughed at myself, shrugging my shoulders. "I'm going home now. I hope I'll see Bérnard. If there is a meeting this afternoon, I wish you would come."

He shook his head. "I am only sorry I cannot be with you and the French students all through this battle. But I would not last a week...I want to decide for myself when I leave..."

"We must find a way for you to talk to Bérnard and meet Remi Guitry, our leader. The group is socialist. But yesterday, you convinced me that it must be socialism with democracy or it's no good."

"You are right, cherie. Perhaps I can help them avoid a terrible mistake."

"Teo, listen," I said, my words rushing out, seeking release. "All the trouble in the world seemed random before, but now I can see it's connected. Paris is on fire, Vietnam drags on, Moscow threatens the Czechs, and students everywhere reject their governments. So now we all swear and dress like slobs and throw off religion and morals and...and I lost my virginity last night..." I stopped, breathless, tears in my eyes.

Teo was laughing softly and shaking his head. "Well, I'm glad we can love each other with all this trouble in the world," he said. But...that's a lot of connections..."

"I do love you, Teo, but the connections are still there, even for us. It's the international youth revolution, isn't it? And that includes the sexual revolution..."

"Yes, you see clearly, cherie. For us...quel destin merveilleux."

THIRTY-FOUR

SEVERAL HOURS LATER, tens of thousands gathered around the Lion of Belfort in the center of Place Denfert-Rochereau, where the students had agreed they could safely convene. Bérnard and I had left the house separately, then gone along with the group after a brief meeting where Remi Guitry appointed several stewards as our service d'ordre. I listened on as he instructed them to hold hands at the sides of the crowd to keep it in check as we marched. Many other groups were doing the same. We would show the French people how disciplined we were. Following the example set by other student groups, Remi refused to march out in front. "All our members are leaders," he said.

At the foot of the stone Lion, I stood in awe of the sheer numbers of people. My first French demonstration— manifestation, as they called it. I'd never seen anything like this crowd in Berkeley—only on television. I knew civil rights and antiwar protests in Washington D.C. were far larger than this, but in the middle of a noisy, crushing throng, this felt huge. And I felt blessedly anonymous.

"I can't see. Who's speaking?" Annette whined.

"At least you're taller than I am," complained a chubby boy named André.

"All I can see is Bérnard's *fesses*," Gabi said.

"Hey, why are you staring at Bérnard's derrière!" Frederic protested.

"I'm short, that's all. Too short...!"

"It doesn't help to be tall," I said.

"Never mind. Shut up all of you." Remi was laughing. He raised his beautiful baritone voice so others could hear: "What does it matter if we can see?" he shouted over the speaker. "He is a person like you or me, a valuable voice. The ideas are important, not the personality. Can you hear?"

"If you shut up we can," shouted a boy from the edge of our group. He was booed by Remi's pals all around me and I joined in, a lump in my throat because Remi's idea of a revolution was precisely mine.

I listened now, seeing nothing but the hair on my comrades' heads. My arms were sore from elbowing others away, from being bumped and bumping back. I hated the unrelieved noise and stink, and I had to remind myself that I was not there to have a good time. Words like liberté, societé, and others indistinguishable from one another seemed to fly one at a time over the multitude and peck me on the head, like birds with sharp beaks.

By the time the speeches were calling us to action, I had begun to let the spirit of the crowd lift me above my petty annoyances. Everyone was bubbling over with the week's public opinion successes. Scattered in the crowd were the "adults"— professors, of course, but also workers and intellectuals. We had been heard!

We began to move, starting sluggishly with a little jostling, then gradually, the smooth flow of bodies gathering speed. Despite the presence of many of the older people, it was the students who set the tone, marching in the general direction of the university, walking fast and often in step with one another. Remi's appointed stewards joined hands with those from other groups, guiding the crowd away from the quartier latin and the police. We stopped once at the Luxembourg Gardens and were directed down streets converging on the Seine. We crossed the river and ended up in the Place de la Concorde, then marched with arms linked down the Champs-Elysées.

As we strode down the famous thoroughfare, I felt my cheeks flush with excitement and pleasure. By ten o'clock, L'Etoile, the "star" of the moneyed Paris establishment, was filled with the red and black flags of communism and anarchism, and we were singing the Internationale under the Arc de Triomphe. I sang with them as well as I could, not knowing the words, but managed at least to hum the tune, my arms around two strangers whose faces I knew from our group. We smiled at one another as we marched in rhythm, the whole thing finishing a little off-key with "...L'Internationale sera le genre humain." Not long after, the crowd began to disperse. We were all exhausted, both from the long march across town and from Monday night—their Monday night, I mused, and mine.

Over breakfast Wednesday morning, we learned that our tactics of peaceful protest had been successful. I was thrilled! Nonviolence had prevailed! The government was considering when to reopen the Sorbonne. And Nanterre, too. Like magic! Bérnard was beside himself, whooping and jumping around after we heard the radio news. "There are one and a half million members in that union," he cried. "If they are with us, the revolution has begun!"

"What union?" I raised my voice to be heard over his uproar.

"For heaven's sake, Bérnard," Elizabeth said, "get hold of yourself." Only the five of us, with Cecile and La Petite Jeanette, were downstairs. The children gazed wide-eyed at Bérnard, but they were giggling, picking up his exuberant mood.

Bérnard sat down. "The CGT," he explained. "It's the Conféderation Générale du Travail. It's both a union and a political party. The French Communist Party. Didn't you understand the radio news? They were writing editorials against us just days ago. We had to sneak around Remi's father's schedule to hold our group meetings in their house. But by this morning, they came out on our side," Bérnard explained, his brown face ruddy with excitement. "So everything has changed. They are behind us! Together, we will change France!"

"Remi's father? What's he got to do with this?"

"Remi's father is a union boss. A leader in the CGT." Suddenly I'd lost my appetite. Remi's father and Remi, Teo and the Russians, communists and the revolution were all having fist fights in my stomach. "Teo hates the Communists," I mumbled.

"Don't worry," Bérnard said with unusual gentleness. "The French Communists are not the Russians. They do not hate Americans."

I followed Elizabeth out the door, pondering what Bérnard had said about the French Communists, and making a mental note to ask Teo about it.

I sat all through my school session, but participated little. My mind kept wandering to events on the street. What was going to happen? I wondered, rifling through all the possibilities from morbid to completely exhilarating. For the rest of the week, I decided, I would skip class, but go to the café for news and discussion.

Elizabeth rushed up to me just as I had located Teo in the café crowd. "I absolutely must speak with you," she insisted, then awkwardly apologized to my boyfriend for stealing me away from him. Her voice warbled dramatically and I could see tears starting to form.

So off we went down the Boulevard Raspail, Elizabeth beginning right off the bat with how distraught and puzzled she was about Laurent's "positively irrational" decision to join the rebels. As we walked home from L'Alliance, I tried to help her comprehend that Laurent would see his own future as bleak. That France was woefully underprepared for its postwar population boom and that even Laurent's lycée was intolerably overcrowded. "He's a bright guy," I reminded her, "who wants to go to a college where he can learn something."

"I've heard all that from Bérnard," she growled. "And I'll listen patiently to Laurent's complicated explanation of current events and to yours and Irena's until I go quite batty, but I still worry about Laurent doing something foolish. No matter what one believes, one must consider the consequences, mustn't one?"

"I guess one should, but sometimes one simply can't." I parodied Elizabeth's speech patterns as I had gotten into the habit of doing, a gentle mockery at her display of shock. Perhaps I needed to know there was someone in Paris who was even more naïve than me. As usual, she ignored my tone.

"In England, we say you can't fight city hall."

"We say that where I come from too. But this is even bigger than that. By extension, the fight is with the parents who elected that government, and then their values, their lazy acceptance of the status quo, their lack of imagination in fulfilling their dreams in a reasonably free and open society, and even their sexual morality."

Elizabeth shuddered. "You're all crazy! You're protesting everything there is here and you're going to ruin Paris in the process." She speeded up, and I trotted on to catch her.

"Elizabeth, when will Laurent return from Alsace?" I asked, making my voice as sympathetic as possible. Following his schoolmaster's advice, Le Grand Laurent had gone home to Alsace that morning to discuss the "youth revolution" with his parents.

"He hoped to be going for just two nights." She paused, and as if she already knew the answer, she asked, "Are you going out tonight?"

"Yes, Elizabeth. I'm going out with Teo."

"I don't mean that."

"I know what you mean."

"Is that true?"

"Of course it's true!" I forced myself to sound insulted. Elizabeth had every reason to mistrust me. And Elizabeth wasn't even the enemy.

She glanced at me sideways, clearly annoyed.

"Janet, I know you like this revolution. You've made that perfectly clear. You're beginning to sound just like Laurent and even a bit like Bérnard. But do try to keep out of trouble. I'd hate to wake up one day to find they've sent you packing."

When we entered the first house, everyone was gathered around the dining table, listening to the radio and asking Bérnard questions. He had admitted to being out the previous two nights. Mme. Bouleaux was furious. She threatened to turn him out on the street, but everyone else, including Margot and Hélène, agreed once again that the police were to blame.

The discussion spun around to the French Communist Party, which had just followed public opinion and affected a complete about-face in support of the students. Now la famille had a fear that outweighed the student unrest: that the Communist Party would take advantage of the students' issues to bring trouble to the country as a whole.

"Communists or not," said Bérnard, "you have to agree that I am responsible for myself and have the right to make my own decisions."

"You are the age of majority, Bérnard. We will not be responsible," was all Mme. Bouleaux could say. Since I knew that she did feel responsible for me, I decided that I was not ready to take on a political argument that might get me sent, as Elizabeth had said, "packing."

When Wednesday evening came at last, Bérnard and I, along with Gabi, Frederic and Laurent, back from Alsace and more sure of himself than ever, quietly exited the houses and met outside on Port-Royal, where we bundled up in our warmest jackets. No one said a word about what Margot and Madame did or did not know. Together, we walked to the Place Denfert-Rochereau to meet again around the Lion of Belfort. Groups of lycées students and their teachers had joined the masses. Le Grand Laurent went off to stand with them, defying his parents' clear orders and as jolly as if he were at a school party.

This time I assumed I knew what to expect from the manifestation, but everything from the mood of the crowd to the weather was different from Tuesday night. The speeches were few, then just as the rain began to come down, we received the order to march. Everyone followed along in good spirits. Slowly, with little shoving, we walked the short distance to the Luxembourg Gardens, then stopped. The rain had softened, but I was soaked. I shivered, straining on tiptoes, seeing only caps and shoulders. Then, angry words were passed back that Georges Séguy, the French Communist leader, was telling us all to disperse.

"Sont-ils fous...? Are they crazy? Disperse?" Remi Guitry was scowling. Students lingered in the drizzle, convinced the revolt was over.

"Trust the Party," shouted Bérnard. "They would not send us home if they did not have a better plan."

"Better plan...?" The question, fragmented by catcalls, hovered over us as a reminder of our original intentions. The Sorbonne was still off limits, but the students had already begun to wander off. Bérnard grabbed Remi and after a few words between them, they headed my way. "There's nothing more happening tonight," Remi said. "It's time I met this Czech fellow Bérnard has been talking about. Let's find a telephone." Bérnard suggested that the district of Montmartre would provide a perfect cover. There were still a few foolhardy tourists in Paris and the nightclubs were open for business. Teo had been listening for the phone in his apartment hallway. He answered before the second ring. He agreed to meet us at the exit of the Anvers Métro station in Montmartre.

Around 10:30 p.m., we three emerged from the Métro. Teo was waiting for us at the top of the stairway. He gave me a quick peck on the cheek. He was tense. "Don't look," he whispered, his lips lingering close to my ear. "Miroslav is here, so this is just a nice, social get-together." Then he reached for Bérnard's hand. "I know Bérnard from the house," he said jovially, "but who is this new fellow you're bringing me?"

After a brief introduction, we began to trudge up the twisting streets of Montmartre. Soon the majestic dome of Sacré-Coeur came into view. The bleach-white cathedral was floodlit like a beacon guiding us to a safe shore. The sky was a scramble of clouds and stars. We sat near the top of the steps that descend the hill across the street from the cathedral. A group of young guitar-plunking hippies howled at the beacon moon. My old dreams of Paris seeped through my newly-built defenses and I gawked, imagining the eyes of Hugo and Picasso, the feet of Gene Kelly and Leslie Caron. I sighed, feeling wistful as the unreality of the setting rippled through me. "The cathedral is so beautiful at night," I murmured.

"Yes, of course it is," Bérnard responded in a loud, sardonic voice that grated on my nerves. "Who would imagine? Sacré-Coeur Basilica is a memorial to a bloodbath. Built by the National Assembly and the Catholic Church in the 1870s. A way to remember the horror of civil war. French against French. And you might be interested to know. L'Internationale also originated from these events. The prized marching song of the fucked up May Revolution," he spat out angrily.

"The Cathedral and the song, too...?" I cried. My voice trailed off.

"Paris is not the romantic paradise you expected, is it?"

I smiled into the shadows. "I wouldn't say that," I mumbled in English.

"So, maybe France is not even worth fighting for?" Bérnard asked, testily.

"A happy future is worth fighting for in any language," Teo soothed. "Say, I thought I knew French history fairly well. Why did they choose Montmartre for the memorial?"

"The bourgeois Republican government left some big guns up here when they fled Paris after their defeat in the Franco-Prussian War. A month later, everyone suddenly noticed the guns. The government wanted them. So did the workers..."

Remi cut in, "The workers were starving during the war, and much of Paris was destroyed. Instead of helping them, the government passed laws making it harder for them to recover. So the workers became a mob, took the guns, and the Commune was established. The Communards, just people like the students today, governing the country." He grinned, rubbed his hands together. "Merveilleux!" he exclaimed.

"I don't understand," I interjected, "were the Communards like the Communists?"

Bérnard grumbled. "No, not a proper party like the Communists. Remi just told you. They were a loose group, like the students. They lasted for two lousy months. You are as romantic as a tourist, Remi. The Communards didn't know how to run a government..."

"They would have learned, given time. And at least they promoted the human side..."

"Eventually, the government came back with troops." Bérnard turned back to Teo and me. "Defeated them. And the Communards were as vicious as any of the government troops. Thousands were slaughtered on both sides."

"History doesn't always repeat itself," Remi said, his long legs and arms squirming uncomfortably over the steps. "The students wouldn't kill..."

"Remi wants the Communist Party to stop interfering so that we can all become martyrs. Let's just give the Party a chance!" Bérnard shouted at his friend. "At least they're not the rabble, like the Communards."

"Why are you always yelling, Bérnard!" I yelled over the guitars. Teo hissed something unintelligible and rubbed at his forehead.

"And the students?" Remi cried. "So to you, we are canaille? Is that what you mean?"

"No, but they'll never make a government alone..."

"I know that, but..."

"Even with student movement's popularity, less than half of the French people support them in polls."

"Well, you can't count on the Communists, Bérnard. With twenty-two percent of the vote, they're interested only in protecting their democratic respectability."

"Is somebody going to tell me what's been going on!?" Teo reached out to grab each of my comrades by the arm. The two flinched at Teo's grip and his sheer bulk, still eyeing each other with malice. I spoke up. "You two are basically on the same side. And anyway, neither of you has any control over matters, at least not tonight, so why don't you just shake hands and be friends again, so we can start telling Teo what happened tonight."

Remi reached over and grabbed Bérnard around the shoulders, and after a melodramatic scowl and moment's hesitation, a punch and a punch in return, Bérnard was reaching for Remi and the two were hugging. Only I noticed then that the hug wasn't just the quick cheek-cheek affair that most French men used to show genuine affection. They were sitting there on the steps of the cathedral and clinging to one another. Tears had formed in the corners of Remi's eyes and his face was lit up with an angelic smile. Bérnard's hands moved quickly, graspingly up and down Remi's body. I didn't remember ever seeing a homosexual face-to-face. If I had, I hadn't recognized them as such. Now here were two whom I knew as friends. Neither boy had been effeminate, and I had formed the opinion that perhaps the attractive Remi was destined for greatness. Bérnard had seemed to be dating Remi's sister Annette. But now it was clear that Annette had agreed to serve as a cover. Bérnard's real passion was Remi.

"That's better," Teo said, stretching his arm out to touch Remi's sleeve. The two broke from each other with sheepish faces.

"I guess you knew all along, didn't you?" Bérnard asked hopefully. "About Remi and me?" I shrugged my shoulders.

"Why not?" I said, more embarrassed for myself than for my friends. "If that's what you feel, then that's what you feel."

Bérnard sighed. Remi was assessing Teo's reaction. "We're okay here," Teo said. "You're friends of Jeanette's. We're all friends. Comrades. Now, please..."

"...tell me what happened!" the three of us chimed in.

"Tonight, my worst fears were confirmed," Remi began, his lip pushed out petulantly. "The French Communists told the students to go home. They said they'd take care of everything for us. I know the French Communists, like my father and his friends. They are unbelievable cowards. You think they are smarter than the students, Bérnard. But they do not know anything about taking over a government, much less running one. They are going to make some shady deal with de Gaulle's people, try to placate us with petty concessions that will not change anything." Then he added bitterly, "But I tell you, it will not stop the students."

"You won't be happy until you're lying in some ditch somewhere with your brains in the sewer," said Bérnard.

Remi scowled, his hand automatically going up to the scrape at his hairline where a gendarme cudgeled him Monday night before he managed to slip away.

"I am glad you're concerned about my head, Bérnard. But my brains will not be worth a bag of shit if France does not change."

"I don't know whether Remi is right or not," Teo said. "But whatever the CGT does next, I'm glad this happened tonight, because now you will see yourselves as on a different side of the battle from the Party."

No one spoke. The breeze was beginning to give off a chill. I moved closer to Teo and shivered. He put his arm around me. Remi and Bérnard sat on the step beneath us, sitting apart, not touching. How sad! I reflected. A few moments before, they had shown too much, and now were afraid once again to be honest lovers. Those two would always feel like a species of tropical fish in a tank: beautiful, exotic, but separated, suspended in the heavy medium of social judgment and on perpetual display.

I prompted, "Would this be a good time for Teo to tell you more about socialism?"

"We need to find a noisier place to talk," Teo said.

In the cathedral square was a bar where the hippies howling at the dome of the Sacred Heart had come indoors, seeking a warmer, windless venue. We found a corner table and ordered a liter of red wine. There we spoke calmly, our voices controlled to ensure that the recorded music would mask our discussion about ideas, actions and history—and about communism, Czechoslovakia, and the new France.

I sat at my little table, writing Aaron about the past two evenings—the Place Denfert, the march to the Right Bank, and the Communists' betrayal. I told Aaron to be sure to keep my letters, now more than ever, wondering what these dates in May would mean to historians.

I set my pen down. Aaron Becker would hold this very stationery in his hands, sitting in front of the hearth in his tiny, woodsy cottage. How close he was to his graduation! What would happen to the letters when he left the country? I wondered. Surely, he would find a way to return them to me!

I asked myself for the umpteenth time why I continued to write Aaron, and as always, came up with the same reply: a friend, a witness, a person who knew me well, but now, I realized, not as well as before. With an inexplicable lump in my throat, I lifted my eyes to the window and beyond, to the budding trees in the courtyard. And then, for the first time, I considered what Aaron might have felt as he read about Teo in my letters. I hadn't written him about Monday night, and he certainly had a right to know! Now I was omitting last night's amazing revelations in Montmartre, simply because Teo was so critical to them.

Did Aaron suspect by now that Teo was my lover? There had been nothing in his letters that led me to feel I was hurting him by telling him about my friendship with Teo. Nothing at all. Perhaps he had found a new girl back in Berkeley. I didn't know whether to hate the idea or hope for it! Perhaps that was it...after all, he was an attractive guy with as much libido as, well, Teodor Pelnar. I felt a small shock of sexual energy push through me like two prongs of an electrical plug. Feeling both confused and foolish, I realized that I was hungering for both men at once.   Shoving that feeling away, I focused on my clear record of my role in the May Revolution. "My life here has been a journey from childhood to adulthood, from silence and fear to opinion and assertion," I wrote. And in the writing, I realized that the journey was far from over. With the Sorbonne still closed, who knew what terrors and triumphs lay ahead for our petit groupe, and for me.

THIRTY-FIVE

LONG, SOLID SHADOWS of ornate buildings filled the Place Denfert-Rochereau. We positioned ourselves about five yards from the Lion of Belfort's platform. No one was at the microphone yet. It was Friday, May 10 at 6:40 p.m. Across the city in a stately salon near the Arc de Triomphe, peace negotiations between the United States and North Vietnam had just commenced. I imagined their voices through the suffusion of sound at the Lion's feet—powerful, contentious voices debating the future of so many individual lives. Private Matthew Magill's life.

Thirty thousand of us were expected to march against the Communists' order to disperse. We would fan out along the streets en route to the coveted University—still in government hands despite their promises. Around me, the many voices blended into garbled rhythms. Through the crush of bodies, I saw a couple kissing passionately. He was rubbing her derrière, palm down on her stretch pants. Silently, I prayed that Teo wasn't sitting alone in his room, fiddling with his radio dial and worrying about me—yet I knew that was precisely what he was doing.

I shifted my feet, staring down at my dirty American Keds, tipping awkwardly on the bumpy cobblestones. Around them ranged the thin leather flats of a European generation, prim and tidy. Where in Paris would we be marching an hour from now? Three hours? My heart thudded. My breathing came unsteadily.

Suddenly, there was Laurent's blond head working its way through the crowd from his high school CAL—Comité d'Action Lycée—a jolly grin on his face.

"I see your head is still bandaged," Bérnard was laughing. Gabi reached up to touch Laurent's forehead gently. Laurent slapped her hand away.

"Ow, leave it alone," Laurent scowled.

"I'm just trying to be sympathetic..."

Bérnard was still snickering. "He's afraid you'll pull it off. Perhaps you'll find what is beneath the gauze is not as impressive as the dressing itself. Laurent's badge of honor."

"It is still a wound," Laurent pouted.

"And I might add, one of the few genuine wounds among your peers."

"Quiet, Bérnard," said Remi. "Can't you see the boy is sincere?"

"Please don't call me a boy. It's demeaning."

"Only if you take it that way," I chimed in. "Laurent, did you see Elizabeth before you left the house?"

He hung his head and scowled. "She is so dramatic," he said. "She grabbed my arms to make sure I was listening." He imitated her voice in a most unflattering falsetto. "'Oh mon Dieu, Laurent! What good is your fighting one night going to do? And you might be arrested, or even killed!'"

"So what did you tell her?" asked Frederic.

"I said, 'I'm sorry. I do not want to leave Paris. But soon I'll be at the University. And what if nothing has changed? I feel as if I should fight with them, even if for only one night and even if it means having to go home!' She became somewhat hysterical at that."

"It's important, Laurent!" Remi declared, raising his voice and eyeing Bérnard and several others in the group, "that you and your comrades are here."

"Thanks, Remi," Laurent beamed. "I'm off to join my school fellows now. See you as we march!"

Just then, the handsome head that I knew belonged to Jacques Sauvageot, leader of the National Union of French Students, rose on the podium above the crowd and began to shout vigorously. Free Our Comrades. Free Our Comrades. The crowd's chorus followed his lead and I joined in, shouting as loud as I could. What a gorgeous guy Jacques was—like a movie star with a personality to match. Sauvageot's speech focused on the question of education, protesting that students were expected to have critical intelligence but were not allowed to exercise it in their studies. I listened with all my might, occasionally nudging Bérnard for help.

"We cannot have a socialist university in a capitalist society," Sauvageot proclaimed. "In this, we are in solidarity with students all over the world. And the Vietnamese people. And German students, liberation of the third world..." His aim was to destroy the university as it had been, and it was clear to me that a university such as the one Bérnard had described to me was not worth saving. And the messed-up world we unwillingly inherited was not worth saving either. Sauvageot railed against negotiating with the government. Each time the crowd started in again, my own clapping and hooting escalated.

Sauvageot didn't speak for long. He soon passed the podium to a plump-cheeked man who seemed older, perhaps in his late twenties, and too well-dressed to be a student. "Have I seen him before?" I asked Bérnard.

"That's Alain Geismar. Leader of the professors' National Union of Higher Education. We call it SNE Sup." Bérnard raised his hands to clap vigorously. SNE Sup swam in the puddle of my brain along with the other guppies: CGT, PCF, FEN, and UNEF.

Geismar was easier to understand. Calm, but very defiant. He was quoting statistics. "Seventy percent who attend a French university fail to complete courses. The University of Paris has not changed its organization in over a century."

"And it was no good then!" shouted Bérnard. He turned to me, his face lit with excitement. "Do you understand?" I nodded.

Geismar waited for the crowd to settle down, then continued. "This is the first time we have seen a revolutionary struggle on this scale within a capitalist nation. We have no reference model. But we know what we stand for! We don't have to choose between these artificial sides that Le Générale speaks of, between his side or the Communists. We can debate and act independently. And the French Communist support for the students is a sham...!" The crowd exploded and my hands automatically flew to my ears, but my unheralded laugh was joyful, confident. Only Remi had known, I thought. Only Remi had predicted it.

The applause still hadn't died down when Dany Cohn-Bendit got up to speak, initiating another round. By now, we all knew him. Recognized him. Dany le Rouge was a small, compact young man with bright orange hair and clear blue eyes looking like flashes of daylight, even from a distance. He was larger than myth, yet I felt like I was listening to a close friend.

I had learned that Danny the Red was a Jewish student raised in France after fleeing Nazi Germany with his parents. He had returned with his mother to Germany in his teens, but had recently adopted France as his country. Now he was a college student like the rest of us, yet what a life he'd lived already! They called him the "Robin Hood of the feverish days of May."

"The Sorbonne is occupied territory," he shouted, spitting forcefully into the microphone. "It is occupied by the enemies from the right and left—both the government and the Communists. But the University belongs to the students, for if not ours, then what purpose does it serve? It is our duty to take it back." I felt his gesticulating finger thumping on my chest. I willed myself to breathe.

Suddenly, he quieted. He urged the petits groupes to call themselves "Revolutionary Action Committees." With that simple change of title, my group's importance seemed to expand. "We offer a permanent challenge to teachers, authorities, and imperialists," he told us. His face was stern and stoic, as if he knew his message was understood by thousands, by tens of thousands, by the whole of France and possibly the world. But then, he startled us by shouting at the top of his lungs, "We begin with the University. We begin—we begin right now. Allez...allez..."

The crowd around us began to move and we moved with it. We were going to "take back the Sorbonne." Like Joshua's band walking around Jericho, we would overpower de Gaulle's forces by our sheer weight and determination. Perhaps by sheer noise. A short, smelly French girl with mousy hair and lots of makeup was pushing me, eager to get moving. I pushed back and she grinned. "Let's go..." I grinned back and laughing together, we inched forward down nameless avenues in the general direction of the Seine.

Along the way, windows were opened and people applauded from their houses and apartments. "They are listening to Europe One and Radio Luxembourg," shouted Bérnard. "Margot and Mme. Bouleaux are probably listening right now." From between open shutters I saw hands waving and waved back.

Up front, a group had started to sing L'Internationale. I reflected that this anthem to Teo's rejected communism was still a dignified march with a message that seemed appropriate to our cause, and to my feelings. The catchy tune flowed back and picked up strength as it rolled our way, until it reached us and we added to its intensity. I still did not know all the words, but I sang la-la to fill in the gaps. We were walking with our arms linked, everyone in high spirits and full of energy, and by the second verse I was singing my la-la's to the rousing march rhythm in as resonant a voice as my tiny soprano allowed. The full feeling in my chest surprised me. By the second time around I could join in with most of the words, "Debout les damnés de la terre," I sang. If my friends and I were the damned of the earth and I had been buried my whole life, at least now, as the song commanded, we were rising together, resurrected.

Dozens of flics were waiting for us on the corner of St. Germain and Boul' Mich', a front line blocking our route, armed for combat. The metallic faces of hundreds more were gathering in the open space behind the line. They barked orders that we understood only through their fierce tone and the implacable line and the convincing signals of fixed bayonets. The crowd was forced to the left and after an hour of marching, we found ourselves nearly back where we had begun. I heard shouts from up ahead, passed on back. The leaders understood the ruse. We were being lead in circles, blocked off from our strategic objective: the Sorbonne. Remi punched a tight fist into his open palm. I clenched my own sweaty palms and followed him forward.

The crowd poured into the Luxembourg Gardens. Night had come and I had to watch carefully and walk fast to keep up with our Revolutionary Action Committee. We halted on the steps above the pond, in clear view of the leaders below. Out of breath, I unzipped my brown car coat and waved the bottom of my tee-shirt to fan the air over my stomach. Rocking from side to side on my Keds, I waited and watched for what would happen next.

The leaders stood on the low wall surrounding the pond, issuing orders we could not hear. Word was passed back: "Break up into small groups and occupy the quartier latin!"

Communist Party officials were up on the fountain ledge, shouting counter-orders. Disperse! There will be bloodshed! We saw, not heard, the official's splash as someone toppled him into the pond.

Without pausing to clap and snicker with the crowd, Remi was running into Rue Gay Lussac and calling for us to follow. He stopped short, weighing options, his blond hair glowing in the lamplight of the broad avenue. My rubber soles gripped the pavés as I halted behind him. I could feel my heart pounding, as much from fear as from the run.

"This street is too open," Bérnard shouted. Remi was already moving ahead toward one of the narrow, climbing streets. Within minutes, he found our spot.

I was surrounded by a blur of decisive people. Everyone seemed to know what to do. My head bobbed back and forth and I watched them, unable to move. Groups of comrades had begun struggling together against the weight of a car, leaning their bodies in with collective groans against the shiny massive machine. Cheering filled the street as the car toppled onto its side.   My hand shot out and grabbed Remi's sleeve. "You said this would be peaceful. That they would never oppose us!"

"They are idiots!" he shouted, his voice rising hysterically. "This will finish them for sure!"

"But what if it finishes us?" I screamed. "They're an army, for God's sake!"

"So you want us to go home? Just leave? Let them run our lives however they want? You're angry with me? What? WHAT?!" He was backing me down, his hands flying over his head, furious. And his anger was like a flame that caught on my clothes, burned through my skin, into my heart. I turned away to lay my hands on a gray fender to pull with the others. It toppled. Everyone jumped back and rushed right on to the next car. Two more went down to my side, the lot surrounding us for protection as if they were covered wagons on the frontier.

I backed off and stood very still, feeling dizzy. My throat was dry except for the mucus that lodged there. My thin frame was a constant in a world spinning out of control, but my eyes stayed clear as I moved toward Annette's bleached white head, towering over Gabi's orange one. They hacked at a billboard. Annette shouted, "Pull!" and I stepped in next to her and together the three of us pulled it down. Several of the boys came along as if on cue to carry it away. They mounted it on top of a turtle-turned Peugeot. I pictured my own father's precious Lincoln Continental. Another symbol of capitalism.

I stayed with my friends and followed Annette's lead. With every reverberation of concussion grenades from the Rue Gay Lussac, we heard screaming and the expressive roar of angry comrades. I could smell the sweet, acrid tear gas wafting in from that direction. I groped inside my car-coat pocket, fingering my red western bandana. Remi had advised us to keep this item on us for protection against the gas.

We worked harder and faster, saying little to each other. We were all dripping with sweat. Our hands were bruised from pulling at objects that didn't want to give way.

"We have youth and speed," shouted a young man whose black hair extended out from the bottom of his motorcycle crash helmet in thin sweaty strings. "They'll never win!" His bravado was playacting. He pulled at branches from a tree until someone brought an ax to chop it down. I wiped at my nose with the bottom of my tee-shirt to keep myself from crying out at the sight of the sapling going down. Destroying cars hadn't bothered me, but this felt like a war casualty. "We have learned something about guerilla tactics from the peasants in Vietnam," the young man bragged to the girl with the mousy hair.

My mind tore away to Matt! Like a flashbulb illumination, the TV image of young men dying in jungles flashed before me.

Then a rush of noisy students was coming down the street. They were young and running wildly. Again I froze in fear. "The Rue Gay Lussac has fallen," they shouted. I spotted Laurent among them.

"Bérnard! It's Laurent! It's the CAL students!" I shouted, searching wildly for Bérnard. He had already seen them. The high schoolers jumped behind our fortifications, shouting about the grenade-throwers and hand grenades on Gay Lussac. Then a new noise filled the narrow street. The CAL students had brought an air hammer with them. They began to cut away at the cobblestones. Annette and I, along with the girl with the mousy hair and a high schooler, formed a four-girl link in the chain, transporting the stones to the barricade. The Barricade! As always, the very word brought up associations of the 1870 war and the Commune. There was a school book illustration, an aerial view of an entire city in shiny orange flames. Flat and odorless. How different this was, to be hot with the moment but out in the cold open air, the scene unlimited, three-dimensional, noisy, chaotic...

When our fort was erected, the throng stood behind and atop it admiring our handiwork. Within minutes, the flics were marching up our street, but before I had time to be afraid, I watched them stop in confusion. Then they were retreating again.

A woman opened her front door above a stoop. She shouted out the news: at 10:00 p.m., Radio Luxembourg had tried to mediate between the students and the Rector of the Sorbonne. The police had retreated because they awaited orders.

The woman offered us sandwiches and soda pop. Someone passed me a little triangle of cheese. La Vache Qui Rit—the laughing cow. I ripped open the tin foil eagerly, then found after one bite that I had no appetite. I wondered just how long it would take the flics to reverse themselves again.

We barely had time to speculate. The woman emerged from her front door. "Rector Roche has not agreed to the students' demands," she said. "Not to reopening the Sorbonne nor to amnesty for the prisoners. Interior Minister Christian Fouchet has given Prefect Grimaud the order. He is determined the students will not reach the Sorbonne."

People scuttled around, took positions on and behind the barricade. Annette had come over to stand by her brother's side. Their eyes met for an instant. He gave her a quick hug, then climbed to the top of the fort.

We sat in the semi-darkness of the street lamps—I had found a seat on the flat of a ripped out shop sign—waiting for the flics. I read the sign and gasped at the irony of it. Le Parc, Vêtements des Enfants. This was definitely not a stroll in the park, I thought. And I am so very far from my childhood.

The sounds of the night wafted around us, occasionally lifting like a fog with the moan of a single, human sufferer. André, a short, stout comrade with a thick quilted coat, whispered in the dark. "Jeanette, did you understand what Professor Geismar said about foreigners this week? Did Remi discuss this with you?"

I shook my head. At that moment, I didn't remember what any of the leaders had said that week. "Maybe Remi had other things on his mind."

André snickered, then puffed himself up with the importance of his message. "Geismar said that the police would let French students go free after a demonstration. But not the foreigners. If you get arrested, you may be deported. Of course, if we achieve our demand for amnesty, foreigners and workers will be included."

I sighed deeply, too tired to think of what to do with this information. Suddenly I remembered Laurent's philosophy. I whispered to André, "Well, at least I'll have one glorious night on the barricades." He smiled, and I returned it, for an instant feeling thoroughly French. Then my shoulders jerked with an involuntary shudder, more from the cold than from the thought of arrest. I leaned against André's quilted sleeve, and calming with the passing moments, did not remember falling asleep.

It was after 1:00 a.m. on André's watch when the woman with the red cardigan brought us a tray of steaming cups of hot chocolate. I reached for one but there was not enough to go around. "Ecoute!" called the woman. "Listen everyone! They are cleaning up and reconnoitering after the fall of Gay Lussac. Europe One has estimated over 50, perhaps 100 barricades are still up in the small streets. Wake up!" the woman warned us. "The flics will be back here for you soon!" With that, she fled into her apartment, shutting the door tightly behind her. Milk bottles of the baking soda and cold water mixture were distributed. We soaked our bandanas in it, then covered our faces like bandits.

Our eyes focused on the vanishing point up the tiny street. We each grasped a primitive weapon in our hands: a stone, a pop bottle or a tool. In the quiet stillness, calmed by my nap, my heart beat patiently. The battle was inevitable. All around me, I heard the padded subterfuge of street cats and boys and girls shifting in their places, trying to stay warm and awake.

Suddenly the flics were there, marching toward us as they had before. Huge, wet black hulks, glistening in their own lights. Detestably snug in zipped leather jackets. To my right and left, a few personal missiles flew forward along with isolated war cries. I bent my arm back at the elbow and threw my stone. It sank to the ground.

A deafening blast of air and objects picked me up and I landed on my side with a jarring pain.

When I forced my eyes open, there was Remi scrambling back up to the top of the barricade. His lesson grazed my consciousness: a concussion grenade didn't actually hurt anyone. My legs moved, everything moved.

Suddenly I was wide awake and furious, with a pile of stones to throw. My arm gained power, my wrist confidence, dead aim. A flic took it on the shoulder and howled. Another explosion rocked the street. I pitched at them again and again. People were shouting, hoarse and hysterical. Merde! Here are more of them! Hold on! Parts of our barricade, built up over our heads and seeming so indestructible, had caught fire. Then the wind shifted and the flics retreated in their own gas, crying out and covering eye burns.

Our boys were laughing and hooting, brandishing chains and iron bars. The flics charged, running back toward us zealously. Their cudgels and rifle butts rang out on metal and cobblestones before finding their marks, tearing flesh, cracking bone.

This time I began to move away as some others were doing. No conscious thought, just backward motion. A few of the girls and most of the boys stood their ground and focused on Remi's commands. Bérnard and André and others running out of the shadows dragged the burning cars so that they blocked the street completely. The tear gas was so thick and the shouting so loud that no one could see the bulldozer until it was grinding over the barricade.

Concussions blasted down the street from the opposite direction. People were running that way, but I backed up against a house, not knowing which way to go. I crouched down.

The flics were still advancing, slowed by the fighters on the barricade but now supported by water cannons and the bulldozer. The heavy-duty vehicle was like a faceless monster from a science fiction movie, followed by faceless, helmeted robots with long, spindly legs, hurtling across unearthly piles of rock. I shrunk down into the shadows as the machine rolled past my line of vision. A girl bumped into me, stumbled and sat down hard on my hip, then bolted away. It was Gabi! Where was Frederic? There was no time to speculate. Water dumped from buckets came flying through open windows. Some found their marks on the heads of the enemy. Furious, the flics were throwing tear gas grenades right back into the open windows.

Behind me the door of the building was shut tight. The sidewalk was littered with smashed shoes, pocketbooks, and broken eyeglasses. Bleeding students lay everywhere.

Down the row of house fronts, the blackness of a breach snagged my attention. When it seemed a clear moment, I scuttled across, fast and low, to a weedy alleyway, and wedged myself into the narrow space behind a row of trashcans. I stretched out on my side on the ground, making my body as thin as possible between the cans and the cold wall behind my back. I tucked my head beneath my hands, as if that could prevent anyone from seeing me. Centuries of rot in the earth wafted up through my bandana and into my nostrils but I dared not move a muscle. A dry heave forced me to be aware of my situation. There was nothing left of my supper the night before to regurgitate. It was the smell. And fear. I had wet my pants, but was so soaked from drizzle and sweat that I couldn't even remember when I'd first noticed the creepy sensation. My body shook all over, from cold or fear or shock—perhaps all.

A girl's piercing scream forced me to peek out from a small rectangle of space about the size of a cigarette pack. A trashcan not ten feet down the row from me rattled and my eyes inched up to glimpse André's head. A policeman spotted him and shouted for his cohorts. Together, three of them lifted the trashcan and dumped André out onto the street from about six feet up and he passed from my view. Just then one of their lock-up vans, the hideous black Marias, screeched to a halt on the street. I watched as they tossed André's chubby body in with so many others. It occurred to me that if the Maria got through, the barricade had come completely down. The contingent with their lock-up moved on down the street. All that remained in my little sector was the sickly, yellowish gas that still hung in the air.

I was aware enough of my own condition to consider emerging for help, but after what I had witnessed, I was afraid to move from my safety zone. "I'm okay," I told myself now. "Oh God," I whispered so softly that only God and I could hear. "This must be what it feels like." And then I started to cry. To shake and cry silently in a hole behind a trash heap and to hear one word, one name: Matthew. My big brother Matt. For it seemed to me then that if one war was like another, one war did not justify another. If this was even a small bit of what Matt had gone through, day after day for many months now...

Still crying, but assuming I was alone at last, I started to lift myself up but crouched down again when the chimera of a young girl darted by. A thin, helmeted shaft came up after her and a matraque, one of the terrifying rubber batons with iron rod at center, cracked over her bare head. Not too hard—the flic had held back his strength. She still stood, but while he held her there, swaying, a tall figure came from behind—it was Laurent! He grabbed the arm with the matraque. Pulled the arm away from the girl, who fled to the safety of darkness. Now Laurent stood alone before the flic. With tears still stinging my eyes, I found myself out on the edge of the street, flinging away my bandana, shouting Laurent's name to let him know I was coming and to distract the flic.

Then I was there, pulling futilely at the matraque, two against one, but it was no good. I felt the blow on the side of my head just after Laurent went down, and I watched the ground and Laurent's prone body rush up toward me. Laurent's back was still and hot under my stomach. The flic was shouting for partners, for vans to take us away. Aware of my own consciousness, I closed my eyes and waited for the inevitable.

Footfalls plodded away down the street. With Marias long gone, our attacker was running off behind his gang, leaving us for dead or at least harmless. Furtively, I surveyed the area. Struggled to get myself up. Pulled at Laurent with all my might. He was unconscious. He should be out of the center of the road.

A round little person with short black hair crept up by my side. After a few moments, she mumbled something in French that I could not fathom. She felt the pulse in Laurent's neck. "He is okay," she said. Together, we tugged him back over to the safety of my alley. "Wait here," was all the girl said, then disappeared back down the street into the shadows.

What could I do for Laurent? I tucked my brown coat collar up under his chin, hoping that might keep his body from going into shock. The Red Cross and hospital orderlies were supposed to be out in force, risking truncheons to rescue the wounded. My own head throbbed. I moved closer to Laurent to keep us both warm.

From off in the distance, an isolated children's choir sustained the melody of L'Internationale. The sky over the Mouffetard district was lit with street fires despite police hoses and rain, like a colorful water show I had seen at the New York World's Fair. Daddy and Matt and I went together. When was it? Four years ago, yes. Mother was with her parents in Boston. I remembered the exhibition's vibrant hues and the perfume of caramel corn. The cries of amazement at the beauty of the rainbowed configurations of spray. The warmth of Daddy's arm wrapped around my back. His other hand resting lightly on Matt's shoulder. Our faces glowing in eerie light.

Laurent was moaning softly. I pushed myself up onto my knees and used the rain to wash the blood from Le Grand Laurent and the tears from La Grande Jeanette. I searched desperately for anger, willed myself to feel it, but I came up only with the clutch of pity. I burrowed my eyes into Laurent's damp neck and let my tears flow. None of us, none in the human race, I thought, are very grand tonight. Pitiable humans—flics and comrades and the bourgeois woman who gave me the Laughing Cow that I could not swallow. How many times in this century have freedom's brave defenders been in harm's way? And now again, not attacked by evil Nazis but by the enemy within, who were willing to hear the cries but afraid to listen to the words of the next generation of French citizens.

THIRTY-SIX

AT 7:00 A.M., I was sitting naked on a low, wooden stool in the bathroom, inspecting bruises, cuts and scratches coated with goose bumps and American First Aid Cream. My bottom was the only warm part of my body, and the only part that didn't hurt. After washing myself three times in the damn cheap bourgeois' freezing tub, I gave up. Even after washing away the stink of the street, nothing was going to make me feel clean.

The patch of sky outside the tiny window had faded to gray. I stood up and yawned, carefully touching the cool, wet hair over the painful lump on the side of my head. I was weak from exhaustion, but wondered how I would ever fall asleep. With every vision of the night streets, a heartbeat of blood and pain rushed up into my wound.

When I walked out into the hall, wrapped in my towel, Gabi and Elizabeth were on the landing. Hélène's family was still asleep in their beds and Gabi's finger crossed her lips. We all hugged, then they followed me into my room and we shut the door. Tersely, I let them both know that Laurent got a bad bump on the head. "He'll recover," I whispered, "but he's in the hospital. I'm not sure if they arrested him or not, but they could hardly take him off to jail in his condition." Elizabeth gasped and drew her hands to her mouth. I was amazed, then, to see Gabi put her arm around Elizabeth. "Did you not hear Jeanette say he would be fine?" she asked. Elizabeth put her hands down and nodded. Reflecting that the revolution made strange bedfellows, I asked about Frederic.

"He's in his room. A policeman grabbed him too, but he intimidated le flic into letting him go. I am very proud of him for his bravery," she said wearily. "Bien sûr, it helped that the policeman was nearly a decade younger than him."

"Gabi, I honestly don't know how you ever got Frederic involved in the first place. To come to the group meeting."

"Frederic is not idealistic. I told him it was a practical matter. When he graduates, does he want to make a fair wage or not? Does he want to be a mindless bureaucrat, aspiring to someday be an exploiting boss? He considers this a fight for his future and..." her smile was sly. "He knew Madame would not approve. And you, Jeanette? Were you hurt?"

"My head..." my hand went instinctively to the sore spot. "There were so many students there in the hospital...the nurse called it 'superficiel.'" As I pronounced the word, I thought about Teo. How worried he must be! I wanted to telephone him as soon as possible.

Gabi shook her head. "Too noisy. You will have to do it when everyone wakes up."

Teo was still on my mind when I dragged myself out of bed just before mid-day dinner. Finding fresh clothes in the armoire, I glanced at the ravaged pile I'd tossed on the floor. I removed the peace symbol pin, now scratched beyond recognition, from my coat lapel. A wave of nausea hit me as I relived the moments of crawling along on the rough, smelly ground of the alley. For a moment, I held the pin in my hand, and thought about how many friends had admired it. Nobody else had one like it. Then I leaned the pin against Madame Bouleaux's hand-bound volumes by Dumas on my bookshelf—the author was my old companion from Berkeley days, just like the pin.

It was time to eat, and I didn't have the nerve to absent myself from the table. My landladies were sensitive to the views of students, but no more sympathetic with street actions than Daddy and Mother Magill would have been. As Margot sat down after serving the cheese and fruit and Madame solemnly switched on the radio, I suddenly knew what I wanted: a French citizen's explanation of what I had witnessed. I looked Margot in the eye and asked her for her interpretation of the news.

"You seem to know more about France than the French do," she said, shrugging her shoulders. "If you need an interpretation, ask your comrades on the street..."

"I'm sorry, Margot, if I upset..."

"Upset? Mais non, la Grande Jeanette." She arched her eyebrow and pursed her lips. "Why should I be upset if someone who lives under my roof wants to put herself in the hospital? You are a stupid girl."

I finished my dinner, keeping the possible retorts to myself, knowing that I had gotten off easily with "stupid." After dinner, feeling desperate, I went quickly and quietly to the phone.

The conversation with Teo was agonizingly brief. The phone in Teo's apartment corridor was as public as mine. I told Teo I needed time to rest and recover, so we agreed to meet Monday at L'Alliance.

Sneaking away and up to my room, I lowered myself gingerly onto the pillow and with all my clothes on, even my shoes, once again fell into a deep sleep. When I awoke, it was dark outside. I had slept past supper. I lay still, remembering the crushing pity I had felt at the battle's end. Then suddenly, it came to me that if I could lie in the street feeling pity, not anger, then there had to be hope. Sure, we needed new ways to protest nonviolently. Weren't there always new ideas among people with good hearts? Surprisingly good ideas even came from "stupid" people like me. I smiled into my pillow. I knew I was far from stupid. I had a lot of learning to do, but now, I had also found my public voice. Too excited to remain alone with my thoughts, I swallowed a couple of aspirin tablets and walked out to the hallway and down to Gabi's room.

"Jeanette! Awake at last. There is good news! Prime Minister Pompidou has announced the release of all students involved in the protests."

"And Bérnard?" I asked hopefully.

"He hasn't shown up." She hugged me tight. "Are you okay?" she asked.

I sighed. "Yes. Worried, that's all."

Back in my room, my mood fluctuated between calm determination and the desperation I felt for news. What had happened to Bérnard, to the injured André, and Annette, Remi, and the others, whom I had last seen standing their ground on the front lines of our barricade?

I slept fitfully again that night and awoke on Sunday morning with a headache, the sniffles and a sore throat. With a silent scowl, Margot made me honeyed tea and brought it on a tray with dinner up to my room. I spent the day nursing myself in my little bed-nook, writing letters I wasn't sure I could ever send and worrying about my comrades.

There was still no word from Bérnard. But at least I was cheered by the news reports. Public opinion was now more solidly on the side of the students. Forced to concede, Pompidou had ordered the police to disperse, the University of Paris reopened, and amnesty for all. This time, the students had truly won all of their minimum demands.

Monday morning, the third day since the Companies Sécurités had obliterated the barricades, I was feeling a little better, and I was hungry. In the salon of the first house, a crowd fluttered around Laurent, who had just been released from the hospital. The blinds of the casement window had been drawn and Madame's antique lamps were lit only in a far corner away from the patient. Breakfast was spread in the adjacent dining room, with pitchers of hot coffee and cocoa and scoops of butter and homemade jam for the egg-shaped bread rolls and crispy croissants. I poured a cup of hot cocoa and grabbed a croissant, its soft, fat saddle already so buttery and sweet that it needed no spread. Munching and sipping, I stayed in the background while everyone else ignored Margot's feast and stood wide-eyed over Le Grand Laurent.

The young hero of the night was not his cheery old self. He sat up tall on a brocaded chair and permitted his audience to inspect his head, but spoke in a voice that sounded like Bérnard's: low-pitched, his words tense and staccato. When he reached the part about my help in his rescue, I felt as if he were talking about some other person. But yes, there were memories. Shadows rushing by. Echoing voices. Stink. Pain. Distress. And the eyes glaring at me now gave me the uneasy feeling that I should be clapping my hand over Laurent's mouth.

"So, Jeanette," Mme. Bouleaux faced me with her arms folded, "shall we telephone your parents as we have already telephoned Laurent's? With news about the ungrateful, radical American girl who has been a guest in our house?"

"In two of our houses, Maman," Margot added. "In Paris and on l'Île de Ré."

"Alors! What do you say, la Grande Jeanette?"

Everyone in the room was staring at me. I heard a gentle groan from Laurent's lips. "I'm sorry, Jeanette..."

"Never mind," Madame said, "this is not your problem, Laurent." She had regained her composure. Her air of command. I settled the creamy cup of cocoa on the little round table next to me, stood up, and walked over to face her. My voice was clear.

"I apologize, Madame, for any inconvenience or fear I may have caused you. If you must phone my parents, then you must. I do not intend to participate in any more battles. It was terrible..." In the corner of the room, I heard Yao-Yao quietly meow and realized with relief that the children were not there. I pushed myself up straighter and continued. "But I do not apologize for participating. I will always act for what I believe and act with my comrades. We did not cause the battle, but we have won the war. Our three demands have been met—"

"You are all crazy!" shouted Jean-Louis, clearing a path to me with flailing, pudgy hands. "You have your university and your amnesty and the police are held in check, but now seeing the way clear, your radicals and communists are stirring up the workers' unions. Spinning new demands, have you heard? They will never rest until they topple the General's government..."

"The General's fascist government must go!" Laurent's shout cut him off. With a sharp movement, the patient buried his head in his hands. Suddenly, everyone was rushing past me to converge on Laurent. After a few frightening seconds, I watched Laurent's head pop back up, his eyes clear. I backed into a corner, looking furiously from Jean-Louis to Laurent.

"You irresponsible children don't even know what you want!" Jean-Louis spit the words at Laurent, as if this one boy was a direct threat to the entire nation.

At that, I came quickly out of my corner. "What we want?" I asked. "As if the elimination of the violent French police state wouldn't be enough to want!"

"Bravo, Jeanette!" Laurent's eyes were suddenly full of tears. Laurent tried to continue, but members of the household seemed infinitely more interested in being heard than in hearing what Laurent had to say. Gabi urged Laurent to calm himself, then swore at the special forces of the Companies for their brutality, which had left two dead and thousands injured. Jean-Louis declared indignantly that even with amnesty, many anarchists were still in hiding, apparently with the bourgeois families whose values they were trying to overthrow. Hélène advised that Laurent should have more ice on the bump. Margot was already running off to get the ice pack before the words were out of her sister's mouth. Frederic was announcing in an unnaturally loud voice that Laurent was lucky to be alive. Madame was asking Laurent where the hospital bill would be sent.

Elizabeth pulled me out into the foyer. She was visibly shaken by the sight of the welt that had risen under the sticky mass of her boyfriend's fair hair.

"I've decided to forgive you for deceiving me," she said. "Heavens! I know I wouldn't have been half so brave as you were, Janet. Oh my, I need to compose myself. I'm truly grateful you were there to help Laurent as you did."

I sighed. "I'm not a heroine, Elizabeth. I'm just like Laurent. I was there because I believe in a fair and free world."

"Laurent certainly is a bloody fool but I love him dearly..." She started to weep, so I put my arms around her, wondering how best to comfort her in the days to come. I was afraid that Laurent's one night of glory had come and gone, and Elizabeth would soon be quite alone.

My own open question was promptly answered. Madame marched into the foyer and stood eye-to-eye with me. "I will not call your parents, Jeanette, if you will promise me no more participation."

"I told you I have no intention..."

"I do not want to telephone them." Madame interrupted. "I trust that you will be sensible now." She retreated into the salon.

Elizabeth smiled through her tears. I sat down heavily on the stairs, and my friend sat next to me, as if weary of fighting her own battles. "Madame is plotting to solicit older boarders for September," she informed me. "I heard her shout at Margot, 'No more teenagers!' She wants a line on some prudent Japanese students."

I snickered. Was this Madame's personal revolutionary action?

My attention was snagged by a stirring in the salon. Just then Laurent hobbled past us without comment, assisted by Margot and Hélène, out the door and presumably to his bed in the second house.

Elizabeth and I left immediately for L'Alliance, already late for school. I was afraid that Teo would go off to class and I would miss him. The pain in my head and the shortness of my breath slowed me down, but Elizabeth stayed with me, a worried expression now perpetually on her face. From far up the Boulevard Raspail, we caught sight of a crowd outside. "The doors must be locked," I said, straining to see. When we reached the iron-spike gate, we stood together reading the posted notice. The school would be closed indefinitely, "In Sympathy with the Students of France."

"This is significant," declared one of the students. He twisted his head to make sure he had an audience, his thick glasses reflecting the quiet light, then he continued in a serious tone. "L'Alliance receives funds from de Gaulle's government. If they take the students' side, they must be willing to risk their allotment from the culture ministry." The crowd responded with the usual "ahhs" and "oh làaas." They hadn't known.

Teo stood to one side, listening. "I'm sorry we couldn't talk longer on the phone..." was the first thing I said. Teo put his arms around me gently and held me there, not moving. It was as if he were afraid I was fragile and would break if he tightened his grip. He tipped my chin up and I saw deep concern in his eyes. "You are sick," he said.

"It's nothing. Petit mal de tête et rhume." A little headache and a cold. "Laurent came home from the hospital this morning. The whole story is out..." His eyes went over my shoulder. Claire Caplan stood behind me, waiting patiently.

"You were there, weren't you," she said in English, more a statement than a question. I nodded. "Well, I wanted to say goodbye. I'm getting out of here. I'm terribly sympathetic with the French students, honestly, but this is not what I signed on for."

"Are you going home?"

She shook her head, scratched at a spot on her flabby cheek. "Not yet. I'll go to Italy. It's supposed to be gorgeous in June, and besides," she grinned, "I hear the men are more aggressive with American women than they are in France." How much I would miss the company of an American and a strong woman friend in Paris! I hugged her and wished her luck. She handed me a little piece of paper with her parents' address in Boston. "Keep in touch," she said, and backed off into the crowd of students.

Teo tapped Elizabeth on the shoulder, "Let's get away from here." He put one arm around her and the other around me and guided us toward the Bouleaux house. Miroslav followed at a safe distance.

We heard the shouting as we entered the courtyard. "It's Margot and Laurent," Elizabeth said. "He shouldn't be getting so excited."

Mme. Bouleaux approached, carrying her purse and some mesh shopping bags over one arm. She stopped when she saw Elizabeth. "I'm sorry, child," she said. "I know you are his friend. But Laurent has disobeyed his parents and he has been injured for his foolishness. He must be sent home to Alsace today."

"Oh no! So soon?" Elizabeth cried, rushing past Madame and into the first house.

Mme. Bouleaux shrugged her shoulders dramatically. "C'est ça. Hallo Jeanette. Bonjour, monsieur," she sang out. "You should see the boy! He carries a big fruit on his head! Only God knows why he is alive." Then without waiting for a reply, she swept past us through the courtyard. "Au revoir, Jeanette. Bonjour, monsieur." And she waved at us over her shoulder and disappeared under the archway.

"Do you want to see the 'big fruit'?" I asked Teo.

He frowned and shook his head. "Can we go up to your room? We have never done that before. Are there any rules against it?"

I glanced at the third-story shutters of my room, crisp in the mid-morning sun. "None that they told me about. And they certainly gave me enough rules."

We met no one as we climbed the stairs to my room. Jean-Louis and Hélène would be at work. The little ones had been sent off Sunday to Jean-Louis's parents to get them out of Paris. I entered my room ahead of Teo and flopped down into a chair. Teo bent double to kiss me on the cheek, then searched my eyes. I blinked wearily, struggling to keep them open. With a shrug of the shoulders, he sat down across the writing table. "Alors, what are you going to do now?" he asked. "I mean, about the revolution."

"I'm waiting for word from Remi. I've heard many of the leaders are in hiding, despite the so-called amnesty."

"Yes, vraiment, nothing is settled yet."

"I should go and search for people in the action committee. But it's odd, just as our goals are possible, I can't get myself to move. I did nothing but lie in bed this weekend."

Teo's face looked as anguished as I imagined mine to be. "What can I do to make you feel better, cherie...?"

"Nothing will ever make me feel better. You should have seen it Friday night, Teo. It was the Commune. People were bloody...it was so vicious. And completely unfair. "

"I worry...you know this could get even more dangerous. With French workers starting to strike and their new demands stretching the government's patience."

"In America, the workers would never respect the students enough to join them. And they would never dare align with the Communists, not since the Cold War."

"The Party in France is French, not Russian," Teo said. "I understand why workers here would follow the Communists, who have a strong history as their champions."

"But you fear, like Jean Louis, that the Communists will take over here?"

"Not so much," he replied. "De Gaulle still has his support with the bourgeousie. I am worried more about you on the street, cherie. This is becoming une mauvaise herbe. Growing quickly, in surprising directions. Are you registered with your American Embassy? Do they know you are here?"

"No! Who would ever think of doing that?"

"A European. Especially a Central European. All Czech citizens overseas must register with their embassies."

"Well, I guess it's a good idea..." I struggled to keep the quiver out of my voice.

"But I can see you need to rest first. To recover."

Teo left before the midday dinner. Laurent was still resting in his room. Margot had brought him a tray of food. His train was due to leave in a couple of hours.

Around the dinner table, we all listened anxiously as Margot spoke about food and gasoline shortages, and cash withdrawal limits. It was good that she and Maman had stocked up, had cash, bottled water and candles, a supply of food. The turmoil, she feared, had just begun.

As Margot wound down, Mme. Bouleaux cleared her throat, then announced, "This afternoon, there will be a mass demonstration through the city. A peaceful march, I have heard. The route passes by the front of our building. You may want to stand on the side and observe," she warned, "but once you join them, you will be stuck there, perhaps for many miles. Now everyone, eat. It is important to keep up our strength!"

Just as dinner ended, Bérnard walked in the door. Hastily, he reported that everyone in our group was alive and free, though André was still in the hospital. Then he addressed himself to Mme Bouleaux, avoiding Margot's angry glare. "Don't worry, Madame," he said, "I am here long enough to collect my belongings. I am paid in full here. I have found another place to stay. Adieu!"

And with that Bérnard headed over to the second house to grab his gear. When he returned to the salon, I walked with him as far as the archway. "Are you staying with Remi?" I asked.

"No, he doesn't want me. His father is ranting all the time!"

"Did Remi have to agree to stay off the streets?"

"Remi's father makes the deals, not Remi," Bérnard replied proudly. "But I can't stay there. I'm temporarily with another Sorbonne student who has taken in several of us. It's a party day and night. An exhausted party, but a party. I'll be okay."

THIRTY-SEVEN

LATER THAT AFTERNOON, I stood with Elizabeth as she saw Laurent off for the train. A moment after the taxi disappeared down Port-Royal, Teo arrived on foot. Elizabeth stood there, tissue in hand, "composing herself," obviously not wanting to walk back into the courtyard by herself. "Stay and keep us company during the *manifestation*," I coaxed. "I promise to stay on the sidelines."

After only a few minutes, a mass of marchers strode down the street toward us, eerily quiet, given their numbers. It was a gray, overcast afternoon, the sky reflecting the sullen spirit of the protesters. We stayed back behind the line of monitors, the appointed service d'ordre who held hands along the curbs, forming a human chain that separated participants from observers. One could not cross the street without becoming a part of it. My stomach knotted, telling me to keep back, to control my own feet and keep my brain and view clear. I didn't want to be jostled. Didn't want to be touched by the shoulders of strangers. But however black and blue I felt now and however much I still hated crowds, I reassured myself that the sound of those footsteps was justification enough for my involvement and the suffering of my friends. The University of Paris had reopened, but the real gain was here, marching down the street. The support of the French people. The determination of the French workers and the promise of real change.

Manifestation, I realized, was an apt word in English as well. The event was a physical manifestation that ten million French people had stayed home from work, en grève—on strike: all forms of power, water, transportation and communications would be affected. Factories and mills were quiet, tourists stranded, garbage rotting in the streets. Even entertainers were on strike. Television and radio would carry only the news.

From radio reports, we knew that even greater numbers were marching over from the Right Bank, then down Boul' Mich'. Even on Port-Royal, the tremendous, controlled throng formed a torrential tributary heading toward the corner of Montparnasse to meet up with others and further expand the stream. I was mesmerized by the scale of the march, often dozens abreast, and they just kept coming. I marveled at the control, given the numbers. A half million? A million or more? All of Paris? All of France? And such an odd alliance: workers, intellectuals, housewives with their children, men in business suits. All types and ages, many carrying colorful banners or flags, all there to support a gang of college student protesters.

Or so it seemed, until a clump of older workers, stretching the bright colors of a CGT banner low across their bellies, moved purposefully apart from the students. The service d'ordre cut off a group of students, halting them until the CGT had gone on. Teo took my arm to draw my attention to this action. I gasped, my anger against Teo's hated communists once more welling inside me. Then, in an almost instantaneous reaction, some of the younger workers doubled back to reach the students. We observed in amazement as the students threw their arms around their new comrades, laughed and made a few derisive comments. Then they walked on amiably together. A bewildered service d'ordre did nothing to change the new configuration.

I sighed with relief, and Teo squeezed my hand. "This is the new order in France," he smiled.

Elizabeth had missed the defiance of the young workers, but heard Teo's comment. "Apparently, they are not all for the same things," she said, the pitch of her voice rising nervously. Her usual mannered combination of irony and shock was taking on distorted proportions. "Look! Look at their banners." Shapes, stripes and slogans floated by in a colorful array of opinion. Some lauded de Gaulle, others held his lifeless effigy on makeshift gallows. Some were for educational reform, others were for social reform. The communists wanted their say, but so did Catholic labor unions.

"All these complaints," Elizabeth snapped. "Whatever is wrong, let's just gripe to the government."

"Well, who else's fault would it be?" asked a paunchy, balding little man, listening from nearby, one of the hundreds of hand-holding links in the chain containing the protest.

"I don't know, but I do wish it would all end," Elizabeth said.

"Listen to those footsteps, Elizabeth," I said, putting my arm around her waist. "Don't they tell you anything?" We listened together, a dozen, two dozen beats. Acres of heads bobbed in the faded sunlight.

"Yes, I know they're accomplishing something," Elizabeth's jittery voice broke my reverie. "But frankly, I want the museums and theatres to open up, and our school. I wonder if Laurent didn't deserve his exile from Paris! He wasn't sympathizing with me at all, nor with his parents." She wrapped her arm around me and held on as if she sensed that I was about to pull away. Then she drew out an embroidered hanky and wiped her nose like a proper war widow.

Teo glanced over at Miroslav, who stood a few paces behind us, leaning up against a storefront with a Gaulois hanging from his fat lips. I was surprised to see Teo's eyes bright with tears.

"What's wrong, Teo?" I asked. He moved up to slip between Elizabeth and me.

"Not a thing," he said, staring into the crowd of marchers. "It's...it's powerful. They are so orderly and controlled. Yet so many of them, free in expressing their various opinions. Something quite beautiful, don't you agree? Merveilleux."

"Yes, exactly. I do. But evidently your friend is quite bored," I said. A few yards away, Miroslav lit another cigarette and stared at the sidewalk beneath his feet. His pants were green and orange plaid and he wore a long-sleeved cotton shirt of drab purplish brown, like a rotting eggplant. I felt nauseous just knowing Teo had anything to do with him. I blurted out, "Doesn't it just drive you crazy to have him there all the time?"

"Yes. And no. I'm used to him. He's my guardian angel." He blew on his hands to warm them, still soaking in the miracle of the French manifestation, then added, "My dark angel."

With the strike expanding daily, the government and the unions were in haggling sessions. Prime Minister Pompidou and his Générale were holding on, but among the students, their impending downfall was discussed as if it had already happened.

To Elizabeth's delight, L'Alliance Française re-opened after the manifestation, evidently satisfied that the students' demands had been met. But my real learning began the evening that I strode through the medieval portals of the Sorbonne alongside members of my action committee. The courtyard was plastered with portraits of Marx, Mao, Lenin, Trotsky, or Che and slogans of the May Revolution. "Be realists—demand the impossible" was my favorite. "All power to the imagination" was another. I didn't like the negative ones, like "Injustice, Inequality, Idiocy," the play on "Liberty, Equality, Fraternity." Even less the one scribbled all over the Paris Métro, summing up the absurdity of existence: "métro, boulot, métro, dodo," meaning "subway, work, subway, sleep." Had my existence ever been less absurd than it had been this spring?

I watched as clumps of big, healthy-looking young guys in working cottons and leather jackets entered the university at a slow, hesitant pace, looking around before each step. Student leaders approached them with warm smiles and handshakes, letting them know how eager they were to hear the workers' viewpoint. Factory and office workers had never been inside the Sorbonne, nor the Odéon—the Théâtre de France—which had also opened its doors for discussion by the revolutionaries. These hard-working, good people had been shut out of France's most humanizing public spaces for their whole lives! The thought made me furious. I only saw men, and silently wished that their wives and even their children had joined us.

I trailed my comrades down an aisle in the Sorbonne's cavernous amphitheatre. Students, professors, and other intellectuals were still arriving, waving red and black flags, shouting and laughing and already arguing politics. Soon the auditorium, rising three tiers above us, was packed. Bérnard was trying to tell me something and I couldn't even hear his voice. With a look of frustration, he jabbed his forefinger in the direction of the passage that ran above rows of seats on our ground floor level. There, I saw some scary types in Eisenhower caps and shoddy, threadbare work shirts standing in the half-light. Their faces were broad, their hair and beards scruffy, and their expressions defiant and tough.

"Who are they?" I shouted directly into Bérnard's ear. The crowd was being urged to quiet down for the discussion. "The unemployed," he replied. "Some call them canaille, you know? like no-goods." Rogues, I thought, or even criminals. It crossed my mind that if you could not find work, you might become a hardened criminal, just to survive. Now they finally had the chance to tell their side of the story.

After what seemed to be an older student's short lecture on a point of labor history, the debate began. Everyone who had something to say was permitted to speak, each for three minutes. The crowd occasionally "voted" off a poor speaker or a naysayer with their hisses and boos, but just as often demanded that the speaker continue. Genuine democracy! I thought, picturing us all in togas, sitting around in one of those marble amphitheatres in ancient Greece.

The most vocal in the huge crowd were the students, arguing with the young workers and with each other over programs and proposals to reform France. What kind of society did they want? How might they reinvent their country? What kind of role did workers want in their factories? These questions were viewed from every conceivable angle. I struggled to get only the basic ideas expressed in the debates. Too much emotion, speed, and simultaneous expression. And too much ardent desire on my part to catch nuances still beyond my capacity. But as soon as I so much as knitted my brow, one of my comrades with command of English would lean in to translate an important point. Later, I thought with an intake of joy, they will ask me my opinion about this or that debate. I itched to get into one of the small classrooms or out to a café, where I knew I would be able to take part in the conversation.

A worker with a tucked, pressed blue shirt and dark, slicked-down hair was passed the loudspeaker. He and his comrades knew as much about running the factory as their bosses, he declared. They wanted to be respected when they contributed ideas about how to improve production. This is the way he and his friends had been talking, when the CGT was out of earshot. If all workers ran their factories, he asserted, then a union of all these individual unions might run France!

"This man is an Anarcho-Syndicaliste," Bernard rasped in my ear. "They are all for complete self-management, autogestion, you understand? This is like asking for a full moon thirty days a month. It sounds beautiful, but it would wreck the planet." I sniggered, able to see his point, but I wondered...I had never even considered that a worker would feel confident about running his plant!

An office worker for the government introduced himself— so many of these in bureaucratic France, I thought. I was amazed to hear that he felt just as the factory worker had about his ability to contribute to the goals of his team. But no one had ever asked for his ideas, and such discussions were regarded negatively, even suspiciously, by his boss. He was not for autogestion, but for cogestion. He did not understand why the CGT could not fight for the right of all working people in France to dialogue openly with bosses about production and the outcomes derived from their labors.

After just a couple of hours of listening, I was exhausted and gagging from the smell of human excretions that I preferred not to identify. I excused myself, telling Bernard that I was going to find the toilettes, then go home. I refused his half-hearted offer to walk with me, happy to walk home on my own, to have the time to myself to think through what I had witnessed.

All week, these large meetings continued. Some days I went directly from school to the Odéon with various combinations of students from L'Alliance. In the evenings, I walked with Bérnard to join our action committee for more Assemblées Générales or plenary sessions, held every night in the giant amphitheatre, or now more often to meetings on specific topics, held in smaller classrooms. By the following weekend, we heard that 175 Action Committees were now all operating independently, but willing to do battle again together if necessary. I was attached to the idea of non-violent exemplary actions, such as helping the neighbors to form their own neighborhood action committee, and approached Remi about that after a few days.

"Your French is not good enough, Jeanette. I am sorry. I know you would like to help."

"Is it that terrible?" I asked, swallowing hard and trying not to show how hurt I felt.

Remi licked his lips and stared down at his fidgety shoe. "It's not just that," he said. "It is that you are a foreigner. It is sad to admit this to you. Workers are not like students. They do not trust foreigners." He chucked me under my chin and I smiled. "Anyway, there is always more hunger for leaflets, posters, even longer pieces. You are good at those, so you can keep working on that, can't you?" I nodded, grateful that Remi had found a meaningful place for me. And I knew that my comrades were listening to my ideas.

Meanwhile, in the press, the Communist CGT objected to the students' open meetings. The union was busy negotiating with the government behind closed doors. Ignoring their pleas, the students continued to meet—strident, enthusiastic, non-stop deliberation, open to everybody.

Everybody, it seemed, except Teodor Pelnar. Even Irena showed up, announcing that the Polish government could do what they would with her—she was determined to stay and to participate. We could only surmise that nobody was watching her every move.

"Please tell Teo," she instructed me, "that the news connects our nations. So many student battles at Columbia University in New York and here in Paris that the newspapers are ignoring Central Europe. But I had a letter from home. In Poland, the police are beating students in the streets, while in Prague, the students marched to the Polish embassy to protest treatment of Polish students."

"And the Polish students are also against the Vietnam War?" I asked.

"No, little one. They protest the government's anti-Zionist campaign to drive out the few remaining Jews. Can you imagine? So many evils in the world..." she clucked her tongue against her big square teeth.

Teo was cheered by the courage of Czech students and their new sense of free speech, but he followed news from home as if he stood before a prison gate that was about to be slammed shut in his face. That week, we learned that Soviet Premier Kosygin had arrived in Prague unexpectedly. The next day, Grechko's eight-man Soviet military mission had crossed the Czech border for an "exercise." If I had ever doubted that Teo would one day return to his own country, his physical absence from the French political situation was proof enough that he was saving himself for Czechoslovakia.

As the endless discussion persisted during the week after our big battle, we got further away from the heat of the streets and more complaisant with our hard-won conquest over the University's courtyard and lecture halls. Splits between the various group ideologies resurfaced at the first General Assembly of all the protest groups on Sunday, May 19, nearly a week after the whole country had gone en grève.

The Assembly had just concluded. About a dozen of us were gathered at three tables pushed together outdoors at Le Choix on the Boulevard Montparnasse. Bottles of wine were passed around, loosening our tongues. Bérnard had awakened to the fact that the students needed to assume a role in the government's negotiations. Flinging his hands into the air in a dramatic display of anguish, he exclaimed, "This bavardage"—all this talk—is never going to get us anywhere!"

"It's not supposed to get us anywhere," Remi said, folding his hands calmly on top of the table. "We're talking. Ideas take time. Agreement takes time." Bérnard pinched his fingertips together rhythmically in front of Remi's face like chattering mouths, and Remi swatted at them, laughing.

"But we haven't got much time left," said Annette, fiddling with a strand of bleached hair with one hand and pouring herself a glass of red wine with the other. "Remi, you have to be realistic."

"Be realistic—demand the impossible," Teo quoted the May slogan, smiling cheerfully. We had arranged for him to join us after the Assembly. I squeezed his hand, loving him all the more because he was able to feel comfortable enough to join the discussion. Suddenly, I realized that I'd said nothing myself. I wanted to take a side.

"It's one thing to want to talk forever," I said, "but with the government pressing the students for their program..."

"...and the students unable to agree on a cohesive vision..." Bérnard took up my truncheon, "well, you see the problem, don't you, Remi?"

"It's time to raise the issue of state power," declared Céleste, my comrade with the mousy hair. "We need a complete change of the social structure."

"We need to get rid of that old man!" interrupted her boyfriend Claude.

André, who had been released from the hospital with orders to stay in bed for another week, bent his head and shut his eyes. He had suffered a serious concussion and a broken arm, but he hated to miss even one more day of the revolution. Everyone was looking his way with concern. When he raised his head, he made a plea. "Please don't let the government and the communists decide everything without us."

"It will never happen, Andre," Céleste said. "The young workers are making such beautiful progress! So many have occupied their factories and organized their systems. If they can distribute food, and provide defense, shelter, and even entertainment, they are living proof of their ideas! And all the CGT want to give them is filthy money. Like a bribe to keep them quiet!"

"Calm down! We have time!" Remi sat up tall, raising both hands to calm the group. Then, in a quiet voice, he reassured us, "Don't worry so much. The workers are moving forward, and the bourgeois are still supportive of the students."

"How long will they be with us when there is no gasoline, no city services...?" Suddenly, everyone was shouting again. "We have no more time!" Bérnard's voice rose for just an instant above the din. "We need to negotiate with them. To compromise...!"

"Debate...!"

"Demand...!"

"Dis...gust...ing..."

Teo bent over and whispered in my ear. "The French are brave fighters, but not intelligent governors."

I pulled away from Teo, the thought sizzling through me that I didn't need another cynical Aaron Becker. My reply was a loud retort to his distain. "The debate itself is a miracle. The students and workers are re-building a society from the bottom up. In France, in the Western world, this unity has never happened before! This is the reason things will change, don't you see?" Comrades were mumbling and it was a moment before I realized that they had accepted my outlook. They agreed with me, even Teo! Relief swept through me. "Nothing is over," I continued, "nothing is lost. We will find our way."

A few days later, the workers' demands rose like smoke, vague and noxious, from the ashes of the Paris riots. Like the students, the workers had expanded their program to include a change in regime and in the system. The city was thoroughly en grève.

L'Alliance closed again, and so did the tourist haunts, museums, and shops. Paris was disappearing under multiple veils, her skies overcast and stained a sickly yellow, her streets drab and quiet as a graveyard. The stench of yesterday's rotting produce hung motionless in front of houses like quarantine signs nailed to door posts. Water and electricity, which had been supplied to the Bouleaux household by a backup reserve, were now running low and operated sporadically. The house was cold and dark except for the sparks that flew as angry snippets of conversation were exchanged.

Worse than any of this, there was no communication with the outside world. No postal service, telegraph, or telephone worker was on duty.

On Monday, May 20, I re-read a letter from Mother, received before the weekend, before the postal strike, a missive so cheery that I had to remind myself that Paris was in a state of turmoil. Jean Magill was on the other side of the world with her special divining rod in the category of worry facing west, across the Pacific Ocean, toward Vietnam. I wondered if my parents ever read any news at all about Paris—but then I remembered the Paris Vietnam negotiations and I knew that my mother's cheerfulness was a thin disguise.

After re-reading Mother's letter, I cornered Elizabeth after dinner about an urgent afternoon excursion. It had been a week since Teo had suggested the long journey to register with the American Embassy. Elizabeth agreed to join me, and we decided to stop at the American Express office on the way.

French students, we knew, were penned in to the Latin Quarter, but our passports were our tickets through the police cordons, over to the Right Bank. As we walked, we sidestepped piles of shattered glass and blackened shards. Masses of overturned, burnt-out hulls of cars, pushed to the side and left to rust. Uncollected garbage overflowing their gray and yellow plastic cans. Elizabeth was horrified that spray-painted slogans had abraded her most beloved, elegant shop windows. To me, more depressing than the destruction, or the fact that I had participated in some of it myself, were the upended paving stones and whole streets that the police had hastily cemented over in an effort to eradicate the possibility of more barricades.

Two hours later, we reached the British Embassy where Elizabeth wrote her name, her Paris address, and her parents' name, address, and telephone number in a ledger. At our next stop, we learned that American Express buses would be leaving the next day for Brussels and Geneva. This might be the only transportation out of the city—presumably the drivers would soon join the strike. With this information on our minds, I cashed a big check and we hurried further along on the Right Bank to the American Embassy. The front of the building was quiet. I rang a bell and a young uniformed man opened the gate. He was nearly as big as Teo but with his hair trimmed so close that his oiled scalp glistened. Two other young guards let us use the restroom and gave me a pencil and paper.

Dear Mom and Dad,
First off, I know this won't do much good, but DON'T WORRY!!! These nice men in the U.S. Embassy are letting me send this letter A.P.O. They're even paying for the American stamps. It's very quiet here now. The student demonstrations are over and we only have the strikes. There are American Express buses to Brussels for $12. I can be

there in 3 hours if anything happens. The worst thing is that communications are gone, so I can't wire, write, or phone unless I walk these two hours to the Embassy or leave France. Who knows, maybe tomorrow everything will be settled. I'll let you know if I decide to make a change. Meanwhile, it's just boring here with everything closed. The worst that can happen is that this turns into a European tour. Where would you suggest? Bye for now.

Love, Janet.

I wrote Matt and Aaron similar notes, but in Aaron's, I added a line about my mutilated Berkeley peace symbol pin displayed on my shelf as a token of my commitment. I knew that Aaron would understand the code: that I had participated. I omitted the line that was calculated to create the illusion of a connection that really wasn't there: "Where would you suggest?" What he might like to suggest, I feared, would be Canada.

As I scribbled my note to Aaron, I had to remind myself that he was really going to receive this one. Throughout the week of the strike, I had continued to write him, telling myself that I had developed a habit that I could not break. The conclusion of each letter brought a lump to my throat. I shook away the vision of Aaron that I had missed and cried over, and concentrated on stacking the latest letter in my little box of stationery, hiding it carefully underneath the clean sheets that I would write on tomorrow and the next day. For I would write. Aaron's practical self would be the first to say that my letters were "lunacy."

THIRTY-EIGHT

"THIS PLACE IS NICE," Teo gestured broadly, spreading his eagle's wings half-way across the expanse of my room. He had become a frequent visitor, coming nearly every day now. "And no one bothers us. It is our sanctuary."

I nodded, but then hugged myself, lost in my thoughts and feeling a chill.

"What's wrong, cherie?" Teo asked.

"Nothing, exactly. I've been contemplating my future."

"Come, let's get comfortable over there," Teo eyed my bed. "I want to hear all your most radical thoughts."

We lay down on my bed. I began to tell him again about my antiwar group in Berkeley. He was holding me so close that I could barely keep my hands from reaching under his cotton shirt while we spoke. But he kept his hands still and prodded me only with questions. I told him that I had come to realize how little the students back home were accomplishing, when compared with the students of France.

"In Berkeley," I said, "I had no idea how to play a role, except to obey orders. Now I know I would go straight to a leader like my old roommate, Barbara Borovsky, and try to convince her that real leadership means listening to your followers' ideas. And if she wouldn't listen, I'd go to someone else, or call a small group meeting myself..."

"And you could do that?" He smiled, enthusiastic about this new self-confidence.

"Oh laaaa," I rolled over, shaking my head and circling it with my arms as if fending off attack. I felt the big hand stroking my hair and neck. "I...I want to help make my country a better place," I said, turning back his way. "But...oh, Teo! How can you, I mean, forgive me...but I have to ask...?"

Teo laughed out loud, amused as ever by my curious nature. "Why not? Ask, ask..."

"I've never understood something. If your parents are such good communists, how did you start to break away from them and from their beliefs? The fact is, most American students never do protest. And though I did, it was against the war. I never actively protested against my parents' way of life or the whole political system. Do you see the difference?"

He nodded, "Of course, cherie."

"How can you do something that is opposed to everything your parents believe in? That may even get them into trouble?"

Now it was Teo's turn to roll away, avoiding my gaze. "I wish I could explain," he mumbled, then lay there silently for a full minute. Finally, with my squeeze of his shoulder, he turned to face me.

"Tell me..." I said, gently.

"You make me remember things. I never tell anyone. It's too dangerous."

"I am no danger to you, Teo. Don't you know that? Please tell me." Squirming restlessly, he propped himself against a pillow, his arms stiffly at his sides. Clearing his throat and closing his fists, he began to talk.

"To understand what Czechs like my parents feel for our homeland, you have to know that in the days before the Second World War, there was only one city on the continent to rival Paris for beauty and refinement: the Czech capital city of Prague. In its days as a Republic, strollers on the broad, tree-lined avenues or along the banks of the Vltava River would enjoy aromas from prosperous restaurants—onions and dumplings, roast pork and sauerkraut, sausages and beer. I am hungry just talking about it! And...the concert halls and marketplaces were filled with well-dressed, busy men and women. Adding to the air of the elegant city were the scents of perfumes, leathers, and of course, the modern perfume: auto exhaust.

"By the time I knew Prague, the Parisian rival was like a beautiful woman married to a bully. Her face is distorted with resentment. In 1968, the people of Prague are kicking at the sheets, declaring to the Soviet bedfellow, 'I will not smooth the bitterness from my face, not until you leave my bed.'"

"But how were you aware of all this?" I asked. "How did you learn such things?"

"I have one important memory, cherie, and I will tell it to you. My family lives in Holeckova, a privileged neighborhood, not far from the center of Prague. This district used to belong to wealthy merchants and doctors and lawyers of the Republic. No apartments, only big houses, with many trees and low stone walls to separate property from sidewalks and streets. Our house is much larger than the 120 square meters permitted to owners, so we must rent four rooms to widows. There are many widows in my country. When I was growing up, some widows got old and died, but there were always more to take their place. By the time I was 7 or 8, I didn't bother to speak to them except to be polite...but I am getting off the subject." He frowned and rubbed his eyes, which briefly registered confusion.

"That's okay," I said softly. "I want to hear it all."

He took a deep breath, then began again. "It was the winter of 1958 when I came home from school enthusiastic about the class outing to the gigantic statue of Joseph Stalin which still towered over the city. The teacher had boasted that it was the only such statue still standing in the Communist satellites of the Soviet Union. Repeating what she had said, I told my mother proudly, 'We Czechs are the only true communists!' My papa Alexei was at work. Katya was at the high school.

"It was then that my mother Marta took me by the hand, and led me into the pantry adjacent to the kitchen. Down the dimly-lit aisle at the back of the pantry was a door, always kept locked. 'To an electrical unit,' my father told me one day when I rattled the rigid handle and asked what lay beyond. I was a young child who had received a satisfactory answer from a father I adored." Teo snickered, then cleared his throat, remembering.

"Marta led me through the pantry. She unlocked the door, and we walked by flashlight down a stairway. Just twelve steps, I counted, as if I needed to know their number in order to find my way up again. As we descended, she began to speak. I still recall the words easily. I have heard them many times since in my mind.

"She spoke like this: 'My darling son, I want to teach you that not everything is as it appears. Czechoslovakia is not as it seems. You have heard some lies, some truths too, in your school. But there is always, always,' she repeated, 'more than one way of judging the world in which you live. My son, you are dearer to me than life. Now is the time to teach you that what you think you know, you may not know...' and she talked like that, careful, slow words that did not sound to me like my mother's true voice.

"When we reached bottom, I smelled stale tobacco and wine and had as much trouble breathing as seeing. What I saw first in the basement, by the light of my mother's lampe électrique, was the face of a clock, stopped at ten. The face was as large as a street lamp, with a violet blue enameled frame, encrusted with tiny pearls and flat stones inlaid and carved into miniature suns and moons and stars. I ran my hand over the surface of the clock. It was clean: who had dusted it? My mother smiled encouragingly. 'Do not be afraid,' she said. My hands flanked the clock and I tried to lift it, but it was too heavy.

"'It says ten, like my age,' I said. 'But why has it stopped? There is no ticking.'

"'It's a wind-up clock,' my mother told me. 'And I don't wind it, so it's stopped.'

"'But you wipe it clean?' I asked.

"'Yes, Teodor, from time to time,' she admitted. Then I began to investigate objects beyond the clock. My heart was beating fast. Even then, I knew I was being shown something important. I made a point to remember exactly what they looked like. Up high, there were battered suitcases and pieces of old lumber and stone, broken pottery and elaborately-patterned tiles. On the lower shelves were artifacts of all colors: a crystal candelabra covered with a layer of yellow grime, too intricate to be kept clean; a peacock fan with molting feathers; and gilt altars, crucifixes, reliquaries... I remembered that my mother's family had once been Roman Catholic. Reliquaries were for the superstitious. We had studied in school about the false religion of the Pope in Rome.

"Colorful objects, 'like a carnival,' my mother said, smiling, fussing with vases, a violin and bow. She lowered and opened one of the suitcases from the middle shelves and patterned fabrics fell out, beneath was a dark woolen suit with a jeweled stick pin in its lapel. As my mother worked in silence, drawing things out and holding them up for me to see, a wine-red cravat clung to the pants and a matching slash of burgundy fell to the basement floor. I bent to retrieve it. 'What's this, mother?' 'A cummerbund' she said. 'Men wore it for a belt, around their middle, over the suit pants, like this...' She wrapped it twice around my slim waist."

Teodor paused and laughed, lost in his memories. "Yes, I was very slim then. Then my mother said, 'Your grandfather was quite a large man.'"

"'My grandfather?' I asked. But of course! I must have had a grandfather!

"'My father,' she replied. She did not say his name. Then she opened another suitcase and from it drew one article of clothing: a long dress the color of raspberries. She held it up against herself, and I reached my hand out to touch. 'Pretty?' she asked gaily. 'Uh-huh,' I said. I was bewitched. I had never seen anything like this. She held the skirt up and beneath was a magic cloth, a finely netted mesh, raspberry like the shiny, sturdier fabric over it, but with little multicolored stars twinkling in the torchlight. I took in my hand to rub its roughness between my fingers. 'Why do they make it so pretty when no one can see it?' I asked. Marta draped the gown carefully over a suitcase. She put her arm across my shoulders and together, we sat on a larger suitcase, upended in front of the luscious garment, as if we were staring enviously through a shop window.

"My mother said, 'The slips beneath would show when a young lady danced and twirled.'

"'Did you dance, mama?'

"'Yes, but only once in this dress, at a big party given in my honor when I was sixteen years old. I stood at the top of the stairs and my father held my arm and I felt like I was floating down, down, into that room full of happy friends. So many people were there! A small orchestra played dance music. My brother, Jiri, played the violin with them, two songs...' she pointed up behind me, '...that violin, there. But that was much later in the evening...' her voice drifted off. I stared at her expectantly, wishing for more of her happy memories.

"I came down the stairs," she continued. "All the young men waiting to ask me to dance. My father kissed my forehead and told me I seemed as plump and pink as a juicy, ripe berry.' "My mother's eyes were moist and I heard in her voice that memory had drained and caught in her throat.

"'Are you sad, Mama?' I asked.

"She took a deep breath. 'I have good memories. Beautiful...that is what I keep down here in this secret place. It was a happy time in my life, Teodor, and it was before the Germans came and before the Communists came. We were Czechs then, just plain Czechs.'

"'Papa said the Germans killed Uncle Jiri. Is that right, Mama? He was the one who played the violin?'

"'Yes, Teodor, the Germans killed him, and then the communists killed my father.'

"I moved away from my mother's arm, feeling uncomfortable. 'Why?' was all I could utter.

"'Because my father thought they had a better way to live, a free system, where everyone worked at what they wanted to and there was prosperity for some but not for all.'

"'But that's capitalism, Mama. That's bad!'

"'I met your father, Teodor, and fell in love with him. He was as loyal to his country as my father. He felt that communism was a better way for us, with more justice for more people. He believed in it as my father believed in capitalism. I was caught between. When they came for my father, I was already married with two babies. Alexei was a member of the Party. My mother and a friend drove to our house with the car loaded up with these things, secretly, by night. Because your father loved me so much, he permitted my mother to bring these things to our basement—clothes with pretty colors and violins and clocks and even jewels—to keep them hidden here, a mausoleum of the bourgeois Republic. Alexei agreed that my mother had a home with us. You remember Grandma Ludvica? She used to live with us.'

"'Yes, of course I remember,' I said, puffing out my chest.

"'Yes, you were already six when she died.'

"My mother was quiet, allowing me time to search through the objects. She began to sing me a song, a happy dance tune. Then a patriotic song. We held hands in the tiny space and pumped them up and down in time to the music and we laughed together. Outside Prague was gray with winter and neglect, the clothing that people wore was drab, the houses were gray stone or faded and streaked yellow stucco. Street plantings had withered, and the Vltava River was the color of the quantities of dark beer my father drank every evening, winter and summer.

"Throughout all the seasons, I had been studying the facts in school. Now, after the songs, I asked almost slyly, 'So mama, which is better then? Communism or capitalism?' And with a practiced guile, Marta said, 'Well, we have a communist government. Your father has a good job. We have a nice house and you go to a good school. But we are Czech, Teodor. And all these things in this basement are part of your past, your history.' She rose and began to fold the dress neatly back into the suitcase.

"'They teach you good things in school,' she spoke as she worked. 'There are some things they don't teach you. Always remember the lesson of this place: everything is not as it appears. There is always more than one way of seeing the world. Is this trash down here...or a delightful carnival of colors? Communism? Capitalism? It is best to just remember, Teodor, that we are Czech.'

"Then she knelt so that her eyes were level with mine. She told me that when we ascended the stairs, we would lock the door. I must not talk about it or ask questions, she said, but I must remember the carnival. I must not provoke, but I must keep my eyes open. Things were always changing, and they would change again. When they did, I must not be afraid. 'You will be there,' she said, 'with the colors and the music in your mind.'

"What my mother showed me in that basement beset me, not so much like a carnival as like an atomic bomb..." his big hands flew up to draw the shape of the explosion in the air above my Parisian bed nook. "...a brilliant, illuminating flash of light, which reduced my idea of our society to deformed remnants of what I thought I understood so well. The loss of my innocence was behind the basement door. But that was my mother's purpose. Not a flame extinguished, but rather thoughts without end, the smoldering of anger and bewilderment to stay inside me.

"It is May of 1968 and it is Spring in Prague and the people and the country are changing." Teo's face was sad now, like the Bouleaux children when the pretty painted Easter eggs turned out to be just ordinary whites and yolk inside. He cleared his throat again and sighed. "When I met the Prestup, I wanted to come face-to-face with the true hero of my mother's carnival," he said, "and to ask him how I, Teodor Pelnar, could be of service to my country. He gave me only that one small task, to carry money across the border whenever I go home. I thought surely there would be more that I could do."

Teo and I lay quietly for a few minutes, stretched out on my bed in our peaceful sanctuary. A calm space opened between us that could only be filled by our lovemaking. Teo pulled a rubber from his pocket and I laughed, partly from relief. As always, I could never feel passion without a crippling fear of pregnancy. It had become my automatic response. Free love, they called it. But nothing was for free.

Loving Teo on my own narrow bed felt much better than it had in the hotel. There were no witnesses down on the street, no pressing appointment, no wondering about right and wrong, should I or shouldn't I. Just Teo's big hands, smoothing away all fears, stinging new places that extended from the surface, down deeply into every part of me, until I thought of nothing else. Pleasure then, to begin with, but as Teo's body collided with my bruises, my mind began to drift uncontrollably between his warm body and the cold, cobbled streets of Paris, the damp jungles of Vietnam. In the end, Teo was busy with his own need. I stroked and kissed my lover patiently until he finished, then lay still in his arms, filled to overflowing with a throbbing sensation of melancholy and longing.

We lay still, my arm extended across his chest. He stared at the ceiling, eyes wide open. I lifted my leg and set it down heavily on top of him, and he ran his hand along my thigh, fingertips first. I shivered with pleasure. "Teo, I do love you."

"Hmm. We are good with each other, cherie," he said. He had not realized that my passion had failed me. I felt myself blush, then berated myself for my shame. Wasn't I still depressed by struggles here and at home? And wasn't I as new to this activity as a newborn to life? I sighed, felt relieved that he did not know. He had closed his eyes and I followed his example.

Within minutes, my body relaxed. Wisps of soft, sheltering fog were moving toward us from the edges of the bed and my heartbeats quieted so that I forgot to listen for Teo's. Then, I heard a voice that I imagined to be that of Marta Pelnar. "They teach you good things...some things they don't teach you..." her voice sounded as if she were speaking to me from under the sea, garbled, inconsistent, "...always remember...carnival..." Then the submerged voice came up for air and it was the voice of my own mother. Even in my half-sleep, I knew Jean Magill never could have uttered Marta Pelnar's words.

Mother's blond hair was over my head, shining in the lamplight. She was putting me to bed. I took off my glasses, folded them carefully, and placed them on the nightstand. Already at six or seven, I had those glasses. Pink frames for a little girl. A smart, skinny, near-sighted little girl whose mother tucked her in without looking at her. I was different from her, so different that she loved without looking. At least, I had to believe she loved. She said nothing, kissed my cheek, gave me a nice, big hug and switched off the light.

In the room with Teo, I opened my eyes and this wonderful giant was resting on his elbow, staring down at me. I felt calm.

Suddenly, that vision of Marta Pelnar, then of my mother and my childhood self, loosened and untwisted in me like a feisty knot. Without ever meeting her, I felt that Marta must be more like me than my own mother. My past and future were retied, joined in a new, perfectly logical shape. Before my mind's eye was a mirror reflection of myself, complete with contact lenses, what I had become and what I could be. "Everything is not as it appears," I said to Teo, enjoying my secret for a moment.

"Are you having important thoughts, cherie? Let me know them."

"Teo, there's a tent at your carnival with a fortuneteller," I began. "She's just shown me my past in her crystal ball. And it's opened up a vision of my future." I searched his inquisitive face to make sure he was following me, then declared, "I'm going to be a political activist in America. I'm going to spend my life working for my country. I suppose you thought I always intended this, but I did not understand what I could do until this past month, and I didn't know how I could deal with my parents' objections until just this minute."

"I know your group has taught you things. But what happened just this minute? I don't understand, cherie. We were asleep!"

"So I will explain," I said, hearing Marta's patience in my own voice. "When I was a little girl, my parents told me over and over again that I was a 'Smart aleck,'" I said in English. "They meant that I was too smart for a girl. I know now that I was no genius, certainly not, but there was some difference between me and the rest of my family, like it was them against me. And they emphasized it. They made me feel like it had to do with good grades in school or asking good questions or speaking up at the family dinner table.

"I don't know why they wanted to do this to me. Before Berkeley, my friend convinced me that it was all a show to make my brother feel better about himself. He convinced me that it was okay to be different, because someday I was going to do something significant with my life.

"Then, just now with my eyes closed, I saw you and your mother, and me and mine. Your country and mine. And...all I could see was the terrible waste..." My speech halted as I swallowed the lump in my throat, determined to make myself clear. Teo squeezed my shoulder and nodded encouragingly. "I see how lucky we are in America, and we are wasting it," I continued. "I'm going to make Mother and Daddy understand that politics is an American career. That I am doing it because I respect their way of life, not to rebel against them. This is what I must do, as an intelligent person who cares about America."

I propped myself up on my arm. Teo lay back on the pillow and I gazed down at him, our positions reversed. After a moment he said, "Yes, yes that's fine. But..." he frowned, "does that mean you go back to your Berkeley roommate? What do you do now?"

"I don't need Barbara Borovsky, but I do need comrades like I have here. And no more secretarial status...I can think for myself," I laughed, feeling the joy of self-assurance. "There are so many things I can do! Start by gathering the facts. Then write about them. Speak about them in meetings. I know I will never be able to speak in front of big crowds. But I can write speeches for others to give at rallies. And ask people for money and signatures for petitions. But what I really want to do is to take part in the next step. The compromises. The results. Here, the student movement has such power, but makes no appeal to any political or legal organizations. And for that I need to finish my education..."

"You'll be going home then?" Teo asked anxiously.

"Eventually, Teo...I don't know when yet." I lowered my head, snuggling into the soft spot beneath his shoulder. "Maybe I could work for America from Paris..."

"Or Prague?"

I laughed. "You really want me to see your city, don't you?"

"I want you to come home with me," he said. And there it was, rentrer chez moi, no real word in French that was "home" instead of house, maison. But the phrase floated from the lips of this godless man into the air between us like a church steeple. Prague. Église. Chez moi.

I sighed, took a big breath and blew it out. "Whatever our city, I don't want to leave you, Teo." He tugged at me and kissed me passionately in the center of my ear and the vibrations ricocheted off my brain and shot down through my body. We held each other, burrowing into the soft mattress, and surprising myself, I pulled him inside me with all my strength, loving him until I burned.

THIRTY-NINE

AT SIX O'CLOCK the next morning, Mme. Marie-Claire Bouleaux was banging on my door. "*Wake up! Wake up, Jeanette*! We are in danger. Beware!" I heard the shouting and wondered if I had understood Madame's words correctly. I dragged myself out of bed and opened the door, dressed in my flannel pajamas. "Please, Madame, speak slowly."

Elizabeth came up behind Mme. Bouleaux in her pale pink nightgown trimmed in white lace. She was shivering. "Elizabeth," said Madame, "run and get a robe on or you will catch cold!" Elizabeth disappeared as ordered. "Idiot girl. In that gown with no heat!" She turned her attention back to me.

"You will want to know this. On the news this morning, they announced that the National Assembly is to vote today. Pompidou's government could fall. The communists could take over all of France!"

Elizabeth had come up behind Madame again, hugging her robe around her. Madame was explaining urgently, "The Chinese are said to be behind the whole thing. The *Red Chinese*, Jeanette! We are frightened! We might leave any minute now for l'Île de Ré or go to our cousins in Switzerland."

Margot had come upstairs and stood next to Madame Bouleaux. They were both fully dressed in nearly-identical dungarees and thick brown wool sweaters. "The house will be open," she spoke up, "or you may come with us to l'Île de Ré, right, Maman?"

"Yes, yes, of course. But we don't know yet what we shall do," shouted Madame, raising her arms in exasperation.

"Quiet, Maman, you'll wake Hélene and Jean-Louis."

"I can't be quiet!" I had never seen Madame so upset. In fact, except for her fuming about Gabi and Frederic's romance, I had never seen Madame lose control as she did now.

"Please..."

"Okay. I am sorry. But after all, we are citizens of France. It is different. The communists do not like Americans. Or the British. We cannot be responsible...! Perhaps you should leave France right away!"

"It's your choice to stay or to leave," Margot said calmly, "but the money you have paid us is forfeit. Do you understand?"

Madame was very quiet.

Elizabeth started to cry. "I don't want to leave. This just ruins all my plans. But if I'm in danger...? I need to talk to my dad, but I can't call him because of the strike. I guess he would want me home. And my mum..." she could not go on. I brushed past Mme. Bouleaux and put my arms around Elizabeth. The eagerness of these landladies to help and advise disgusted me. We would leave and be out of the way and they would keep our money. Or mine, at least. I was suspicious of the motives behind this little early-morning melodrama. For a few moments, I sized up first Madame, then Margot, trying to analyze the situation.

Finally, I forced a smile at Elizabeth, my arm still around her. "You don't have to go," I told her.

"What?" she sniffed, as surprised as if I'd just pecked a kiss on her cheek.

"They said you were welcome to stay. So don't go, if you don't want to." I glared at Margot and then over at Mme. Bouleaux. "The French government, no matter which party is in control, will not care about one 16-year-old girl from Sussex."

"Oh Janet...is that true? You're right! Of course I'll stay," she said, so excited that she had spoken in English.

"Français!" shouted Madame.

"Oui, Français," she corrected herself hastily. "You're right, Jeanette. I want to stay in the worst way. And you? You'll stay?" she asked.

"Yes, Jeanette? Are you, an American, considering the feelings of your dear parents at such a time?" asked Mme. Bouleaux.

I sighed wearily. "We did learn yesterday that the very last American Express buses will be leaving Paris tonight."

"Oh, please don't go!" Elizabeth cried. "Don't you want to stay in Paris?"

"Of course I do, but the Red Chinese...my parents...maybe it would be best if I left for a few days. The buses go to Brussels. It's only four hours and twelve American dollars away. If things get better, I can always come back."

"And if things don't get better in France, you'll go home from Brussels?" asked Mme. Bouleaux. I agreed, and Madame continued, businesslike, "Let us know if you want to return. You have a place with us through the summer months. You have our phone number and I'll write down the phone number at l'Île de Ré. Do you have paper and pencil?"

As soon as our landladies had left, I got dressed and began packing. Elizabeth stood there, watching me, still hugging the robe around her body. "I still don't understand why it's safe for me to stay and not for you," she said petulantly. "First Laurent is gone, and now you."

I ignored her, working vigorously, dragging clothes out of drawers, folding, smoothing, pushing the air out of piles of fabric. "I'll leave my big suitcase and pack the small one for light travel," I mumbled to myself.

"I guess you just don't love Paris like I do," Elizabeth scoffed.

"Of course I do."

"Then you'll be back soon, won't you? Well...or..." she had driven up her voice a full octave, "...should I go ahead and ship your big suitcase off to the States when the strike ends?"

I shut a drawer and faced Elizabeth. Somewhere between Madame's uncharacteristic alarm about the communists taking over and Margot's cold, glint-eyed pronouncements, I had made my decision.

"You may end up shipping it to the States, or it might be to another address in Paris. You might as well know. I'm not going to Brussels."

"But you told Madame and Margot..."

"I'm not running away from the revolution."

"You lied to..."

"I don't care. As long as they have my money, they're just as happy to be rid of me." I took a big breath and blew it out noisily. "I'm so sorry, Elizabeth. Please don't be frightened for me. I have my reasons for staying here. There's so much happening in Paris..."

She drew back. "Have you gone dotty? Nothing is happening in Paris. Everyone is on strike..."

"I want to see where the political situation goes, first hand. The students aren't just going to disappear, no matter what happens with the government. I want to know if things can change for our generation. And if not, why not."

"But if you want to be a political person, wouldn't it be more logical for you to go home and help out there?"

"I'll worry about America later. Anyway, the college students go home for the summer and the Vietnam talks are going on here. Nothing I can do at home will be more useful than what I can do in Paris."

"But what can you do...I don't understand?"

"I know sometimes I'm impulsive, but in my group, I'm a relatively calm voice..." I grasped for words. "Maybe I can make them reflect, not just react to violence with more violence. And besides..."

"Yes?"

"I want to stay with Teo until he has to go home."

Elizabeth's face relaxed. "Oh, now I see...I thought that might be it."

I reached over to close the top of my small case with a bang, then sat back down, patting the seat of the other chair so that my friend would sit with me. "That's not it, Elizabeth. It's not simple. Everything I told you adds up to it."

"But you are in love with Teo, aren't you?"

I paused with a dramatic sigh, more to clear my heart of turmoil than to impress Elizabeth. "I'm hoping he'll be in Paris for a while longer. Then I might go to Prague with him. But we're not going to be together forever. Because you're right...I mean...eventually, my fight is back in America."

"Does he know you want to come to him?"

"Not exactly, but he encourages me to make my own choices. It's always been like that with us."

I rose again and began working hastily to arrange things in my big suitcase. From behind me, Elizabeth cooed, "This is so romantic. Maybe you'll end up marrying him."

"Love doesn't always have to end in marriage. We don't live in the dark ages."

Her nose tilted into the air. "Of course I know that."

I smiled at her. "Elizabeth, we'll be friends forever, won't we?" She nodded enthusiastically. "So...I have a favor to ask. Please don't tell Margot or Mme. Bouleaux or anyone else where I'm going. I don't want my parents to know, not yet. I just can't deal with their fears and prejudices right now. The postal strike is convenient."

"And what if the postal strike should end?"

My first thought then was of all the letters that might arrive—letters from Mother and Dad and Matt. And from Aaron Becker. How could I cut myself off? And yet, like it or not, I was cut off, cut off completely. On my own. My hands tightened automatically into fists. "Just stuff the letters into this suitcase. Anyway," I added more softly, "you know I'll be all right with Teo, don't you?"

Elizabeth stood up and put her arms around me. I hugged back. I was sure I would miss her more than she would miss me. "Yes, of course. Teo's a good boy. He'll take care of you. And I won't tell a soul if you don't want me to. But remember to tell them yourself, when the strikes end."

≈PART SEVEN≈
Berkeley

FORTY

MY HISTOLOGY TEXT, all 492 pages and $36 of it, lay open on my sheepskin rug. I sipped at a can of A & W Root Beer and stared at information about the composition of chordate tissues, but it was hard to concentrate knowing that Marshall Magill would soon be at my door. When Mr. Magill called to say he was flying into Oakland that evening and wanted to talk to me about Janet, I felt as if someone had punched me in the chest. I couldn't have been more shocked if my mother had phoned to say that Daddy Becker would be paying me a visit.

I'd had all day to examine my shock as well as my fawning reaction to the call from Mr. Magill. My submissive tone, I discovered, was not wholly insincere. True, Janet had ceased to keep me from the appropriate hours of sleep and my equilibrium during daylight hours had returned as well. But I had not heard from her for nearly three weeks, not since the Embassy letter written when the French postal service had gone on strike, and I admit that besides simply missing the contact with her several times a week, I was becoming more than a bit concerned.

I scrutinized the daily news for developments in Paris, both about the peace negotiations and the revolution. When the students succeeded in making an alliance with ordinary French

338

workers, it was heralded by some, decried by others, as a first in world history. From California to Columbia University, and in far-flung cities like Rome, Berlin, Warsaw, Mexico City and Tokyo, leftists of all stripes were thrilled. Despite my blind hope that any change at all might improve my situation, I didn't embrace this bit of history, not for Janet and not for France. I was no socialist. What I felt was more of a chill than a thrill.

Within these three weeks, however, reports confirmed my earlier cynical prediction, and set my mind at greater ease where Janet was concerned. Pompidou's government had narrowly survived a parliamentary effort, led by the French Communists, to overthrow him. While negotiations were in progress on a broad range of complaints, the de Gaulle and Pompidou duet still played in the halls of power.

Mr. Magill's taxi pulled up at 7:45 p.m. and having been on the lookout, I tread my narrow brick path and stood at the top of the stairs, leaning as nonchalantly as I could against the planter box while he paid off the cabbie. I shivered a little from the cool breeze, but I could smell the pines swaying above me and thought with a tinge of satisfaction about how undeniably unique he would find my modest student digs.

"Hello, Mr. Becker." A formal greeting. A cordial handshake.

"Welcome, Mr. Magill." I turned my back on him and led him to my door. Inside everything was tidier than it had been during four years of finals seasons. The kitchen was spotless, Dork's cage had been given its ritual ablution, I'd swept and dusted and shaken the pretzel crumbs embedded in the shag rug into the hearth. The fire crackled in a friendly way, filling the cottage with the pleasant air of forest campsites. I offered him a chair and a cup of coffee, both of which he accepted gracefully.

"Nice place you've got here," he said, glancing up at the skylight and beamed ceiling. He lifted his glasses and squinted at my aquarium, perched between the volumes on my bricks-and-boards.

"Thanks. It's comfortable. I've got everything I need here. Worth the extra lab job to pay the rent...I'm going to miss it." Mr. Magill smiled politely at my chattiness, making no comment on my plans. He blew into the coffee cup without tasting, then wiped the steam nervously from his nose with the back of his hand. I shut my mouth, waiting for the man to let me know why he was sitting across from me in my nifty cottage.

The quietest damn minute went by. He took a sip of coffee. He lifted his eyes from the cup. When he spoke, his voice was tense and sincere. "I'd like to tell you how I came to make this trip here and just what I had in mind."

Then, believe it or not, Janet's father began to describe the layout of his Beverly Hills master bedroom suite and what happened there one night. What I didn't tell Mr. Magill was that Janet had taken me through those private digs. I remember rushing squeamishly past the king-sized bedroom set to Mrs. Magill's closet, where Janet, in a rare display of materialistic hubris, seemed proud of her mother's custom drawers with little places for jewelry, scarves and all that. As Mr. Magill spoke, I could picture the entry to a mammoth closet just beyond his wife's side of the bed. Beyond the dressing area was the bathroom, with its view of the patio, the garden, the pool and cabaña.

Now Mr. Magill was telling me more that I already knew. From his side of the king bed, a door led to a small den that he called his "sanctuary," where he shed his business suit and tie each evening into his own roomy closet, then sat in his recliner with the automatic massage mechanism and adjustable positions. Janet had let me sample those positions, with her in my lap. If you kept going through Mr. Magill's den, you arrived in the same spacious bathroom, with the view of the patio, the garden, the pool and cabaña.

All that description, in order to tell me about an incident that happened in the suite late one night. And as I listened, I kept in mind that Mr. Marshall-businessman-Magill was a skilled manipulator, and I'd better be damn careful. This was no ordinary bedtime story: there was an agenda here.

"We were like two possums," Mr. Magill began after describing the floor plan. "I'd been laying there awake for hours after bedtime and Jean had too. Only I didn't know it then. I figured she was asleep. There we were, side by side, both of us trying not to toss. Around three o'clock in the morning, gently I pulled back the covers and tip-toed around through the den. About five seconds later, Jean slid out of bed on her side, careful not to wake me up, so she assumed, and headed through her dressing room to the bathroom. Let me tell you, neither of us had to go to the toilet. Somehow, we both had the vague notion of looking ourselves over in the mirror. Seeing what these past few months of worry have done to us." He paused, wanting to make sure I was getting it.

"Insomnia," I said. "It's miserable."

"Right."

I shook my head, sincerely sympathetic, remembering my own sleepless nights—long, excruciating and lonely.

Mr. Magill took a big gulp of his coffee and set the cup and saucer down on the table.

"So, you ran into each other?" I coaxed.

"Not into each other...we reached for the light switches and had this little battle going, on-off-on-off, until finally I yelled something like 'stop it for Chrissake' and we called a truce with lights on."

I smiled appreciatively at his narrative. I could just hear Mr. Magill's gruff voice breaking the silence like a blister on the smooth skin of the night.

He continued, "So Jean admitted that she hadn't been sleeping very well lately and I said the same. We talked about sleeping pills and ended up settling for Tums. So, there we were, kind of laughing and groaning at the same time. I said to Jean, 'It's those damn kids. Both of them. In fact, all of them, all around the globe now. Just what do they expect to get out of all this? A better world? Hah!'"

"And she answered me that they're being manipulated. I lost my temper. I yelled pretty loud, 'The hell they are! They're manipulating us!' Jean always keeps her voice understated when I yell. Low and slow. That was her voice when she told me that she didn't care about all the kids in the world. She just cares about our kids."

Mr. Magill ran his hand through his thinning hair, took a deep, dramatic breath, and slurped his coffee. I was fidgeting, fighting to keep my legs and feet still. I was trying to be patient with him, but couldn't ignore the question: had he picked me out to be a surrogate for his shrink, or what?

"That was when I went for the Tums," he finally went on, "and we faced the mirror cabinet, side by side, and chewed and scrutinized ourselves and each other. I told her how funny it was that I'd had this urge to look in the mirror, and she said 'me too, isn't that something? To remind myself how old I'm getting.' And I told her, 'I'm too old for this....'"

I pictured Mr. Magill trying to rub out the puffy half moons under his eyes with his knuckles. The American face that saved the world from Hitler...the brave, broad forehead, the jowls suspended from a strong, square jaw. "Too old for what?" I asked.

"For worrying about kids in the middle of the night. What did you think?" he snapped. "So, you know, Jean started to cry. I hate that. She said she just couldn't figure out how we arrived at this point in our lives. It seemed like yesterday, we had two beautiful, sweet kids, a boy and a girl, just like we'd hoped, and now they were far away and we were cut off and didn't even know, day by day, hour by hour, whether they were in danger."

Mr. Magill's fist came down into his hand and he shouted, "Goddammit, boy, Jean's not the only one who can't figure it out. I've never felt so powerless in my life! At least if Janet would write to us..."

"She can't. There's a strike..."

"Well, she wrote us once from the American Embassy. To tell us about the strikes."

"Yeah, she wrote me, too." I had practically memorized the little note, but there would be no recitation for Mr. Magill. Janet had written that her peace button had been demolished—her way of telling me, I surmised, that she had been out there with her group. I knew that most of the protests had been quashed by the police teamed with the French Communist Party, and the radicals were in retreat. But the strikes had dragged on and the trouble in Paris was far from over.

"Okay," Mr. Magill was saying, "but it's been three weeks since that little message, and even when she did write, she didn't say much. Why do we always find out what she's doing after she's done it?"

"Did you ever try talking to her about her political beliefs?" I asked.

"Jean would be the one, not me. But Janet's so book-smart, Jean just trusted her to do the right thing." Marshall laughed a bitter laugh. "Jean said that after all, Janet did leave those rabble rousers in Berkeley to go to Paris as we requested. And I couldn't help it, I said, 'Paris. What an incredibly stupid idea.' That just made her cry again."

Mr. Magill examined my face in the firelight. "Jean was the one who knew that you two had broken it off, but that she still keeps in touch with you."

"She broke it off. We're just friends, Mr. Magill."

"Call me Marshall," he said. He pushed back from the table and crossed his legs. Without intending a parody, I found myself following suit. Now he stared dejectedly at my knees.

"Hey, Marshall," I said, "I'm sure you both figured Paris was the best idea given the circumstances. You saw the Berkeley protests and you just couldn't take two lost souls in the family at one time..."

"Matt's not a lost soul!" he shouted. "He's a soldier fighting for his country! And he's damned proud of it, too..."

"He's fighting for some South Vietnamese person's country."

"Oh, now, don't start in with me! You've told us all about it, remember? In front of all our friends." I flinched at the reference to Matthew's farewell party. "And now!" he said, his voice rising to a ridiculous pitch, "Jean's starting to sound like one of you!"

"No shit!" I coughed into my hand, choking over this bit of news. Could this be what his agony was all about?

"When I criticized her Paris idea," Marshall continued, "she stood up and started walking in a circle around the bathroom and then settled in front of the mirror again and stared into her own face and told me that she's joined 'Another Mother for Peace.' She couldn't look at me when she said it. I mean, it's not that group that's been packing soap and candy and razor blades into packages for the troops. That's what I supposed she meant, at first. But this is the bunch at the high school. They sold the cards last year that said, 'War is not healthy for children or other living things.' For medical relief for Vietnamese civilians. They are really against the war."

Marshall stood up and in one quick step was standing over me. "For heaven's sake that kind of thing only prolongs the war. Gives hope to the other side. I told her, they make Johnson's job impossible! And you know what she said?" I shook my head, pulling it back from his beefy forearms as far as I could.

"She said that the other side doesn't need any more hope than they already have! I told her she didn't know anything about politics and she shouted at me. She said that I don't know how to get out of this thing anymore than she did, and that she was trying this way!"

My new buddy Marshall caught his breath. Moved back a step. "I can't take much more of this...this craziness," he said. "That's when I thought about you. If you might not be an avenue to Janet. Maybe even to Matt. I'm betting you're all writing to each other. Jean and I are the only ones left out in the cold. Wandering around in the dark at night bumping into each other." Marshall stood up straight, creating an illusion of pride that seemed totally weird under the circumstances. "Somewhere along the way," he said, "we absolved ourselves of responsibility. We allowed ourselves to become powerless. Well, I knew I would feel a lot better if I did something, anything, even if it meant coming to see someone who I've never really, well...discussed things with before."

At this point, I would have had trouble keeping a cynical smile off my face were it not for his urgent tone, the pathos of the details, and most of all the repeated reference to his children.

Marshall was finished with his bedtime story. He sat back down and finished off his coffee in one gulp. "Would you like another cup?" I offered.

He set the cup down, his hand shaking slightly. "No thanks." Then abruptly, he asked, "When was the last time you heard from Janet?" I knew that question was coming.

"Three weeks, same as you." Then I told him what I knew he wanted most to hear: that I'd had no indication that Janet was interested in the Parisian revolution other than as a casual observer. "She doesn't consider this her fight," I lied.

"But three weeks!" Mr. Magill said. "She could at least get another letter through somehow. And what's she doing there all this time? The country is at a complete standstill. Her school could not possibly be open and operating. Things like museums and tourist sites are closed. And those strikes! Postal workers, taxis and buses and the subway, even the garbage collectors. It can't be very pleasant!"

"I know, I've been following the reports too," I shook my head. "The whole country...I can't imagine what it would be like if even one American city was frozen like that."

"Would never happen," he bellowed, swinging his fist down heavily through the air but then giving it a light bounce on his thigh. When I saw that fist, I realized the degree to which the distraught father was still in control and decided not to debate his point. I began to eye my textbook, still lying open to schematics of chordate tissue sections.

"So, there's nothing we can do but wait it out," I said.

"And what if the one month becomes many? No, I'm worried about the situation. A friend of my wife's was in Paris and actually took a taxi to Switzerland. Janet even indicated there were ways out of the country. She could have gotten across a border by now, to where she could telephone us."

I shrugged my shoulders, trying to keep myself from squirming in my seat.

Then Janet's father scowled, tapped his knuckles together and began to exert his accustomed sense of authority in the most tactful words he could muster. "Aaron, it's time to just go get her and bring her home. She's got her whole life to go back to Paris if she wants to, and if the country comes to its senses. I'd like to offer her a ticket and a ticket back over there when things calm down. You see what I mean? But I can't do that if I can't even contact her."

"So then, the problem is, how do you contact her?" I said. Again, there was silence between us. "Through the U.S. Embassy to the French family?" He shook his head. And even though I could tell he was working his way up to something, I was surprised by what came next.

"Aaron, would you like to see her come home?" It was a question I had not even considered as a possibility.

"Yes, I would," I said automatically. "I wouldn't have said that a month ago, because I felt that Janet was where she wanted to be. But now, yes, I would like to see her home and safe, if you put it that way."

Marshall Magill leaned forward, his arms on his thighs, pushing his stare into my mind as only a man sure of his power and position vis à vis the sucker he's talking to can do. "I have a proposition for you, Aaron. I know you'll be finished with exams soon. When you are, I'd like you to go over there and find her. You speak some French, right? You can find her and talk to her and bring her back. Or send her back, if you'd prefer. I'll cover all the expenses. What do you say?"

My heart was beating violently against all the possible and impossible obstacles to his proposition, those he knew about and those he didn't. "Like I said, Mr. Magill, Janet and I are just friends now. I mean, our relationship is not what it was..."

"But you care about what happens to her, don't you?"

"Yeah, of course...and I'm flattered that you would trust me to help."

"Well then, it's settled. I'll proceed with making the arrangements and getting your ticket and the information you need. When is your last final examination?"

"Just a minute, Mr. Magill. The world is a crazy and dangerous place right now. There could be a war in France. And...she may not want to come with me. She has another boyfriend now...at least he might be a boyfriend..."

"No!"

"I probably shouldn't have told you that. It was told to me in confidence."

"A revolutionary?"

"Not at all. He's a Czech boy. From what I gather, a real nice guy."

Mr. Magill covered his eyes with his hand, then slid it up to his forehead, wiping away sweat. He mumbled, "This is getting more complicated all the time."

Suddenly, he had that determined expression on his face again. "Complicated. And urgent. She could go running off behind the Iron Curtain with this boy and we'd never see her again!"

"I don't think she'd cut herself off forever. She would at least let me know..."

"That's my point! She would let you know. Hot damn, I was right to come to you!" he struck his palm with his fist and beamed with self-righteous glee. "She trusts you, boy, and you can save her!"

I focused on the floor between the two of us. This guy was a master bullshit artist, but he was off his rocker if he thought I was going to take his side against Janet. If she trusted me, then all the more reason to be trustworthy. I kept my analysis to myself. "You've got the wrong guy, Mr. Magill."

He nodded slowly, smiling as if he hadn't heard me. Then he rose and headed for the front door, opened it with a flourish, then swung around to face me. His vitality seemed to swallow up more than its share of my cottage. "I know France is a bit rough right now and you get spooked..." and he stopped short, whatever words he had intended to add crammed into his throat. "I'm not gonna beg, but I'm damn close. You weigh this carefully, please. You may change your mind. If you do, call me immediately." He flipped his business card down on the window seat. "Anytime, day or night. I'll be happy to talk with you if you just want to talk. Or if you decide to help us out." Then he strode over to me and grabbed my hand, more for a squeeze than a shake, and he was gone.

FORTY-ONE

DESPITE MY RESOLVE to put Daddy Magill's visit behind me, disturbing images oozed into my mind unbidden. Janet's parents, with a son in Vietnam and a daughter in Paris, simply reeled as their tight little playpen world, full of shiny toys and innocent self-righteousness, fell to ruin. The slats had been lowered, all four sides at once, and they were going to have to crawl out with the boogie man right behind them. Part of me wanted to say "tough beans," but I had my own terrors. As the days went by, the ease with which Janet had sent word from the U.S. Embassy began to fester. Why hadn't she gone there again to write or even to phone? She might have contacted the Magills, if not me.

Shaking off morbid theories that would get me nowhere, I focused on the end of the school quarter. Despite my need to flee the draft, I'd applied to Cal's doctoral program in biochemistry and had been accepted by the department. Maybe a miracle would happen. I wanted to hold back the muggy days of June, but before I knew it, my papers were done and my finals just a few dozen hours of hitting the books away.

On June 5, the French postal strike ended. When Bobby Kennedy was murdered the next day, I consoled myself with the good news from France. But by Friday afternoon, I still hadn't heard from Janet or Marshall. I fingered the old man's card for about ten minutes, finally tossing it into a drawer. If Janet needed me, she knew where to find me, but it was obvious that she did not need me. She did not want me. I was a free man, like it or not.

Restless, I wandered outside my cottage, kicking a clod of dirt off the brick path, obsessing about Janet, the French quagmire, political violence, the assassination, JFK, MLK, now RFK. Bobby's murder was a stunner. Who would be next? Thousands of poor people had set up a shanty town called Resurrection City in our nation's capital. The D.C. protest was the aftermath from MLK. But with this latest atrocity, I noticed that the campus and the nation were shocked into silence, quieter than it had been in weeks. There were no uprisings or even murmurs of protest. Disbelief clung to voices, the mood somber and respectful.

I'd walked up the path and around Neil's small yard, the sun blinking through the pines. A jazzy bass beat from Neil Strand and Joanna Larkin's stereo issued a welcome as if it were Morse code. That rhythm and just a whiff of their onions in oil swept away some of my despondency, so I turned on my heel and strolled over to their door. My friend opened up to my hang-dog expression.

"What the hell happened to you?" Neil inquired, running his fingers through his stubby blond curls. Joanna stood behind him with a knitted afghan wrapped around her shoulders. Their faces were flushed, but both were dressed, so I assumed that I hadn't interrupted anything more serious than a little cuddling while the stew simmered. I could smell an oniony concoction in the kitchenette. No meat, of course.

"Too much news and not enough," I said. "It's all scary shit."

"Bobby was never one to dwell on failure," Neil said.

"Why don't we all sit down," Joanna coaxed. The edge of her afghan came around my shoulders as she guided me to a chair at the kitchen table. Lit from behind, her hair tumbled in golden curls over the red and green of the comforter. She was not a beauty. Her squinty blue eyes and pug nose would have been better on a face less bold and square and set between cheeks less rough and reddish. But to Neil she was gorgeous and more importantly, to herself. Inner strength was a beautiful thing. I wanted her to fold me into that afghan and keep me close.

I shook my head. "It was the first primary I'd ever been able to vote in," I began, "and he was my candidate. There was a good chance he would have been our next president. It's hard to fathom the enormity of his death. The meaning of it..."

"Death..." breathed Joanna, "is for eternity. Reincarnation is bullshit."

"Or in this case, way too slow to take effect before the November election," Neil smiled sheepishly. The two had taken seats opposite me, their hands entwined on top of the Formica table. "Look, Aaron. Joanna and I were just talking about a trip to the mountains. The weather accommodates. We all need to clear our heads. Why not a last fling before the finals crunch? Can you swing it?"

"I couldn't intrude..."

"Don't be ridiculous," Joanna said. "What're friends for?"

A couple of hours later, we were on the road to Sacramento in Neil's 1962 VW, singing songs from our quintessential American youth, like I've Been Workin' on the Railroad and Home on the Range. Neil had a choir boy's soprano when he boosted it just a couple of false steps up from his tenor and Joanna's voice was as low as Eartha Kitt's but a little flat on every note. My baritone with Neil's tenor was a blend, but the loopy combination of the three of us would have been unbearable had I been sober.

Behind us, the smoggy sunset over the Bay was fading to the color of ferrous mud, but up ahead the night was clear and cold. Although the traffic was heavy, it was moving right along at a regular clip. By the time we drove into Sacramento around 8:30, I felt somewhat restored. Neil found a Motel 6, where he graciously picked up the tab, $12.92 for two rooms.

After dropping our gear, the three of us piled back into Neil's VW and went in search of a grocery store. The guy at the motel desk had directed us to one that stayed open for the few night owls in the California State capitol. We stocked up on wheat bread, potatoes, Tang, chipped beef for me, canned beans, apples, and of course, marshmallows, graham crackers, and Hershey bars necessary for the s'mores we all remembered from our scouting days. By the time we finished stuffing it all in the empty pack we'd brought, I was starving again, and just about to pick up a box of Nilla Wafers for the night when Neil was at my side asking, "Hey, Aaron, ever try these?" He was holding up a package of garden variety Morning Glory seeds with a stilted picture of a violet-tinged flower on its cover.

"What do you mean 'try them'? Eat them?"

"Yeah. I hear they give you a terrific high. I've been meaning to get some. They have a whole line of groovy vegetable and flower seeds over there. Must be a lot of gardeners in this area. But these are the ones that're supposed to be the send off."

"Are they digestible?" I asked. By now, Joanna was on the other side of me and I directed my question to her, trusting more to her good sense.

"I've heard they are fine as long as we soak and rinse the pesticides off them first," she said. "Leave it to the industrialists to poison your garden flower seeds."

"Maybe it's because they don't want us to get high on them," I reasoned. "If you try to take a trip, they just poison you. Cheaper for them than a court trial."

They both smiled grimly. Joanna said, "I've heard these are safe trips. And more interesting than grass."

"At least with grass you know what you're getting," I said, scanning the seed rack. "Are you sure...?

"Jesus, Aaron. Wasn't there a first time for pot, too?"

"Yeah, but everyone I knew..."

"Live a little, buddy. You're with friends."

I forced a conciliatory grin. "Right, of course. And you're not idiots. I'm sorry."

"Don't be sorry," said Joanna. "You're a questioning person. Now you've questioned. Get a pack for each of us, Neil." We headed for the checkout stand. I grabbed my Nilla Wafers and followed along.

Just after sunrise, we headed out toward Eldorado National Forest. We drove past fields of boulders and spring herds, calves standing close to grown females in acres of silky green. There were little towns like Cool, California and Placerville. We got closer to the gold country, driving alongside the American River where Joanna suggested we stop for a break. We feasted on the clear air and swift river as much as on our cheese sandwiches and carrot and celery sticks. Then Neil and I sipped on beer while Joanna played her harmonica. Soon we were back in the car again, this time Joanna at the wheel and Neil perusing the auto club map. We stopped at the ranger station to get hiking and camping permits and directions to the Mokelumne Wilderness. "Why Mokelumne and not Desolation Wilderness?" asked Joanna. Neil was now consulting the smaller map that the ranger had given us.

"I don't like the sound of that name," Neil replied.

It was mid-afternoon by the time we stopped, now deep into the forest, Neil and Joanna intent on finding a patch of ground where no humans had ever tread before. We parked at the end of a dirt road, unable to proceed any further by motored vehicle. Hefting the satisfying weight of our packs, we set out with Neil in the lead.

A narrow path trickled down a steep hill under trees so thick that the late sun was all but blocked out. Then across a meadow, treading softly, silent homo sapiens amongst chattering larks and crows and scurrying field mice. Back under the trees, the eyes of deer peeked at us from behind moss-covered trunks of cedars and pines. But in the space of a few minutes, eerie quiet and a steady, fine-grained drizzle slowed us down. The pristine forest air had become damp and moldy, its details lost in early evening gloom. We listened for goblins with every slippery step. I was relieved when we reached a meadow at the bottom. "Is this a good place to camp?" I asked hopefully. "It's starting to rain."

"This isn't rain, it's just a low fog," said Neil. He opened out the trail map, its moist creases looking like extra paths in the primordial expanse of the mimeograph paper. "We're not there yet."

"Where? Where's 'there'?"

"Not to worry," he said, "when we reach it, we'll know where our 'there' is."

"Neil wants to be the next Gertrude Stein," Joanna deadpanned.

Across another meadow was another path, heading down an even more precipitous slope, down a longer grade, through a denser, more cobwebby forest. "Are you sure we didn't somehow end up in the Desolation Wilderness?" Joanna asked, her voice as rocky as the trail.

"You'll see," Neil sang out, "this is going to be glo...rioso." So we began to half-trek, half-slip down this hill in the increasing "low fog" while I struggled with my pack, which kept wanting to hurtle itself over my head and get to the campsite a few yards ahead of me. Mold spores filled my nostrils and my socks had begun to squeak inside my hiking boots. I was worried about the weather. I envisioned our footpath being washed out completely overnight so that in the morning, we would be unable to find our way back to the car. Or a torrential downpour washing mud into our tents, flooding our "wherever" campsite and turning it into our final resting place.

Mokelumne. It was so dark that we had begun to feel our way down the hill, grabbing onto trees to keep from slipping as we went. No one spoke. You could hear every point of contact between the three of us and the rooted foliage. Suddenly, I wondered how it would be if Janet were next to me, trying like hell to be a good sport. Without much of a stretch, I began to imagine Matt squishing his way through the muddy jungles of Vietnam with danger behind every dripping tree.

Neil called out, "Stop!" scaring the shit out of me. "Let's get out the flashlights," he commanded. His troops obeyed. He took Joanna's pack in his arms and held it in front of his chest while Joanna and I fielded the lights. They were nearly useless in the density of the forest.

Another eon and finally, the vegetation thinned on one side of the path, a narrow ledge with a rock cliff going straight up on our left. My naturalist sense told me that we were walking, walking for miles, not into the kind pristine nature that poets like Neil sang about, but into the kind of harsh reality of isolation and wildness that we scientists analyze and tame. I was tired and achy and sweaty and hungry and dirty, and if we were trapped at the bottom of this forest for the rest of our lives, Neil was just going to have to share Joanna at some point. After all, this route had been his idea, hadn't it?

As it turned out, Neil's map had it right. We soon emerged from the vertical forest, flashlights first, into a Disney fantasy of a campsite. Before us was a glass-smooth pond, no rain dotting its surface, with the rising moon reflected from it as a clear, half-circle of white light. Frogs were croaking their nighttime ballads. Newts were sneaking into the mud, sinking into sleep. But pine needles dusted the level ground on a narrow strip of beach opening out of the woods. With the soles of our boots, we discerned that the ground was moist with lifting fog but not at all flooded, a perfect place to pitch tents and start a campfire.

While Neil and I lit a lantern and set out our supplies, Joanna set to testing the pond water for potability, then crushing and soaking the Morning Glory seeds. We built a smoldering fire, roasted potatoes and onions in tin foil and heated the cans of beans and beef. The smell of salt and smoky barbeque juiced my mouth as the three of us worked together to pitch our two pup-tents over tarps. I spread out my sleeping roll inside my tent, calling over to Neil and Joanna in the most obnoxious tone I could muster when I heard the two of them cavorting inside theirs. "Now hear this, all fuckers cease and desist. Little brother is watching you."

"Find your hand, you sniveling little brother," Neil shouted back. "And next time bring your own camping equipment...ouch! Sorry Jo..."

Neil had brought a bottle of rotgut, but I stuck with beer. We gobbled our meal, speaking only to congratulate each other on our campsite and our culinary prowess, punctuating our mouthfuls with "mmm" and "oooo" right up on through the s'mores. We toasted those 'mallows to the most golden of browns before squishing the mess between the layers of graham cracker and chocolate. As we each went for a second s'more, the pace slowed and we began to chew the Morning Glory seeds. With self-conscious chuckles, we watched each other for first signs of lunacy after ingesting whatever narcotic was supposed to be addling our brains.

Within minutes after eating the seeds, Neil seemed to crumble up like his rain-soaked trail map. He fell asleep with his feet in the door to his pup tent and his head on his jacket in the direction of the campfire. Joanna stroked Neil's kinky blond hair, singing something that her grandmother taught her. I'd heard it before.

"O, Vermeland, my heart cries in longing from afar,
For thee O most precious spot in Swee-den..."

My body was beginning to feel detached from my head. Otherwise, I felt very relaxed and awake and could not understand how Neil could be so fast asleep.

"Too bad Neil is missing the moment," I said, interrupting Joanna's song. As if I hadn't spoken, she continued in her vapid contralto:

"Though years have past since I've been gone,
You're still my guiding star,
The hope all men cherish for an Eee-den..."

I was focusing on the moon, which had climbed to about 60 degrees from the horizon. It was a small light bulb in the pond, illuminating a furry row of treetops. Or, I wondered, the rippling back of a giant brown bear? I squelched a nibble of panic that had bit into my gut. Joanna blew out the lantern light and began to play her harmonica. Leaning against my pack, I listened to the mournful sound, breathed in the fragrance of firewood and firs, and was calmed. At the high notes, Neil stirred and crawled onto Joanna's thigh. She ignored him as she had ignored me and continued to play her instrument as if she were a nymph alone in the moonlight. I was stunned by the beauty of this place, yet incredibly sad because Janet was not there to share it with me.

I imagined her face staring at the same moon from down on my thigh, her thick, black curls wrapped around my fingers. I stared intently at a particular spot close by where the moon polished a pile of stones several feet high to a bright sheen. Heaviness filled my chest—weight, like stones on soft gravel, or like Janet's head on my thigh—then without prelude, the stones grew like intractable tumors into a Parisian barricade, and all around the pile, a maroon jungle rose where Matt tilted back his trimmed Irish blond head and raised his classic horny young face into the white light. My muscles snapped to attention. Something was sneaking around in the dark. I peered across the pond, searching for white glowing eyes in the moonlit trees. The complaint of Joanna's harmonica was scratching at my nerves.

"Joanna, can you stop your playing a minute? I hear something out there." She lowered the harmonica and held it still in her lap. Neil pitched straight up. Rubbed his eyes. "It's bright as day out here," he said.

"It's the moon," Joanna soothed.

"Shh!" I quieted them. "Do you hear it?"

"What?" they both asked at once, their heads whipping around.

"It's over in the water." I whispered and began to crawl on all fours toward the pond. "Crocodiles. Oh my god! It's croc..."

"Crocodiles?! There's no crocodiles in a pond in the Sierras. Maybe it's the Loch Ness monster..." Neil was laughing. Joanna shushed him.

"He's scared. Can't you see that? Aaron, come sit close to us. Neil's going to recite one of his poems." She had risen, lowered her gentle hands onto my shoulders, and turned me 180 degrees. Her wide fearless gaze pulled me in.

"The sky is filled with colors," Neil cooed, laying back on the needle-strewn ground, arms outstretched and smiling at the sky as if he were a sunbather on a summer day.

"Watch out!" I shouted, suddenly knowing what I heard was incoming firepower. I tore myself from Joanna's hands and flung myself on top of Neil, who struggled against my protective instincts.

"What're you doing, you idiot?"

I whispered into his ear, straining for clear enunciation. "The Cong, it's not cro-crocodiles in the pond. It's the Viet Cong."

"Get away you fool..."

"You'll be blown to bits!" I yelled, tightening my grip on his prone body. I was frantic, crying, desperate to hold Neil beneath me.

"They're no bombs," Neil insisted. "Just searchlights with rainbow colors. Shit, Joanna, help me get this guy into his tent." The two of them yanked me off Neil and guided me to the flap of my tent, shoving me inside. "...in here there's no colors, you'll be okay," Neil reassured me. "The tent's your home, the tent's your friend..." I curled up into a fetal position and the two of them went outside to fool around in the rainbow bath.

On the slanted inside walls of my tent, even with my eyes closed, I could see the flashes of colored light, blue, red, orange and white, like flame. I saw burning villages and then candles in windows and then those little Halloween candy corns and then ghosts and skeletons and all the while the colors were coming from the north, south, east and west with loud swishing, like

355

water rushing through a spout, overflowing in a storm. Why swishing? I became curious enough to begin observing myself under the spell of these weird impressions, even while experiencing almost unbearable dread. Then the sounds converged just over my head and opening my eyes, I fled from the tent.

There were Joanna and Neil, stretched out on their backs, their extended bodies covering the width of the tiny beachhead. I sensed them as two lovers electrically grounded by the slightest touch of the hands between them. But how could they be so oblivious to the danger? I rushed toward them, shouting loud as a banshee but I couldn't hear my own voice. Still, I had to warn them! "Sleek, sharp, slick, fast..." I shouted these words over and over again as if they were a mantra that would protect us all. Neil was groaning and Joanna was rising, and she took me in her arms and gave me a hug and sat me down with them. I was crying and she was stroking my head, as calm as if there had been two different species of Morning Glories, mine the anguished, hers and Neil's producing an inexplicable calm in the face of my assault. "God dammit!" I shouted. "Do you know I'm wet? I mean, it's not pee...it's...it's...I don't even know when I came..."

"Oh yich! The violence of war is such a turn-on for men," Joanna chided, "even though they don't like to admit it."

"And in my opinion, it's been too long since you had any, my friend," said Neil, "but I'm not sharing." He eyed Joanna ominously. Her petulant tongue popped out of her mouth to tease him and earned a laugh from Neil. She flapped the pink, wet eel at him again with a sly grin and when he flapped his back at her, they moved to kiss, dragging me along like a rag doll until I was in the middle of the two of them kissing. I was starting to get another hard on and instinctively I knew I didn't want to be where I was. In a loud, rather harsh voice, I said the first thing that popped into my head. "Did you know that I was Samuel Pepys in a former life?"

"How do you know?" Neil broke off the kiss to ask, laughing. He pushed us both away.

"I was," I shouted. My fists knotted, then before I knew it, they were pounding at the sides of my head. When they dropped, the words gushed out, my mouth a storm drain after a deluge of emotion. "I write letters in code...Christ! I can't stand this shit...Pepys and me and Janet and that fucking diary. Pepys' diary was in coded shorthand. Deciphered after years and years. How long will it be before I understand Janet's diary? How long?"

"I thought you said it was your diary?" Joanna interrupted.

"Janet's...I want to understand now...oh..."

I was crying again and shivering with the cold. The two of them had dragged me back over by the fire while I babbled. They wrapped a blanket around my jacket, sat on either side of me and kept their arms around me. Joanna asked me what some of my good memories were from my freshman year at Cal. An obvious ploy to change the direction of my lunacy. I fought back nausea and the desperate desire to shriek. I struggled to cooperate.

Gradually, the campsite beach strayed and melded with my freshman reminiscence and pushing through the thicket of memory, I emerged on a clean, salt-smelling beach over in Marin County. My classmate Raymond Chan and I were up for the tides at 3:45 a.m., out on class assignment for Stevens' intro to invertebrate zoology. Joanna's ploy was working.

"There's nothing better than the rhythm of the surf. The sky above it just sss...sliding into day," I said. I could smell salt air and clams and abalone cooking over the open fire. We had finished the required analyses and dissections. This weird breakfast feast crackled, while I strummed my guitar. "Great breakfast...that was the best," I mumbled dreamily.

"Ya gotta sleep before you get breakfast," Neil was saying, a touch of a dad in his voice.

"Naa, not breakfast now, it was then, on the beach, abalone and stuff." I sighed, staring into the ebbing campfire. Neil and Joanna's arms were still wrapped around me and I could feel their fingers and arms playing behind my back. An image of Janet in her hippie rags kicked me in the stomach. The taste of her skin was in my mouth...or was it Wonder Glow? What a great name for a makeup. Great name for Janet's skin, her cheek. The colors had subsided. My eyelids drooped. Still depressed, but returning to the mode of partially detached observer, I wanted to reassure my friends. "I'm okay now. Just slee..." I gulped, then coughed. "...sleepy."

"Let's get you back into your tent, then," said Joanna.

Curled into my sleeping bag, I pictured the Viet Cong to the west, Janet to the east, or was it the other way around? Then Matt, Janet, Bobby, MLK and...me. Each of us a lovely-hued searchlight, lost at distant, isolated spots on the bright moonlit field of heaven or the curved, fragile surface of earth.

FORTY-TWO

AARON BECKER, well-organized, rational science student, brushed his teeth with his finger and some of Neil's toothpaste, because he had forgotten his toothbrush. I hated that.

It was the morning after and the only one who had a hangover was Neil, from the rot gut. A rosy dawn yielded to a clear sky, and my anxiety over being trapped by a washed-out footpath evaporated with the last vestiges of moisture from the humus. After some Sanka and Nilla Wafers, we dragged washcloths over the dinner dishes and hung the remains of our food in a pack up a tree. Walking single file, we struck out on a hike around the pond, skipping the flattest stones we could find along its glassy surface. From the far side of the pond, we headed up along a gurgling creek, talking about the experience of the Morning Glory seeds.

"You were pretty far gone, Aaron. Do you remember it at all?" Neil asked.

"Yeah, I remember every lousy moment of it. Thank you guys for helping me keep my sanity."

"Is that what we were doing?" Neil laughed. "I thought we were keeping you from killing us."

"Hell, no! I wasn't going to kill you. I was protecting you. From the Cong, from the crocodiles, from exploding bombs..."

"...and from the pretty colored lights?" Joanna finished.

"You think I would bump you off? You've got the map out of this place, for Christ's sake." They chuckled dutifully. I laughed, not wanting to admit that I'd been scared out of my mind. And sad, angry, and missing Janet. Then I said, "Seriously, though, it was the pits." We marched on in silence for a full minute before I decided to ask, "You had fun, though?"

"Yeah, I liked it."

"Me too," Neil agreed. "I guess you've got some heavy shit going on and it all came out with the seeds."

"Sorry I was such a lunatic last night."

"No harm done."

"No more seeds for me." We trudged on, heading uphill, hearing only the buzzing of insects and our own panting breath. Suddenly, I cut into the meditative moment with more anguish in my voice than I'd intended. "It just keeps hitting me that I've got to get through exams. Can you imagine? Finals? It's my senior year at Cal and the quote-best-years-of-my-life-unquote are drawing to a close. But I've got people I care about in danger zones. I'm evading my own danger zone by running to Canada, and I figure that ties up the loose ends. But ever since that decision, I've felt...well, frankly, like a piece of shit."

"No ends were neatly tied up for you last night, man," said Neil, stopping to study the burl on an oak by the side of the trail. "Look at this..." He ran his hand over the curved mutation.

"It's sensuous and I love it," Joanna spoke up, "but if I don't keep going at a steady pace, I start to pant and lose momentum."

"We'd better keep going," I said. We started out again, Neil taking the rear, Joanna in the lead. "I was in the middle last night, just like this." I laughed and shook my head as I sidestepped an outcropping of granite. "I was being attacked and at the same time observing the attack like it was on someone else. So...so I'm reading Janet's letters about violent demonstrations in Paris and the unexpected letter she got from Matthew where he admits the war is morally fucked, and then there's MLK and civil rights riots and antiwar protests and another Kennedy murdered. Stuff this whole fucking semester. And then Janet just kind of vanishes. And I'm fine, just fiiine," I drawled. "But then why, last night, did I feel like all of it was happening to me?"

"Because you care about those people," Joanna said. "And you're afraid for them, not for yourself, because you just said you were free and clear now."

"But if the whole world goes up in smoke, then what's left for me? So, isn't that fear for myself? Just more selfishness?"

"Don't berate yourself, Aaron," Joanna said. "You're human, and worrying about others doesn't automatically translate by some twisted means into selfishness."

"Hell, I don't want to care..."

"And if Janet goes up in smoke...?"

"Aww fuck!" I shouted into the glistening treetops. I could not bear the sound of Joanna's words. "Okay," I said gruffly, swallowing hard. "Here's the crux of my problem: how does one fit a normal life into the social chaos all around? Somehow, I've got to focus on final exams."

"But you do care," said Neil. "And admitting it would be better, and admitting that you care about your exams too. You'd be surprised at the capacity of the human spirit to absorb pain and go on living, as you say, a 'normal life.'"

Joanna picked it right up, "You ought to try writing Janet at least one non-flippant, straightforward letter with your sincerest feelings about what's happening to her and all around the world. No more Samuel Pepys."

I sighed, remembering my delirium from the previous night. "No can do," I said.

"Why not?"

"Because Janet writes me in her coded diary about some guy named Teodor, and we're in the friend category now. I don't want to be a chump."

"Ah!! You hadn't mentioned that one," Neil slapped a hand on my shoulder.

"Sorry. Some things even you can't know...but now you do. I didn't tell you about Janet's father, either. He came to see me. Wants to give me a ticket to go find her and bring her home for him, but you can see that I can't do that either."

"It wouldn't be cool to write her, leave alone run after her," Neil agreed.

"It wouldn't keep your masculine pride intact," Joanna snapped, making the two of us stop in our tracks. "You guys are all alike. How do you know that Janet isn't linking up with some guy out of desperation, because since she left Berkeley, she's never had a straight, uncoded word from Aaron Becker about his intentions? How do you know she didn't cry every night because you never said you were joining her there. She may not be capable of being the first to speak straight, or even be aware of her own feelings. But then, she's reaching out to you, writing you. A lot, right?"

"Was until the French postal strike. Long, descriptive letters every few days. A diary."

"In code. And yours back. At least you're aware of your feelings now, Aaron, right?"

"I guess."

"You guess." Her flat echo felt like a slap across the face.

"Forget it. I'm not writing her any mushy letters. She's the one who broke it off, then got crazy radical and was exiled. Then started writing me about some other guy, for Christ's sake!" We walked along silently for a few minutes. I was relieved that Joanna was going to leave it alone. We started talking about the forest, the gold rush, the National Park Service, poems about nature, Gary Snyder, the relationship between real science and literary allusions. Intellectual stuff, transforming the conversation, leaving my heart back behind us on the trail.

By midnight, after the long uphill trek and drive home, we reached our neighboring brown shingle cottages. In the Berkeley sky, the stars were covered by masses of clouds, ruddy reflections of city lights.

Once my goodnights and heartfelt thank-yous had been said and my cottage door was closed, I shed my pack and immediately began to search through some of Janet's final letters. When I thought again about Marshall Magill's offer, it struck me that he had swallowed his pride and flown all the way from L.A. to ask me for help. Feeling weak in the knees, I dropped into a chair by my table. Suddenly, manipulation appeared more like desperation, my defenses lost their texture, and my remorse opened up as wide and crooked as a door on one hinge.

I assumed by now I'd memorized Janet's letters, yet I couldn't remember where, exactly, she was in her philosophy. I rifled through them, ignoring Dork, who was making an awful racket at the sight of me.

Here was her distress, exuded between lines of Sproul Plaza rhetorical language, upon listening to her new friend Bérnard describe the origins of the May Revolution in the Vietnam War. And here were earlier letters, depicting the horrors that communists had wrought in Teodor Pelnar's country. Janet must be confused, I thought. Since before Berkeley, she had decided that socialism was the light at the end of the tunnel. The benevolent society where poverty, oppression, and racism would be abolished, and we would all abandon our mutual exploitation and live in peace and prosperity together. The French students' hope for the same Nirvana is intense. But that image has been so demolished in the morass of Teodor's details about Czechoslovakia that Janet feels like a ship at sea with no anchor. She mocks herself as a "worry-wart" – coded mockery which asks the question: How does one fit a normal life into the social chaos all around?

Gripping her letter in my fist, I rushed out the front door, across the patio to Neil and Joanna's.

Neil admitted me before my second panicked knock. "Sorry, but I just had to..." My friend was ushering me in, pushing me down into a chair. Joanna was kneeling at my side. "Here's what she wrote," I said, searching for the place on the page.

"Your ironic sense is the balance to my serious nature, which is to take everything to heart." My friends were listening intently. I gave up trying to control the tremor in my voice. "Janet may see that nature as her problem," I said, "but to me, it's her strength. The world needs Janet more than it needs me. If it weren't for Janet, who would care?"

Neil's hand rested lightly on my shoulder. "It's hard to find the words to describe a soul, Aaron. But I do believe you've done it."

"Not just a soul, but the connection between souls..." Joanna's voice faded as I swallowed hard and cleared my throat.

"I want Janet to know that I need her to be just who she is. That I can't share her depth of feeling, I dare not. But I value it. I miss it. How can I let her know?"

"Go and find her, Aaron," Joanna whispered.

"Yes..." I could barely breathe. Both Joanna and I had known the answer to my question before I had asked it. "I've got to get over the chump thing. And my fears about the street actions, the protests. The only thing that matters is that I'm there for her if she needs me." Joanna and Neil glanced at each other and back at me with somber smiles. Affirmative. All systems go. I pushed up from the chair and paced the room, then turned to face them. "I've been as dense as my idiot parakeet."

"You've been a Dork, I agree," said Neil.

Joanna pushed at his sleeve with a reproving look. "It's good to see you facing the truth," she said. "And our friendship means a lot more when you're being honest with us."

"How could I be honest with you when I didn't know myself?" Halfway out the door, I stopped to give them each a hug. Then I hurried back to my cottage to search in my desk drawer for Marshall Magill's business card.

≈PART EIGHT≈
Paris

FORTY-THREE

AS FAR AS MARGOT and Madame Bouleaux were concerned, I was starting out for the American Express office and the last bus to Brussels. Teo would meet me, I assured them, and he would help me on the long trek across to the Right Bank. I had said my goodbyes to the two landladies, and to Frederic and Gabi. Hélène and Jean-Louis were at work—could they be the only people in Paris not en grève? Bérnard and Laurent were gone for good, and Elizabeth was waving to me from the third floor window. I felt both guilty and sad that I hadn't been able to say goodbye to the children, my tutors and companions during so many pleasant hours. They remained with Jean-Louis's parents in the countryside.

Hefting my small suitcase, backpack and guitar, I headed across the courtyard under the delicate spring leaves of the plane trees. Margot was standing at the door, her apron a bright starched shield tied over her drab cotton dress. When I reached the edge of the courtyard, I turned back to wave one last time. Her brow rose sardonically as she lifted her palm in farewell. A lump unexpectedly knotted my throat and ambushed my breathing. Margot Chabert had been my first hostess, and my advisor, confidante, self-appointed protector, talented cook and French language taskmaster. She had also been a busybody, social saboteur, political enemy and straitjacket, my own personal General de Gaulle.

As I entered the arched foyer, I gazed up at the diamond pattern in relief overhead and remembered the awe that decoration had once inspired in me. If I had been in love with the idea of Paris since my childhood, I had fallen in love with the physical presence of Paris at that moment. Such a simple thing, the décor of an ordinary apartment foyer, but that was the point, wasn't it?

Now I pulled my gear back through that cavernous space toward an uncertain Paris and a clandestine life with Teo. Up from wonderland, I thought, out of the rabbit hole. In the next moment I was on the sidewalk, the sun warming my face. I noted the instant of my liberation: it was 10:30 a.m. on Tuesday, May 21. I was nineteen years old and on my own in Paris, France. I was blessed with freedom and someone to love. The spring light dallied with the treetops. The day ahead was boundless...but what did that mean? That anything could happen? I took a deep breath and blew it out smoothly, deliberately in control. "Here I go," I said aloud.

I would walk first to Remi and Annette's, because it was just a few blocks away. My plans were vague: perhaps phone Teo from Remi's if the phones were working or take a taxi to Pigalle if I could find one. Or get help with my bags and guitar from someone on the action committee.

I was surprised to see our little group standing listlessly around on the street in front of the skinny little house with the blue shutters. Why weren't they meeting inside? "Hallo, Remi," I said, feeling shy as all eyes turned my way. I dropped my burdens on the curb. "Has something happened? Why are you all out here?" The others gathered around us as if they were a bunch of drowsy cats, and I had just brought a big trough of Friskies to the middle of the quiet street.

"Much has happened to us, but what is this?!"

"I separated from the bourgeois household," I replied, trying not to sound proud.

"Ah! Oh lá lá!" Bérnard laughed. "Excellent ..." There was laughter all around.

"Very good," Remi approved. "But...do you have a place...?"

"With Teo," I cut him off. His smile grew as bright as his golden hair. "But I'm desperate to hear what's going on. Why are we outside?"

Remi's smile faded abruptly. "You know. My papa is a Communist union leader. He forbids us to meet in the house."

"But why? Even if it is superficial, aren't we supposed to be on the same side?"

Remi sighed. "A lot has happened these past couple of days. A group of Trotskyist students marched all the way from the quartier latin to the huge Renault auto factory in Boulogne-Billancourt. There they symbolically transferred their banner to the striking workers. The CGT had forbidden them to go, but they went anyway. My papa's party has lost control. They are jealous of all the attention the students are getting in the news." Remi's beautiful lips shriveled up in disgust. "They don't want us taking any action. They don't even want us debating at the base, which is our whole strategy."

"No one wants to listen. Just like the government!" shouted Bérnard, then added, "No...worse. Because they are such cowards."

"Absolutement!" declared Céleste. "Georges Séguy announced that the CGT is not prepared to take steps to end capitalism. Can you imagine?"

"Isn't he the same one who made us disperse from the Luxembourg?" I asked.

"That's the one," Remi replied. "He continues to praise individual students but insults the students as a whole. He calls us a 'petty bourgeois' group.' Papa worships him, and today he told me, 'The CGT must take over from here, mon fils. They will get you what you want.' Such reassurance! Get me what I want? How can they get me what I want, when neither they nor I know yet any of the details about what I want or how to achieve it?" Remi raised two hands to the bright sky, then dropped them heavily to his sides. Exasperated.

"But with or without the CGT," Céleste said, "we continue to occupy the Sorbonne and L'Odéon and to debate day and night about the future of France."

Everyone began to grumble at once. Remi waved his hands in the air, signaling for us to pay attention. "Mes amis! On Sunday, you know, we had the general assembly in Charléty Stadium. Nearly 150 Parisian action committees sent delegates. C'etait fantastique...at the assembly, for once, we were in harmony. We agreed we must be political. But then today the CGT announced they are starting their own action committees, as they say, to 'channel the movement into parliamentary waters.' First step to selling out to the government."

"But how can they...?" I burst out. "They can't just steal the movement from the students...!"

"Don't worry, Jeanette," Remi laughed bitterly. "The communists won't stop us as easily as they believe. Our general assembly had value as propaganda. Most of France is striking now—all the big stores, the textile mills, the government ministries, even the professionals and scientists. They are wise to the CGT game, to hold political advantage by steering clear of real change."

"But no clear direction has been taken," said Bérnard. "We must come to agreement among ourselves about the forms of socialism. I think most workers prefer cogestion, as we do, n'est-ce pas...?"

"What the hell is that?" asked Claude, tugging at his long strings of hair.

"You don't know?"

"Pardone mon stupidité, monsieur le bâtard..."

Remi began to explain, putting a new spin on what I already understood. Claude, I reflected, was more action than talk. He hadn't been listening. The radical anarchist groups insisted on nothing less than autogestion, which meant that both the students' and workers' assumed complete control of management. Our action committee agreed that a complete systemic change would never be possible, perhaps not even preferable from an economic viewpoint. But cogestion meant mutual respect, open discussion, shared management. Remi's explanation to Claude confirmed how excited I was about these ideas.

"But shouldn't the workers be debating these things?" I said.

"Of course! The workers and the students together. That is what the students want. And meanwhile, my father has told us we cannot use the house to meet."

"So we will go to the Sorbonne!" I burst out.

Bérnard took up Remi's story. "Well yes, but we were using the house to help organize the neighborhood action committee. Mostly the wives of striking workers. Cohn-Bendit said we should be an 'exemplary' movement. Leading everyone by example."

"Of course I know! I made the small poster for the Métro announcing a meeting..."

"Oui, c'est ca," Remi continued. "That's the one. And you remember that the location for the meeting was this house. We were to meet here to guide a discussion about politics, social problems, current events, history, all that."

"Ahhh...merde!" Bérnard swore. "The wives will not come to the foreign land of the Sorbonne. They are comfortable here in the neighborhood."

"We will have to postpone the meeting," Remi said.

"I can contact the women," Céleste offered. "I'll let them know we're looking for another place." Remi and Céleste began to confer and then she strode off, first in the direction of the Métro to write "postponed" across my little poster.

"Come, let's go to our University!" Bérnard shouted.

"All of you go on and I'll meet you there," Remi said, rubbing his chin and obviously trying to formulate a plan. "I'm going to help Jeanette get up to Teo's house first. But you go with the others, Bérnard, okay?" They all agreed on a classroom to meet, and Remi turned to me.

"He lives in Pigalle," I said, anticipating his question.

"Ah yes, the ghetto of the poor Central European. A long walk. Let's get started." He grabbed my suitcase.

Annette sidled up to us. "I'm hungry," she said, lifting my guitar case. "Let's start our long walk after a stop on the Rue de la Huchette."

My stomach growled. I wrapped my hand around Annette's arm and whispered a grateful merci.

After lunch, I telephoned Teo and got through to the phone in his hallway. He was relieved to hear from me. "I was thinking all morning about your next move," he said, "and I decided that this was the choice you would make." I laughed joyfully into the telephone.

The three of us trudged across the Pont des Arts and up the hill, all of us panting and complaining about the Métro strike as we began our final ascent. It was late afternoon by the time we entered the Place Pigalle. The district was already blushing under gargantuan, garish tubes of neon. Beat City, Club Havana, Sweet Spot, more English than French, beckoning with the promise of grimy pleasures. I bounced by my friends, wanting to display an air of confidence. Surely, I prayed, I will always have Teo to walk with me here when I go out at night. Then Teo was moving toward us through the thickening crowd. His expression flickered, lit by skittish neon tints. He thanked my gallant French friends earnestly and shook their hands, then hoisted all the gear himself and walked me up the hill, past a tiny, moldy Romanesque church, to my new home on the Rue Antoine.

FORTY-FOUR

TEO'S STUDIO was easily taken in at a glance: narrow bed, steamer trunk, sink and hotplate, piles of books everywhere, a table with two unmatched chairs. The bay window extended far off to the side, leaving the room with only three walls. My smart, neatly-dressed lover seemed out of place in this cramped, off-kilter space, its contents limited to the bare necessities. He dropped my things near the door, closing it behind us. The stink of urine and garbage from the stairwell gave way to the moldy odor of a wet dog. I drew closer to Teo, my hands fingering the small white buttons on his shirt as I scanned the room. This was Pigalle, not just the rowdy streets and the sex clubs we had rushed past on our way up the hill, but life with a giant man inside this small, shabby compartment. The words "you made your bed, now lie in it" flashed against the sudden darkness of my mind like the tawdry neon tubes lighting the streets nearby.

My lover was smiling down at me, his mouth just inches above mine, blinking away tears of happiness. "You see?" he asked, a hint of pride in his question. He pointed to the square table in the center of the room, where he had set two places with the type of heavy flatware and clunky, off-white china used in

French diners. A hotplate supper awaited us, which he had prepared from two cans and cut-up salad vegetables. A bouquet of fresh violets in a chipped coffee mug graced the table. As I took it all in, Teo shifted his big frame across the room with one stride and pulled out my chair. I hesitated, then spied those violets again. Gratitude stabbed me and I rushed to give him a grateful hug, but before I could get my arms around him, he was kissing me with all his considerable might.

We sat down at the table and Teo spooned food onto my plate. On the wall behind us, the sink, miniature fridge and two-burner hotplate served as his kitchenette. Cubby holes spilled over with cans, pots, spoons, and cups. Next to the kitchenette was an armoire with its doors missing, stuffed with everything from Teo's rumpled shirts to paper, pens and books. Nothing was the least bit organized. A stray notion grazed my consciousness: Aaron Becker would not have approved. I itched to straighten it all up myself.

I focused on my plate, picking out an edible bite. What to say? Out came, "Well! You got fresh vegetables! You know what I like."

"Yes, I do know!" Teo scooped up his dinner enthusiastically. "But you see, I get them in the neighborhood, fresh every day. The farmers and grocers here are too poor themselves to starve us with strikes." He ratcheted his grin down to low wattage, crunching on lettuce. I sniffed the canned beans and the beef stew. Elizabeth's word for canned goods came to mind. "Tinned." They smelled metallic. I tasted a bit of each, then smiled sheepishly over at Teo, relieved to see him concentrating on his own plate. Berating my nose for smelling dog food, I dug in, finding that I could avoid choking if I alternated between bites of meat and fresh carrot.

Searching for something to divert my attention, my eyes wandered toward the black night outside the window and around the room. The rounded bay pushed forward asymmetrically to the left, merging with the long kitchenette wall, then gave way to the second of the odd three walls, the one with the door. One narrow bed extended from the third wall toward the center of the room with a battered trunk at its foot. A nightstand with a lamp and shade as aged as an artifact from the Musée Cluny completed the arrangement. As nonchalantly as I could, I asked, "Where will I sleep, Teo?" It seemed a reasonable question, given the size of my boyfriend and the size of his bed. Teo stifled a cough and slurped some beans.

"Can't we fit in the bed together, if I hold you very close?" He wiped his lips with the waxy French napkin, scrutinizing me and the bed, then moving back to me again. Perhaps he was calculating the space in his mind, but had forgotten to count himself into the measurements. "I'm willing to try," I said. We resumed our meal, changing the subject to the news of the day.

When we had finished, Teo motioned for me to stay in my seat and went to put the kettle on the hotplate burner. "Would you prefer coffee or tea?" he asked.

"I'll take some tea, merci," I replied. Then I chuckled. "Are you going to wait on me all the time?"

"No, just for this special welcome. After all, I want you to feel at home here."

"Will you expect me to wait on you, then?" I asked, shamming suspicion.

He had come to stand above me, amused by our volley. "Well, you see, I am from a socialist country. Our motto is, 'each gives according to his ability, each receives according to his need.'" I laughed heartily.

Suddenly, he was down on one knee. "Teo, what on earth...?"

"Jeanette, I have no ring, but I am sincere with you. Will you please be my wife?" I was dumbfounded, still calming myself from the hilarity of his comments on our housekeeping. Should I take this seriously or not? But Teo's smile had faded. He gazed at me expectantly.

"Teo, I don't know what to say...? I mean, you don't have to do this...."

"No, please believe me. I want to do this. I love you, Jeanette."

"I know you do..."

"Do you love me?"

I sighed. "Why doesn't the tea kettle whistle right now?"

"I don't understand..."

"Please, Teo, get up. Come on." I had taken his hands and guided him to his feet. We stood holding each other's fingertips. "I'm truly honored that you would ask me. And I do love you.

Because I am moving in here, it seems like we ought to be married..." He started to protest but I put my hand up against his lips. He was frowning at me. "But I cannot lie to you, Teo. I cannot marry you because we are not going in the same direction. Isn't that right? I'm going this way and you're going that way..." I pointed my forefingers in opposite directions, one to the window, one to the door.

"Someday?" he asked timidly. "When we have worked out all the many difficulties?"

"When 'someday' comes, we will see who we are and what world we are living in."

Teo blew out a noisy breath. After a few seconds, he nodded and repeated, "Okay, okay." I searched his face for signs of relief. I was sure I detected some of those twitches, alleviating some of my own guilt pangs. That was when the kettle went off. Without another word, Teo went to retrieve it.

"Where is the bathroom?" I asked.

"We share, like in the pension. The W.C. is downstairs." As an afterthought, he added, "The shower room is next door to it."

"One floor down?"

"Yes, but the stairway is just to the left out the door. It's very convenient."

Teo would not have called it "convenient" if he had realized that standing there in the darkened stairway, blocking my path, would be the rotund, sweating figure of his friend Miroslav. I stopped in my tracks when I saw him, then backed myself up to the top of the stairs. Without so much as a nod or a hello, Miroslav climbed the stairs, brushed past me and proceeded toward the room where Teo was cheerfully preparing tea. Tempted as I was to follow Miroslav, I knew nature would not wait for me another minute. I fled downstairs and into the toilet.

I could hear them shouting, even with the door closed and one floor down. I pulled the cord to flush and slowly made my way back up the stairs, marveling at the paper-thin walls, which must leave all tenants privy to their neighbors' intimate secrets. I stood outside the closed door, listening to them yell at each other in strange guttural words. There was a sudden scraping of furniture on the floor and banging and bumping, which I took to be some sort of pushing each other around. In any picture of the two of them I could conjure up, only Teo could be the winner. So my heart thumped away, more excited than frightened. I stood back from the door in case Teo tossed Miroslav out into the hall, and I waited. Feeling my funny bone oddly tickled, I wondered absently if the obvious threats and cussing were in Czech or Slovak. But my amusement drained away when a word popped out at me, the only word I recognized, and the word was America. The door opened and just as I had predicted, Miroslav was shoved out of the room from behind by Teo's big hands. He dashed past me as if I weren't there.

The steamer trunk was halfway across the room. One chair was on the floor. Teo was rubbing the side of his face. Miraculously, he had tea on the table.

"What was that all about?" I asked, quietly closing the door. Teo stared at the tea as if he found comfort in the civilized nature of the setting. "It was nothing."

"Please, let's not start off with secrets..."

"Always more questions with you!" he shouted. "Do you know you drive me crazy with your curiosity? Do you? I'm sorry. But there are things I cannot tell you. You must accept that."

I backed up, struck mute by Teo's outburst. He scowled, his lips stern.

My heart rattled in my chest. My mouth was so dry that I could barely speak. "Are you sure you...you still want me here?"

He sighed, ran his fingers through his hair. After a moment, he had finally calmed himself. "Yes, of course, Jeanette. The danger is not grave."

"What does that mean exactly, 'the danger'...?"

He glared at me. "Another question. Do you even hear yourself ask them?"

"Okay, okay!" I shouted back, my voice cracking a bit as I tried to sound more angry than afraid. "I'm not a moron! Je comprends! When it comes to Miroslav and your country, I'm supposed to crush my curiosity and my fear..." and I used the word "écraser" because that awful crush is what I felt he was asking of me. "And you wanted me to marry you?"

"I'm sorry, so...but...this cannot be otherwise, cherie." His palms turned up, an appeal for pity. We glared at each other for a moment, then he glanced idly down at the supper table. "We'd better have the tea, or it will be cold." He held my chair back for me. I shrugged. What else could I do? Certainly then, I did pity him. It was not his fault that Czechoslovakia was repressive. I sat down to tea.

We sipped in uncomfortable silence. What could I say to show him I accepted his secrets? "This tea is excellent," was what I came up with. "You are a gracious host."

Teo grabbed my hand, gave it a kiss. "My beautiful Jeanette, I am sorry I shouted. I was upset, but everything will be fine."

"Okay, Teo. I trust your judgment," I said.

"And now, I have a question for you, not about marriage I promise, so this time I will get the answer I wish."

I smiled, "I hope so."

"At some time, as I have told you, I will decide to go back to my country. And you want to see Prague, don't you?"

"Yes, of course," I responded immediately. I had considered this possibility many times. I couldn't see anything that could go wrong on a brief adventure. "It would be wonderful, Teo. And I'd like to meet your family and friends, especially your mother."

He finished his tea with one gulp, then scowled into the empty cup.

I read his expression more clearly than magic tea leaves. "They won't want to meet me because I'm an American," I said quietly. "Isn't that it?"

His head jerked up. He switched on a positive, almost cheerful tone. "When they finally meet you, and they will meet you, they will love you. Especially my mother." I forced myself to radiate trust. Shouldn't I trust Teo? But I suspected after what I had heard from the hallway that his confidence was a brave front.

"So, here it is," he continued, leaning forward, his face flushed. "When I go, I would like to be of service to the Prestup."

I remembered. "The money. You will carry money across the border for him."

"Exactly." He squeezed my hand. "I am pleased that you remember this. So, if you come with me, you can take the money more safely. They will never search you. And even if they do, they will never question the idea that an American girl could possess large amounts of money. Don't you see? It will be difficult for me. It will be safe and easy for you."

"Yes, I can see that," I replied. "And I do want to help you, Teo."

"Then it's agreed? We will decide together when to go."

"I...this is too complicated to decide right now. But I'll think about it. It sounds like something I could do."

"Okay, cherie, you think about it," he said. "You are good at that."

The bed proved to be more of a problem than Teo had anticipated, and not just for sleeping. In the end, we dragged the thin mattress onto the floor because we were afraid the bed would collapse under the strain. Once we got down, we found ourselves stretched out, separated, each of us with a leg, a shoulder and an arm on the cold floor. I felt as dilapidated as the old mattress, my spirit emptied, first by the shouting and then by the bed.

"Why don't we just buy a bigger mattress tomorrow? We can do without the springs and supports. This old bed is ready for retirement, don't you agree?" Teo lay there, lips squeezed white, saying nothing. "Well...?"

"What?"

"What about my idea? About the sleeping arrangements?"

"Don't worry, I can sleep on the floor. You can have the mattress."

"That's not the point. Why not just...?" I swallowed a sharp gulp of air. Could it be that he didn't want to put out the money for a temporary arrangement? "Teo," I began again, "I might be here for weeks. Wouldn't it be worth it...? Or am I welcome here for just for a few days?"

"I have no money for it."

"Not in your..." I surveyed the room, took in the seediness of the stained, gray walls, the scratched furniture, the blotchy lampshade. "Teo, there's something I don't understand."

He rolled over on his side to face me, began to play with my hair, his expression kind once again. "Give me your question, cherie."

"If your father is doing important things for the Communist government, and your family lives in a nice house, why don't you have enough money to live in a better place than this?"

Teo gave out a groan, left off twisting strands of my hair and rolled onto his back, his whole body tensed. "Do you know what socialism is?" he asked the ceiling.

"Well, everyone shares. A fair system..."

"Yes, but in order for everyone to live decently, no one can be wealthy. It means that no one has very much. My father gets a little special consideration, it is true. We are more comfortable than some others. But no one has the extra money that it seems every American student in Europe has to play around with. That is what you need for sending sons and daughters to study abroad. That is a luxury. We have no luxuries."

"Perhaps that is better," I said, imagining a country where there would be no Beverly Hills and yet no Watts either. "And once the playing field is leveled, then everyone could come up together, get richer inch by inch, the whole country together..."

"Unless you are a Soviet satellite."

"Ohh..."

"The Czech Republic before the war was so strong that it took 15 years for our Soviet masters to drain us dry." He asserted this with a strong note of pride in his voice, but his tone changed abruptly when he continued.

"Now there are Czechs and Slovaks without food for their children. That is part of what our quest for freedom is about. In a Soviet satellite, you don't ever get richer. You only get poorer, as you said, the whole country together."

"Ohh...that's terrible!"

He sighed, then whispered, "We should cheer up. I have heard it said that sex is the opiate of the masses." He brushed his lips against my hair.

I laughed. "A self-serving parody if I ever heard one..."

"It doesn't serve you, too?" I rolled over and saw that he had assumed the artificial expression of a large, wounded mammal. I folded myself meekly into his embrace and suddenly the mattress seemed to expand around us. The odd shapes of the walls straightened up like soldiers and their surfaces fell away. Teo's hands were unbuttoning my shirt and mine were unfastening his slacks. Everything of the room was gone except the sounds of our breathing, and our flesh and bone. Then something scratchy caught my bare shoulder and I realized that not one inch of either of us was on the mattress. He must have noticed too, because he lifted me with his powerful arms almost into the air and right back down on top of him. He slid us both back over onto the soft, bumpy mattress and smiled up at me. "Better, eh?" I giggled. "Yes yes..." I whispered as I leaned in to kiss him. And running his gentle, open hands all the way down from my breasts to my thighs, he pushed me down so that our bodies were aligned with the forces of nature.

FORTY-FIVE

A PRIVATE RITUAL defined our household. At the close of days filled with meetings, marches, and heated discussions on street corners or in cafés, Teo and I would lie down together on his narrow mattress and spend a quiet hour, our arms around each other, listening to news broadcasts on a portable radio. Teo fiddled with the dial, pausing at the independent French stations, the BBC or occasionally Radio Free Europe, static free in the quiet night.

Like all rituals, this one was girded with implicit rules.

No kissing, no touching below the waist, no sexual distraction.

No talking, except to discuss alterations to the radio: the subtle movements of Teo's thick fingers on the radio dial; the position of the black box or the flimsy antennae.

Holding each other permitted, once the channel was clear: the pressure of arms and hands signaled distress or support for the distressed.

Eyes to be saved for dire circumstances, when the warmth of touch was simply not enough.

We learned many things during those nightly ceremonies. About events and realities in Czechoslovakia, in France, in Vietnam and in the States. He listened for news from the Soviet bloc, I for activity in Asia. We learned what was essential for the next day's discourse in the streets and cafés and to make rational decisions, day by day, about what to do next. But more important than the political lessons was what we discovered about one another. I learned to gauge both the direction and degree of my lover's reactions to the news through the pressure of arms or the care on his face. What frightened and confused him. What boosted his hopes or left him gloomy.

On Wednesday, May 22, the news broke that Dany Cohn-Bendit, the red-headed student leader whose charisma I had enjoyed at rallies and debates, had been expelled from France as an "undesirable alien." Officially, he was still German, but certainly he had more right to be in France than I did. I heard the news with trepidation. As much as I resented interference from the "adult" communists, in my heart I had welcomed their resistance to further violence. Now the expulsion had given the students an excuse to take to the streets again, bringing their friends among the workers and intellectuals with them. I told Teo that I must be among them. If there was one thing I couldn't put up with, it was the injustice of expelling Cohn-Bendit by calling him l'étranger. As I spoke, Teo was knitting his fingers until his knuckles were white. "Please don't be worried about me...I have to go..."

"Not that!" he blurted out. "I mean, okay, I am worried about you, but it is just that I want so much to go myself!"

That night, I didn't even try to catch up with Remi and Bérnard and the others. I had been with Teo all day and had no idea if they would still be at our meeting place at the Sorbonne. I caught sight of the crowd on Boul' Mich', heading toward the Palais Bourbon. The crowd was shouting angrily, waving fists. There was no traffic, no opposition from the police. In fact, it was unnaturally controlled except for thousands of Frenchmen and one American girl, marching toward the Bastille crying, "We are all undesirables..." That affirmation of Cohn-Bendit's right to remain in Paris was soon transformed into "We are all foreigners...," and finally "We are all German Jews!" I shouted with them, gleeful with each change. We came within sight of the medieval fortress, the prison of the revolution for which the French national independence day is named: the Bastille. The sight of it made me angry with the whole bloodied history of the world, with all its prejudices, all its idiocy.

Powerlessness breeds anger. The angry mood was palpable. It was the first time I had marched among a group of complete strangers. Suddenly I noticed the raised fists and angry mouths all around me and I flashed back to our night on the barricades, to the smell of gas and the sticky feel of Laurent's blood.

Nauseated, I began to move backward, like a person who has stepped off a conveyor belt and left everyone else moving on. A few minutes later I was at the very edge of the crowd. Tomorrow I would find my group and work with them. Tonight, I had done my part. I turned around and headed toward home, glad that I had no pack to carry.

The next day, a girl I had never met delivered a note from Remi with a message about the action committee's plans. Teo invited her for breakfast, but she said she wanted to take our return message back to Remi. Natural communicator that he was, determined to remain inclusive about his little band, our leader had set up a message service, where members of the group fanned out all over the city and delivered mail like the pony express. I was delighted.

"What does he say," asked Teo, trying to read over my shoulder. I moved the letter over and we read together.

Our action committee had been out there at the Bastille the night before. The crowd was being estimated at 50,000. I could just see the satisfied smirk on Remi's face as he composed the communiqué. We would meet the next night at the Gare de Lyon. It would be exactly two weeks since our decisive battle. Hastily, I scrawled a note: I will be there.

When the sun went down, Teo and I threw the mattress back on the frame and lay down on our sides, his right arm wrapped around me and his left hand working with the radio dial on the nightstand. We heard that Pompidou could no longer follow de Gaulle's "wait and see" policy. He had called all the unions and communists to round-table negotiations over the weekend. Nearly ten million workers were involved in the strike.

On Friday afternoon, I followed Remi's instructions, joining my action committee at the Gare de Lyon where a short march to the Bastille was to begin. Still proclaiming ourselves to be German and Jewish, our throng arrived at the Bastille to find the entrance blocked by police. We halted and a hush overtook the crowd. Transistor radios were tuned to listen to de Gaulle, speaking as if on cue to the huge mass of demonstrators.

The old man proposed a referendum through which people would give him what he called a "mandate for renovation." Or else he'd resign. What a threat! Hadn't he already been given chance after chance to renovate his poor excuse for a decent

University and a democratic government? The crowd was waving white hankies, calling out "Adieu, de Gaulle, Adieu, Monsieur le Générale" and I reached into my jeans pocket for a clean piece of Kleenex to wave.

There was trouble up front. The police were deliberately pushing their truncheons up against the demonstrators, giving them no choice but to push back. This had happened at other demonstrations, but this time I had a clear view of the provocation. The gendarmes—those flics—were faceless in the shadows of their helmets. And they were big men, much bigger than the chain of protesters opposite their column.

Before we knew it, skirmishes had begun and we began to back off, on the run again. We split off into small groups, staying along the boulevards this time. I followed Remi, others followed Bérnard. There were too many of us and we were too scattered for them to control. Remi was sure that the police would once again be trying to take the precious territory of the Sorbonne and its environs. We headed back to the quartier latin and there met up with Bérnard and the other half of our group.

Saving the Sorbonne was now our only goal. Again we brought out air hammers and pulled up what was left of the ancient pavés, again we built our barricade, not so high this time. When the order came around to pile the top with combustibles, I felt as if I had awakened from a trance. Branches and trash, from fruit peels to oil-soaked rags, appeared as if from out of nowhere and were thrown up into the air, landing accurately atop the piled stones. Was there a flammable stockpile somewhere? I wondered. Had this been planned in advance? Remi was on top of the pile, dodging missiles and arranging the load. I heard someone whistle through his teeth. Bérnard was gazing up at our handiwork with heartfelt admiration. "That's one dangerous pile of shit," he said loudly enough for Remi to hear. Our leader beamed down at Bérnard and gave him the victory sign, two fingers raised.

I stepped away, recognizing that a game was being played and that some knew the rules and others didn't. I knew I wanted Dany Cohn-Bendit back in France. I knew letting the Sorbonne fall to the government would be the end of everything. But was that it, then? Was that all we could do? Defend the same territory over and over again while the communists and Pompidou made secret deals?

The police advanced slowly from far down the street, as if they were as weary of the battle as I felt just then. One of the flics raised his Plexiglas shield to rub sleep out of his eyes. They had been out overtime for weeks, tripping over rubbish and corralling rebels only to have them released again.

Remi and Claude stood at the top of our barricade with torches lit. The police approached and saw the threat, but they kept coming. The two clambered down and bounded backwards, throwing their torches on top of the incendiary pile. The garbage caught fire and the police retreated, running to fetch the fire department. It was over more uneventfully than I had feared. Yet as I trotted down the street, following my friends away from the fire, a new perspective crept into my consciousness. This was no occasion for celebration. There was no reason at all to raise our two fingers in victory.

While I was watching torches fly onto our barricade in the quartier latin, rebels on the other side of the city were setting fire to the Bourse, the French stock exchange—symbol of French capitalism. May 24 was dubbed the "Night of the Bourse." Fighting had broken out all over France, not just in Paris. A policeman had been killed in Lyon.

After the Night of the Bourse, a whole week went by without a battle. I had never felt confident about going into the bustling Sorbonne alone, so I went there now only for specific meetings. Most days, Teo and I trudged long distances, heading for the obvious public places to run into our friends—a frequented café, the steps by the Seine, my old neighborhood near Remi's house or up along Boul' Mich'. Despite the strike, I stayed alert, careful to avoid the route traveled by Margot Chabert or Mme. Bouleaux.

Wherever we walked, we were amazed by the sheer numbers of silk-screen posters plastering every available segment of wall. The Sorbonne students at the École des Beaux-Arts and École des Arts Decoratif had established an atelier populaire to tell the story of our struggle. Action estimated more than 350 different designs transformed Paris into a festival of activism that spring. At every turn, the simple, powerful graphics and clever slogans lifted our spirits—and indeed, our spirits needed lifting.

On Boul' Mich', we ran into Remi and Bérnard, who affirmed what we already knew: the activity was all up at the level of the government and union negotiators now. The students still met inside l'Odéon and the Sorbonne courtyard day and night, but student debates were as circular and inconclusive as ever. I had seen for myself that many of the University's occupiers were filthy, sick and sleep-deprived, and that their ranks had been infiltrated by unruly teenaged thugs. All this was depressing news, but worse was Remi's admission that he had no idea what was next for our action committee.

FORTY-SIX

I WAS GETTING USED to life in the little studio. Teo was a quiet man, not difficult to live with. On the other hand, he had to live with me and my sporadic blue moods. I was struggling to accept the failure of the May Revolution to speed the end of the Vietnam War, but more often our new living arrangements set me off: the disgusting canned meat, a greasy sink, a spider crawling up the blotchy wall, some impenetrable Czech phrase escaping from Teo's lips, or the sheer dominance of his presence in the cramped space. Then there was sex: there was always a bone-cracking moment when I wasn't sure if Teo's body wasn't more dangerous than the barricades. Sex, I was surprised to learn, could be disappointing. Or there could be too much sex. Or perhaps the worst, sex so absolutely formidable that it reminded me that I would be spending decades—the rest of my life—without Teodor Pelnar.

My secret hope? That the postal strike would continue indefinitely. I had spent quite a few sleepless nights worrying about the news I might miss about Matt. But now, shaking off disturbing thoughts about Vietnam, I couldn't help but be struck by the irony of connecting with my brother just before the strike began. I had been able to get one letter out to him in which I described the French students' concern about Vietnam—their Indochine. I would have liked to receive the letter I knew he must have written in return. At the same time, it was a relief to be spared dealing him the truth about my life in Paris.

Somehow I couldn't imagine telling Matt about the barricades, much less about Teo. My brother fought a war and in the process, became involved with Lue. It sounded like she was a confidante, not a lover. But what if she were? Teo and I were so much more to each other, and yet my life with him would not be condoned by my brother.

The other side of my life, the public side, could put me off as well: rumors of another impasse at the peace talks, a radio report about street violence, or conversations with friends about the students' endless bickering or the Communist Party's sabotage of our dreams.

I had no temper, but my ugly blue moods seemed to permeate every corner of the studio—Teo's studio, I often reminded myself—and Teo's own sensitive spirit. Clearly, it was within my power to put Teo into his own dull mood, and sometimes I felt like a puppeteer whose fingers have gotten hopelessly entangled in the strings. Teo did occasionally cut those strings himself, turning his back on me and retreating into silence. But he never walked out...except one night, and that desertion had nothing at all to do with my curdled disposition.

In the middle of that night I was awake and obsessing futilely over the future of the revolution. It had been hours since we'd made love and I assumed Teo, his head burrowed into his rolled-up jacket, was fast asleep. I lay there, conjugating French verbs, hoping the exercise would bore me into dreamland. I listened to the usual cracklings from walls full of roaches and mice, and rolled over onto my side as if I could turn my back on the creepies. I stared at Teo's broad back, conjuring pictures from the wrinkles in his skin.

Then with one swift, smooth motion, Teo rose and dragging his pants and jacket behind him, quietly slipped out the door. I sat straight up. He wouldn't have taken his clothes to the toilet. The fusty air rippled in the dark cave of the studio. My heart beat like bats' wings. I felt as if it could fly out of my chest and down the stairwell after Teo. Bewildered and afraid, I listened intently to the fading of his steps. After a minute of silence, I lay back down, my eyes frozen open, with only the creepies for company.

The two of us set out the next day to scrounge for supplies. Heading down the hill under a bright, endless spring sky, we crossed the river at the Pont des Arts. Traffic was light and the prevailing odor of the day was garbage. Teo seemed not to notice. He whistled cheerfully, held my hand loosely and swung a cloth grocery bag at his side.

We stopped at one of the few windows on the Boulevard St.-Germain not shielded by corrugated cardboard. Teo examined a row of the latest model adding machines. "I wonder how they work," he mused. I made no reply. "You seem pensive today, Jeanette. Tell me your meditations." Teo cocked his head, smiling playfully.

"You don't want to hear them. Believe me, you don't." My nerves were squishing my muscles together and the sensation reminded me of how scared I had felt, lying there alone the night before. I hadn't decided how to bring it up, but Teo squeezed my hand, his air of innocence egging me on. "Okay, then," I shouted. Peeking around at passersby, embarrassed, I lowered my voice. "I saw you leave last night."

The bag drooped in his left hand, but he held fast to mine with his right. "I'm sorry," he said sincerely. "I thought you were asleep."

"That's not the issue...!"

"...I know I know. Ach! I have to go in the night to see the Prestup, so Miroslav is asleep. We are making plans about the money."

"You could have told me that."

"Of course. I'm sorry, please forgive me. I should have said...I will go again."

I pursed my lips and nodded slowly. Of course he would go again. And what was there to say to that? We walked up the Rue de Seine where we bought pale-spotted fruits from a street vendor. Peaches and plums, miraculously there in the middle of the strike, plump and fresh.

Up toward the Boulevard, the bag swung cheerfully again, but as we walked, the easiness of Teo's explanation made me as uncomfortable as a persistent itch. Something didn't add up. Something about our first intimate night in the hotel room. I wasn't concerned about his seducing me. I considered that it was time, that I had given signals, that everything was mutual.

But why had he needed me as a decoy in Montparnasse if he could have gone in the night from Pigalle?

I pulled him down to kiss him on the cheek, manufacturing coyness. "Teo, so...tell me again why you needed me as a decoy on our first night of lovemaking? Couldn't you have just gone from your studio as you did last night?"

"Well, cherie," came his jovial reply, "I didn't know the Prestup so well then. He didn't trust me..." he broke off.

I heard the nuance immediately, but held my tongue in check. In a heartbeat, I connected his supple words with the shrill reality. He had said, quite clearly, 'hadn't known the Prestup so well then.' But he had told me that they were total strangers! That he had gone to meet with the Czech dissident for the very first time. If he had known the Prestup before that night, then what else was he fabricating?

"Teo, I'm just curious," I tried to sound as naïve as I could, "did you know me first or the Prestup first?" He dropped my hand and swung around to face me, nervously switching the bag back and forth between his hands. "Why do you ask that?"

"Because I want to understand."

"Because you don't trust me. My motives."

"I appreciate your political motives, but what about us?"

"I love you, Jeanette," the words blew from his lips in a hoarse whisper. "I do, I do. Believe me, please."

"I don't know what to believe, but I suspect...tell me now, Teo. Now!"

"Okay, yes, yes." His thick, hardened tone slammed into me with a thud. "I met the Prestup first, and of course he suggested it would be useful to have an American friend, any American who would be on our side. But I loved you right away and I knew right away you were on our side! The truth...other Americans don't care about Czechoslovakia, but you do..." and his face was flushed pink, his pale gray eyes filmed over and his chest heaved as I had never seen it heave before.

"Calm down, Teo. It's okay...shhh, it's okay," I squeezed his shoulder and he threw his arms around me, dropping the bag, and I watched two of the tender little plums roll into the street. Who was this man, holding me so tightly, crying, begging? I found it hard to breathe, let my body go limp.

He released me and I narrowed my eyes on his. "So, alors, what are you saying? You're telling me that you got lucky. Lucky because you actually wanted to be with me. But even if you had detested me, you would have been willing to seduce me and convince me to take the money to Prague for you. You would have done that?"

"You have to understand what it is like to live in a country that is not free..."

"So you've told me, many times," I said with as much scorn as I could muster. I turned on my heel and ran across the broad Boulevard against the red light, dodging cars that honked angrily. I hurried up the Rue de Tournon, not looking back. Skirted the Palais and entered the Luxembourg Gardens, afraid to stop running. He would be behind me. Following me. He could easily have caught me...must be keeping his distance, spying on me.

But when I paused by the big pond, completely out of breath, I was disappointed to see him nowhere among the sun-splashed walkways.

I found a seat on a splintered bench. My hand went to my face where I was surprised by my own tears and heat. Then I thought of Remi, not Bérnard, but Remi. An honest mentor, a friend I respected. I would find Remi and ask him what to do about Teo.

I stood and walked briskly through the iron spike fence on the Boul' Mich' side of the gardens. This time, I checked left and right before I crossed. But to the right was Gay Lussac, and I remembered the run behind Remi the night of my first street battle, and suddenly pictured his blond, bobbing head, his hand signals. Remi on top the barricade. Remi's anger and his angelic countenance. I backed off from the street and plopped down on a cold cement wall, leaning back onto the row of iron spikes. I reached into my pocket for a tissue and blew my nose. Two more and my face was finally dry. And I knew exactly what Remi would say.

That we are all in this together, the youth all over the world. It is an international youth revolution: Remi and the action committee, Dany Cohn-Bendit, Jerry Rubin, Mario Savio, Barbara Borovsky, Jeanette Magill and Teodor Pelnar. We are all caught between the personal integrity that we respect in others and seek for ourselves...and the deceit, treachery, heartlessness, and anarchy that might just, if we are brave, achieve our long-term goals.

For Teo, to sacrifice oneself meant sacrificing his "self." Temporarily doing something he could never have imagined himself doing, in the name of his cause. Remi would ask me, "What is a seduction or a betrayal, compared to some of the things you have done, Jeanette? Tearing up Paris to save your brother in Vietnam, hurling stones at soldiers to soothe your anger, living with a man from behind the Iron Curtain while your American boyfriend took the ultimate stand, packing his bags for a lonely life in Canada!" Then I realized that perhaps most egregious of all was that I had dismissed the feelings of my parents, letting them wonder and wait until what...? The revolution is over? A new France has been achieved? I knew I simply did not have the courage to tell Mother and Daddy the truth. I no longer recognized myself any more than I did this fellow I slept with, this bête doué.

With the same agility he had used to sneak out in pursuit of the Prestup, Teo slid onto the cement wall and was by my side. He waited for me to acknowledge his arrival. I peeked sideways at his shoulder, then quite unable to speak, took a deep breath and knocked him roughly with my elbow.

"Have you been thinking, cherie?" he asked. His voice was calm, but not confident. A rush of sympathy streamed through me.

"Yes. I've been wondering what Remi would say."

"Ah yes, and what would Remi say?"

"That we have all sacrificed some of the true aspects of our characters in the name of the revolution. For me it is in the name of peace and for you it is in the name of liberty. So, I've been wondering if authenticity is actually important between us. Maybe it isn't."

"Please, Jeanette," he interrupted. "Do we not understand each other in all the most important ways?" Teo's gaze, sad and earnest, met mine and lingered, and before I knew it our arms were around each other and we were kissing. The expression, "kissing like there was no tomorrow" flitted across my mind.

Then we were holding on, our hearts thudding like the last trace of our kiss. I wanted to tell him that I was not ready to lose him yet, even if I had never had all of him. I struggled for the French words to tell him that the world we knew had flattened out, stood upended and was about to flip over. When we transitioned to the other side, I felt sure it would be better, had to be better. But it would be way too late for me to be with Teo in the new world order. Perhaps some day, with an Iron Curtain drawn or more likely blown to bits, we would be alive to find each other. Because I was sure that the portions of our "selves" lurking beneath the conditions of 1968 were in love.

All of this kept issuing in spurts from my brain, but all I could say was, "I believe that we love each other."

"Yes, cherie," he responded, "and that is the part we must obey." In another moment, Teo rose and tugged at my hand. We strolled off through the Luxembourg and paused at the rippling pond. Hugging myself in the stinky, chilled air, I told Teo again how the Communist Party official had been pushed from his platform on the pond's circular edge into the shallow water. As we derided what had become a common enemy, I realized that if ferrying money across the border was the one positive thing I could do for Teo's cause, I should do it. How could I risk for American boys like Matt and Aaron, for the French, and not for the Czechoslovaks? But enough had been said today. We continued on our rounds, each of us with a hand on the cloth bag full of ripe fruit swinging between us.

Our lives together continued as if my awakening to betrayal had never happened—walks across Paris, practical errands, café conversations, meetings with comrades, home studies and lovemaking. Teo went out in the night again, on a schedule, now kissing me sweetly on the cheek before rising from the floor. That kiss was our only communication about the matter, and that was fine with me. With each kiss, I knew the time for committing myself out loud to transporting the Prestup's money was growing closer. Aaron Becker's words came back to me and made sense: about taking care of myself so that I could use my adult talents to do important things my whole life. But I had decided, hadn't I? Desperately, I sought the courage to agree to this meaningful task. I tried to picture myself on a train, at a border, on a corner waiting for a dropoff, and always my visions were of Nazis, on a screen in black and white.

One morning in the last week of May, sitting with my pen and paper on a moldy churchyard bench, I permitted myself to forget that my letters to Aaron Becker had become nothing but a self-reflective diary. I couldn't see his thin-lipped crooked smile anymore, but I could see his dark, velvety eyes and I let them penetrate my mind as I crafted my words. I rationalized that any secret emotion that felt good and hurt no one couldn't be all bad. I had told Teo that I just needed some time on my own, and with his understanding heart, he had shooed me out, "Go, of course. Have a nice chat with yourself."

Gazing at the pigeons picking at seed in the raggedy grass, I recalled, as I so often had, Aaron's letter about taking care of myself. I longed for Aaron's good sense in deciding what to do about Teo's errand. I rested my pen in my letterbox, for just a moment wishing myself back to our carefree dating days. Surely that innocence must be far more distant than the few months that had come between us. How I missed talking to Aaron, and holding him, yes, kissing him too, but most of all, his hungry expression in those romantic moments. None of that had disappeared. I knew that no matter how many incredible Teos there would be in my life, no one would ever take Aaron's place in my heart. This seemed disloyal to me, and terribly confusing and even a little immoral, but there it was. I would have to accept this defect in my character and to live with my secret. So I would write my pretend letter. I picked up my pen, struggling to collect my thoughts.

"Dear Aaron,

It is impossible to explain the feeling of disillusion-ment that has flooded my days like a deluge sweeping down the streets, obliterating the Paris of our dreams. Yes, there are still people who care about the important issues. But the Revolution that focused on these things has been usurped by the rats caught in the floodtide. And believe it or not, I'll admit now that the rats are the Commies, just as Teo has always told me. Commies, Fascists, they are all the same. They are all old fat white guys, willing to send their youth to the slaughter, just like in America. And although the students here are better at listening and sharing, they are too disorganized. As Bérnard has been warning us: the various French factions are full of ideas but cannot unite to propose any viable alternative to the Gaullist regime. I'm sorry to report that I have not discovered in Paris any magical and quick, nonviolent means of creating social change.

So, you see, when Teo asked me to help the Czechs fight their communists, I thought: This is something we can do, a meaningful action. It gives him, and by extension me, a feeling of power. Not a raving egocentric kind of power. More like an absence of powerlessness. He's asked me to carry some money across the border, something that should be relatively simple for a "rich" American. I want to do it, but I'm frightened. Can you separate whatever you might feel about Teo and me, and give me your opinion? Oh, Aaron! I need your opinion and you are so far away. Studying for finals. I picture you in the glow of your fireplace, prone on your comfy sheepskin rug, your book open and a look of concentration on your face. Concentrate on me, once in a while, will you...?"

I set down my pen and gazed down a neat row of poplars, then up to their pointy crowns. Aaron had expected his opinions to be my own, and paradoxically, I had both required and resented his protection. If he were actually here now, I realized, I would bristle at his advice. How different Teo was from Aaron! Teo had let me be. Even though Teo hated the communists, and I was a socialist and consorting with socialists of every stripe more vituperative than I, he spoke his opinions as if that's all they were: his opinions, take them or leave them, "cherie." With Teo, it was easy to grow up, to make my own decisions and to take responsibility for my actions. I was grateful to him for all he had enabled me to do.

But with Teo, I realized, there were no burdensome expectations because there was no future. He let me be because he made no claim on me. I did believe he loved me, unless he was the best actor in the universe. But it didn't matter if I was exactly the person he wanted me to be. Aaron had hoped for so much more.

I packed my letter-diary away for another day, tucked my pen and eraser back into the box. I had missed Aaron and cried for him, yet I had discovered that I could survive without him. This gave me confidence that someday I would feel the same way about Teodor Pelnar. I would be sad, I would rant and cry, I would mourn, yet I knew I would go on. Dry-eyed, I hoisted my pack, feeling strong and self-reliant, striding with my head held high, all by myself through the streets of seedy Pigalle.

FORTY-SEVEN

IN THE DEAD OF NIGHT, Dany Cohn-Bendit, his flaming hair dyed brown, reappeared at the Sorbonne and held a press conference. But it was too late for his leadership to have any impact. Prime Minister Pompidou had gathered union and employer delegates at the Hôtel du Châtelet outside Paris. After 25 hours of bargaining, the unions got some compensation for the days they missed in the strike and a slight wage increase that would soon be eaten up by inflation. Almost nothing they had asked for was in the document they signed. They did not get shorter hours, a full employment policy, a return to more advantageous (and more "socialist") health and social security policies, nor even freedom to pursue their union activities. The workers were openly furious with the French communist Georges Séguy and vowed to continue the strikes, but no one had any intention of seizing the government—not the communists, not the students, not the other factions.

The grand finale to this exhibition was de Gaulle's cheap little trick, designed to scare the hell out of the French people. First, he cancelled a meeting of ministers and disappeared for six hours. No one knew where he was, not even his closest allies. Rumors hobbled across the city like wounded pigeons, and the police were massed at the Palais Élysées as a precaution against attack from within or without. Then le Générale mysteriously reappeared to warn the people: it is his regime or "totalitarian communism." Those were the choices, the only two choices. Soon, we knew, he would call for a general election.

Alerted by the radio, I walked downhill to the Champs Élysées, staying at the edge of the gathering crowd, searching for a friendly face. I stood under a sky as slate gray as the rooftops, listening to a speaker called Mendès-France, the man with the pleasant, patriotic name whom everyone seemed to like. Still professing to oppose de Gaulle, Mendès-France called for a "popular government" with new policies, without saying who would govern or how this would be achieved. His speech concluded uneventfully. He stepped down. The socialist

Mitterand, who I knew had been defeated by de Gaulle in the 1965 election, climbed the portable platform.

I searched the crowd for Remi, hoping for news from the second student general assembly. Someone had to be more effective than these empty grandstanders. I heard cascades of initials escape easily from the lips of Mitterand: CFDT, FGDS, CGT, PSU. Then Annette's large blond head appeared on the other side of a group of workers in their blue shirts. I made my way over to her. "Where are the others?" I asked.

"They're here. Somewhere. I went to visit my grandmère this morning so I came late. She is sick in the hospital."

"I'm very sorry. Is it bad?'

"Oui. Very bad. I am afraid she may not live to see the new France," she finished sarcastically. She frowned at the podium and asked if I wanted to find some lunch together. Relieved, I followed her out of the crowd. Cafés were the one institution that hadn't closed down completely. If they did, I mused, that would be the end of France.

There had been no student general assembly yet, but that night at 9:00 p.m., Mitterand and Mendès-France went to the French National Assembly to make a statement to the press about uniting the "whole left," including the students. Had the students ever been consulted? I wondered who had been designated to represent the students.

Late that day, Remi called our group together through his messenger service for a large, sullen march up the Champs Élysées to the Arc de Triomphe. No one in our group was taken in by the statement about uniting the left. The marchers were a mix of people, as many supporting de Gaulle now as against him. Gabi and Frederic appeared just long enough to explain that they would not be marching with us in the future. Now that the French Communist Party had usurped the students' cause, they could not justify their support, not even to themselves. It was a sad farewell, lots of hugs all around. Without their saying so, I knew they'd never betray me. Never tell Margot and Madame that I was still in Paris.

Ironically, the day after our march, the last day in May, was the last day of the May Revolution. Georges Séguy announced that the French Communist Party would not impede the election and would negotiate to end the strike. The voting age in France was 21, so that just as in the United States, people my age, people serving in the army and paying taxes and marching for better universities, would not be allowed to participate. De Gaulle's people were in charge of the election. The strike was the primary weapon for change, so in effect, Séguy's French Communist Party ended the battle that day. Now everything was on de Gaulle's terms.

Remi was not ready to give up. Before we left the streets, he gave everyone the address and directions to a new meeting place for that night.

Before twilight Saturday evening, I left Teo in Pigalle and began the long trek across town. The streets were still quiet and reeking of trash, but De Gaulle's clever plan to persuade the gasoline truck drivers back into Paris just in time to put more cars into operation for la Pentacôte—the three-day weekend— buoyed the bourgeois mood. There were lines of cars at corner stations, and people still on foot seemed to bounce along with confidence again. I passed through the St. Germain district, past Le Riverside, where Teo and I first bear-hugged on a dark dance floor. Remi's directions brought me to a spacious, fourth floor apartment not far from my old school.

It was June 1, the first day after the revolution, so I knocked on the door expecting to find pinched faces and ominous pronouncements within. Instead, as I entered the apartment I was surprised to be greeted by an energetic bunch, down on their hands and knees consulting over large tracts of poster board. Rugs were rolled back and boards spread out on top of a protective layer of last week's Le Monde. The room was crowded with the faces of strangers, more of them, in fact, than of us. Remi rocked back on his knees. "Can you help?" he asked. "These are to show Sunday at the general assembly. Perhaps we can turn things around."

"You're dreaming, Remi," sneered Claude, working at the far corner of the poster.

"Shut up, you fucking cow," André retorted.

"This whole thing began with dreams, so why not?" said Bérnard.

"Whose place is this?" I asked Remi. He gestured toward a boy with short black hair, thick-framed glasses and a pimple festering in his scraggly mustache. I had never seen him before.

"It's Paul, who leads this other action committee. Let's just say he's a friend of a friend. It's the only way to go on. My old man has had it with us."

"I'm not surprised. But maybe all together, we can regain momentum."

"That's right," Remi said. "Show the CGT that they can't decide unilaterally to end what we started. We will try to shame them into standing with us against the government."

Remi's voice was as earnest as a priest's and his optimism was infectious. I grinned and rubbed my hands together. "I'm ready to see that. So where do I start?"

"Over there, next to Annette."

Annette set me up with equipment and instructions, and we chatted for a moment about her grandmère who apparently was making a miraculous recovery. Then I got to work, painting slogans, large colorful renditions of grimacing flics and bayonets and more slogans. I was already quite absorbed in my creative task, French words buzzing all around me and jagged rock music blaring from the radio behind the buzz, when cursing and angry voices snagged my attention. Remi was facing Paul, his hands flying in the air above them both, "But we did just as much work on them as your group did."

"We're an action committee, not a group!" Paul's voice was hoarse—the revolutionary's laryngitis.

"Alors, okay. I'm sorry. So are we."

"But you are not anything at all. You're part of our committee now. And you're new—so block that signature out..."

"We're not merging with your group! Don't you listen? We've got our own committee..." shouted Remi.

"You must be part of ours now..." Paul said, pushing his glasses up on his nose with a scowl.

"Jamais de la vie"—not on your life—"so, if you want, you sign yours and we'll sign ours."

Annette interrupted. "Why don't we put all of our signatures on all the posters? Won't that look stronger?"

"But my people did all the work," Paul interrupted Annette, "and we paid for the materials and this is our meeting place!"

"Hey, we paid our share and painted our share!" Remi snapped back. "And what's this about your people? Do you own them, like slaves?"

"You asshole! You...fucking idiot! I'm talking about my committee...and it's supposed to be yours now, too. That was my understanding."

"We should put on the name of a new parent group," Bérnard spoke up. "Show we've joined forces with something larger than ourselves."

"Yes," I chimed in, "solidarity is more important than anything..." There was more buzz all around. I felt as if I were sinking, watching these self-absorbed children split into factions, just like in Berkeley, wrecking our potential to continue.

"But our group stands for a broader concept than yours!" Paul was shouting, his fists tight and his glasses starting to fog up. "Did you see how the Central Strike Committee ran everything in Nantes? They had the power. They decided on the roadblocks, gas rationing, food distribution, defense. They had the students, factory workers, farmers, truckers, even housewives, all together, all politically conscious. That is revolution! That is our goal! For Nantes to happen all over France! We accept that total social chaos must precede real change. Total! Absolute! No compromise!"

"Is that your last word, then?"

Paul snickered. "Hell, you guys are barely even revolutionaries. You were even happy that the CRS fired rubber bullets at us, that there was so little bloodshed!"

"Rubber bullets?" I burst out. "What does he mean, Remi?"

Remi turned toward where I was up on my knees, paintbrush in hand. "The flics and the CRS used rubber bullets against us. Paul regards that as a form of government repression."

"And humiliation! The government doesn't even permit us to risk our lives for our cause!" Paul screeched.

Remi glared at Paul unblinkingly. His voice held the controlled intensity of the great orator. "Would the students have been victorious today if more of us had been blown away? If that's what you believe, then there is nothing more to say to you. Some of us will be at the general assembly Sunday. We do have our own opinions, though they are different from yours."

Paul stood with his back curved like a cornered cat. After a moment of heavy breathing, he straightened up and spat his command into Remi's face, "You'll be carrying posters with our signatures or you can just take your rabble and get out of here now!"

"Like I said, Remi, you're dreaming," Claude grumbled. He put down his brush and came to stand behind his friend. Bérnard had joined them and the rest of us followed.

Remi headed for the door. He turned to Paul one last time.

"We were on the barricades, same as you," he said, "but it is you who are tearing them down. You are more vicious and self-serving than the worst flic. But we won't give up. We'll be there Sunday, with or without the fucking posters."

"This is our party here! Go fuck yourself..." As we made our exit, all of Paul's group began chanting their leader's obscenity at us. "Va te faire enculer!"

Out on the street, we quickly said our farewells, agreeing to meet in the Sorbonne courtyard the day after the general assembly for a debriefing from Remi and André, who would be our delegates.

It was dark, and Remi and Bérnard volunteered to walk me home. Annette came with us. They wanted to stop for a drink, but I asked if they could please find their café after they dropped me off. We trudged across the Pont des Arts. No one spoke. Beneath us skiffs and river water slapped the stone embankment. How many times had I crossed that bridge lately, and for what?

"Is it really over, Remi?" Annette asked.

"It's over...temporarily," he replied, trying to sound brave. "But I'll be at the general assembly and at every march and battle left to us. And I believe our efforts will have some lasting effect."

"I just hope for one thing: change at the University," said Bérnard. "If we just get that, I'll be happy."

Remi smiled at his friend. "Perhaps, the University. The conversation has begun. But real change? It's possible, but ...who knows what? And who knows when?"

Suddenly, I stopped walking, swung around and put my hands on my hips. "Who knows when...?" I mocked. They stared at me as if a five-foot-seven-inch crow had just stepped into their path. "How can you stand it?" I shouted down the street. "We had no clue about how to make this work. To compromise.

To carry it forward. Oh!" I stamped my foot and clenched my fists, full into my tantrum. "To have come so far and to lose! I can't comprehend it, not here in Paris with all we've gone through!"

It was Annette who stepped forward and put her arm around my shoulders. I struggled just to catch my breath. "We screwed up," she said. "You are right. But the establishment will not forget us soon."

We had reached a narrow, climbing street, with only the lamplight from the next intersection illuminating our faces. Silently, my friends formed a circle around me. "Annette is right," Remi said, his voice gentle and soothing. "Our success has been to make people aware of our issues, and sympathetic. We didn't speak with one voice. That was a problem. But many things were said that made sense, even to the bourgeoisie. Many people who never listened to us before have listened this time and blame de Gaulle."

I nodded, trying to control my high, quaking voice. "So, it wasn't all wasted?"

Remi shook his head, whispering, "No, no, no... The only way to change things is inside the political arena and students are on the outside. But you see what happens when students try to grab power? Paul's vision is of anarchical groups connected by a central organization. But he doesn't recognize that what he is after is a conquest of state power. A state machine, with a military and police." He kicked at a loose stone in the street. "So very delusional."

Then he looked up and met our eyes again, finally clearing his throat. "We have been heard by those inside. Even in free nations, young people have never felt the freedom to speak out until now. At this moment in history and all over the world, we can express any ideas, any beliefs, and know we will be heard. This is another form of power! Now we have established our right to it, and this is just the beginning."

We huddled there, all of us trying to be comforted by Remi's words.

Finally, we resumed our climb, passing the tiny Romanesque church in my neighborhood. It was almost time to say goodbye. "What of this can I take back home?" I asked.

"People only listened because of the police violence. But I hate the violence..."

"That was a problem for you," Remi sympathized. "But a little of it goes a long way."

"Yes...I appreciate the tactic..." my voice faded.

"Even the best police-baiting theatre is not worth it if your side can't agree on what they want," Bérnard said bitterly.

Remi tapped me lightly on the arm. "But in America, the problem is different. The factions can agree that the war must end."

I took heart from Remi's passion. "Our factions squabble just like they do here," I said. "They mix peace goals and civil rights and the class struggle...but I'm determined to bring home the lesson about solidarity and repeat it a million times if necessary. The war will end only when the concept is focused and clear, not broad and socially destructive like Paul's."

"We would have changed the University if it were not for bums like that egotistical, greasy Paul," Bérnard said.

We reached the small square and paused in front of Teo's apartment. "Please don't think you're leaving me without hope," I spoke up, my small voice echoing on the moldy stone walls. "Merci pour ton amitié." I hugged each one of my friends, and they walked away, through the lamplight and into the shadows.

FORTY-EIGHT

ANOTHER WEEK WENT BY, the first week in June. L'Alliance Française re-opened, so Teo decided to spend mornings in class, while I went with my comrades, marching defiantly and shouting slogans that I knew to be false, making theatre as best I could. We proclaimed the fight was not over. "Ce n'est qu'un début. Continuons le combat!" This is only the beginning. The fight continues! With strikes dragging on into a third week, workers all over France seemed as unwilling as the students to give up their dreams. The third and final general assembly, as expected, failed to streamline the action committees into a meaningful direction, but in any case it was already too late. The moment had passed. By the end of the week, various services and sectors had resumed work.

Thursday, June 6, began like any other day. Teo and I breakfasted on dry, brown bread and jam and canned juice, then went out into the sunshine to kiss goodbye for the morning. But as soon as we were down in the street, we sensed something was wrong. A teenage boy whose face we knew from the neighborhood ran like a blown spider across the square and disappeared into the candy store downstairs from our studio. Teo and I glanced at one another and without a word, followed after him.

Inside, Marcelle, the stocky proprietress whose leftist political views were known by our neighbors had crumpled into a chair behind the counter and was crying her eyes out. The spindly teenager was shouting at her in rapid French. He stopped when he heard us enter and held up his palms, hopelessly. "I can't help her. She is inconsolable."

"Why? What has happened?" Teo asked. I noticed that the big Philco radio on the counter in back of the candy cases was still lit up, but its volume had been lowered. Marcelle greeted us, then between sobs, she uttered words that I hoped I had not understood correctly.

"Kennedy...shot. Robert...Bobby...assassinated like his poor dead brother..."

Teo put his arm around me instinctively. He asked Marcelle to please repeat it very clearly for us, but she could say no more. "I'm sorry..."

Back up in the room, we flung ourselves onto the mattress with the radio between us and sunlight streaming in through the bay window. Another Kennedy gunned down, this time near my home. On the BBC and Radio Luxembourg, they called him Bobby. Bobby's rousing speech that all but guaranteed his presidential primary win in California. Bobby exiting the Ambassador Hotel in Los Angeles through the kitchen at midnight. A young Arab named Sirhan Sirhan. A gun. A gripe. A shot at close range.

All day long we lay there, listening to the same reports with occasional minor additions, as if Bobby's blood were being spilled on our mattress a drop at a time.

Somewhere toward the end of the day, we learned that Robert Kennedy had not been the only one to die that day. Outside Paris, there had been a battle in which students had fought alongside workers against the gendarmes for control of two automobile factories. Three workers had been killed, but the strike had not been broken.

"The French workers' strike will come to nothing and the anti-war effort in America will probably die from body shock," I told Teo bitterly.

"There are other American candidates against the war, n'est-ce pas?"

"Yes, but only Bobby..." and I stopped to take a deep breath, to get control of my shaky voice. "Oh hell, I'm as bad as Marcelle."

"As good as Marcelle..."

"We needed a real hero of a leader. Only Bobby had the power...and now he's gone."

"My mother says there are no heroes, only corpses," Teo mumbled. What he said barely registered. I was focused on the Kennedys and King, wondering if there was anyplace left in the world that was truly free.

By June 10, the strikes were completely over and the electioneering was in full swing. De Gaulle was scaring the population with Commie stories and the opposition fighting back very weakly. We understood that they simply didn't want to rule. The election was set for June 23. All day, in retaliation, mobs of students continued to light fires and destroy property. I stayed away, convinced that their anger and petulance were achieving only De Gaulle's goals, not ours. We listened to reports that down on Boul' Mich', the police charged brutally, arrested 1500, drew down 72 barricades. I knew what it had taken to get those fortifications up, and what it had cost to lose them. Five police stations were attacked, but this was either a desperate attempt by groups like Paul's or the work of thugs taking advantage of the battle's cover to vent their own rage.

That night, a curfew was imposed on the Latin Quarter. The next morning, the government banned all radical leftist organizations. We knew it was only a matter of days, at most, before the police re-seized and evacuated l'Odéon and the University.

After our radio was switched off, Teo announced his intentions to return to Prague before the elections. He set his departure date at June 20—nine days away. "Why now?" I asked, sitting at the table with my hands folded up in a tight knot. "Why would the failure of the May Revolution chase you back to Prague?"

Teo pushed his chair back with a noisy screech. He stood up and gazed down at me. "It has nothing to do with the May Revolution, Jeanette. At home, Dubček's speeches are getting more pro-Soviet, not less." He began to pace around the table, his mind someplace far beyond this room. "All the old conservative Stalinists and Novotný's men have been expelled from the Party or resigned, but Dubček is giving way...it is agonizing to hear it. Why is he backing off?"

I started to speak, but he stopped pacing abruptly, speaking passionately. "I'll tell you: The Russians, East Germans, Poles and Hungarians are assembling their troops just outside and even inside our borders for what they are calling 'maneuvers.' Practices. Practicing for what? Well, Dubček needs supporters, people who will speak up and back his reforms..."

I saw quite clearly where Teo was headed. "What a waste!" I cried.

"What do you mean?"

"You're so bright and have so much to offer. You could go back and...what? Get arrested?! Have you ever considered the possibility of defecting to France?"

Teo's head shot back as if I'd slapped his face. "You must be joking, Jeanette. Would you ever defect permanently to France? Leave your family and friends, and your culture. The food and the music and all the rest that you grew up with? Even if your country was not democratic, I doubt you could decide to leave, to never return. That's what defecting would mean for me."

I sat very still, I could not answer. Could not admit that I had, at one time, planned to stay in France forever. Had never once felt nostalgia for the place I had rejected. For family and friends and the physical trivialities of life in California. I pictured my parents and the room I grew up in, safe and warm, hot pink and American red. My mother working in the kitchen alongside the housekeepers, the promise of a roast beef dinner filling the air as I walked in the door from high school or the library. Daddy in his recliner, grinning at something inane on TV, his gold filling winking at me under the glare of the bullet lamp. The "ohhs" and "ahhs" of approval when I appeared in the foyer, dressed up for my senior prom. A hug from Mother. What were these things worth? Perhaps not enough...but never, ever, ever to return?

Suddenly my mind flashed on Aaron, our dreams and plans. It was Aaron waiting for me when I appeared for my prom. And it occurred to me for the first time that more than all I had learned from Teo or the May Revolution, and even more than Aaron's change of plans, it was my empathy for Aaron's tortuous decision to defect, to disappear from home for the rest of his life, that had made me gradually stop regarding France as my permanent home. My heart was trapped in my throat.

Teo had taken a seat, watching me from across the table. "You have not forgotten your promise to come to Prague with me. To carry the money for the Prestup..." He said it like a statement of fact, not a question. He knew I had not forgotten such a request.

"I'm...still not completely sure. I do want to help you and your people, but I want to ask you something. Have you told your parents you will be coming home?"

"I telephoned them days ago, as soon as the strike lifted. While you were at a meeting with Bérnard and the others."

"You didn't tell me..."

"It was around the time Kennedy was killed. It wasn't important."

"Anything you do is important to me," I said, trying not to sound recriminating. "So, now you're telling me."

"Because now I have set the date before the election."

"And your parents...?"

"Of course, now they want me to stay here! Because de Gaulle can't lose and the strikes are all but over. My mother believes that Dubček is no hero. And on that point we agree."

I recalled Teo saying something about his mother once before. About heroes... "Is that when your mother said heroes are corpses?"

He sighed. "She said Dubček is one of a long line of men—foolish idealists. Her brother died fighting the Nazis, her father died fighting the Communists, her husband was willing to die to fight Capitalists and now her son against the Russians. She said that women don't stand up and stick their chests out and say,

'This is what I believe! Shoot me!' And that was when she said it, that a hero is nothing but a corpse."

"You can understand how she feels, can't you?"

"Do you agree too? You, of all people? Out on the barricades. Alors, I can't see the value of a life in chains. I'm going home and fight if I have to!"

A painful, empty space opened up between us and despite a brave attempt, I began to cry.

"Please, cherie." He took hold of my fingertips, his elbows resting on the table. He kissed them, then sheltered them with both of his warm hands. "Come with me and marry me. We should not be apart. Together we will make my country a free and wonderful place."

"I can't, Teo...I mean, I'll come just to get the money across, I will. But then I have to go home. I have my own country to fight for in my own way."

I shook my head slowly. I sobbed and let the tears fall onto my arms, Teo's hands, the table. Teo's face crumpled, as if he had not heard me agree—at last!—to do his political errand. As if he would not move a muscle until I agreed to marry him.

"I don't want to leave you, Teo, but I can't live in your country and you can't live outside it. There's no use in my coming. Your family, your government...I wouldn't be tolerated. It would only be torture. You know this."

It took only a few seconds, then tears rolled down his cheeks and gathered in the corners of his lips. He let go of my fingers and scraped his chair back, then turned away and swiped at his face. "Well, it would do no good to beg you..." I lifted my hand to his shoulder. How high and broad that shoulder was! He accepted it and bowed his head into his chest. Then this big man drew a handkerchief from his pocket to blow his nose.

Suddenly I felt an overpowering need to talk to my parents. It was wild and irrational, contrary to anything I had felt, even as a child. I had never been one of those kids who begged to call home from summer camp. But this wasn't summer camp. This was my life and they were part of it. Late the next afternoon, when it was morning in Beverly Hills, I would go to the post office and place a call home. There I could count on a good connection, an unrushed, private conversation. I still had no idea what I would say to Marshall and Jean Magill, sitting over their morning coffee and searching the newspapers for far-flung news. I would not worry them with my brief trip to Prague, but whatever else I said about my life in Paris, it had to be the truth. And the truth about my essential safety, I hoped, would reassure them. When I had accomplished that, I wanted to come back to the studio and let the honest words for Matt, formed in my mind over the weeks, float effortlessly down onto my stationery. As for Aaron Becker, it was June 12, classes were out, and I was quite sure that I was no longer in possession of his address.

≈PART NINE≈
La Cité de la Lumière

FORTY-NINE

THIS WAS NOT HOW I'D PLANNED IT, avoiding the draft by heading into a revolution, my escape financed by Janet's old man. A little too much intrigue for my blood. Somehow my vision had been more along the lines of kill two birds with one stone: give my middle finger to the U.S. military as I flew off to a pre-arranged rendezvous with a woman who awaited me with open arms. And just a little perspiration above her upper lip, ready for me at last.

Hell, every time I'd thought about this affair with the Czech guy I got so angry that an involuntary gggrowl circled in the back of my throat. But the anger had burned to white ash and sat cold as a morning-after lump of log when day after day went by without word from Janet. Now I was all forward motion, propelled by fear. If only I'd find her in one piece, I'd be forgiving because I knew that Teo the Czech was—had to be—a fling. Something a young American woman just does when traveling in Europe, part of the itinerary: Monday the Louvre, Tuesday the Eiffel Tower, Wednesday get laid by a dashing, exotic European.

As I stood in the customs line at Orly Airport, I felt as if I were sleepwalking. Everything was in place, flawlessly imagined. The row of tired, impatient travelers, the stout French official in the blue uniform, crisp words resonating like English spoken through the mouthpiece of a trombone. "Are you traveling for business or pleasure?" His rubber stamp was poised above my passport, waiting for my reply.

"Pleasure." The word cracked immaturely as I spoke. I felt heat rise to my face, certain that my story could be read there as clearly as a feature printed in Le Monde. The stamp came down. "Welcome to France, Monsieur."

As I emerged from the building, I wasn't sure if my eyes were watering from the glare of the midmorning sunlight or the lump in my throat had just gotten too heavy. I was in Paris, everyone around me was shouting in French, and this was not at all how I'd planned it.

As the taxi pulled up to 95 Boulevard de Port Royal, I was suddenly aware that it was June 14 at exactly 11:30 a.m.— coming from the same flight, the same hour that Janet had arrived at that spot on a much colder day, three months before. Lucky for me the cabs were back in business.

My memory was racing as I pulled out my gear and paid the driver. Was this a lunatic's wet dream or what? There was the tall Parisian baroque building with the curvilinear digits over the archway. There was the tunnel-like passageway with the diamond-pattern from peak to wainscot. And then out into the sunlight again, the fairytale garden with the identical three-story houses. The forest green shutters. Paths. Birds. A quiet space shut off from the rush of traffic beyond the thick outer walls. Everything was just as Janet had described it in her letters. Everything in its place, except of course, Janet Magill.

Sifting through the possibilities during the long flight over, I'd decided that the Bouleaux homestead was the place to start. I certainly wouldn't go to the police until I'd exhausted every other possibility. It seemed logical to retrace Janet's steps, and for Janet it had begun in this courtyard. Anyway, I wanted to see the place—her room, the main house, to touch what she had touched and speak to the people she had known and befriended or despised. I would try to understand better what she had been through—with luck, that would lead me to her.

I rang the bell at the first house and there was no answer. It crossed my mind that maybe I should have tried the third house, hoping to find the more pliant Hélène and avoid the acerbic attitude of Margot and her avaricious mother, the formidable Madame Marie-Claire Bouleaux. But what if they had all left the country, fleeing the Youth Revolution? I felt the grip of panic in my stomach and was checking out some of the neighbors' doors. Perhaps they had gone to l'Île de Ré? Yes, that must be it!

Suddenly, the door opened behind me and a square-shouldered woman with pale, freckled cheeks and drab, blunt-cut hair stood there, not saying a thing. One hand was still on the door, the other on her hip. She assessed me, head to toe. I stared back. Finally, she drawled, "Ouiaaa?" This had to be Margot.

"How do you do?" I said in a formal English that I hoped she'd understand. I knew my French would be useless this early in the game and in my state of mind. "My name is Aaron Becker. I am a friend of Janet Magill. I am looking for her."

As if in slow motion, Margot's face twisted into a sardonic smirk. "These American girls." She clucked her tongue and shook her head, still staring at me. Her English was strangely accented—something about Alabama, as I recalled—but almost perfect. "We warn them and try to protect them. But she has done what she wants. We are not responsible. We already spoke with her parents."

"Yes, merci..." What to say next? I was jet lagged and the Janet-associated emotions were packed down in my gut like the stuff in my suitcase. I ordered myself to focus. Took a deep breath. "You assumed Janet flew home and then Mr. Magill telephoned you to tell you she hadn't come. Mr. Magill sent me to find her. I was hoping you could help me."

Margot laughed heartily. It was a throaty, ugly sound. "They sent you? Why, monsieur? Are you an American private eye?" She laughed again, could not stop. "Humphrey Bogart?"

Hilarious. I was just another drôle American. The light approach would go a lot further with this woman. As irritating as she was, I stood there, smiling calmly, waiting for her to finish having her fun. She was so damn smart. Maybe she would have an idea about Janet after all. Getting it out of her would be the project.

"That's me! Sam Spade." I drew a dix francs piece out of my pocket and flicked it with my index finger. It went high into the air and I caught it, flicked it again and again while I talked. Margot had stopped laughing and stared bewildered at my dull brass coin. It was a trick I'd taught myself back in the fifth grade, before my dad had left, before Janet had grown up gorgeous, before I'd lost my nerve. "I'm working for the dame's old man, I am," I said in a fitful Bogart. "And I could use a little assistance, lady. See what I mean?"

"Well, Mr. Spade or Mr. Beck or whatever your name is today..." She sighed, but kept a tenuous smile on her lips. Did I detect a little flirtatiousness, a twinkle in her eye? "I would love to help you for some of that monnaie you are putting up in the air so cleverly, but I'm afraid I have no clues. As I explained to Mr. Magill, one day in the middle of the Revolution, she packed her bags and left. I assumed she was frightened. We all were. We had talked about Pompidou's government falling, about our fear of the communists. And communists and Americans don't mix, like l'huile et l'eau, you understand?"

"Like oil and water," I replied. I palmed the coin. "So you assumed she was scared enough to return to America?"

"C'est ça. As I already told to Mr. Magill this week on the telephone. I assume the decision to send you came after that conversation." I nodded, though decisions had been made before, his then mine. She stood there in the doorway. I felt the dix francs in my hand and wondered if, for a price, she would let me spend the night.

"May I see Janet's room? Maybe I can figure something out."

"Searching for clues, Monsieur?" Again that nasty smile. Sour, Janet had called it. I called it rancid.

"I don't know your name."

"Margot Chabert."

"Madame Chabert..."

"Margot..." she corrected me. I considered a gentlemanly bow but stopped myself just in time. Bogie would never bow. I gave her a little salute.

"Margot, then, I'm bushed...tired out. As you can see, I've just arrived in Paris." I pointed down at my suitcase. "May I stay in Janet's room tonight? I will pay you, of course."

Margot sighed impatiently and rolled her eyes upward, but kept smiling. "The room has been cleaned. You will find nothing there, Monsieur Beck."

"Becker. Call me Aaron. Please, Margot. I have no place else to go now anyway. Maybe an idea will come to me."

"Do you want a meal, as well?"

"Why not? Are you a good cook?" I knew, of course, that she was terrific. Maybe I'd learn more around the dining room table.

"The best cook in Paris!" She cackled. Then abruptly, she switched to a businesslike tone. "We are not a hotel, but...since you come from Janet's parents, I will allow it."

Over to the third house and up the stairs we went, with the recitation of house rules of which Janet had written. She opened Janet's door with a flourish and stepped back to let me in. I could feel the landlady observing me from behind. I walked to the middle of the room and lowered my suitcase. The furniture, objects, architectural features, and décor were as familiar as if I were an old man revisiting the scene where I'd first had sex decades before. I felt like an intruder. I turned to confront Margot.

"How much?"

"Forty francs," she said, crossing her arms in front of her chest.

"Ridiculous." I shot back. "I am familiar with prices here in good times, but they should be reduced. Tourists have cleared out of Paris."

"Forty francs, monsieur, and the dinner I am cooking right now included, of course."

"Janet left you with over two thousand francs..."

"...that," she shouted, "is not your business! Is that what you're after? Coming in here like this...with phony excuses!"

"No! No!" My voice rose over hers. "Not at all! No!"

"Because I explained to Mr. Magill..."

"I just want to find Janet. I'm sorry! I should not have brought that up. I need a place to stay and your price is exorbitant!"

"My price is what?"

"Unfair. And my hunt for Janet might take me a long time..."

"Will you stay here? A long time? I don't want you here for a long time, monsieur."

Now it was my turn to laugh. Gently, though. I could see she had become a bit frightened of me.

"Why not? Don't you like me?"

"You are okay, Sam Spade." She shrugged her shoulders and pursed her lips.

"Janet was paying about 30 francs a night. Forty is too much." I folded my own arms and glared at her.

"But she was a regular boarder."

"Who has disappeared. And I am here on behalf of her parents, and not asking for anything but a room at a fair price and a taste of your delicious supper." I stood waiting, scrutinizing my adversary. She sighed a long, dramatic sigh.

"Oui, alors. Thirty francs a night. Minimum and maximum three nights, paid in advance."

"Deal," I said, already regretting the payment of anything in advance to Margot Chabert.

Once alone, I opened my suitcase and checked to see if everything was still there. My beat-up bag had no lock. Not that I possessed much of value, but what there was I would need. I felt a great distrust of just about everyone in the world and edgy about my finances. Marshall Magill had offered to give me whatever I would need to find his daughter. Once I'd accomplished that, however, I would be on my own.

I walked to the window and raised the shade. Out in the courtyard, the morning was peaceful and sunny, and despite a kind of intense mental tug-of-war, I turned back around to the interior. There was the table where Janet had written me all those letters, her one-franc tulips, red and pink, suspended over aerograms like colored lights over a party. It had been a private party, an intimate, shared experience between the two of us, but now the party had been crashed and I suspected that the trespasser had taken her off. Janet and her tulips were gone and the room seemed lonely. I walked over to the sink and splashed the ice cold water on my face and daubed it dry with the clean linen towel hanging above the basin. Margot had fetched the towel from a cupboard in the hallway and returned to hang it there, all the while informing me that it was 11:50 a.m. and dinner would be at 1:00 p.m. She would send someone to wake me if I wanted to lie down and rest after my long journey.

I knew I must be exhausted from the flight, but I could not keep still. Beginning with the armoire, I systematically explored every inch of the room for clues. Why was there never, in real life dramas, a little ball of paper or a matchbook left in the wastebasket with the forwarding address? Why were all the decent damn clues left accidentally-on-purpose for the private eyes? Hell, they were professionals. They weren't supposed to need the lucky breaks. I was just a poor sucker on a fool's errand—I deserved a clue. My search ended at the bed, where I scanned the floor, the corners, the bedclothes, even the walls, hoping for anything to give me my next move. Janet had lain here. I flopped on the bed, face down, too tired to cry, too tired to jerk off.

The next thing I knew, there was a timid knock on the door through which I heard a soft voice with a British accent. "Time for dinner. Are you awake, Mr. Becker?" In an instant I was up with the door open. Elizabeth!

"You're still here!" I burst out. She backed away from the door.

"Yes, do you know me?"

"You're Elizabeth Prior, aren't you? I mean, Janet's letters." I was so excited I could barely speak.

"Yes, and I know who you are, too. Janet's friend Aaron Becker. But we must get down to dinner. Perhaps we can talk tonight. I'll be working all afternoon."

"Of course," I said. "Just let me use the facilities and I'll be there."

Elizabeth smiled. "I guess you got a lot of details in those letters that Janet was always scribbling."

"Yes, I did. And I might add, it's nice to see a friendly face."

It was after ten o'clock at night when I heard that knock on the door again, and this time it was more of a muffled scratching. I'd made it through the dinner by focusing on the feast and doing a lot of listening. The group was small and except for the little boy named Laurent, I was the only male. Margot introduced me to Madame, to her son Laurent and her daughter Cecile, and to Gabi, the new family member. I guessed that the missing Frederic was at work or school. She sat me next to Elizabeth. They seemed happy to leave politics behind. It was as if the May Revolution had never happened and a major national election was not a week away.

Fortunately, there were no awkward silences. They had Frederic and Gabi's wedding to discuss. This was planned for the end of August, when everyone in France would be on their way home from vacances and their friends and relatives would be able to attend. The venue would be on l'Île de Ré, on a piece of empty land they owned called Pré Nouveau. I flashed on the Easter egg hunt. Mme. Bouleaux sitting in the tall grass surrounded by excited grandchildren. The chicken's head in the refrigerator. Janet's anger growing with every letter as she came to understand that these people were even more conservative, bigoted and bourgeois than her Beverly Hills parents.

They were speaking French, alternating between an excited rapid blur and the slow clarity that Janet had so appreciated. I was surprised at how well my French was holding up, at least once Elizabeth whispered hints about the general direction of the discussion. Elizabeth kept quiet except for her prompts to me, cleared the table and didn't even say goodbye.

I went up to my room to bide my time and had fallen into a deep sleep when Elizabeth turned up at my door. I could see that she wanted to get inside fast. We sat at the table, whispering in the dark.

"You've slept past supper."

"No wakeup calls for supper? Well, I won't starve after that mid-day meal."

"No..."

"So, how are you, Elizabeth?"

"I'm doing all right. But I'm bloody well not here to chat."

"That's fine by me..." I leaned forward across the table, hoping for some evidence of collusion.

Elizabeth leaned in closer until we were just inches apart. "Margot told me that she did not, under any circumstances, want me to talk to you. She said I was to let you go about your business and that you would be gone in a few days."

Suddenly I was wide awake and on edge. Her mood of intrigue, sitting there in the dark, dredged up Margot's sardonic, "Sam Spade."

"Don't worry. I won't attempt to talk to you when they're around. But I could use some help. I'm trying to find Janet."

"Yes. Margot didn't say, but I knew that must be why you've come."

"Why doesn't Margot want to help?"

"Because Margot just hates Janet. At first, she respected her and treated her like a queen, but Janet continued to sneak around and defy her. And now Margot and Madame are also afraid they'll be blamed for her activities."

"You sound like a friend to Margot yourself."

Elizabeth shrugged her shoulders. "I have to get along here...but I do feel that Janet's a dear girl."

"And now she's missing. Her father asked me to help find her. He sent me to..."

"Oh...oh là! You mean she hasn't told her parents where she is?" Elizabeth's eyes were visible even in the dull light from the courtyard lamp, round as the "oh's" she'd gasped in French.

"No. Margot told the Magills she was supposed to go to Brussels, then head home. Since she never phoned or showed up, we all assumed she'd either gone off with her boyfriend or with the revolutionaries. She hasn't contacted us. So my question is a simple one. Do you know where she is? Because if you do, I promise I won't take any steps until we discuss it. You'll be my partner. I only want to make sure she's safe."

Elizabeth sat back in the chair, and rubbed her forehead as if she were wiping away sweat, though the room was cold. "Please understand, I don't want to betray her friendship. But like you, I'm concerned for her safety." She hesitated and I waited patiently. Then she sat up straight and seemed determined. "I'll tell you what I know," she said. "Please understand, well, it's not much. But there are some possibilities..."

"Possibilities?"

"Like Prague..."

"Oh shit!" I barked.

"Shhh... Excuse me?"

I ignored her shocked tone, but lowered my voice. "Any others?"

"Oh...well...or with Teodor Pelnar here in Paris. Do you know about him?"

"I do. She wrote to me," I said.

"Janet hasn't been to school. So she could be with her little band of revolutionaries or camping out in the Sorbonne or in prison..."

I slumped back in my chair and gave a long, low whistle.

"Okay, Elizabeth. Let's not deal with the possibilities just yet. There are too many of them. Just tell me everything, the way you saw it, from the beginning of May."

Elizabeth began by telling me about the May Revolution and recounted many things I'd read in the press and in letters I'd received before the postal workers went on strike. She asked me if I had known that Teodor Pelnar was from Czechoslovakia, and that he was as determined to free his country from the Russian Communists as most American and French students seemed to be to free their countries from the Capitalists. Then, she described an encounter Janet had suffered on the barricades, and that her own boyfriend, Laurent, had been forced to return home to Alsace because of that incident. There, she stopped to reflect. "That was the beginning of the end for Janet. She was very disturbed about that night."

"Was she hurt?"

"Not really. Just bumped and bruised. But she was hurting on the inside. She talked about the connection between the May Revolution and the Vietnam War."

"She wrote me about that."

"That was why she joined them, I suppose. Mme. Bouleaux rants that it's all just an excuse for a communistic government to take charge. And I just want it all to bloody well go away and for my boyfriend Laurent to return ...ohhh..." Her voice crescendoed up and she shook her hands out in the air as if they were soaked in gasoline.

"So what happened after the barricades?" I interrupted, struggling to sound patient. "What did she do then?"

"Then things just went downhill in the city. Everything was en grève, you understand?

"Yes, the strikes."

"The next thing we knew, Mme. Bouleaux woke us up at six o'clock in the morning, panicky about the communists. I was ready to flee Paris and very sad about it, but then Janet said I didn't have to. Just like that! That if I loved it here, I could just bloody well stay and wait it out. And so I did and now I'm so happy because I'm back in school and everything will be back to normal soon, I'm sure, after the elections. And I owe it all to Janet!"

"Elizabeth, did Janet say anything to you about leaving the country?"

"Not in so many words. I expect the problem was that Teo might be forced to go home and she might consider going with him. I haven't seen him at school either, but that doesn't mean he's not there. We're not in the same degré, and I don't go to the café with the others..." She stopped speaking as if she remembered something, and emitted a wonderful "oh làaaa!" Her even teeth sparkled in the half-light. "Yes, that's it! He's here..."

"How do you know?" I leaned forward, forcing myself to keep whispering.

"Because Teo's spy is here! It was several days ago, but I saw him skulking about the school. Oh, it's hard to explain...we just went back this week. I rush home after school to help Margot with dinner, but I'm sure one day I glimpsed that ugly man who follows Teo around!"

"But where is Janet?" I cried. "Why isn't she in school?"

"Shhh...do you hear...?" There were noises downstairs, someone rushing up. Elizabeth stood and backed away from me. The door hit her from behind.

"Elizabeth," Margot rasped. "To your room, tout de suite!" Elizabeth scurried around her mistress without a backward glance.

I stood up, the better to confront this contrary woman. "She was helping me..."

A tight-lipped sneer crept across her features, eradicating freckles and goodwill. "You are on your own, Sam Spade. You are not to bother this young girl again."

"Janet might be at the school, Margot. Can you help me with directions?"

"Why do you not understand English, Monsieur? You must figure out the fate of your stupid little fanatic all by yourself!" She slammed the door. Someone yelled in French from downstairs. A child cried out. Margot cussed her way down the stairs.

Elizabeth did not return, but I was encouraged that I might have an answer. I sat back in my chair and stroked my forehead. Then my temples, then my neck. I was developing a whopper of a headache. I pushed back my chair, dropped my elbows onto my knees and bowed my throbbing head as if I were praying. But I was not praying. I was making plans.

FIFTY

WAS THIS REALLY ME, Becker the lab rat, and not some TV actor hiding in a doorway, spying on a big hulk of a man and his greasy sidekick? I watched them trudge up a TV cobbled hill. The streets snaked around, so off I went, moving in short sprints to keep tabs on them. It was high noon and shadows from the buildings lay like jagged stumps on the narrow sidewalks. I was carrying my suit jacket over my arm, had loosened my tie. Whatever I needed to deal with that day, I figured it would be wiser to do it in the suit of clothes I brought along for job interviews, the only gear I possessed that would separate my identity from the student rebels. I consider myself a liberal guy, but I am not a revolutionary. I wanted no pretense. Janet would never admire me for pretending to be what I was not.

My first sleuthing job of the morning had been to tail Elizabeth to school, but about a block from the Bouleaux's, she stopped and I caught up with her. "You're a peach, Elizabeth."

"Never mind." She peeked around and over my shoulder. Her neck bent as if to make herself small. She whispered, "I've thought this through. You'll come down into the Métro with me. I'll show you how to get around or you'll never be able to follow Teo."

"Great idea. Then to school? You'll point him out to me?"

"I won't have to do much pointing if we see him at all. You can't miss him. Just look for the biggest young man at the school and that will be him."

I winced. "Shit. So I've heard."

"Pardonez-moi?" Elizabeth said out loud, reacting to my cuss. I took a breath and backed off. There was the Elizabeth that Janet had described. Somewhere between cool wit and haughty disdain. I guessed that an apology was in order.

"I'm sorry for swearing. Janet mentioned his size. I'd hoped she was just trying to scare me off."

Elizabeth's brows warped sympathetically. "Well, he is extremely large, but he's not tough."

Elizabeth helped me negotiate the subway, explaining that with the strikes over, Teo would use public transportation to cover the considerable distance between the Boulevard Raspail and the Pigalle, the "bad neighborhood" where she knew he lived.

Once she went off to class, I had three hours to scout out the area, the Métro, the school, the types of building entrances where I might hide myself—and to get something to eat in the deserted school café. I took my place on the court, sipping and munching as nonchalantly as I could. What with the noise and jostling of the throng descending from the school building, I didn't spot Teo the Czech until he was already standing at the counter inside the café, paying for two big pastries. He headed out immediately, his pastries in a cloth bag swinging from his hand and his "spy" walking by his side. I followed them underground and we arrived, as anticipated, at Place Pigalle.

Teodor stood out like a brawny, real life TV superhero, off the set and out of costume. But the thoroughfares were teeming with people of all ages, nationalities, shapes, sizes, and colors. Horns wailed and fierce activity screamed at me from every direction. So, even with the sun high and bright, it took all my eagle-eye skills not to lose them. I counted on the crowd and storefronts and all the mundane and tawdry commerce to give me good cover.

Soon they were out of the Place Pigalle and heading uphill through narrower, quieter streets. There were shops with signs in English like Beat City and Sweet Spot, and I wondered how Janet had found herself in this hookers' paradise. My attention re-focused on my quest. The two were passing the clunky stone apse of a church, its arched windows black as night inside. There I risked coming out into the open. They turned the corner into a tiny, backstreet square, where I watched them disappear into a brown, scratched-up door next to a candy shop. What to do?

I crossed the street and stared at Teodor Pelnar's door. It had been sanded down roughly and was waiting for a paint job. I entered the candy shop to its left, stalling for time.

The doorbell was still tinkling as I asked the woman behind the counter for some caramels. It's a candy word I was sure of. There was no one else around, no sound once the door was closed except for the radio announcer's voice from the big Philco on a shelf behind the woman. She was a bit older than my mother. She had short gray hair cut bluntly all around and wore a pink cotton dress, covered down the front by a frilly apron. As she opened the glass case, her glance flitted up and down absentmindedly between me and my caramels. She was listening to the radio announcer, who clearly had something important to say.

Deftly scooping some cello-covered caramels into a little brown bag, she asked me if that was enough. I nodded and she placed the bag on a scale. I peered out the window to make sure I was not missing anyone leaving the sanded door. Wouldn't it have been nice if Janet just happened to walk into the candy shop at that moment? She loved chocolate. I remembered her eating sweets with French names. Petit Fours, Bordeaux. The woman handed me a little slip with the price and I was going for the money when she gasped and turned toward the radio as if it were a TV set.

"Qu'est-ce que c'est?" I asked. What is it?

"Sha, sha!" she said, waving me off from behind her back. My hand plunged into a pocket, fingered francs nervously. I was listening to the radio like the candy lady, but could get no sense out of the few words I discerned. It made me realize how much slowing down the Bouleaux had done for my benefit. Finally, the woman shut the radio off. She stood with her back to me, trying to compose herself, then turned to reveal she had not succeeded. Her face was flushed, chaffed to scarlet with its square gray frame of hair. Her eyes were watering up. "Please, Madame. Tell me what has happened!" I enunciated in French, trying for a sincere tone that matched her mood.

"Vous êtes Americain," she said. A flat, nonjudgmental statement. "En vacances?" Did she have to interrogate me to translate the radio news? I stewed.

"Oui, madame. But what news?"

"The gendarmes are conducting searches," she continued, speaking so that I could understand. "Arresting all the leaders of the student revolution. It is over for good this time. The government has won. The old man survives."

My first reaction was to fear for Janet. My second was to envision the Czech Incredible Hulk in chains, and Janet free to come away with me. But no, she would do no such thing. I saw an image of her thin forearms, thrust toward the police, asking for her own chains.

"That is terrible news," I said, not sure whether it was or not. I wanted to be sympathetic. It seemed to me inevitable and long overdue news, but terrible all the same. I understood this country even less than the one I'd left behind.

The door behind me tinkled. A thin-cheeked teenager stuck his head in and shouted excitedly. The woman replied and he rushed back out across the deserted square, leaving the door ajar. The town crier, I mused.

My gaze was still clinging to the boy when I saw Janet Magill run at full speed out the sanded door. My reaction was instantaneous. I started for the door of the candy shop and the woman behind me shrieked, "One franc twenty!" I threw two francs out behind me and they clinked on the concrete floor. I mumbled "Excusez-moi" and ran out after Janet.

I was aware that Teo the Czech was behind me. It took only a quarter turn and a millisecond to spot that guy. Miroslav—I remembered his name—was following as well. But I fixed my sights on Janet, racing down the hills, around curves, negotiating the cobbled streets more adroitly in a pair of Keds than I did in my loafers.

When we reached the crowded Place Pigalle, I suddenly realized that I'd been lucky that she hadn't turned to see if Teodor was following her. If she did now, she would spot me—and I decided that I did not want her to just yet. My mission might have been Mr. Magill's, but my immediate goal was my own. I wanted to enable Janet to conclude whatever she had begun, simply because it was clearly important to her. That wouldn't have been Mr. Magill's first choice. If Janet saw me, it would halt the natural progress of events. I slipped into a doorway and let Teodor and Miroslav pass me by. The two had followed after Janet unaware of my presence or my mission. I would follow them instead.

We all raced downstairs into the Métro. The three sat at the other end of the car, about two dozen passengers between us. It didn't matter. They were focused on each other, silent and glaring. Two train switches later, and I was relieved to see the trio head up into daylight. We were at the Rue Monge, wherever that was. No time to consult a map. Once again, I sprinted and hid. Teodor's tall, fair-haired head and broad shoulders were easy to follow on the quieter streets. I let them move far up ahead of me.

Then, as suddenly as she had run from the apartment in the Pigalle, Janet stopped in her tracks and let Teodor catch up with her. She was shouting at him in French, but I couldn't hear the words that were coming fast, much faster than mine would have come. I saw her arms and hands flail around in a passionate, disorderly way. She was telling Teodor off, telling him to take his disgusting "friend" and go away. I could only imagine the words.

Moving closer, I slipped into the shadow of a doorway. Some of her verbiage sounded like what she had shouted at me, so long ago in a bedroom in Beverly Hills. That had been the first time I'd ever heard Janet Magill swear, seen her get that angry, lose all control. Now this language had become part of her ordinary vocabulary, even in French.

I peered out from my spot in the doorway across the broad Rue Monge, and could barely contain a mammoth smile. God, if she wasn't gorgeous. Try as she might, Janet would never look like a proletarian. Her charming dark curls set off her pale, delicate features. And she couldn't conceal the streamlined elegance of her body, not even under a large shapeless tee-shirt and jeans and with a stance as aggressive as a Cossack.

I am really in Paris, I thought, trying to believe my own eyes. Janet is right there in front of me. I pinched the doorjambs and tried to keep the natural juices from flowing. I reminded myself that I was not here as a voyeur, but as an unwilling and untrusted participant.

Teodor shouted back and his deeper voice was audible. I caught the word "gendarmes" and "pas fou" and "cherie." He wanted to protect her, then. His heavy arms flapped in the air like those of a giant eagle about to lift off. He didn't approve of her activities. I imagined her retort. "I can take care of myself, thank you!" Teodor stood in his place as she moved on.

I couldn't wait any longer or I would lose her. I began to move along behind her from across the street. I was quite exposed when I passed Teodor, still facing Janet. Then I glanced back and caught Teodor's eye. The alarm and exasperation that he had displayed during his discussion with Janet instantly turned into bewilderment. Some curiosity. No fear. Boldly, I marched on ahead of Teodor and Miroslav.

Janet turned left onto a side street. I followed her, keeping close to the buildings on the right. The apartments on the street were typical of Paris, with faded stone façades and fancy, false balconies. Wedged in between the buildings were a couple of narrow houses with dark shutters. It was a quiet and contained bourgeois neighborhood, like a small town buried and forgotten in the heart of the metropolis.

About a block down, on the left side, a diminutive squad car and a police van were parked halfway up on the sidewalk, engines still running under rolling, hungry lights.

I glanced back. Teodor was still behind me and I assumed, Miroslav somewhere behind him. Like dominos pushed by some invisible god bent on satire, they slipped into doorways and I stepped into my own, just as up ahead, Janet disappeared behind a jamb directly across the street from the police vehicles. Here we were, the Eternal Triangle plus our chaperone, ranged out along an obscure street, hiding from each other as much as from the gendarmes.

A lot of things were happening at once. The police were trying to drive two French boys and a girl from one of the shuttered houses. Their prey were resisting, wriggling, and shouting indecipherable epithets and slogans. Several housewives were coming out onto their doorsteps. Some were cheering for the students, others for the police, like spectators who have placed heavy bets at a wrestling match.

Then, Janet rushed forward. The policemen were having difficulty managing to lock handcuffs onto the wrists of the two French boys, both slight and one as blond as the other was dark. They had dark circles under their eyes and cuts on their faces and arms. Janet and the other girl, who seemed big enough to wrestle the cops to the mat, were beating on the police with their fists and shrieking. Janet stomped on one's foot but her rubber heels were ineffective. The attempt brought a villainous snicker and he threw Janet aside like a rag doll. She sprang back up and latched her arms around the neck of the shorter boy, screaming, "Bérnard." The other girl had her arms around the tall, blond boy and again, there was no handcuffing these guys.

From behind the wheels of their vehicles, the drivers were revving their engines. When they awakened to the difficulties of their cohorts, they emerged, middle-aged and paunchy by comparison to the tight-bodied girls and boys. Their heavy brows and jaws registered weary resignation. Janet kept backing away and then dashing forward to harass. I was sure they were going to throw her into the van with the others. All four of them wielded sticks and began to beat the girls away, striking out blindly, while grabbing at the boys. Screams replaced taunts. Newspaper photos of "nonviolent" students being dragged out of Sproul Hall my freshman year crashed into my consciousness through the sight of the physical struggle in front of me. I peeked out and down the street: Teo the Czech and friend were nowhere to be seen. Maybe Teo was still hiding in a doorway, paralyzed by the fear of deportation. My heart thumped, demanding action.

Now, I have never in my life, regardless of hormonal lunacy, even considered risking my neck to save a damsel in distress. "Oh dammit to hell," I said out loud, and with a vague plan in mind I was about to step into the street when from behind me the door swung open. A tall, thick, fortyish housewife with phony gold beads around her neck jabbed at me with her broom, shrieking incomprehensibly. The woman must have worked nights in the opera chorus. I dodged her weapon, but her voice rang out and bounced off the stone houses and down the canyon of the street, and even in my state of mind I could discern, "Help! Police! Another one! Here's another one over here! Help!"

Not stopping to seek the source of the distraction, Janet made a break for the side of the house and disappeared into an alley. The police at last had overpowered the rebels and were shoving them into the van. Still yammering, my attacker backed off as one of the policemen headed our way.

Suddenly, all I'd risked to be here flashed in front of me. This moment was why I had come. Focusing on my plan, I realized that Janet might hate this tactic. Probably not thank me. But slugging a gendarme was not going to get us anywhere. "Us," I told myself, and it sounded right. Keeping all my faculties under tight control, I breathed with a slow, steady rhythm. I assumed a self-confident posture and straightened my tie and jacket. And smiled. A calm, natural expression. Friendly, but not too broad.

As the gendarme approached, the neighborhood quieted, listening to the woman's hysterics so absurd in light of my calm and harmless demeanor. The gendarme's head bounced back and forth between us. The student rebels stared speechless from the back of the van. The rules were being broken and no one recognized this intruder in his Sunday suit. Except possibly Janet Magill, peeking out from behind the house. A patch of sunlight lit her slender hand.

The woman from my doorstep quieted, holding her broom aloft and swinging it gently like a flag of surrender. Nothing else moved. A dog barked from a distant place, signifying a barrier between domesticity and insanity.

Ignoring everyone but the policeman, I made a little bow and in very slow, plodding French, even slower than it had to be, I began to speak:

"Your Honor. Allow me to introduce myself. I am Monsieur Becker from the United States. I have my passport in my underwear if you would like to see it. I assure you I can retrieve it without embarrassment to the ladies present."

The cop smiled back, began to laugh and swallowed a sigh.

"No need, Monsieur. I can tell you are American..." he replied in French.

"I just arrived in your country yesterday," I interrupted him. "That too is stamped in my passport."

"Then what...?"

I waved away his question and continued to speak. Relaxed and polite. Like the Boy Scout I have always been, but guarding my own free speech until the time was right. "I am the stepbrother of one of these young women, and I have come to make sure she is safe. And to bring her home to the United States."

"And perhaps you can explain, monsieur, who are they?" the policeman asked, pointing to the van.

"I cannot say who they are," I said, "but that one," I pointed at Janet, "is my sister."

"So these rebels, they are not your brothers?"

"No, monsieur." I chuckled appreciatively at his sarcasm, then took the plunge. "But they are the children of good French citizens," I said, "who live in this charming Parisian neighborhood." I paused to sweep my hand across the canyon as if I were the tour guide and not the tourist. "And whatever they have done, I am sure they can rely on Your Honor to treat them with humanité while you bring them to justice. Après tout, in France, in America, and all over the world, we are watching you on television." He was scowling and I held my breath, waiting to see if I'd overstepped the boundaries that this policeman had the power to set. He turned toward the little band over near the vehicles, then quickly back to me. I had resigned myself to being thrown into the van.

His voice came calm and smooth as a block of ice. "So, will she go peacefully with you?"

Janet had come out in the open, standing like a statue except for the tears rolling down her cheeks. Her dazed and beaten eyes filled my heart and my own eyes began to cloud over. I forced my attention away from her, not wanting any of them to see the constraining heat that was rising in me, most unfraternal in either Centigrade or Fahrenheit.

The gendarme standing with me now signaled for his cohort to bring Janet to us. Number two took her by the arm and she moved forward with him. In Janet's posture, I perceived stability along with new awareness: there was no place to run to and there was no reason to run. It was all over for Bérnard and her other friends. It was all over for the May Revolution. The month was June, school was out, and here was her old friend Aaron Becker, defending French revolutionaries and explaining in rotten French that she was his stepsister and he'd come to Paris for her sake. Janet's tears had been wiped away.

"Hello Janet. It's good to see you again," I said, automatically reverting to English.

"How did you...? I don't understand..." is how she greeted me. She shook her head as if to clear away cobwebs.

"You will soon, I promise." She glanced down the street, squinting. Hoping to see a familiar Czech face. "It seems he's retreated," I continued. "We should do likewise."

She glanced back over at the van. The dark, wiry boy—Bérnard—was staring at our huddle from behind the bars of the paddy wagon. His head jerked down, avoiding Janet's gaze in a gesture of resignation. Behind him, the handsome tow-headed boy kissed his cuffed hands and waved them at Janet with a wink and a grin. The cop had let go of the big bleached blond girl, who was backed up against the house, surveying the whole scene with a defiant expression. Janet kissed her hand and waved it back toward the golden boy in the van, then at the girl. There was no defiance in Janet's demeanor, no hope either. Just resignation, like that of Bérnard, now gripping his prison bars with both hands.

"Let's get out of here," she said. We got the nod from the number one gendarme and with Janet out ahead, we started to walk back down the street, accompanied by some verbal taunts from the neighbors. Janet did not turn back, and so neither did I.

FIFTY-ONE

JANET HAD LEFT ME to wait for her at Café Bonaparte, outdoors and in full view of Saint Germain des Prés. I pulled off my tie and shed my coat onto a hook by the front door of the establishment, wanting Janet to recognize me from our dating days. Maybe I should order a drink, I thought. I could see the full bar inside. Something to dull the image of Teodor and Janet together, hanging like white, freshly scrubbed underwear on a rod in the john of my mind.

My ex-girlfriend had gone up the broad Boulevard to find a telephone. Considerate girl that she was, she didn't want Teodor to worry that she was trapped in some jail cell. She was hungry, she would tell him. And she needed time to talk to her American friend.

There was a little gated park by the cathedral that might have been a better place for us to sit, but evidently, Janet really *was* hungry. I turned the used teacup still on the table in circles by shoving the loop with one finger. I let out a noisy stream of air and glued the flat of my hand to the table to keep it still, berating myself for clinging to a ridiculous sense of hope.

425

Just as I was about to hail the waiter for a scotch, Janet appeared across the square, her pink tee-shirt peeking out above the familiar navy poncho. I noticed that the shirt was frayed and spotted at the neck, and I wondered if being a hippie had converted her to the ranks of the unwashed. I was kneading my napkin into a croissant as she swung a chair around so that we faced each other.

We greeted one another oh-so politely. "Would you like a sandwich, Aaron?" she asked. "I'm starved."

"No, thanks. I'm not hungry," I said.

"No? Too bad. Their paté is terrific here. Better than at that famous place, over there." I squinted across the square at the green awning and read the name out loud: "Aux Deux Magots. I've heard of it. Are you still a tourist?" I asked. She shrugged her shoulders, then summoned a tall, skinny waiter with a polite little wave. Very American. The guy came ambling by as if he just happened to be in the neighborhood. He cleared our table, gave it a swipe with his towel, and whipped out his pad and pencil. Janet ordered her paté and a cola. As the waiter turned to walk away, I grabbed his sleeve. *Une petite gaucherie.* Tough beans.

"*Whiskey,*" I said.

"Seagrams, monsieur?"

"*Quelque chose moins cher.*" Less expensive. Just a mean shot to take the edge off, I wanted to say.

"I don't remember you as a drinking man," Janet said. "Can it have been that long?"

"I'm not usually a drinking man...but, yes, it has been that long."

We remained silent, sizing each other up.

"It's good to see you, Aaron. There's so much I want to tell you."

"Catching up on the letters never sent?"

"Maybe. But sometimes, as I was writing those letters, I realized that if I didn't tell you things they seemed less real. Like airplane or hotel reservations, you know? You make them, but then you have to confirm them or they get lost."

The waiter approached holding his tray aloft. With a deft hand, he placed a shot glass of nondescript brownish liquid and a glass of cold water on a napkin. He centered a cola on another napkin for Janet. Then he served her the plate of moist paté on crisp lettuce leaves and a basket of crunchy bread. Hmm. Seems I was hungry after all. "I'll have some of that, too," I told the waiter. "Just like that. *C'est ça.*"

"This is a high class place," I said, taking my scotch to my lips and swallowing a big gulp. I coughed it down and Janet giggled.

"You make a terrible tough guy."

"And you make a terrible starving student." We smiled at each other.

"Honestly, Aaron, everything here is so cheap. This paté would be a fortune at home."

"But not cheap for them. It's only cheap for us."

She gazed appreciatively at the paté, then shrugged her shoulders. "Might as well enjoy it while we're strangers in paradise." She began to spread and eat. "Why don't you start by telling me how you found me."

"Okay, you eat, I'll start," I agreed. "The truth is that your father came to Berkeley to ask me to find you, and I declined. But when the postal strike ended and I didn't hear from you, I changed my mind. I started at your boardinghouse, then went to the school and followed your boyfriend home. I saw you on the run, and I decided without hesitation that you needed to reach your destination and to do whatever it was you needed to do."

"I appreciate that," she said. "I don't know what I would have done..." her lip trembled for only an instant before she visibly shook off the memory of her friends. "My father would not have approved of that decision," she declared.

"Your father did pay for the ticket and ask me to find you. But he and your mom weren't the only ones worried about you. We were all a little crazed. I don't mean to be critical, but couldn't you have telephoned?"

"I'm sorry," she said. "I did telephone, but it was just night before last over there."

"Then...I was already on my way! Didn't they tell you? Didn't they say I was coming?"

"Never mentioned it," Janet said. "We had an awful lot to talk about. I guess they had their minds on other things."

I sat dumbfounded, feeling screwed by the Magill family, one and all. Then it hit me that if she had phoned in time, and they had told me, it would only have been to withdraw the offer of the ticket.

But I didn't feel like cutting Janet any slack. "Why the hell did it take you until day before yesterday to call?"

Janet's voice was thick with resentment. "At first there was the strike. Then, I hoped they would just continue to blame the strike for my silence. What would I have told them?" She paused and raised her palms up, empty. "That I have been consorting day and night with revolutionaries? That I have moved out of the safe house they arranged for me and am living with my communist boyfriend in a slum?"

"I thought he wasn't a communist," I interrupted.

"He's from behind the Iron Curtain. Same thing to them, don't you think? They would have had heart attacks."

Amazed that I hadn't had my own seizure from the direction of the conversation, I acknowledged the truth behind her fears. The waiter delivered my order. "So, what happened when you talked to them?" I asked quietly between bites.

"I told them everything. The truth. First, I told them how much I love them and apologized for the pain I've caused them. Actually, I continued to apologize over and over again throughout the conversation. But I told them I was healthy and satisfied with the decisions I've made here in Paris. Then, I explained what I've been doing, giving them time to react and calm down every few seconds."

"How did they take it?" I asked.

"I had to keep reassuring them that although we have differences, I am positive that they respect my right to explore and learn for myself. That they love me as much as I do them, and that's why they want me to become a self-reliant adult."

"And did they buy that bullshit?"

"It's not bullshit, Aaron! Okay...in a way, you're right...they did *not* respect my rights, but I decided that by saying that, I could remind them that they *should*. And it worked. I wouldn't say it went smoothly, but it was...tolerable. And you can't believe how good it felt to be honest."

I sighed and took another sip of my whiskey. "I'm ready for some of that honesty stuff myself. Why don't you start by telling me what went on today."

She shook her head as she chewed the crisp bread vigorously. "Not good," she said, swallowing hard. "I can't start the story at the end. She pushed her plate away and leaned forward. "For you to understand, you have to hear some of what's happened to me since the postal strike began. I'm not the sweet, fearful, innocent high schooler you took under your wing in Berkeley."

"So I've noticed."

"Don't be angry, Aaron. I had to grow up sometime, didn't I?"

"I kind of hoped we'd be together when that happened," I said. "*While* it happened."

"Anyway, it happened another way. Do you want to hear or not?" she answered, swerving adroitly away from my tone.

Of course I wanted to hear. For starters, how did a girl who hated crowds, feared violence, and lacked any kind of self-confidence in the public arena transform herself into someone who stomped on a police officer's foot with her Keds? I listened intently as she described conversations she'd had with the radical students at the house, Laurent and Bérnard, and the Bouleaux's opposition to their activities. How she'd spoken up at the *petit groupe* meetings and how that had changed her perception of herself and what she might accomplish in her life. Finally she admitted to nights of terror when she was caught in the middle of bloody, skull-cracking battles.

We talked for over an hour, the words flowing as smoothly as if the months of nightmare had not happened and we'd been sitting, hands warmly clasped, at the Bear's Lair. Our waiter came by. "More whiskey, monsieur?" Calm now, I ordered some tea, and Janet finished up her lunch. With her last bite, I encouraged her to continue her story. She explained the politics, because to me the whole thing was a confused mess that had accomplished nothing. I began to follow all of the threads that had woven themselves so tightly into the May Revolution, and why they had unraveled in recent days. Janet gradually began to wind down. "To tell you the truth," she said, "everyone was worn to a frazzle and no one could agree on how to turn the events into permanent change. But nothing will ever be the same in France. The ideas are out there now."

I considered for a moment, not only what she said, but how she said it. Saddened, but without the petulant whine and the dithering language that I remembered so well. Her demeanor was poised and self-confident, like she knew who she was and had assessed clearly her gains and losses. "It must be very depressing for you," I sympathized. "And for your friends."

"My friends...I don't suppose you can think of a way to find out what's happened to them."

"We can go to a local police station, but I doubt we would learn anything."

She shrugged her shoulders. "I ran across town today with a vague idea that they might come hide with us..." Her voice faded.

We watched a couple take the table next to us and listened to them order in broken French. The summer tourist horde had arrived on schedule. The café was busy, but I wasn't ready to leave. And in the tradition of the French café, I realized, no one was rushing us. There were still things I needed to comprehend.

"This must have been tough on you," I continued. "But it seems to me like you've won your own personal revolution this spring."

She smiled. It was nurturing. Irritating. "I have, Aaron. Feeling comfortable expressing my ideas to people. Moving in with Teo. All that. France is still in chains, but I am free."

"And now, after the revolution and talking to your parents?" I fished.

"Today on the street," Janet said, "just standing there with you for the first time since forever, I realized how I must look—like a Kodak snapshot of who I am and how I've changed. My strength. My independence. It didn't happen overnight, and I've been afraid so much of the time. My friends helped me through the fear, and helped me to make my own decisions. And I'm responsible for the consequences. That's my current definition of freedom."

"That's very grownup." I felt my insides tighten until they ached. "And what have you decided to do next?"

She answered with a bounce that startled me—her old enthusiasm. "Go home to Mother and Daddy."

"What?!"

"It's weird, but I've come full circle. They need me. It's a chance to meet them face to face, adult to adult. To get to know each other. I feel sure that I can be there until Matt gets home. Just be there and be me. And in the end, they agreed."

"Shit...who would've thought? But...what about college?"

"Oh, I'll go back after Matt comes home. But not to Berkeley. I want a small, quiet campus where I can get lots of units quickly and get through. I'm going to study history, then go to law school or whatever it takes to get inside the system. I might work in government or the diplomatic corps or maybe as a lobbyist. Lobbyists don't have to speak in front of large crowds." She laughed at her weak point. "Whatever I do," she continued, "I want to hold onto my own ideals. I'll be on the lookout not to be co-opted by the system."

"Do you really believe you can make a difference?" I asked.

"I guess you can't help being skeptical, Aaron. I have to admit, when I was home, if I'd considered a career like that at all, beyond my total lack of self-confidence, I would have been just as skeptical. My opinion of the U.S. government was abysmally low. Getting away, I've had a chance to compare it to a couple of other governments first hand, and yes, I'm sure I can make a difference."

"And what about the radical groups back home, like your ex-roommate's?"

"I'll choose my own groups, thank you very much."

"Be careful, Janet...there are still some crazies out there. More dangerous stuff going on at home now than ever."

"Will you *please* stop treating me like a parent or a self-appointed guardian!?"

I was silent, absorbing her anger, and I knew it hadn't started with today.

Suddenly, Janet laughed out loud. "I've changed, Aaron. But I should have realized that you haven't." I watched her as she seemed to survey the diners around us for the first time. She turned back to me and shrugged her shoulders. "Well," she said, "you did stick your neck out a bit further than usual today."

"I'm not afraid. I'm just not stupid," I retorted. I was aware of the tremendous anger that had been rising in my gut throughout this friendly little conversation. I had to let off a little steam or the whole pot would explode right there over the teacup. "Shit!" I leaned forward into her face. "Do you have any idea how *worried* I've been about you all these months?"

She stared at me as if I'd lost my mind. She shredded her napkin almost to dust. Finally, she found her voice. "Now I'll be home safe," she whispered. "You'll be roaming the world, and you'll forget all about me."

If her response had been coy or teasing, I would have snickered, sworn lifelong loyalty, and let it rest at that. But her tone was deadly serious, tears forming in the corners of her eyes with "you'll forget all about me," and I found my own tears were blurring the sight of her. Vexed, frustrated and finally raging, I let loose with a yell, as if only the sound of my agonized voice could restore my vision: *"Christ, Janet! Why-did-you-write-me-all-those-fucking-letters?!!!"*

Janet's entire chair jumped back. There was a brilliant flash of silence, then customers resumed chatting and dishware rang out. We sat there dumbfounded. "You sent me a *diary*," I said bitterly. "Fuck. Why me?"

"I needed you with me," she cried, "no matter what you think."

A weird, high-pitched noise escaped from my lips. An animal in pain. My whole body deflated. "Couldn't you have written about your boyfriend in one of those little blank books with the flimsy keys and kept it to yourself?"

"Oh, Aaron, I've hurt you...I'm so insensitive. I'm so sorry!"

Part of me wanted to pull my chair around, to put my arm around her. My butt stayed where it was, as if it had a mind of its own. "Yes, insensitive...and self-centered. All wrapped up in your Paris revolution and your Paris romance, while I've been cooped up in my room with my copy of *Newsweek* and your goddamned perfumed letters."

"I'm so sorry," she repeated more forcefully. "I felt as though we'd truly become friends. Just friends...you never said anything..."

"Are you dense? *Yes*, we were friends, but weren't we more?"

"I couldn't help it. I was here. You weren't."

"You fell in love..." I sneered, still lashing out.

She nodded vigorously. "Yes. I did."

We were silent again. There was, in my opinion, nothing left to say. But Janet spoke, and if I'd had any sense, I would have stuck my fingers in my ears. "I apologize, Aaron, truly. But I want you to know that I'll always love you..."

"Like a friend." My voice turned the "friend" concept into dog meat.

"*Not* just like a friend."

"I'm trying to understand, dammit...!"

"Why can't you understand? I was alone here, there was a revolution. Teo is a wonderful man, gentle and strong and committed to a huge cause, and I was never going to see you again..."

"I was going to come here," I cut her off. "We were going to meet after graduation, remember?"

"With no money for the ticket, as you kept telling me and telling me? And once the revolution started? *You*—the cynical, safe Aaron Becker? Always saying 'stay out of it, don't be stupid'? Huh! I can't even believe you're sitting here right now. Let alone that you saved me from the *flics*!"

For an instant, we were absolutely still, confronting each other across the table. Her harsh, hot green eyes stung me like two alien insects. Then I was crying into my hands. Not because I loved her and had lost her, but because I knew she was right in assuming that I was capable of going off on any safe road, whether or not she'd be on it.

I sucked in a big breath and grumbled, "Goddamned Vietnam War."

"Goddamned Vietnam War," she echoed, still staring at me. "But you came, Aaron." Her face was still wet. "You came for me."

Then she reached out for me. I dragged my chair her way and we put our arms around each other, hugging, holding on for dear life.

"You came..." she repeated, squeezing onto my chair.

"Too late..." I whispered. "Too goddamned fucking late."

"So can you forgive me?" she asked.

I shrugged. "Hell, I'm ... Yeah, sure. Yeah. We've all been doing the best we can, under the circumstances." She returned to her own chair. We backed off and I reached for her hand. Then I remembered that I'd brought her a gift, and for the first time, I really wanted to present it. "Here," I said, pulling a small package out of my pocket. "For you."

When she opened the little box, she gasped. On a bed of cotton there lay an enameled metal pin, an open-worked, blood-red peace symbol. Janet's entire body slumped over the gift. She seemed to melt into it as she grasped it, opening and closing her fist to examine it. I cleared my throat. "You wrote me from the embassy that your peace button was ruined," I began. How many times had I rehearsed this speech? "This isn't intended to replace it, but I figured you'd want another, direct from the heart of protest in Berkeley, California. It's some sort of metal alloy. The salesgirl assured me it'll be practically indestructible. Nothing is foolproof, of course."

She reached for me and we hugged, long and tight. Her thank-yous were heartfelt as she hugged me again and kissed my face an inch or so to the right of my lips. Then she pinned my gift to her poncho.

Suddenly, reality set back in. "It's a damn good thing I came to hear this last letter in person," I said. "I'll miss you. Again." We separated, still holding each other's arms, and I continued. "I have to stay in Europe. At least until the war is over. And maybe then-some."

She observed me with some degree of gloom. "Seems absurd, Aaron. You. The one who always loved a hearth and a home of your own, starting out your life as a wanderer...and me, the adventurer, headed back to California."

"Absurd," I agreed, a lump in my throat, saddened all over again at losing a woman who knew me so well. I forced cheerfulness into my voice, "Maybe I'll travel a bit, but I'll have to get work soon. I've got great letters of recommendation. I can be a lab tech anywhere."

"It's tough to get work here. That's part of what this revolution was about. I'm glad my dad came through for you, but asking for more than the ticket might have bought you some time."

I shook my head. "Couldn't do it..."

Janet's hand covered mine and I turned my palm up to grab on. Her hand was soft and warm and I felt the faint beating of her heart encased in delicate wrists. "Anyway, mission accomplished. I found you, and you're safe."

"Thanks for finding me..." her voice trailed off.

"We do have some time, now, don't we? You can show me your town."

She stared down at the edge of the table, still holding my hand. "Actually, there's no time. There's one more thing I have to do before I can go home, though. I promised Teo." Her eyes fell to the floor. "It doesn't matter...this isn't the Paris we dreamed of."

"I know. I read all those damn letters, remember?" My lip trembled uncontrollably as I tried to reconcile myself to saying goodbye to her for good. I squelched my curiosity about the "one more thing"— none of my business. Then I had an idea. "Would you like to get out of Paris? Together?" I asked gently.

"Yes, out of Paris! Oh Aaron, that's it..." she squeezed my hand. "After all, you're *here*. What about...oh, this is it! My ticket to the States is from London. Why don't we meet there, say, in a week? We can leave each other messages at the main office of the American Express ..." She stopped mid-sentence, then whispered, "But out of Paris. What a good idea."

"You need to get away from everything." I swallowed hard. "Everything that happened to you here. Especially with the revolution winding down."

She sighed. "The revolution is definitely *over*. They say the Sorbonne and l'Odeón and the whole Latin Quarter was retaken by the government yesterday. And the Renault auto-workers, the last holdouts, voted to return to work. I still can't fathom it, even though I witnessed every debilitating slip."

From the nearby waiter's station, a clatter drew my attention to rows of glassware glistening in the sunlight. Across the street was a building façade with a shitload of sculptural cheesecake. "Paris *is* beautiful, though," I said wistfully. "Maybe someday we'll see it together."

"'Someday' is a word that I have officially expunged from both my English and French vocabularies." She put both hands on the table and pushed back her chair, stretching out stiff arms and legs. I froze, not ready to say goodbye. Her words, *I promised Teo* flooded my mind like the shot of whiskey. What could that be about?

"So, Janet, why don't you introduce me to Teodor Pelnar?" I asked, trying to keep my voice as smooth as still water. She gaped at me with pity and I laughed out loud. "Don't worry! I'm not trying to torture myself. I'm just curious, that's all. I've seen your revolutionaries, now I want to meet Teo the Czech. It's only natural," I lied. I tried my best to smile.

"But right now? Would you really?"

"If it doesn't bother you...and if he's not the jealous type."

Her brows bent. "He'll be a little jealous..." She considered. "Well, if you want to, why not?" She removed her new enameled peace pin and pushed it down into her pocket. "No use making this more difficult than it has to be."

"Are you sure this is okay? I mean, for you?"

"Yes, it's fine. I want you to come. Maybe just to prove to me that I haven't dreamt these past few months," she said. "Come. Be my witness."

FIFTY-TWO

WE WERE HIGH UP in an odd-shaped little room, its front window on a broad, convex wall from which extended one ridiculous shard of a bed. The foot of the bed was a couple of feet from where the three of us talked, Janet and I seated at a table, Teodor Pelnar on a large metal trunk. Around us were the trappings of a student's subsistence. It was the tower room. The penthouse? *Mais non*...I felt like I was sitting inside the shell of a peanut.

"No. I didn't want to get arrested," Janet was saying, alternating impressively between languages, helping us both to understand. "I heard the news and I ran out to find Bérnard and Remi to tell them they could come hide with us."

"In this room?" Teodor asked, incredulously.

"Oh, so I'm crazy," Janet said, dropping her head into her two hands. "Maybe I just wanted to see them before they were taken. To say goodbye."

"Don't worry. They won't be in jail for long," Teodor said. He turned to me. Dragging his French and peppering it with English words, the big man explained that Janet's friends were the leaders of a minor student organization. Socialists, with anarchist tendencies. The police would force Bérnard to leave

Paris, to go back home to Nice. "So perhaps Jeanette wanted that last hug," he concluded wryly.

"*Zut merd*, Teo, don't be an ass. You know that Bérnard is a homosexual. Anyway, they won't be in the history books like Savaugeot and Cohn-Bendit, but they were heroes to their friends. They stood for openness and fairness. Rare commodities in this world."

I couldn't stop the "whoa, lady!" that blew out of my mouth. "Hey, Janet. Looks like you've learned to swear in French."

"That's not all this woman has learned to do."

"Teo, quiet!" Janet sighed dramatically. "Anyway, I haven't told you, but this morning while you were at school, I had a call from Annette." She turned to me. "That's Remi's sister. She told me that their father caught Remi and Bérnard in bed together. She was sure he was going to do something drastic..."

"Oh *merd*! No wonder you went running..." Teo said, sympathy opening up his broad flushed face.

"Then, when I heard about the roundups of the leaders, I knew..."

"So your friend's own father turned him in?" I asked, incredulous.

"Bérnard moved out of the Bouleaux's and into hiding a while back, but the police have been gradually closing in on the rebels and Remi decided it would be safer for him at his father's. Things have been going badly at home ever since Bérnard moved in. Annette told me that Remi's father blamed Bérnard for convincing Remi that the communists had sold out the student rebels. He assumed Bérnard was the ring leader, when in fact, it was Remi all the time."

"And he didn't want his daughter Annette to be Bérnard's girlfriend," Teo added, shaking his head. "I can imagine the explosion when he learned that Bérnard's girlfriend was his son Remi, and Annette was covering for them."

We were all quiet, absorbing the full extent of a family's disaster. My gaze roamed across the shabby little room and landed on the night stand: a giant box of functional and expensive American Kleenex squeezed in next to a dilapidated lamp and a grimy portable radio.

"You can see why I was so panicked," Janet continued. "But I'm glad I went. I may never see them again..." Her voice was tight, her hands clasped between her legs. "Oh Aaron...I was shocked to the point of fainting when I saw you standing there! I'm furious with you for being such a kiss-up to the *flic,* but I *am* grateful to you for getting me out of that mess...I knew I couldn't help them."

"What is a 'kiss-up'? Is it like kiss? What...?"

"Being so polite to the police."

"What I said wasn't actually so polite. I spoke up about my main concern. That none of you get beaten to death."

Janet's lip curled up in disgust. "The police here are vicious. *Incroyable.*"

"How did you find us?" Teodor asked.

"I followed what I knew from Janet's letters. I went to L'Alliance Française this morning and when I saw the biggest guy there, I knew it had to be you. Just adding one and one and getting two."

"I saw you immediately," Teo said, scowling. "No problem." Janet's eyes had been locked on mine, a sensation I was enjoying. Now suddenly her head jerked and she looked up at Teo.

"So why didn't you stop me?" I asked.

"Curious. Anyway, you are no threat." He looked me up and down contemptuously.

Janet cleared her throat. She held up her hand, signaling Teo to let her speak. "Teo, you should thank Aaron for helping me this morning."

"*Cherie,* do you understand why I couldn't be the one...?"

She halted his speech, both palms up. "No need for that, Teo. I understand..."

"I understand too," I said. "Fear of deportation must be terrible... Say, I can't even imagine..."

"*Alors, merci, Monsieur,*" Teo said earnestly.

I turned to Janet. "You really told 'ol Marsh and the lovely Jean that you were living in this garret with *him*..." I gestured toward Teo the Czech.

Janet hooted. "Is that what this is? A garret? I never thought of that." She surveyed the place as if seeing it for the first time. "I'm not saying the call was easy." She turned to Teo. "I hope you don't mind. I want to tell Aaron more about the call home. In English, okay?"

"Okay, okay...no problem. You want some tea?" We both declined and he rose to get some for himself.

"At first I felt sorry for my mother," Janet continued, "but she had an unbelievable surprise for me. She told me that she'd joined Another Mother for Peace! I'm proud of her. It's the first strong, independent stand I've ever seen her take. Why are you grinning at me like that?"

"I was picturing your father listening to the two of you go on together."

She laughed heartily. "Well, he got his two cents in, but considering this was Daddy, he was pretty quiet about Mother's activities. I guess they've been all through it together already. And he made it clear he's still against anything antiwar. The only thing I didn't tell them the truth about was Matt's changed attitude. I figure that's got to come from him."

"Good girl."

"So by the end of the conversation, I felt sorriest for Daddy. I'm sure he feels like it's Armaggedon, the way I've behaved."

"And he didn't threaten you or try to control you?"

"Of course, but I stood my ground. In the end, I'm sure I made him feel better, because they were both concerned about what I'm going to do next."

"I'm sure they were happy about that," I said. Janet shifted in her seat, smiling at me steadily. She was about to continue when Teo sat down with his cup, his voice breaking up our private communication like static ruining a radio melodrama.

"Well *next*, Monsieur Becker, next she will take the train to Prague, *avec moi*. We go Friday. Before the *élection présidentiel*."

"Teo, please..."

"She will see my city," he said, and then..." A flicker of a sneer passed over his lips and he grew a couple of inches as he drew himself up. "Jeanette has promised to help me in my work for my country's freedom. She will carry money across the border for me. Easy for American, dangerous for me."

"Teo, stop!" Janet rushed from her chair and sat by Teo on the trunk, pushing at him with her hip so he'd share. He moved over, set his cup on the floor and watched her expectantly. Janet sighed and put out her hand to cover one of Teo's big paws. "Shouldn't we keep this a secret?" she implored. She gazed at him innocently, with deeply trusting eyes. My heart sank to my feet. Then she turned to glare at me, as if any of this was my fault. "Now you know," she snapped.

"So...this is the mysterious 'one more thing' you have to do before..." She held up her hand and I shut my mouth. I guessed she'd rather I didn't mention London.

Teo lowered his voice to a whisper, "I'm sorry, *cherie*," he was back to French. "This fellow threw me off." He'd put his arm around her and they were pecking at each other, Janet assuring him that I wouldn't change a thing in their plans.

438

Then I was mumbling to myself. Something didn't seem right about this assignment. She was helping him, I understood that, like one last gesture before they parted. Something meaningful for a place worth fighting for, even if the French Revolution had turned into a debacle. "'Dangerous for me, easy for an American,'" I repeated. "Why is that?"

"Because Americans all have the money," Teo said, fingering air as if it held president-studded paper.

"But what about this guy, Miro...Mirslavic..."

"Miroslav!" Teo shouted, then glancing shifty-eyed at the cardboard walls, lowered his voice. "How does he know about him?" he asked Janet. "What have you been telling him?"

"I saw that guy when I was following the both of you today," I cut in, suddenly sure of my logic. I switched to English, knowing I'd never be able to say all I wanted to in French. I had to make Janet understand, and the hell with this big Czech. "If this Miroslav is around, Janet," I said, "he recognizes you and he has your name. It may be easy and safe for an anonymous American to smuggle..." at that word, Janet's head turned sharply toward Teo as if I'd slapped her cheek. But I went on, "Yes, smuggle money across a border, but not a known American." I perched on the edge of my chair, watching Teo tighten and release his fists and reminding myself that he was supposed to be a nice guy.

The refrigerator moaned and some traffic entered the square below. Finally, Janet asked meekly, "Do you understand, Teo? Didn't you realize this?"

Teo nodded and mumbled, "*Je comprends.*" His body crumpled, his downcast face falling near Janet's shoulder. "My promise," he whispered, "and your promise. Ach! Why did I not see this...?"

"Don't blame yourself," Janet said, raising his bulky head by the chin. "You didn't want to see it. You needed it to be okay."

"Please, *cherie*. It *will* be okay. Please do this...for me..." he begged. "At worst, they would deport you."

"At worst," Janet cried, "I would end up in jail. My government might rescue me. But when they traced me to you, Teo, and they would, you would suffer much worse." The tears started to roll down her cheeks and she shook her head, but then blew her nose and sat up straighter, gathering her strength. I knew at that moment that she would not go as planned, and I exhaled, feeling my gut relax.

Teo knew it too. And watching them hold each other, witnessing those tears, those words, spoken with an intimacy I could not fathom, my pea-brain at last acknowledged the notion that these two were a *couple*. In that instant, I knew absolutely that Janet Magill had become a woman. I took in the narrowness of the bed, the chafed skin on her lower lip, the flushed sincerity in her eyes, lifted to meet Teo's. At any moment, the Czech's disappointment would turn into anger at me for spoiling his plans. I imagined a sharp, unbearable pain in my chest, inflicted by a Hun-helmeted Teo standing over me with a thick, flashing blade, a medieval two-hilted job that only the big Czech could wield, dripping with my blood. And Janet tugging at Teo's arm...too late.

But there was no blood, no blade, no pain in fact, just dizziness. The peanut room twirled and I realized I needed to breathe. I gulped some of the rancid air and she was kissing him sweetly and he was whispering. Deliberately, I breathed again. Janet's elegant neck curved around and her pitiful gaze went right through me, as if I were invisible. I knew there was no room for my paltry pain in this lunatic situation.

So the words came out, my voice quiet and steady. "I'll do it." Teo's head jerked up as if I had just entered the room. "I'm pretty anonymous as we Americans go."

Janet rose and walked over to the nightstand for some more tissue. "Forget it, Aaron. This has nothing to do with you. You don't need to be this much of a hero to prove anything to me." She blew her nose and brought a piece back to Teo.

"This has everything to do with me. I'm a European now, aren't I? So do *not* try to talk me out of it," I said roughly. "As opposed to you, I *can* do it. This must be important to the Czech people, and I can see that it is important to the two of you."

"No, Aaron! Not another word about it!" Her commanding tone softened. "You could get in trouble, and you would be all alone. Isn't that right, Teo? Please, tell Aaron," she begged.

Then, in preposterous French and with an earnestness I rarely mustered, I asked, "Teo, my friend? I'd like to help you and your country. What do you say?"

Teo studied me. Janet squeezed his arm, then took his hand. "Teo," she said, "you were hoping somehow to get me to your beautiful Prague. This was your way."

Janet was staring at Teo, but Teo's eyes were locked into mine. He nodded in response to Janet's voice. "*Oui, mais*...I thought a good way, but now you will not come. And the Prestup..." He covered his face and I heard a groan from beneath the heel of his hand. "She is right, *Monsieur l'American*. This is not your business."

"It can be my business if you trust me. I can promise you that I am not a thief, and I am not a coward. And I know a worthy fight when I see one."

Once again, the big Czech uttered, "*Oui, mais...*" but finally, after one more brief hesitation, he set aside Janet's hand. "*Alors, c'est ça...*" With one surprisingly graceful motion, he stood and walked over to the cluttered armoire, rummaged through piles of debris and came up with an envelope. He began to speak to Janet in French and she turned to me with a tremor in her voice. "How do you know you'll be safe?"

"I'll be fine, really. No one will suspect that an American in France just one or two days would have this kind of connection. I've got American Express checks and maps and guidebooks from three European countries in my bag. I'll pick up one more for Prague. I'm a tourist. Please. I know I can help."

Janet nodded slowly and forced a smile. "Well, okay...if you..." She sighed. "Thank you, Aaron." Then, Janet began to translate Teo's French, instruction by instruction. Traveler's checks. Gare du Austerlitz. Overnight train to Munich. Prague by afternoon. Mariánské Square at 7:00 p.m., in front of the City Library. A tiny little woman. A code phrase, "*Vous avez des enfants, madame?*" Then the night train to Vienna and disappear. Obviously, they'd been working on this.

"How much is in here?" I asked, hefting the thick wad.

Teo mumbled in French. "Ten thousand francs," Janet translated, then, almost an afterthought, "that's a lot of money."

"Two thousand American dollars," I calculated. "Enough for a lot of guns..."

"It's for the family of a Czech dissident," Teo hissed.

"Is that what they told you?" I asked.

Janet turned to Teo and spoke quietly. He was reassuring her. But then she was questioning him about something that became clear when he handed over a few more bills. "Your train fare," he said in rasping, guttural English, "round trip. And thank-you-very-much." After a pause he dredged up a more sincere tone. "*Vraiment. Merci, monsieur.*"

With the Czech's cash and envelope shoved deep into an inside pocket, I headed for the door, slinging my suit jacket over my shoulder like Bogart in the final scene of Casablanca and sporting the unmistakable trace of a smile. It was a mean-spirited glimmer, one that wouldn't endear me to the woman of my dreams, but I was satisfied with this small victory: Janet Magill was not going to get on that plane with the Resistance hero.

I opened the door just a crack and peeked out, then turned back to the pair. "Have a nice life, Teodor," I said. "I want to get out of here before Mr. Mir-spy sees my face up close." I peeked once more, then opened the door wide with a flourish. Janet's hand was on my sleeve. As I turned she threw her arms around me. "Be careful, Aaron. I can't tell you how much this means..."

"Shhh. I don't want to hear it."

"I'll wait for you in London," she whispered. "Don't forget...American Express." I crushed her to me, inhaling the aroma of her salty skin, kissing her curls.

Teo the Czech stood there, taking in our little scene, but Janet didn't seem to care. Why should she? She was worldly now. Independent. And she wanted to see me again. I stepped back and kissed her hand, not delicately like a Frenchman, but a rough, good-natured thwack. Just an ordinary American guy—grateful for the moment, saying hello and goodbye again in this year of international insanity, 1968.

About Elise Frances Miller

Elise Frances Miller was born in Los Angeles CA. She is a graduate of the University of California, Berkeley and holds a Master's degree in Art History from UCLA. In Miller's wide-ranging career, she has served as an art critic and reviewer, high school and college teacher, and communications admini-strator at San Diego State University and Stanford University. She began her writing career as an art critic and reviewer for several well-known publications, including the *Los Angeles Times, Art News, The Reader,* and *San Diego Magazine,* for which she wrote a monthly column.

Two of her short stories have been published in *The Sand Hill Review* (2007, 2010), for which she served as guest fiction editor in 2008. These were included in the SHR's tenth anniversary publication, *The Best of Sand Hill Review* (2012). Her many short stories have appeared in the *Fault Zone* anthology series and online publications. Her prize-winning memoir was published in *The Times They Are A-Changing: Women Remember the 60s and 70s* (2013). In 1998, she and her husband moved from San Diego to the San Francisco Bay Area, where she enjoys the region's literary opportunities and her memberships in the San Francisco Writers Workshop, the California Writers Club, San Francisco/Peninsula Branch, Women's National Book Association, and the Historical Novel Society.

Acknowledgements

Thank you to the many intelligent readers who improved the book immensely with their thoughts and recommendations. First, to my mother, who saved my letters from my university years and my journeys, then read the early stages of the novel before she passed away in 2005. For editing, proofreading, and supplying commentary and information at various stages of the project, I am indebted to my first reader, Randee Friedman of San Diego, and to Beth Bruno, Lyn Wyman, Keith Parks, and Susan Englander. Much appreciation also to the team at the U.C. Berkeley library, where much of my research was conducted.

Over the course of three years, I benefited from the weekly critique sessions of the San Francisco Writers Workshop, followed by discussions over beer and/or cherry pie at Left O'Douls. From that group, I would especially like to express my appreciation for the comments of Tamim Ansary, and for selected readings outside the group by Erika Mailman and Alan Venable. Like most writers, I have flourished in the company of other writers. The SFWW and my friends from the California Writers Club San Francisco/Peninsula branch have provided a valuable source of support. It was through the CWC that I met Martin Sorensen of *The Sand Hill Review*, who published my short stories and entrusted me with the duties of the Review's Fiction Editor.

I am especially grateful to Tory Hartmann, my friend, colleague, and publisher for her amazing range of skills from business and technical agility to her own writing and editing panache. I am indebted to her for confidence in this book, and for maintaining her patience and crazy sense of humor throughout the process of getting it in the hands of readers.

I wish to thank my parents, Tula and George Friedman, for imparting to me their love and respect for the written word. To my children—Amy, one of my first and also final readers, and Corey and Katherine, my scouts in Europe, thank you for your love, support and encouragement throughout my years of research and writing about a time before yours.

Concluding with my husband, Rabbi Jay Miller, is saving the best for last. His love and belief in this project enabled me to persist. To him, I dedicate this novel of youthful aspirations, set in the era when he and I were young and formed a "braintrust" to carry forward our plans and dreams for a more just and honest world.

A Reader's Guide for
The Berkeley Girl: In Paris, 1968

Origins and Methods: Researching the
Background, Constructing a Fiction

In 1995, my mother found a cache of letters that I had written during my college years. Among them were what amounted to a 50-page, single-spaced "diary," all written on crackling thin onion skin stationery or aerograms. I had written these to my parents from my two "quarters" in Europe during the spring and summer of 1968.

Re-reading those letters, my interest re-ignited in the American civil rights and anti-war movements and concurrent European protests. I obtained my alumni library card from U.C. Berkeley, newspaper and magazine clippings on microfiche, and haunted libraries and used and antiquarian bookstores, often the only source for out-of-print materials. My research discoveries included the pamphlets, brochures, monographs and journals displayed by radical tablers from Sproul Plaza to the Sorbonne Courtyard. By the new millennium, the Internet became a tremendous addition to my sources. Finally, after sending my grown children on "missions" to take photographs and seek answers to specific questions, I was able to conduct my own investigations in Prague (1999) and Paris (2000 and 2004).

The Berkeley Girl: In Paris, 1968 is a work of fiction. Its characters, scenes and locales are the product of the author's imagination or are used fictitiously. Any similarity of fictional characters to people living or dead is purely coincidental.

However, in order to replicate the scene, the atmosphere, and the spirit of the era, I have used real names from the realms of politics, institutions, organizations, media, music, popular culture, the arts and literature. All American, French, and Czech names of educational institutions, streets and boulevards, public buildings and open spaces, neighborhoods, landmarks, tourist destinations, restaurants, cafés, night spots, etc. are identified by their actual names at the time. U.C. Berkeley professors' names and class titles are identified from the university catalog. The text includes the real names of political, cultural and other public figures. Speeches of actual public figures are approximated, fictionalized and paraphrased in the spirit of the speakers' values, beliefs and styles.

Selected Readings
The Berkeley Girl: In Paris, 1968

Although I found many nonfiction accounts of events, there was little fiction (noted in the Selected Readings section, below, in bold type). The enlightenment and freedom of following fictional characters, especially the very young characters known to be involved in the events of their day, was missing. Ferlinghetti, Jones, Neville, Kundera, and later Roth—all producing wonderful fictional accounts—featured the point of view of characters well beyond their college years.

United States
Chepesiuk, Ron, *Sixties Radicals, Then and Now*, 1995.

DeBenedetti, Charles, *An American Ordeal, the Antiwar Movement of the Vietnam Era*, Syracuse University Press, 1990.

Hoffman, Abbie, *Soon to be a Major Motion Picture*, 1980.

Kurlansky, Mark, *1968, The Year that Rocked the World*, 2005.

Rorabaugh, W.J., Berkeley at War, The 1960's, New York, Oxford University Press, 1989.

Roth, Philip, *American Pastoral*, 1997.

The Tales of Hoffman, Edited from the official transcript by Mark L. Levine, George C. McNamee and Daniel Greenberg, 1970.

France
Alistair Horne, *Seven Ages of Paris*.

Alistair Horne, *La Belle France, A Short History*.

CAW, Magazine of Students for A Democratic Society, No. 3 Fall Issue, Devoted to the Battle of France, 1968.

Feenberg, Andrew and Freedman, Jim, *When Poetry Ruled the Streets, The French May Events of 1968*, State University of New York Press, 2001.

Ferlinghetti, Lawrence, Love in the Days of Rage, 1988.

Jean, Holly, *May 1968: How the people brought an industrialized nation to a halt, why you haven't heard about it and why you should...*, 2005.

Jones, James, *The Merry Month of May*, 1970.

Kirsch, Robert, *Essay: Paris Students Topple Ivory Tower*, May, 1968.

Neville, Jill, *The Love Germ*, 1969.

Protest in Paris 1968: Photographs by Serge Hambourg, Hood Museum of Art, Dartmouth College, Hanover, New Hampshire, 2006).

Ross, Kristin, *May '68 and It s Afterlives*, 2002.

Schultz, Jim, '68 web, jschultz@research.com.

Singer, Daniel, *Prelude to Revolution, France in May 1968*, N.Y., Hill and Wang, 1970.

Spender, Stephen, *The Year of the Young Rebels*, 1968; *Journals, The Thirties and After*.

The French Student Revolt, The Leaders Speak, presented by Hervé Bourges, 1968.

Czechoslovakia

Kundera, Milan, *Life is Elsewhere*, 1973. *The Unbearable Lightness of Being*, 1968.

Schwartz, Harry, *Prague's 200 Days, The Struggle for Democracy in Czechoslovakia*, New York, Frederick A. Praeger, Publishers, 1969. SDSU Library, DB 215.6, S33.

Zeman, Z.A.B., *Prague Spring*, New York, Hill and Wang, 1969. SDSU Library, DB 215.6, Z4 1969.

Historical characters and references

Politics
American:
Eldridge Cleaver, Black Panther
Fred Halstead, Socialist Workers Party presidential candidate
Abbie Hoffman, The Yippies, Youth International Party
Hubert Humphrey, Vice President during the Vietnam War, Democratic presidential candidate
Lyndon B. Johnson, President during the Vietnam War
Robert (Bobby) Kennedy, Democratic presidential candidate
Rev. Dr. Martin Luther King Jr., leader of non-violent equal rights movement
Eugene McCarthy, Democratic presidential candidate
Robert McNamara, Secretary of Defense
Huey Newton, Black Panther
Richard Nixon, Republican presidential candidate
Rosa Parks, refused to sit down in the back of a bus and started the civil disobedience movement
Rep. Jeanette Rankin (R, MO)
Ronald Reagan, Republican governor of California
Jerry Rubin, The Yippies, Youth International Party
Dean Rusk, Secretary of State
Bobby Seale, Black Panther

[political context]:
Barbara Avedon, Founder, Another Mother for Peace
Joan Baez, folk singer, antiwar activist
Sterling Hayden, actor, antiwar activist
Daniel Siegel, a Boalt Hall law student, antiwar activist
Benjamin Spock, pediatrician, author of wildly popular book on raising children, antiwar activist

French:
General Charles de Gaulle, President of France
Georges Pompidou, Prime Minister of France

Daniel Cohn-Bendit, leader of the March 22 Movement, Nanterre campus, University of Paris, speaker for the May Revolution

Christian Fouchet, French Interior Minister

Alain Geismar, leader of the professors' National Union of Higher Education, speaker for the May Revolution

Maurice Grimaud, Paris Prefect of Police

Jacques Sauvageot, leader of the National Union of French Students, speaker for the May Revolution

Czechoslovak:

Alexander Dubček, President, (January 1968-April 1969), Czechoslovakia

Tomas Masaryk, President of Czechoslovakia, 1918-1935

Antonin Novotný, President (1957-1968) and General Secretary of the Communist Party (1953-1968), Czechoslovakia

The Prestup (Pavel Tigrid), Czech dissident, writer and publisher in exile

Institutions, organizations
American
Commonwealth Club
World Affairs Council
Ku Klux Klan
Students for a Democratic Society (SDS)
Student Nonviolent Coordinating Committee (SNCC)
Black Panthers
Peace and Freedom Party

French
Comités Vietnam de Base
Comité Vietnam National
March 22 Movement
National Union of French Students (*UNEF*)
National Union of Higher Education (*SNE Sup*)
All political parties in various countries

Media
Amercian
San Francisco Chronicle

New York Herald Tribune
New York Times
Daily Cal, UC Berkeley newspaper
Berkeley Barb, activist newspaper
U.S. News and World Report
Newsweek
Cosmopolitan Magazine
Rolling Stone, magazine
Pocket Guide to Vietnam (U.S. Govt.)
Boy Scout Handbook
Radio Free Europe

French
Le Monde, mainstream newspaper
Europe 1, mainstream French radio
Action, revolutionary newspaper
Les Cahiers de Mai, revolutionary magazine

Other
BBC, radio
Radio Luxembourg

49756181R00277

Made in the USA
San Bernardino, CA
03 June 2017